# The Inner Conflict of Tradition

*J. C. Heesterman*

# The Inner Conflict of Tradition

## *Essays in Indian Ritual, Kingship, and Society*

The University of Chicago Press
*Chicago and London*

J. C. Heesterman holds the Chair of Indian Civilization at the University of Leiden.

The University of Chicago Press, Chicago 60637
The University of Chicago Press, Ltd., London

Printed in the United States of America

94 93 92 91 90 89 88 87 86 85 54321

***Library of Congress Cataloging in Publication Data***

Heesterman, J. C.
The inner conflict of tradition.

Includes index.
1. India—Civilization—Addresses, essays, lectures.
I. Title.
DS423.H39 1985 954 84-8854
ISBN 0-226-32297-1
ISBN 0-226-32299-8 (pbk.)

To the memory of Clara

# Contents


| | | |
|---|---|---|
| | Preface | ix |
| | Introduction | 1 |
| 1 | India and the Inner Conflict of Tradition | 10 |
| 2 | Brahmin, Ritual, and Renouncer | 26 |
| 3 | The Case of the Severed Head | 45 |
| 4 | The Flood Story in Vedic Ritual | 59 |
| 5 | The Origin of the *Nāstika* | 70 |
| 6 | Vedic Sacrifice and Transcendence | 81 |
| 7 | Ritual, Revelation, and the Axial Age | 95 |
| 8 | The Conundrum of the King's Authority | 108 |
| 9 | Kauṭilya and the Ancient Indian State | 128 |
| 10 | Power, Priesthood, and Authority | 141 |
| 11 | Western Expansion, Indian Reaction: Mughal Empire and British Raj | 158 |
| 12 | Caste, Village, and Indian Society | 180 |
| 13 | Caste and Karma: Max Weber's Analysis of Caste | 194 |
| | Notes | 205 |
| | Index | 249 |

# Preface

This collection of essays, most of which have been safely tucked away in the somewhat remote corners dear to the naturally shy Indologist, would not have come about without the encouragement and indeed the insistence of two friends whose wisdom and judgment I have come to respect. Edward Shils, as usual *suaviter in modo fortiter in re,* quietly disposed of my diffidence and introduced me to the University of Chicago Press. No less indebted am I to Shmuel Eisenstadt, who also encouraged me and whose mastery of the arcane art of the colloquium provided the occasion for the original versions of some of these essays. It is more than a pleasant duty to record my debt of gratitude to their encouragement as well as to their stimulating thought.

I also want to express my thanks to the American Academy of Arts and Sciences, the publishers of *Wiener Zeitschrift für die Kunde Süd- und Ostasiens,* the Indological Institute of Vienna University, Leiden University Press, and Professor John F. Richards and Professor W. Schluchter for their kind permission to revise and republish the papers which first appeared under their auspices. In this connection, I should especially mention my friend and colleague Gerhard Oberhammer, director of the Indological Institute of Vienna University and editor of *Wiener Zeitschrift für die Kunde Süd- und Ostasiens*. He hospitably accepted five of the following essays in the publications edited by him, but most of all I feel grateful for our many hours of animated discussion, in and out of seminars, over a long period of years.

Indology is not a gregarious field of activity. It is a sort of neglected frontier area, sparsely populated by lone rangers struggling along diverging and little-frequented trails. When these rather solitary trails lead to long-standing friendships, the urge to mention a few of these friends is irresistible. Let me name only Hanns-Peter Schmidt, Madeleine Biardeau, Joachim Sprockhoff, Wendy O'Flaherty, Frits Staal, and the late Hans van Buitenen.

Indology may, after all, not be such a lonely enterprise. And by mentioning these few names, I can record at least some of the many otherwise unacknowledged debts I owe.

Publishing, I am told, is an industry like any other. It has to deal, though, with a curiously variegated and generally unruly collection of people who claim personal attention, ample patience, and expert help as unquestionably due to them. I therefore want to thank those at the University of Chicago Press who were concerned with this book for giving it the advantage of their excellent care. It is indeed a most gratifying experience to have been asked to publish with them.

I dedicate this volume of essays to the memory of my daughter Clara—and also to her mother and her sister. It is the only tribute I can offer.

# Introduction

## *1*

To say that a society and its culture depend on tradition is as good as tautological. Tradition, therefore, cannot but share in the flexibility and adaptiveness of culture. It is not only permissive of change, it can even be seen to be the means to formulate and legitimize change. It is not necessary to revise the long-standing and largely inconclusive tradition-modernity debate and to argue once more the resilience and adaptiveness of tradition[1]. Nonetheless "traditional society," if not a term of opprobrium, for all its nostalgic value, still describes a world seen as irrationally resisting change, a world without history other than aberration, decline, and final failure. This notion, though eroded by undeniable economic and technological progress, is still applied with much conviction to India, especially when it comes to her problems and shortcomings. India continues to be seen as the repository of hallowed but obstructive tradition. This seems especially to be the case in the matter of caste, which is considered to hold Indian society in its iron grip. It may be that the lingering notion of India's persistent traditionality owes much to the observer's feeling of having lost his own traditional moorings, which makes him cast around for the certainty of tradition. India thus becomes a screen on which to project our nostalgia for a world we have lost, even when we know that the good old times were not all that good.

Granted, Indian civilization in no small degree contributes to the notion of a predetermined and immutable order of things. Its scriptures do indeed strongly project the image of a monolithic world order, the *dharma,* although man can and will deviate from it. The rule of dharma may diminish as a result of the progressive decadence of the world but the dharma itself is still there as the incontrovertible and immutable model. Man can always, alone if not collectively, return to the rightful path of the dharma's universal order.

This is a powerful ideal. Here it will no longer do to invoke the flexibility and adaptiveness of tradition. The well-known statement on the essential dharmic behavior proper to each of the four ages—austerity, knowledge, sacrifice, and gift—is not meant to give a brief for change. It only reflects man's diminished capacity to live the dharma in full. The atemporal dharma itself, however, remains immune to the changes of the ages.[2] Man will be ignorant and confused because "Dharma and Adharma do not go about saying here we are, nor do gods, gandharvas, or ancestors say: This is dharma that is adharma."[3] But this does not affect the integrity of the eternal dharma. The proper guideline is the conduct of the correct and well instructed, the *śiṣṭa,* who acts disinterestedly and without any mundane attachment. The essential condition of true dharmic behavior is the absence of worldly cause or motivation.[4] In this way, the dharma presents itself as the unbroken tradition of a monolithic and eternal order carried forward over the generations by the disinterested conduct of the śiṣṭas.

There is, then, strong support for the notion of India's unchanging tradition which goes well beyond mere resilience under pressure of changing circumstances. It is even guaranteed against such pressures by the absence of worldly causes or motivations. But it is exactly this unworldliness that brings out a problem. The dharma is universal and as such must take into account worldly concerns and interests, but at the same time its atemporal character requires a total withdrawal from those secular realities. The dharma does not propound a fixed institutional order, as we are all too prone to assume; it poses an insoluble dilemma.

## 2

Tradition is characterized by the inner conflict of atemporal order and temporal shift rather than by resiliance and adaptiveness. It is this unresolved conflict that provides the motive force we perceive as the flexibility of tradition. Indian civilization offers a particularly clear case of this dynamic inner conflict.[5] The conflict is not just handled surreptitiously by way of situational compromise. Once we look beyond the hard surface of the projected absolute order, it appears subtly, but no less effectively, to be expressed by the same scriptures that so impressively expound the dharma's absoluteness.

Perhaps nowhere is this more clear than in the Vedic ritual texts and their curiously contradictory place in Indian civilization, at once hallowed and neglected, like the king who is honored by all and obeyed by none. They are the scriptural repository of the revealed *śruti* and as such purport to be the core and foundation of the dharma. Therefore the conduct of the śiṣṭa—that is, one who is fully instructed in Vedic lore—is the only guideline in the confusion of dharma and adharma. The dharma essentially proclaims itself to be the ritualistic order of Vedic sacrifice. It stands to reason, then, that we take our cue from an investigation of Vedic śrauta ritual. Most of the following essays are therefore concerned specifically with the śrauta corpus or refer to it.[6]

Now it is in the consideration of the śrauta ritual that the unresolved dilemma of the dharma's traditional order stands out most clearly, for the revealed śruti has nothing to say about the world, its concerns and conflicts.[7] It proposes, on the contrary, a separate, self-contained world ruled exclusively by the comprehensive and exhaustive order of the ritual. It has no meaning outside its self-contained system of rules to connect it with the mundane order.[7] This is already clear from the conspicuous absence of *sacra publica*. Therefore the conduct of the śiṣṭa who finds his fulfillment in the śruti is, by definition, free from worldly attachment. The ritual is *adṛṣṭārtha,* without visible purpose or meaning other than the realization of its perfect order, be it only for the duration of the ritual and within the narrow compass of the ritual enclosure. After completing the ritual, the sacrificer formally divests himself of his ritual persona, quits the enclosure, and returns to his worldly life.

The ritual holds out to man the prospect of a transcendent world he creates himself on condition that he submits to the total rule of the ritual injunction. But at the same time, the open gap between the transcendent order of the ritual and the mundane ambivalence of conflict and interest is all the more obvious.

## *3*

In this gap the brahmin stands Janus-faced, attached exclusively to the order of Vedic ritualism and at the same time called upon to play his part in the affairs of the world. His precarious stance is the theme of the second essay, "Brahmin, Ritual, and Renouncer." This involves an investigation of the śruti. It appears that the gap between transcendent ritualism and mundane order is the unique result of a conscious reform. The ritual texts still show, through the cracks, as it were, of the closed ritual system, an earlier and fundamentally different state of affairs. We perceive the original nexus of the potlatch, agonistic sacrifice, combining and opposing the host and guest parties in the sacrificial contests, verbal and otherwise, for the goods of live—contests that were no less violent and destructive for being sacral. In fact, it is the presence of violent death that gives the agonistic nexus of the human and divine worlds its sacrality. Here the brahmin is not yet the exclusive adherent of ritualistic order but a consecrated warrior going out to prove himself in the sacrificial contest. The threatening realities of the original "battle of sacrifice" can still be pieced together from ritual rules such as those that are concerned with heads that are to be buried under an elaborate brick fire altar.[8] It can be shown that the harmless ritualistic abstraction of "the head of the sacrifice" is no other than the victim's severed head; thus the recurrent threat held out to the imprudent contestant in the Upanisadic debates that he will lose his head was more than empty hyperbole. This head was the head of the defeated brahmin warrior who failed to win and to exchange the *servitude et grandeur* of the knight errant for the settled life of the lordly man of substance.

It is the cyclically recurring violence and destruction of the "battle of sacrifice" that appears to have led to the reform of the ritual, specifically, of the sacrificial contest itself. By removing the opposite party, the contest was eliminated. The immolation of the sacrificial victim was relegated outside the ritual enclosure. The sacrificial meal was broken up, and the awesome aspects of the myth that connects the meal with the immolation of Idā, daughter and wife of the human sacrificer's prototype, Manu, were replaced with the originally unrelated flood story.[9] The enigmatic *bráhman* formulations that contained the insoluble mystery of life and death and constituted the weapons in the perilous verbal contest were replaced by the flat and perfectly unenigmatic *brāhmaṇa* identifications of ritual elements with elements of the macro- and microcosmos.[10] Identification is indeed given as the new "weapon" that gave Prajāpati, the Lord of Life and prototype of the classical Vedic sacrificer, his decisive victory over his opponent, Death, thereby putting a definitive end to the sacrificial contest and inaugurating the reformed ritual.[11] The dismembered elements of the broken cycle of sacrificial violence with its ever-uncertain outcome were, through the artifice of identification, restructured into the fail-safe construct of the śrauta ritual. Henceforth the single sacrificer would stand unopposed by his rivals and unimpeded by his partners in his ritual enclosure, creating a transcendent world all his own and, for that reason, unrelated to society.

## *4*

Here the classical brahmin comes into his own. However, he does not do so primarily in a priestly capacity, for he would risk his exclusive attachment to the transcendent rule of the śruti by attaching himself to a patron. Instead he is the archetypal single sacrificer, practicing by and for himself the injunctions of the śruti's transcendent order. From there, the road leads straight to the interiorization of the ritual order. Even when eating his meal, he does so as a sacrifice in the internal fires of the breaths *(prāṇāgnihotra)*, thereby realizing in himself the absolute order of the śruti.[12] The ideal brahmin is a renouncer turning his back on the world in order to find transcendence in himself.

The turning point where the sacral nexus of conflict, violence, and death was cut through can perhaps best be characterized as an "axial breakthrough''.[13] The once unitary world of agonistic sacrifice was definitively broken and thrown open by the rift between uncompromising transcendence and mundane reality. The axial breakthrough did not, however, restructure the world. It posed a transcendent order that, like the renouncer, turned its back on the world. Having no other meaning than its internal, ''rational'' order, it left the world to its age-old devices of magic and meaning, to ambivalence and conflict. The mundane sphere remained very much—in Max Weber's terms—an ''enchanted '' world. But the momentous difference was that the sacral nexus of sacrificial strife had lost its ultimate validity and legitimizing force. These now belonged exclusively to the transcendent order and consequently were taken out of the world. The shimmering potency of the sacred and the numinous was not eliminated but was vitally impaired by the glaring light of renunciatory transcendence—be it the transcendence of ritualism or of another, ''heterodox,'' but no less demanding absolute order.

From this point on, there was no way back to the unitary world order. Though the Vedic ritualists desperately tried to infuse their transcendent order with meaning and relevance, the encompassment of the worldly sphere could not be achieved anymore.[14] It is only man himself—ideally the brahmin—who can make the connection by alternating between worldly life and submission to the rule of ritualism. Or he may opt for the path of renunciation and leave the world for good. Indeed it is on this point that Vedic ritualism exercises its enduring appeal. It does not require man to leave the world once and for all but allows him to return to his mundane concerns. It remains open to man's life in the world even though it cannot encompass worldly life. This may well be the secret of the Veda's pivotal position and the meaning of its being the hallmark of ''orthodoxy.''

## 5

Although the axial breakthrough that split the unitary order did not change or reform the world, it did take away the ultimate validity and legitimacy of the mundane sphere. This is particularly relevant for kingship and the state. Three of the following essays are therefore concerned with the king and his order, viewed not so much as given institutions but rather as a problem, and an essentially insoluble one at that.[15] Briefly, the problem is the universal one of authority and legitimacy. These were originally provided by the outcome of the periodic ''battle of sacrifice.'' It can be shown that the so-called royal consecration *(rājasūya),* like other such Vedic rituals (*vājapeya, aśvamedha,* or horse sacrifice) and even the standard Soma sacrifice *(agniṣṭoma),* hides an original cycle of setting out after the monsoon harvest on transhumance and conquest and returning again.[16] The turning points of the cycle, at the setting out and at the return, were marked by agonistic sacrificial festivals still apparent in the rājasūya's series of sacrifices strung out over a couple of years. In his unremittingly repeated circuit, the king joins two opposite and complementary worlds, the peaceably settled community *(grāma)* and the wilds *(araṇya),* where the consecrated warrior band has its being. In this way, the king (or would-be king) vindicated his power and authority over both worlds—or lost out to his rival partners in the cycle of violence. The king's position of power and authority, dependent on the uncertain outcome of the circuit, was as a consequence unstable and constantly endangered. The ritualistic reform, however, broke the cycle of violence and restructured its disjointed parts into mechanistically devised rituals performed separately by the unaided and unopposed single sacrificer. It is significant that even the royal śrauta rituals are not *sacra publica* but strictly individual affairs in which the royal sacrificer is no different from the commoner. But for the same reason, the realities of the king's world were unchanged. The king's order remained the order of conflict and violence. Even as late as the beginning of the nineteenth century, we come across the conquering and tribute-gathering circuit then known as *mulkgīrī,* "grasping the realm." But although institutionalized, it lacks the ultimate legitimizing value the original cycle held out.

In a comparable way, the *Arthaśāstra*'s description of the process of auditing the state accounts harks back to the agonistic festival.[17] But it also appears that the neatly devised bureaucratic procedure falters and finally founders on the crucial point of who shall control whom. The result is again a conflict in which the king must precariously hold his own among his cosharers in the realm, who in Kauṭilya's formula of the "circle of kings" include not only his allies but his enemies or potential enemies as well. The situation is one of dispersed and conflictive kingship.

## *6*

But if ultimate authority and legitimacy elude him, how is the king to make his writ run, as he obviously does? Part of the answer is in the nature of kingship itself. At the intersection of the conflicting interests and factions, the king fulfills the connective function that the all-pervading conflict requires. His position, then, rests on conflict, and he cannot therefore be called upon to end and eliminate all conflict. But by his connectiveness, he should keep conflict from becoming schismatic. Hence the constantly shifting lines of conflict schematized by Kauṭilya in his "circle of kings." It is again the royal ritual of the rājasūya that brings out the connective function of the king. It shows that the essence of the king's sacral or divine quality—so often ascribed to him by the dharma texts—resides in his connectiveness so long as he successfully fulfills this function.

But as we saw, sacrality has been divested of its decisive potency. It is only transcendence that provides ultimate authority, and it is only the brahmin who has access to it. However, because of his renunciatory stance that gives him transcendent authority, he cannot involve himself with the king on pain of losing that authority and becoming no more than the king. In practice, then, the much-vaunted king-brahmin alliance is a restricted formulation of multiple kingship.

Here we come upon the Indian formulation of the universal problem of power and authority. To turn power into authority, the king must ally himself with the brahmin, but the brahmin must reject the alliance in order to safeguard the authority for which the alliance was sought. While the king stands for the order of conflict, the brahmin's order is absolute, negating all conflict. The one's order is the other's disorder. The two stand at opposite ends from each other, and there is no mediating priesthood. The dilemma is insoluble, as is the dilemma of the dharma.[18]

## 7

It appears that the argument outlined above can be carried forward to the scene of the Mughal Empire.[19] Notwithstanding its strongly marked Muslim character, it was no less an Indian phenomenon, underwritten—to mention only the most obvious feature—by the Mughal-Rajput alliance. One may be inclined to think here of India's well-known "inclusivism,"[20] but we can perhaps be more precise. Rather than an integrativeness that accommodates alien elements that otherwise might disrupt the coherent fabric of Indian civilization, we see here the inner conflict of tradition at work. The open rift between the king's order of conflict and the brahmin's, or the renouncer's, absolute order of transcendence called for and actually welcomed new ways to deal with disruption. It is not so much India's integrativeness per se as it is the inner conflict that allowed the "inclusion" of the Islamic conception of transcendent order. The empire that was ostensibly intended to realize this order does not seem to have been seriously challenged as such.

The Mughal rulers, however, although asserting their claim to universal dominion, were well aware of their limitations. They recognized implicitly an "inner frontier" raggedly and shiftingly dividing taxpaying regulation areas from those held by tributary or rebellious—the two qualifications easily shade over into one another—chiefs or rājās. In many ways, this arrangement recalls the ancient complementary opposition of "village" and "wilderness," of the settled sphere and the sphere of the war band. In this context, an institution like the mulkgīrī circuit easily falls into place.

Like previous regimes, the Mughal Empire was fully and at all levels involved in conflict, even to the point of submergence, referring at the same time to a universal transcendent order. However, this was to change fundamentally with the introduction of the modern concept of the state by the

British regime at the end of the eighteenth century. The essential difference was not its alien origin. The Mughals had also been aliens; nor did the British regime lack Indian allies. The difference was rather that the modern state denies internal conflict and does not know an inner frontier. Instead it is based on the notion of an unbroken and universalist internal order. There are no more cosharers in the realm whose shifting networks of conflict and alliance make up the substance of the state, but only monadic subjects, equal before the law and interchangeable. The modern state, in other words, wants to bring the ideal of universal order from its ultramundane haven down to earth. The inner conflict then becomes explosively schismatic, as eventually became clear in the drama of the Partition.

## *8*

The universal order propounded by the modern state implied a novel, analytic view of society.[21] Rejecting the pervasiveness of conflict, it could only conceive of society as made up of separate, self-contained units. Hence the notion of the self-sufficient "village republic." Hence also the exclusivist census definition of caste as a world unto itself, which disregards the interrelations of castes as well as other, noncaste groupings, such as guilds or brotherhoods. This definition translates the scriptural notion of *varṇa,* but distorts the living realities of *jāti*. Identifying the conflict-free ideal of varṇa separation with the conflictive interdependence of jāti, the modern state sought to establish its universal order. In this way, an inflexible grid was devised to allow the state to rule society, by remote control as it were, through impersonal, mechanistically conceived rules and agencies. It may well be that this view has in a significant way contributed to the idea of an unchanging or stagnating society held in the unyielding grip of monolithic tradition.

This idea seems to have gradually developed and hardened during the nineteenth century, together with the growing elaboration of the state. The high water mark was reached in the beginning of this century with the evermore refined census operations that were specifically directed at recording caste, in the sense of self-contained units. In the same period, the clinching argument for the monolithic tradition of the caste institution was provided by the authority of Max Weber, who ingenuously viewed caste as unbreakably wedded to the karman theodicy.[22] Though it is certainly possible to find traditional statements linking caste and karman, this was not a fundamental doctrine. Moreover, on closer consideration it becomes clear that such a doctrine would be untenable even theoretically.

If we have to view caste in the sense of its census definition as an inflexible, monolithic tradition, it is a tradition of the modern state unknown to the old dispensation.

## 9

The thread that holds the following essays together is the inner conflict of tradition. This conflict is not a peculiarity of Indian civilization. One is, of course, accustomed to the distance, even the opposition, between ideal and reality. But we still tend to view the ideal in a direct line with reality even if at an unreachable distance. India, however, shows us a sharp break in which the two are, as a matter of principle, incompatible. The "axial break-through" decisively split the unitary order of the world into two principles; the turbulent order of conflict and the static order of transcendence. The broken connection can be restored, not by somehow forcing or faking unity, but by man, who has the freedom to turn his back on the order of the world and to opt for transcendence. The only connection is in man's voluntary decision.

From this perspective, we may reformulate the relationship between "great" and "little tradition." The "great tradition" proposes the separative and conflict-free order of transcendence that denies society and its web of relationships. The "little tradition," on the other hand, is the lived-in order of society characterized by conflict and interdependence. It is therefore not exclusively geared to the "little community" of, say, the narrowly circumscribed village. While the renunciation-oriented brahmin is the exemplar of the ultramundane great tradition, the protagonist of the mundane little tradition is the king. The little tradition, then, is the king's order of conflict and connectiveness. Together king and brahmin bear the brunt of the unresolved conflict of civiliation.

Though the two orders impinge on each other, there is no process through which they can merge. Nor does the great tradition gradually supersede the little tradition, as the well-known phenomenon of "Sanskritization" (or "brahminization") seems to suggest. These terms imply not so much a process as a structure—a structure that is determined by the unbridgeable gap between the two traditions.

Here, however, a third "tradition" has intervened, the "tradition of modernity," exemplified by the modern state. Its distinctive feature is the principled denial of the gap between the two orders and the total identification of the mundane with the transcendent order. As the sovereignty ascribed to it makes clear, the modern state cannot be transcended. It is itself transcendent and so is its universalist order. Hence the similarity of the brahmanical and the modern tradition. However, the difference is equally obvious. There is no more room for a countervailing order. Modernity, then, means the integration of the mundane and the transcendent orders into one explosive reality.

# 1 India and the Inner Conflict of Tradition

## I

Ever since English Utilitarians and Evangelicals and Indian reformers set out to modernize India, the problem of misunderstood traditions and miscarrying modernization has been with us. It may, therefore, not be out of place to take a point of view that may enable us to understand the meaning and function of tradition, not in order to oppose it once more to modernity, but rather in order to arrive eventually at an integrated view.

To begin with, we may view tradition as the way society formulates and deals with the basic problems of human existence. In other words, it is the way in which society comes to terms with the insoluble problem of life and death, including such life and death matters as food and water in a world of scarcity.[1] In this respect, of course, it is not different from modernity. Since the fundamental problem of life and death is truly insoluble, it has to be attacked, formulated, and dealt with each time anew under a different aspect. Tradition therefore is and has to be bound up with the ever-shifting present. Hence the irritating flexibility and fluidity of tradition.

This can be clearly seen in customary law and its procedures, such as the much-vaunted simplicity of village or panchayat justice. The point is not its rustic simplicity—in fact its procedures are often far from clear to the unwary observer—but its basis in the intuitive understanding that the participants in the face-to-face society have of the web of social relations and each other's place in it. This intuitive knowledge makes it possible to do without objective rules, precedent, and case construction and yet arrive at decisions (or stalemates) that are acceptable to the participants. But the results, from case to case, will often be far from lucid to the outsider, let alone easily

This essay first appeared in *Daedalus* 102, no. 1 (1973): 97–113. Reprinted, with minor revisions, by permission of *Daedalus: Journal of the American Academy of Arts and Sciences,* Cambridge, Massachusetts.

comparable, for customary law and its proceedings are not concerned primarily with the objective truth of the matter but with the subjective truth of the persons involved, which will differ from situation to situation.[2] Obviously, the worst thing that can happen to customary law is codification. And the same goes for the sometimes hair-raising complications of rights in the soil, the division of its produce, and even of weights and measures,[3] complications that hardly seem to bother the local participants but only come out when the revenue administration wants to describe and fix them in an objective and systematic fashion.

However, tradition cannot be only flexible and situational, for its essential mission is still to deal in a structured way with the insoluble life-death problem in all its situational manifestations. It must, therefore, also offer a plan or order independent of and above the actual situation. It is this transcendent order that provides man with the fixed orientation for legitimizing his actions in the middle of the situational flux. In other words, tradition has to be both immanent in the actual situation so as to keep up with shifting reality and transcendent so as to fulfill its orientating and legitimizing function. Thus, we can understand the paradoxical but traditionally common idea that transcendent law is all the time there, suspended as it were in midair, and that it can be "found" by agonistic procedures, verbal or otherwise.[4] Here also seems to lie the meaning of the urge for consensus. In this way, truth and law are at the same time transcendent and immanent in society. Obviously this is a tour de force, but it can work as long as truth and law are not explicitly codified.

This is no different in the case of the Indian concept of *dharma*. The well-known difficulty of defining and translating this term is the result of its being caught on the horns of the dilemma outlined above. Dharma is the transcendent lodestar and is thus removed from the pressures of man's daily affairs. Or in Louis Dumont's adaptation of Thiers's phrase about the constitutional monarch, "le dharma règne de haut sans avoir, ce qui lui serait fatal, à gouverner."[5] It is therefore based on the Veda, the *śruti*, even though the connection between Veda and dharma is in reality nonexistent; moreover, dharma has to be relevant for an ordinary man in society who does eat meat, marries his cross-cousin, interacts closely with people exhibiting different degrees of impurity, and generally has to act contrary to the tenets of dharma. In short, dharma has to take custom into account. Indeed *ācāra*, "custom," is considered an important source of dharma, and the task of determining what is the right custom falls on the assembly, the *pariṣad*. Of course, this pariṣad should be composed of educated and virtuous men, who by definition will be conversant with the Veda, however little relevance the Veda may have for the matter in hand. In theory, the circle is conveniently closed and everything is as it should be.[6] But the reference to the council or assembly is no less significant, and in the final analysis, the dharma texts cannot but concede that no blame is attached to the man who simply follows the customs of his community even if they are contrary to the dharma.[7] But neither will such a man arrive at the transcendent solution of the life-death problem, for, even after his death, he will remain bound to his community in following births.

## 2

Here I think we come upon the hard core of tradition, namely, its inner conflict. Tradition is determined by the particular form in which it expresses the conflict between its immanence in society and its transcendent aspiration to solve the fundamental problem of human existence. Although this view of tradition as a paradox does not look very promising, it may offer us a vantage-point for our understanding of social and cultural phenomena and processes. Instead of having to explain away the obvious rifts and fissures so as to arrive at a harmonious and coherent pattern, we may exploit the essentially fractured picture for a dynamic view of society and culture as organized around an inner conflict.

Let me try to illustrate this with reference to Indian civilization. The task has been greatly facilitated by Louis Dumont's fundamental work on caste and hierarchy,[8] although I shall have to differ from his main thesis on the place of hierarchy. Briefly, then, we find here two diagonally opposed principles of organization, the one based on hierarchical interdependence and the other on separation and independence, represented respectively by the king (or the dominant caste) and the brahmin. A practical illustration of this situation may be found in A. C. Mayer's study of a village in Central India.[9] The dominant rajputs (literally, "king's sons") of the village who entertain, notwithstanding their royal pretensions, commensal relations with a group of definitely lower "allied" castes—an arrangement that also seems to help them to maintain their dominance through their retinue of "allies"—clearly exhibit a pattern of hierarchical interdependence and reciprocity. On the other hand, there are the vegetarian khatis (farmers) and a few artisan castes that tend to restrict their relations, each to his own caste. These castes can be said to "opt out" of the system of interdependence and to stress their independence. Their "opting out" is equally reflected in the distinct, though far from rare, oddity that whereas some higher castes may accept their food, they themselves refuse to return the compliment, thereby demonstrating their disregard of interdependence. In other words, they follow a brahminic pattern also reflected in a simple, unostentatious life style as against the "royal" style of the rajputs, whose extensive relations require generous hospitality.

Yet the typically brahminized khatis and other castes following the same pattern are placed by the consensus of Mayer's informants fairly low on the ranking scale, below the rajputs and their allies. From the point of view of brahminic values as the touchstone of hierarchy, the fact that the meat-eating and generally unbrahminic rajputs and their "allied" servants are credited with a higher rank is distinctly embarrassing. Professor Dumont observes that "here to all appearances the principle of the pure and the impure is in abeyance," a circumstance which he feels to be fairly unique. He then argues that "this is the point at which . . . power participates in purity, although the latter negates it in theory; or in other words, this is the point at which the solidarity between the first two varnas (of brahmins and kṣatriyas) reveals itself." The solution, however, does not seem to require this somewhat awkward explanation. The trouble is not so much with the reported facts as with the theory of an all-encompassing ideology of hierarchy, which forces us to underplay the real contradictions. Since Professor Dumont recognizes these contradictions which he analyzes so clearly, one wonders why he did not exploit them for his theoretical work instead of relegating them to a secondary level. For if we start by taking them seriously, it becomes at once apparent that we are confronted—as the villager is—with two opposite and irreconcilable principles of organization, the one stressing interdependence, and the other independence. The relevant point is, then, not the unexplained low rank of the brahminizing caste, but rather that this ranking in fact runs aground on their brahminical separateness and independence, which are reflected in their opting out of the regular system of food and drink exhanges. Professor Mayer, therefore, has to put them in his table of castes in a separate block, not under but next to the rajputs and their allies, while the other castes follow under the rajputs.

Lest it be thought that the situation in this village is an exception with regard to the overall system, it may be worthwhile to consider for a moment the strikingly parallel right-left division of castes known from South India. This well-known but so far rather hazy phenomenon has been studied in the field by Brenda F. Beck.[10] The right-hand division appears to be composed of the dominant peasants such as the Gaundar, who "are known in legend, ritual and even by title as the 'kings of the area,'" and the service castes directly dependent on them. They form a closely knit complex, resembling each other in ritual matters and entertaining an elaborate system of exchanges. The left-hand division is made up of vegetarian, brahmin-emulating castes which exhibit various degrees of independence from the "kings" of the area because of their outside contacts through trade and marketable skills. As against the coherence of the kinglike group and its dependents—constituting, as Miss Beck puts it, the "in" group of "allied" castes[11]—the left-hand castes are far more diverse and exclusive, not least among themselves. They do not form a coherent bloc but a plurality of separate, mutually independent units. Consequently, the ranking that is fairly simple and clear-cut within the right-hand bloc tends to be vague if not irrelevant with the left-hand castes, for in the left-hand division the higher castes do not mediate power and prestige for the lower ones as is the case in the right-hand bloc.[12] So here, too, we find an essentially dichotomous picture held together, not by an integrating hierarchy of values, but by the conflict between the two principles of hierarchical interdependence on the one hand and of separation and independence on the other. This case, moreover, is the more interesting because it points up the systematic nature of the dichotomy.

### *3*

On one hand, hierarchy seems to be based on real relations such as become apparent in the acceptance of food and drink, and these relations are tied up with the distribution of power and focused on rights in the soil, which are managed by the "kings." On the other hand, where the brahminic "way out" is followed, not relations, but isolation becomes the key word and hierarchy consequently breaks down. But it would be wrong to see the two principles simply as two different traditions. For notwithstanding their obvious irreconcilability, the brahminic ideal of separateness and independence is still recognized as the ultimately valid one. Thus Mayer's rajputs, when they maintain close relations with the lower "allied castes," are far from denying the ultimate validity of the brahminic ideal that would require them to keep themselves apart. Their excuse is that they need servants, with whom they have to keep close contacts;[13] in other words, as mediators of power and prestige they cannot help having to live in a world made up of relations. Equally, the fact that the brahmin is deemed to be above the right-left dichotomy means the recognition of the ideal he stands for as the ultimately valid one.

So the brahmin and the total independence he represents cap the dichotomous system, signifying that it is still felt to be one, albeit contradictory, whole. But this does not create a system of hierarchical interdependence, for such a system can only be given reality in actual relations. The brahmin ideal, however, rejects all relations in favor of absolute independence. It can therefore only be an outside reference point for each separate group and cannot relate them to each other, either vertically or horizontally.

Nor does this ideal reference point resolve the conflict on the higher level of an all-encompassing ideology. For the brahminical rejection of relations obviously cannot be reconciled with the system of relations that society is based on, nor can it encompass them. The "kingly" order immanent in social relations and the transcendent brahminical order are irreconcilably opposed to each other. This unresolved conflict is the form Indian tradition has developed to express and deal with the insoluble problem with which all tradition is essentially concerned. For, as the oldest ritual texts already make clear, society is felt to be based on the alternation of life and death, and consequently participation in society's web of relations is felt to be tantamount to continual involvement with death. The radical way to escape from this situation was resolutely to turn one's back on society and thereby to overcome death.[14] That this is an impossibility is hardly relevant. The point is that tradition can only deal with the insoluble by being itself an unresolved conflict.

We may then recognize the pivot of Indian tradition in the irreconcilability of "brahmin" and "king," who yet are dependent on each other, for the king will need the transcendent legitimation that only the brahmin can give. But the brahmin, however much he may need the king's material support, cannot enter into relations with the king, for this would involve him in the world of interdependence—a situation that would be fatal to the brahmin's transcendence,[15] in the same way that "governing" would be fatal to dharma.

## 4

What relevance can the foregoing considerations have for modernity? The first thing to note is that there hardly seems to be room for a conflict between tradition and modernity, for whatever room there is has already been taken up by the unresolved conflict of tradition itself. Modernity, then, would seem to find its predestined place within tradition's own essentially broken and contradictory framework.

The indubitable fact of the alienness of modernity introduced by a colonial government seems to be greatly overrated as a source of difficulties, for such a view is ultimately based on the romantic belief in the closed and monolithic character of a civilization as an autonomous organism. That this is not only a belief, and as such is beyond proof or disproof, but rank superstition is sufficiently clear—even the most superficial reading on Indian civilization can demonstrate this—and should not detain us here.

The essential point is that the alien and the modern offer new ways to deal with the long-standing, unresolved conflict and thus are more often than not eagerly welcomed. For modernity is, if anything, dedicated to the devaluing or even the breaking up of organic or primordial ties, which it wants to replace with suprapersonal, universalistic groupings. As we saw already, this tendency is at the heart of the traditional conflict between "kingly" interdependence and brahminic independence. Thus, for instance, the "joint family" has been idealized out of recognition as a badge of cultural identity coming straight out of hoary tradition. Obviously "jointness" may serve as an adequate device where other means of securing labor on the one hand and subsistence on the other are lacking. Nevertheless, brahminical theory prefers the division of the father's estate by the surviving sons,[16] as it usually favors the individual over the collectivity.[17] It is therefore not surprising that modernization, even when clearly derived from the West, and ''brahminization'' (or ''Sanskritization'') are often seen to tie in easily with each other.[18] In this way modernity—in a sense already ''transcendent'' by the fact of its alienness—falls in line with the transcendent legitimation that brahminic theory possesses.

Viewed in this way, modernity would seem to add only a few new possibilities to the old conflict, while the latter remains the same, so that when everything is said and done the overall pattern has not changed. Though this view may be helpful in laying the ghost of the overworked tradition-modernity fight, it is not sufficient, for it comes down to yet another assertion of India's perennial unchangeability grinding all innovation to meaningless dust. On the contrary, it should be asked whether the obvious changes that have been wrought over the last hundred or two hundred years are only of a superficial nature without any significant impact on the overall structure. Or, in other words, whether the inner conflict on which Indian civilization is built changed in form and content.

## 5

Perhaps the effect of change can nowhere be seen in a clearer way than in the sociopolitical sphere; at least it is best documented there.[19] As a convenient starting point we may take the traditional empire, such as that of the Mughals.[20] This, like other traditional empires, was a rambling collection of smaller and bigger local centers enjoying various degrees of power and influence over their surroundings and continually competing with each other for local or regional predominance. For a long time, by far the biggest center was the Mughal power situated in the strategic Delhi-Agra area. But for all its power and prestige, it was in fact no more than one power, albeit a preponderant one, among others. In order to realize its claims, it had continually to ally itself with the local powers, which, of course, expected more than merely immaterial benefits for their cooperation. In other words, the empire lacked the independent power and resources fully to realize its claims, and the price for the necessary cooperation of the local powers further weakened the imperial resources. In order to strengthen its resource base, the empire had to resort to conquest and expansion. But these also required substantial initial investments for obtaining the necessary support, and it has been shown that with the conquest of the Deccan in the second half of the seventeenth century, when the empire reached its greatest expansion, the cost of conquest became so heavy as to be fatal. Conquest meant a cumbersome process of winning over the holders of local influence by distributing imperial resources, including crown lands, before any benefit could be reaped. Thus the empire, though never actually overthrown, naturally and irrevocably shriveled again into a local sphere of influence, or "little kingdom," at the mercy of the new would-be empire builders such as the Marathas, the Afghans, and eventually the British.

In fact the Mughal Empire reflects on an enlarged scale the cycle of the segmentary polity. Such a polity continually alternates between total dispersion of power among the segments that balance each other in an ever-shifting pattern of rivalry and alliance and the effort on the part of particular segments to rise above the mêlée, centralize part of the power available, level down the other segments, and replace them with an administrative apparatus.[21] In the case of total dispersion, there is a potentially unending concatenation of overlapping centers interconnecting wide areas. Such a situation seems to be reflected in the geographical extension of "a regional network of hypergamy which links dispersed and often socially disparate groups within a generalized marital exchange pattern," as have been observed for the North Indian rajputs.[22] The poor man's solution to empire, one is tempted to conclude. Its strength is exactly the dispersion of power so that it can in no one place be attached and finally broken, while at the same time, the continual open or latent conflict between the segments is managed through diffusion without the need for any easily overstrained central institution.

This situation of dispersed power is, of course, not a static one. Out of the flux of shifting rivalry and cooperation, new centers steadily arise and new power concentrations are attempted. When such centers are successful, they break out of the concatenation of overlapping units. But by the same token, their area of influence will be limited, for the wide-ranging horizontal ties on which the concatenation is based have to be broken. Now, even if such a center or segment manages to reduce the surrounding ones and to replace them with an administrative apparatus, the allegiance of the people who man the apparatus must be secured. In other words, the carefully extracted resources that should be concentrated in the hands of the ruler have to be redistributed. As we saw already in the case of the Mughal Empire, expansion offers no solution, for it only heightens the need for distribution. Since, moreover, resources are for the greatest part tied up with the soil and its agricultural produce, the simplest if not the only way of distribution is to parcel out the rights in the soil itself and the power that goes with them. So the dispersion of power is restored once again, if it has indeed ever stopped being dispersed.

## *6*

Under these circumstances, there can hardly be any form of organization except one that is almost exclusively based on comprehensive personal relations. For, since even the source of power—the rights in the soil and its produce—is diffused throughout, power cannot be broken down in separate, specific functions but is parceled out in total, undifferentiated packages. The participants in the network can only be differentiated as to the greater or lesser amount of power—and this too may be fluctuating—but not as to the kind of power. The ruler is, therefore, no more than a primus inter pares; his functionaries are in fact his cosharers in the realm, and there is practically no room for specific impersonal relations as a basis of the polity.

This is strikingly illustrated in the ancient Indian text on statecraft, the *Arthaśāstra,* which presents a compelling picture of a centralized bureaucratic state. But on closer inspection, the realities show through the cracks. The numerous government departments are not connected by lines of command, delegation, and communication. They are all separate units on the same level, and any control or coordination, it seems, has to be personally secured by the ruler. Likewise, the officers of state are presented as a corps of ranked functionaries enjoying fixed salaries. At the same time, however, they seem to be cosharers with the king.[23] A similarly ambivalent view is given of the state: on the one hand, one can easily take the text's description of the state in the sense of a monolithically coherent unit; yet, when considered in the context of the theory of the "circle" of kings—the text's schematization of the segmentary concatenation of centers—the state comes to look curiously fluid and open-ended. For when in the context of the "circle" the elements or factors of the state are enumerated, they include not only the internal elements but also external ones such as the ally and even the enemy. Segmentation does not stop at the boundaries of the state but permeates it. The state seems to be ready at any moment to dissolve in the "circle."

The interesting point is that this text allows us clearly to discern the realities and their limitations, while at the same time enunciating an ideal state of affairs transcending by far the actual possibilities. But both viewpoints are blended into one whole. It is the same contradictory double point of vision we noticed before as the basis of tradition. On the one hand, the unavoidable reality of the "little kingdom" and the segmentary order had to be accounted for, while on the other, a way out toward an ideal state of affairs transcending the fluidity of the actual situation had to be formulated so as to offer a fixed reference point for legitimation.

This double point of vision seems to be connected with the two principles of social organization. Most prominent, of course, is the segmentary organization centered on the distribution of rights in the soil and its produce—in short, the "kingly" model. But an equally important form of organization seems usually to be overlooked in the context of state formation, probably because it operates in the margin of and threatens the "kingly" organization. I am referring to the war band in its different forms, a subject that deserves a separate study.[24] Here only a few points can be referred to that are relevant in connection with state formation. The first point, then, is that, in contradistinction to the segmentary "kingly" organization, membership of the war band is not based on ascription but is freely recruited on the basis of individual allegiance to a single successful leader.

An old and well-documented illustration of this phenomenon may be found in the ancient indian *vrātya* bands described in the ritual texts.[25] In that context they form a problem, because they do not fit into the well-ordered and rational system of ritual expounded by these texts. From the point of view of the inner conflict of tradition, their occurrence in this context is not so strange. Two points are of particular interest. In the first place, the vrātya band is not simply an exceptional feature deviating from the normal system, for it clearly ties in with practical needs. Its activities center around transhuming and raiding expeditions necessitated by the scarcity during the lean season. Thus we are told that such bands set out in autumn after the monsoon harvest in search of food for their men and cattle and return before the next monsoon. The second point is that the vrātya, for all his "heterodoxy," is still the starting point for the brahminical model of withdrawal and renunciation. In this connection, it does not seem fortuitous that in South India left-hand groups were involved in the clearing and settlement of previously forested areas and that "warriors" were generally members of the left division.[26] Here we can observe the connection with the problem of state formation, especially when we take into consideration the transformation of the South Indian polity into a warrior-dominated and warfare-oriented one in the thirteenth and fourteenth centuries.[27]

## 7

Probably the best studied material regarding this function of the war band is that of the ancient Germanic peoples. Authors of ancient Rome had already noticed the difference between the polycephalous (or acephalous) organizations of the settled tribes and the war band's uniting of individual members from different tribes under a successful leader. It is especially this type of organization, based on the association of different ethnic elements under a single leadership, the conquest of land, and the establishment of overlordships in new areas, that seems to have determined to a great extent the essence of medieval kingship.[28]

Of course, such developments are only possible when advantage can be taken of adjoining rich areas and their resources, as in Roman Gallia. The Mughal Empire started in the early sixteenth century with exactly such a predatory war band, led by the founder of the dynasty, Babur. On a smaller scale, dacoity seems to play the same role in rajput state formation.[29] The critical point in such developments is, however, the moment of success, for by itself the war band does not crate new resources but only causes a reshuffle. It may be of interest to note that in early medieval Europe, as in the Mughal case, the principle of a nonascriptive contractual bond with the ruler that also governed the original war band lived on in the organization of the polity—in Europe as feudalism, in India as the *jāgīr* system. But the end result remained the same—segmentary diffusion—for the main part of the resources remains tied up with the soil. This in turn means, as already argued, a reversal to segmentation and the parceling out of total packages of rights and power. Thus the Mughal Empire could only exist as a *Personalverband* based on personal relations.

Yet such traditional empires are at the same time characterized by an orientation to a suprapersonal and durable unity in which power is regulated by rationally organized bureaucratic agencies on the basis of impersonal principles of justice. In short, it is oriented toward a transcendent legitimation that it tries to translate into reality.

The prime example is, perhaps, the third century B.C. Maurya Empire, whose ruler Asoka went to the unusual length of posting the tenets of the transcendent Buddhist-inspired dharma on rocks and pillars throughout his empire so as to galvanize, as it were, his widespread domains into a universalistic, suprapersonal unity. There are, however, no indications that the empire was much more than a segmentary concatenation that perhaps derived some extra strength and resources from its command of important trade routes—the routes along which the famous inscriptions were placed. But the reality of the universal dharma as the foundation of the empire becomes apparent when Asoka claims to have achieved the final victory of the imperial dharma by sending missions propagating the dharma to the courts of all rulers known to him—missions that went completely unnoticed except for their elaborate mention in his own inscriptions. In the same way, we can understand the Mughal Aurangzeb's effort to establish an Islamic polity, as well as the failure to achieve it.

The traditional empire, then, fluctuates in the middle space between two diametrically opposed poles: on the one hand, the total dispersion of power throughout a segmentary and fluid concatenation where the political is completely merged into the social order; on the other, the far-out ideal of a universalistic polity where power is made independent from the social order and is administered according to fixed, transcendent rules.[30] The latter pole is in the literal sense transcendent in that it is beyond the limitations of actual society and can therefore possess ultimate legitimating force. It can only be imagined in an extrasocietal, never-never world such as Asoka's dharma empire, the *'umma,* the universal brotherhood of all believers, as the ideal Islamic polity,[31] or the *universitas christiana*. It certainly has a strong attraction, but its mobilizing potential has to be spent outside or, at best, in the fringe of society which is, in Indian terms, in the sphere of world renunciation. If the pattern of dispersed power may be considered the poor man's solution to empire, the extrasocietal transcendent ideal may be called the poor man's dream of universal dominion.

## *8*

Against the backdrop of the traditional empire, we may now try to understand the change that modernity has brought about in the inner conflict of Indian tradition as it is reflected in the sociopolitical sphere. This change, then, bears on the relationship between reality and the legitimating ideal or, in specifically Indian terms, between the "kingly" and the brahminical, renunciatory order.

As argued, the lack of resources blocked the way toward a change in this relationship. The first requirement for modernity to be effective would therefore seem to be a new base of resources free from commitments to the traditional arrangements. In itself, however, this is not sufficient, for nothing prevents these resources from also being absorbed in the traditional way. Thus, for instance, the extra resources obtained by a successful war (or rather, raiding activities) easily melt away in the existing channels of distribution without causing any structural change. Or, as the *Arthaśāstra* revealingly puts it, the conqueror should give all his allies their due from the war loot, even if he should lose by it, for in this way he will be agreeable to the "circle of kings."[32] What modernity therefore has to be based on, apart from a new resource base, is a new pattern of distribution, a pattern no longer governed by the ramification of personal relations but by an impersonal code of principles and rules. This means that the realm of politics and the stuff it is made of—power and resources—must be set apart and safeguarded against the demands of the traditional order.

It would seem that it is precisely this that the first carrier of modernity in India, the British Indian government, achieved to a remarkable, previously unknown degree. It is, of course, the old but traditionally unattainable ideal. What made its success possible was the simple fact that British rule over India was part of an expanding world power that had its center outside India and drew its main strength from its dominant position in the world trade backed up by a growing industry. Though it needed India in different ways, it was not solely dependent on India's agrarian resources. It could therefore afford to stay away from involvement in Indian society. In fact, it could not only afford to do so, it simply had to work hard to establish and maintain this privileged position, for the first decades of the East India Company's rule over Bengal had clearly shown that its resources and power were not safe from the danger of being drained away. Whatever the philosophy behind the code of rules and regulations of 1795, including the "Permanent Settlement" of the land revenue in Bengal, its aim was unmistakably to disengage the government from involvement in the local and regional segmentary order. The government's resources and power, including the use of force, were reserved and administered according to an ever-expanding, rational system of impersonal regulations.

Obviously this was no simple matter. The problem before the colonial government was how to strike a balance, from situation to situation and from crisis to crisis, between the need for withdrawal and the pressures for involvement. But the pattern was set. The distributive demands that kept being made on the center in various ways from various quarters were no longer met on their own terms but by the formulation and application of objective rules that bored ever deeper down toward the grass roots level. Though in this way the contacts between the modern and traditional orders grew immensely, there could be no integration, far less an overall impact of modernity on the traditional dispensation. The very modus operandi of modernity precluded such a comprehensive impact. It was devised to deal with specific cases in specific ways according to specific rules, so as not to have to deal with total situations and comprehensive relations. In this perspective, a local magnate was not a comprehensive leader of his men but exclusively a legal landowner. Only as such could he have his interests looked after by the government.[33] But this meant also that the specific impingements of modernity—though often dramatic for the persons involved—were met by the comprehensiveness of the traditional order that diffused the effect, closed the ranks, and ultimately, after the reshuffle, remained the same.

This dual dispensation had the great advantage of giving a previously unknown measure of reality to the dream of a universalistic order. But its failure was that it could not come to grips with the comprehensiveness and diffuseness of the traditional order. It could only refuse full access to the center's power so that the traditional order could not gain strength at the expense of the center; the most that the center's reservation of power could achieve with regard to the "little kingdom" was to freeze it and thereby reduce its peculiar efficacy, which lies in its fluidity. But in this way, no fundamental change could be brought about in the traditional order.

Of course the division was never watertight, nor could it be. The government could not operate in a vacuum and there had, therefore, to be considerable "leakages." Thus, there were groups that derived a measure of power and influence through their connection with the government and especially through positions in its extensive bureaucracy.[34] More important however, the simple fact of India's becoming part of an expanding commercial empire with access to the world market made for the development of another independent resource base—or rather a plurality of small ones—in the hands of groups of landlords, cultivators, and commercial entrepreneurs.[35] Such groups easily outgrew the reduced circumstances of the "little kingdom," and even though they were in no position to compete directly with the government, their demands on the center were hard to ignore. The always precarious balance of the dual dispensation became more and more threatened and eventually had to be completely overhauled.

### 9

Here the traditional inner conflict presented itself in a new form. Briefly, the problem was—and is—that modernity operates on the assumption, or rather the fiction, that society consists of an arbitrary collection of isolated individuals, while the unity of the whole is not realized through immediate relations of hierarchical interdependence but mediated by abstract, impersonal rules and principles. This, as we saw, is not new. What is new is the resource base that makes it possible to give the idea a substantial degree of reality. In order to achieve this degree of reality, modernity requires an impersonal, "horizontal" pattern of distribution, which emancipates the individual from the personal bonds of "vertical," hierarchic interdependence characterizing the "little kingdom."

Now perfectly "horizontal" distribution, even if all resources would be spent on it, is an impossibility. The very fact of distribution is bound to create inequalities, for even the most perfect set of rules has still to be operated by people who perform the distribution at different stages and levels and are thereby placed in positions of unequal power. In this way, the system would easily slip back into the segmentary "little kingdom" concatenation and modernity would lose its reality content. In the final analysis, the problem is again insoluble, but it can be managed in new ways; the "horizontal" and "vertical" orders must be allowed to interpenetrate. Obviously, a colonial government cannot allow this interpenetration to come about, since it would irredeemably impair its position. When it comes to that point, it can only react by total withdrawal, as indeed happened. The problem can only be managed by a national polity, for only a national polity can take the risks implied by the interpenetration of the "horizontal" and "vertical" orders. Such a polity, prepared slowly over the previous century or so, came into being in the interbellum period in the form of the Indian National Congress.

It has been customary to explain the success of the single most important figure in this process, Gandhi, by pointing to his expert wielding of traditional religious symbols and ideas, but this is only half the truth. Gandhi, apart from his use of symbols that had also been used by others, was a renouncer, personifying in his relation to the sociopolitical world the inner conflict of tradition. This also qualified him to deal with the conflict in its modern form, but as a renouncer he played a totally unprecedented role. It has recently been pointed out that "the reason, over and above the use of religion in politics, why Gandhi was able to initiate national movements with such conspicuous success was because he recognized the social pluralism of India and exploited the traditional loyalties of different sections of society to draw them into political agitations.''[36] If I am allowed to paraphrase this statement, I would say that he managed to attend to the organization of both the ''vertical'' demands of the segmentary order and the conflicting need for ''horizontal'' unity. That the actions aiming at horizontal unity and therefore centered on universal moral issues were far less successful and showed a far lower degree of control than his earlier, locally restricted ones, which focused on material grievances,[37] was to be expected. Given that horizontal, no less than vertical, unity must be sustained by distribution and that access to the center's power and resources was as yet barred, the measure of reality he gave to horizontal, national unity, if only during the short span of a nationwide agitation, was a totally new phenomenon.

Equally remarkable and instructive are the limits of horizontal, national unity that became painfully clear at the same time. The unity of the nation is apparently not bounded by ethnic, linguistic, or geographical criteria nor even by the extent of existing or potential channels of distribution. The final criterion would seem to be the recognition of a specific formulation of transcendent authority and legitimation. For the Hindu, this was clearly and unequivocally the renunciatory ideal. It was this ideal that was not only referred to but effectively embodied by Gandhi, who thereby could arbitrate conflict and guarantee ultimate unity. Here, of course, Hindus and Muslims had eventually to part company. As long as horizontal unity was only an idea beyond the reach of reality, it had no direct impact. Once it was given reality, it had to have practical consequences, however painful.

This parenthesis on the limits of horizontal, national unity also shows us something of the precarious and explosive situation that arises from the blending of the vertical and horizontal orders into one reality. Everything then depends on the development of an institutional framework for dealing with this situation. Here probably lies Gandhi's greatest achievement, namely, in the remolding of the Indian National Congress so that it could fulfill this function. For Gandhi did not simply give it moral inspiration, which usually fades once a particular action is over, but he played a dominant role in the different phases of its reorganization during the interbellum period.[38] Its remarkable success lay in its capacity to accommodate both the segmentary local and regional demands and the precarious reality of horizontal unity.

This means, however, that Congress had to be the arena of the resulting tensions and conflicts to the point of becoming identified with these conflicts and consequently being threatened with breakdown. However, so far no other organization has been able to take over its function. Even though the position of the Congress is increasingly being called into question, it has shown an unexpected resilience—a resilience that paradoxically seems to be based on its conflictive nature—and it is still there as the indispensable arena of pervasive conflict and national unity. Whatever the fate of India's political system in general and of the Congress in particular—as argued, it is inherently precarious—the main point is that India has been remarkably successful in setting up the institutional framework for dealing with the traditional conflict in its modern reincarnation.

To conclude: successful modernity does not mean the supersession of tradition or the superimposition on it of a different order. It means that the inner conflict of tradition is now fought within the confines of an expanded reality that transcends the limits of the "little kingdom" so as to include ultimate authority and legitimation themselves. Authority and legitimation are no longer transcendent and safe in an ultramundane sphere but part of reality—and therefore constantly called into question. In contradistinction to tradition, modernity must valorize change because the authority of its code of abstract rules and principles no longer transcends reality. Modernity has not solved the inner conflict of tradition, nor can it ever do so. But it has fundamentally changed it by carrying it over into the sphere of a single explosive reality.

# 2 Brahmin, Ritual, and Renouncer

## *1*

In Hindu society, the brahmin stands supreme. Though he is, at least in principle, divested of temporal power, he is superior even to the king. His is the absolute purity, the yardstick of the socioreligious hierarchy, in relation to which the nonbrahmin gauges his own status.[1] He can be said to be the measure of things. Not only do the classical codes of social and religious behavior derive from him, but also, even to the present day, he represents the model that the others strive to imitate, as witnessed by the increase in "Sanskritization" (i.e., the conforming to brahminical norms of respectability) among nonbrahmins, and especially among the harijan.[2]

The reason for this preeminence is generally assumed to be the brahmin's priestly capacity. He has a monopoly of the performance of the Vedic ritual, the most hallowed part of brahminical tradition. However, this priestly capacity of the brahmin is open to serious qualification and his preeminence does not seem to be founded on priesthood, as I shall argue.[3] But what then is the basis of the brahmin's preeminence?

In a discussion of the place of the brahmin in Indian culture, it is natural to turn in the first place to the Vedic ritual texts. Not only is the Vedic ritual at the heart of brahminical tradition, but above all it would seem to me that the ritual texts reflect an evolution that has been decisive for the position of the brahmin and, generally, for the development of Hinduism.

## *2*

Ostensibly the central theme of the solemn *śrauta* ritual is the periodical regeneration of the cosmos, the winning of life out of death.[4] In the classical

This essay first appeared in slightly different form in *Wiener Zeitschrift für die Kunde Süd- und Ostasiens* 8 (1964): 1–31. Reprinted by permission.

system of the ritual, as presented in the brāhmaṇas and the sūtras, the pivot of the ritual is the *yajamāna,* the patron at whose expense and for whose sole benefit the ritual is performed. He is supposed symbolically to incorporate the universe—he is identified with the cosmic man, Prajāpati. The ritual culminates in his ritual rebirth, which signifies the regeneration of the cosmos.

For our discussion, two points are of particular interest. First, though the ritual is a regeneration of the universe, it is not a communal, but a strictly private celebration, centering on the single yajamāna who is the sole beneficiary.[5] Second, the ritual is the domain of absolute purity; the brahmin ritual specialists are pure and the yajamāna has to undergo a purificatory ceremony, the *dīkṣā,* in order to be admitted to the ritual.

However, underneath the classical system, a different, older pattern can be discerned. Here in this older, preclassical pattern, purity and impurity are complementary to each other. The yajamāna, who has undergone the dīkṣā, is not pure, but on the contrary is charged with the evil of death to which he has to submit in order to be reborn. According to the texts of the Black Yajurveda, one should not eat his food, one should not put on his clothes, nor should one pronounce his name. The reason is the dīkṣita's evil, the impurity of death.[6] Being tainted by death, the dīkṣita has to divest himself of his impure self. In this way we understand that, for instance, the twelve-day ritual *(dvādaśāha)* is described as a gradual purification of the yajamāna.[7] By means of the various offerings and the gifts *(dakṣiṇā)* which represent the parts of his body, he disposes of his impure self.[8] Thus he is reborn pure, "out of the sacrifice."

In this light, the relationship between patron and officiant is of a nature diametrically opposed to what the classical theory of the pure ritual wants it to be. The function of the brahmin officiant is to take over the death impurity of the patron by eating from the offerings and by accepting the dakṣiṇās. By gifts and food, evil and impurity are transferred and purity attained, especially if the donee is a brahmin.[9] It is no matter for surprise, then, that the acceptance of dakṣiṇās by the brahmin is surrounded with meticulous care. The need for such care is, moreover, reinforced by the fact that the brahmin is not allowed to refuse the dakṣiṇā; indeed *Manu* 4, 249 deprecates a brahmin who refuses a gift.[10]

This relationship between patron and officiant comes out clearest in the case of the brahman-officiant. Though his role in the ritual is mostly that of a spectator, he is recognized as the most important of the officiants. His share of the dakṣiṇās is as great as those of the other officiants together.[11] In the classical system, his function is to redress the faults committed in the execution of the ritual. He is the *bhiṣaj,* the healer of the ritual, but this must originally have referred to the healing of death. Since the classical ritual does not admit of impurity but only of infractions against a correct execution of the ritual, the brahman's function was transformed into that of redressing ritual faults. In the preclassical system, then, his role was that of taking over death and impurity. The two poles of the ritual, death and rebirth, are resumed in the complementary pair patron-brahman. At the acme of the ritual, the moment of birth, when the dakṣiṇās are distributed, a reversal takes place: the dīkṣita patron sheds his death impurity and is reborn a pure brahman.[12] The brahman on the other hand takes over the burden of death. Whereas the pivot of the classical ritual is represented by the single yajamāna, the preclassical ritual is based on a complementary pair. This pair, through exchange and the reversal of roles, maintains the continuity of the cosmos.

The cooperation of the antithetical pair in guaranteeing the continuity of life seems to be even more explicit when we consider that their exchanges involve affinal relations. In general, the relations between patron and brahmin—or, in abstract terms, *kṣatra* and *brahman*—are represented as connubial. At the classical Soma ceremony, the yajamāna can marry off his daughters to the officiants. Finally, the officiating brahmin represents the brahman out of which the yajamāna is ritually reborn a brahmin. Seen against this background, the life-winning function of the exchanges stands out clearly. The evil *(pāpman),* which the dīkṣita transfers on his ritual birth to the brahmin, can thus produce rich returns. It is, so to say, transformed into *śrī,* good fortune.[13]

## 3

Actually the patron-brahmin pair, surviving in the classical ritual, stands for two opposed groups cooperating in the life-winning ritual. The classical system has limited the number of participants to seventeen: one yajamāna assisted by sixteen officiants. The Black Yajurveda, however, still knows of a group of dīkṣitas faced in the ritual by a group of non-dīkṣitas, namely, at the *ahīna* or Soma sacrifice lasting from two to twelve days. But in the classical system it is not allowed to officiate for a group of yajamānas. Thus the brahmin who is invited to officiate at a Soma sacrifice should ask whether it is an ahīna. If it is, he should reject the invitation.[14] We may safely assume that the cooperation of two opposed groups, which is not mentioned in the White Yajurveda anymore, belongs to the preclassical system.

The cooperation between the two opposed parties seems to have been characterized by rivalry. Indeed, the classical ritual still contains, though under a stylized form, many contests, especially chariot races and verbal contests (e.g., in the *mahāvrata,* the *vājapeya,* the *rājasūya,* the *aśvamedha).*[15] It is typical of the classical ritual that these contests are very much pushed into the background or transformed into liturgical operations in which there is no real contest any more. But the texts still do indicate that rivalry originally took up a far more important place in the ritual.[16] Thus we read of competing Soma pressings, *saṃsava.*[17] Of course in the classical system, the saṃsava is a ritual fault consisting in lack of spatial separation between two Soma sacrifices taking place at the same time, a fault that calls for expiation. But it is characteristic that the form this "expiation" assumes is that of a contest: one must overcome the rival ritual by a greater sacrifice than that of the adversary.[18] That ritual competition was a normal phenomenon is indicated by the fact that the full- and new-moon sacrifices are characterized as *samṛtayajña,* "competing sacrifice."[19] We are reminded here of the rivalry between devas and asuras, who in the brāhmaṇa texts are often described as competing in the ritual. Their (competitive) exchanges of food and gifts suggested by some passages seem to fit very well into their continuous rivalry.[20]

Although in the classical system the rival is rigorously excluded from the ritual, we may assume that he was an essential participant in the preclassical ritual. His participation as the antagonist of the yajamāna still shines through in the identification of the sticks *(paridhi)* which are put on three sides of the sacrificial fire. The middle (eastern) one is identified with sacrifice *(yajña),* while the southern and the northern ones are identified with the yajamāna and the rival *(bhrātṛvya)* respectively: the yajamāna and the rival each on one side of and linked together by the sacrifice.[21] In this way, it becomes understandable that we occasionally still find that the dakṣiṇā is to be given to the rival, recalling the exchanges of food and gifts between gods and asuras. Such is the case in the *sādyaskra* ritual.[22]

Now in the sādyaskra, the original agonistic character of the ritual is still to some extent manifest. The war and racing chariot are still very much in evidence, and, at least according to one text,[23] a chariot race was part of the ritual. Particularly interesting is the legend which is meant to explain the sādyaskra: "The Ādityas competed with the Aṅgirases for the possession of the heavenly world; they considered: which of our two parties will officiate at the ritual of the other, that party will be left behind (on earth while the other wins heaven)." The Aṅgirases then invite the Ādityas to their ceremony, but the Ādityas find a way out by preparing a ceremony that can be performed on one day (the sādyaskra) and consequently can take place before the Aṅgirases' ceremony. Thus the Aṅgirases are forced to accept the invitation of the Ādityas, who in this way win the contest.[24] Less mythological, almost "historical," is a similar story of rivalry told in connection with a variant of the sādyaskra, the *parikrī,* where Keśin Dārbhya and Khaṇḍika are said to compete with each other for the kingship of the Pañcālas. Khaṇḍika hopes to win by announcing the sādyaskra to Keśin; but Keśin retorts by announcing to his opponent the parikrī, which gives him the upper hand over Khaṇḍika.[25]

It seems possible, then, that originally brahmins and kṣatriyas were not closed, separate groups. It has already been mentioned that the yajamāna, to whatever varṇa he belongs, is ritually reborn a brahmin. The kṣatriya's transformation into a brahmin is made even more explicit in the rājasūya; when the king has been anointed and enthroned, he addresses each of the four leading brahmins with "brahman," whereupon each answers with "thou, O king, art brahman."[26] The reversal of roles is further underlined by the king's gift on this occasion of two golden plaques *(niṣka),* his royal paraphernalia which have been used at the unction, to the brahman.[27] The king even gives away what he has conquered at the symbolic, but originally real, chariot race or razzia. In the same way, the conquests made during the year-long roaming of the sacrificial horse are to be given up at the aśvamedha.[28]

Indeed, we hear of kṣatriyas becoming brahmins, for example, the famous king Janaka of Videha. It is not without interest that Janaka becomes a brahmin on being successful in a verbal contest on the meaning of the agnihotra offerings.[29] On the other hand, brahmins do not seem to be excluded from becoming kings and warriors: for instance, the brahmin Paraśurāma, who exterminated the kṣatriyas.[30] It is further interesting that Paraśurāma after finishing his conquests performs a sacrifice, or even an aśvamedha, at which he hands over the conquered earth to the brahmin Kaśyapa, who eventually hands it over to kṣatriyas.[31] If I am not mistaken, the ancient system of exchange and reversal of roles is still discernible here.

## 4

The above considerations seem to suggest that the brahmin officiants in the classical system of ritual, and especially the brahman officiant—to the extent that they eat from the offerings and accept the dakṣiṇās—have taken the place of the rivals in the preclassical system. An illustration of this development is provided by the rājasūya. After the central ceremonies connected with the unction and the communal Soma drinking *(daśapeya),* a particular offering *(iṣṭi)* is prescribed, the distinctive feature of which is the sending of messengers *(sātyadūtahavīṃṣi).* These messengers bring particular presents, which are connected with the king's unction, that is, with his ritual birth, to the rival kings *(pratirājan).* By their acceptance of the presents, the rival kings show their allegiance. Now these presents are at the same time prescribed as dakṣiṇās for the brahmins who officiate at the iṣṭi.[32] This does not mean that the brahmins have brought the kṣatriyas under their sway or have "usurped" their position. We have seen that brahminhood was not originally represented by a closed group of priestly specialists.[33] The bearers of the brahman, on the contrary, were the antagonists in the preclassical ritual drama. In principle, they were the equals of the yajamāna (or group of yajamānas). Invited as guests,[34] they help to bring about the life-death reversal by eating the host's food and by accepting his gifts. The host is reborn a brahmin; the guest, being a brahmin at the outset, takes over death.

The classical system implies that it is each time the same yajamāna who spends his wealth on the brahmins, but the preclassical system called for reciprocity. In order not to remain permanently saddled with the inferiority implied in his accepting the opponent's food and presents, the donee has to reciprocate ("sich revanchieren"). On the other hand, the lavish munificence of the giver has created a vacuum, which must be filled again. Whereas the classical ritual is supposed to produce its results (i.e., broadly speaking, the furthering of life and prosperity) automatically without an intervening agency, the preclassical system based the life- and prosperity-furthering function on periodically alternating exchanges and reversals.

An illustration of this alternating pattern seems still to be contained in *Aitareya Brāhmaṇa* 4. 25. This text declares that in the beginning Prajāpati undertook the dīkṣā and invited the seasons and the months to officiate for him in the twelve-day ritual. Having officiated for Prajāpati and having received his dakṣiṇās, the seasons and the months feel "heavy" *(gurava ivāmanyanta)*. In their turn, they undertake the dīkṣā and have Prajāpati officiate for them. Thus "Prajāpati, (who is) the year, found support in the seasons and months; the seasons and months (in their turn) found support in Prajāpati, the year; they became firmly established in each other." We might say, in other words, alternately the one represents the brahman out of which the other is reborn.

The same idea seems to underly the prescript that "he who, having accepted many gifts, feels as if he had swallowed poison *(garagīr iva manyeta)* should perform the repeated stoma *(punaḥstoma)*."[35] That is, he should in his turn offer a feast. It would seem that this ancient idea is still preserved in the epic, where it is said that through victory over the rival party the "material sacrifice" *(dravyamayo yajñaḥ)* is obtained and that it has to be spent again in sumptuous ceremonies such as the aśvamedha; "this is the everlasting path of fortune" *(śāśvato 'yam bhūtipathaḥ)*.[36]

In other words, the preclassical system of ritual was characterized by what Mauss called "prestations totales de type agonistique",[37] involving an ever-repeated cycle of exchanges.

## 5

Death must constantly be overcome in order to renew life. The preclassical dualistic system of ritual brought this about through the cooperation of the rival parties in endless rounds of "qui perd gagne." This meant that one was all the time doubly dependent on the other. One needed the other so as to be able to shed one's dead, impure self; but, on the other hand, to fill the vacuum thus created, one again depended on the other. *Pāpman,* "evil," had to be passed to the other so as to be reconverted into *śrī,* "good fortune"; but in order to receive it back, one again depended on the other.

It seems clear that the cooperation between the rival parties is as delicate as it is pivotal. In the texts we can still find the fear that the sacrifice that has been offered will not come back again. Thus *Taittirīya Saṃhitā* 6. 6. 7. 3 says that at the end of the Soma ceremony, in the afternoon, the sacrifice leaves the one who has offered it and goes away to the one who has not offered it; therefore special libations are prescribed to hold it. Thus we also read that "the food of him who has given all, has gone to the (other) people" and therefore he must go there to win it back again.[38] The well-known motif of the sacrifice going away from the devas to join the asuras and of the efforts of the devas to win it back seems to bear out the same idea.

Since it is in the last resort oneself that one offers—the offerings and dakṣiṇās, as has been mentioned, represent the yajamāna—it is easy to see that the procedure involved a heavy risk. In addition, the reciprocal obligation not only to give but also to accept the evil, the death of the others, must have added to the strain of the relations between the parties. The continuity of life depended on the others, but this dependence was permeated with the idea of death. It is perhaps against this background that we should see the concept of "recurrent death" *(punarmṛtyu).*[39]

At any rate, it would seem that here lies the crucial point where the development of ritual thought started. The problem before the ancient ritualists was to break through the vicious circle of mutual dependence. They had to find a way permanently to overcome death and secure the continuity of life. The solution that presented itself to them was to short-circuit the bilateral pattern of exchange and reversal by cutting out the other, the rival party. The elimination of the rival brought the cosmic cycle of life and death in one hand; thus the single yajamāna was enabled to deal ritually with death without incurring the risk involved in the ambivalent cooperation with the others.

## 6

This solution seems to be the leading principle that shaped the classical ritual. It is graphically described in the story of Prajāpati's contest with and final victory over Death. The *Jaiminīya Brāhmaṇa*[40] tells this story as an explanation of the classical form of the mahāvrata ceremony. In its classical form, the mahāvrata is a normalized Soma ceremony, but it has preserved a complex of markedly archaic rites: different kinds of contests (a chariot race among others), dancing, singing, drumming, lute playing, and copulation. The *Jaiminīya Brāhmaṇa* relates that Prajāpati and Death competed with each other through rival sacrifices. In this contest, Prajāpati had as his ''weapons'' *(yajñāyudhāni)* the liturgy of the classical, normalized Soma ritual *(tad yad yajñe stūyate, yac chasyate, yat pracaryate)*. The arsenal of Death consisted in the archaic rites *(yad vīṇāyāṃ gīyate, yan nṛtyate, yad vṛthācaryate)*. A long time the outcome of the contest remains undecided, but finally Prajāpati overcomes his rival through the discovery of the symbolical and numerical equivalences *(saṃpad, saṃkhyāna)*. This meant that Prajāpati, by means of the symbolical and numerical equivalences, brought the ritual ''weapons'' of Death under the same denominator as his own ''weapons.''

Indeed saṃpad and saṃkhyāna were the premier techniques of the ritualists in elaborating the classical code of ritual. It enabled them to reduce the inventory of the ritual to a restricted number of liturgical means—chiefly meter, melody, and *stoma,* or serial arrangement of verses into small units *(stotriyā)* for chanting—which, applied in countless variations and combinations, could be made to express any content. Thus we find, for instance, a great number of ceremonies which are only differentiated by their stoma pattern. Thus Prajāpati's victory over Death expresses the breakthrough of the classical ritual. The ''weapons'' of Death, assimilated to those of Prajāpati, have no meaning of their own anymore and can even be dispensed with completely. In the end, only the characteristic liturgical forms of the mahāvrata chant *(stotra)* and the corresponding recitation *(śastra)* remain as parts of a normalized Soma ceremony, the *sarvajit.*[41]

The most important point in the Prajāpati-Death contest, however, is that Prajāpati's victory means the elimination of Death as a participant in the ritual; or, rather, by means of the symbolical equivalences his power can be ritually made subservient. By the same token, the rival is excluded from the ritual. In the same way as Death, he can be dealt with ritually, without his active participation. The *Jaiminīya* significantly adds as the conclusion of the story: ''Now there is no ritual competition *(saṃsava);* what was the second sacrifice (of Death), that waned; the sacrifice is only one; Prajāpati alone is the sacrifice.''[42] Prajāpati, the cosmic man and incorporation of the classical ritual doctrine, is the prototype of the single yajamāna, who performs without the intervention of a rival party and for his sole benefit the ritual of cosmic renewal.

The outcome does not depend anymore on the others, but everything depends on the correct execution of the automatically working ritual. This has led to an excessive development of ritual ''science,'' but nevertheless it was a breakthrough in that it set the individual free from the oppressive bonds of reciprocity which tied him to the others, the rivals. This was achieved through the symbolical and numerical equivalences. Where there was opposition, there is now equivalence. Through the knowledge of the equivalences, the yajamāna not only becomes the cosmic man Prajāpati, but also, like Prajāpati, he assimilates Death. "Death becomes his self," and thus he conquers recurring death *(punarmṛtyu)*.[43]

## 7

The individualization of the ritual, which placed the single yajamāna in the center, stands out clearest in those cases where the texts by their own words indicate that originally the ceremony was performed by rival groups. Such is, for instance, the case of the "concord" sacrifice *(saṃjñāneṣṭi)*.[44] This ritual was manifestly intended to be performed by rival groups in order to unite them under a common leader. "The gods, unable to agree among themselves on the leadership *(anyonyasya śraiṣṭhye 'tiṣṭhamānāḥ)*, divided into four groups—Agni with the Vasus, Soma with the Rudras, Indra with the Maruts, Varuṇa with the Ādityas—Bṛhaspati made them perform the saṃjñāneṣṭi; they turned to Indra; they agreed on Indra as their leader." The classical ritual of course cannot fully admit such a situation. It therefore transformed the saṃjñāna ceremony into a standard type vegetal offering *(iṣṭi)* to be performed by a single yajamāna, who wishes that the others will agree on his leadership, but without their participation in the ceremony. Thus the *Maitrāyaṇī Saṃhitā* continues: "On him who performs this iṣṭi, they agree as their leader." It is to be noted that whereas the explanatory story speaks of a plurality of rival gods performing the ceremony, the iṣṭi is to be performed by a single person.[45]

Henceforth man depends only on his own (ritual) work, his own *karman*. He is born in the world which he has made himself, as *Śatapatha Brāhmaṇa* 6. 2. 2. 27 has it. The world is no longer recreated through the contest and the exchange between the rival parties: the single individual creates it by himself through his own works, good as well as bad. In this conception, it is no longer possible to pass off the evil work, death, to the others; he must digest it himself. In this the ritual helps him; it has reduced evil to the point where it can be dealt with ritually (of course always on condition that he knows the proper equivalences). On the other hand, the new doctrine means also that there is no more danger that the good work—the correctly executed sacrifice—will not return to the initiator from the opposite side. No more does the sacrifice go away at the end of the ceremony; it stays with the yajamāna. Or in the words of *Śatapatha* 11. 2. 2. 5: "Becoming himself the sacrifice, the sacrificer frees himself from death; . . . what he offers becomes his self in the hereafter; when he goes away from this world it calls after him, saying: Come, here I am, your own self".[46]

Instead of the transversal axis of the reciprocal relations with the others, everything is now concentrated on the vertical axis of the individual life, or lives, of the single yajamāna. It is perhaps in this light that we can understand the novelty and the mystery of the Upaniṣadic karma doctrine which

Yājñavalkya could not explain to Ārtabhāga in front of the other participants in the verbal contest in King Janaka's assembly. "Good *(puṇya)* one becomes by good work, evil *(pāpa)* by evil work".[47] One is tempted to think that Yājñavalkya and Ārtabhāga had to go outside to talk about this doctrine because it was the negation of the contest ideology.

Many factors contributed to the rise and elaboration of the karma doctrine, but it would seem to me that the pivotal point is the emphasis on the individual.[48] The life-death alternation which was realized through the agonistic cooperation with the others must now be worked out by the single individual in his successive lives. But this train of thought cannot stop here; individualization implies that the individual had to be all lest he be nothing. Given autonomy, the individual is able—as has already been noted in the previous section—to overcome the life-death alternation. Resuming the opposite poles in himself, he can attain immortality.

## *8*

The individualization which transformed the ritual must also have meant a transformation in the field of social relations—or at least in the ideas governing their representation. In principle, the reciprocal relations between equal parties have been cut; there can be no more exchange and reversal of roles. Consequently the groups stay fixed in their roles. Relations between the groups are no longer defined in terms of homogeneous prestations but become predominatly governed by functional specialization. The hierarchy, which originally was, in principle, rearticulated at the periodic agonistic ceremonies, now becomes permanently settled. Evil, impurity, does not circulate anymore between the parties but is fixed at the lower levels of the hierarchy. Disposal of impurity becomes a hereditary specialty. In other words, we touch here the principle of caste ideology.

Thus the brahmin is no longer the rival on whom death and impurity are devolved and who is entitled to a "revanche." In the classical ritual, we see him as a member of the brahmin caste whose functional speciality is the liturgy. Death and impurity having been "assimilated away," the ritual has become the domain of absolute purity. The brahmin's world is a pure world and consequently his place in the hierarchy is the highest.

On the face of it, it would seem that his purity and his liturgical monopoly eminently qualify the brahmin for priesthood. But here we come up against a difficulty. Purity was attained at the expense of the complementary relations with the others. In order to safeguard his purity, the brahmin had to keep aloof from the others and especially from their food and gifts; he is not allowed to take part in the reciprocal prestations implied by gifts. But to exercise his craft, he needed a patron. On the other hand the yajamāna, more than ever, was in need of the liturgical specialists, not only to eat his food and to accept his gifts, but also because of the hypertrophical development of ritual science.

The result was an all but monstrous growth of the mutual dependence of yajamāna and officiant. In the same way that death and impurity had been "assimilated away," yajamāna and officiant were amalgamated into one single unit. The ritualists who elaborated the classical system seem to have been keenly aware of the difficulty involved in the relations between yajamāna and officiants. Thus, for instance, *Śatapatha* 9. 5. 2. 12ff. discusses the question of whether one is allowed to perform the mahāvrata liturgy for somebody else, which would mean giving one's "divine, immortal self" *(daivo 'mṛta ātmā)* to somebody else. The ritualist Śāṇḍilya then quotes in conclusion the opinion that one can perform the mahāvrata liturgy for somebody else because yajamāna and officiant form a single unit: "The yajamāna is the trunk of the sacrifice, the officiants the limbs" *(ātmā vai yajñasya yajamāno, 'ṅgāny ṛtvijaḥ)*. There is no evil passed on to the other party; both obtain the same benefit.[49] Relations on the basis of complementary opposition being ruled out, relations can only be realized in terms of fusion into a single unit.

Genetically the basis of the rigid unity of yajamāna and officiants may be found in the alliance ritual, which, we may assume, has also been part of the preclassical ritual and which is still reflected in the *tānūnaptra* rite of the classical, normalized Soma ritual. In the preclassical system, the united group derived its meaning from its opposition to another group. The mythological explanation of the saṃjñāneṣṭi, mentioned above, makes it clear that the bond between the devas was established because of their rivalry with the asuras.[50] The antithetical relations have, however, been broken up in the classical system, thus depriving the sacrificer-officiant bond of its meaning. The dakṣiṇās no longer circulate but stay in the same place. The brahmin has to keep the dakṣiṇās and is not allowed to pass them on or to return the compliment,[51] while the depleted stocks of the yajamāna are supposed to be replenished through the automatism of the ritual.[52]

## 9

The rejection of the dualist system of exchange and reversal is manifest in the brahminical theory of the gift. It revolutionized the relationship between the brahmin and the non-brahmin world.

The obligation to give and the obligation to accept presents are, if anything, even more strongly emphasized; but it is significant that the obligation to return the compliment by giving counterpresents is conspicuously absent. In his "Essai sur le don," Mauss noted this absence with some astonishment: "Il faut convenir, que sur le sujet principal de notre démonstration, l'obligation de rendre, nous avons trouvé peu de faits dans le droit hindou

. . . Même le plus clair consiste dans la règle qui l'interdit.''[53] To this effect, he quotes the interesting case of the *śrāddha* ceremony, the banquet in honor of the ancestors, which, as he observes, originally must have been an occasion to invite each other and to return invitations received formerly. This idea still seems in effect when reference is made to many guests entertained at a śrāddha.[54] It is interesting to note that the classical doctrine allows the invitation of the affinal relations.[55] But at the ideal śrāddha there should not be a large company,[56] and it is especially enjoined that the śrāddha as well as other ceremonies should not aim at establishing reciprocal relations.[57] In this connection, it is said that the food and gifts which people offer each other mutually *(saṃbhojanī)* are demoniacal *(piśācadakṣiṇā)*.[58]

Actually, brahminical theory does not and cannot give scope to the gift to the full extent of its meaning.[59] Though it is more than ever meritorious to give, the brahmin has to feel a strong aversion against accepting, as indeed he clearly does. He does not accept the dakṣiṇās in a direct way but by ''turning away'' from them[60] and assigning them to various deities. Further, there are manifold restrictions as to the people from whom, the things which, and the circumstances under which he should not accept. This aversion is not unknown to ethnologists; Mauss refers to analogous Polynesian, Melanesian, and Amerindian customs. But nowhere does it seem so strong as in the Indian case. As Mauss appositely observes: ''C'est que le lien que le don établit entre le donateur et le donataire est trop fort pour les deux.''[61] We have seen why this is so in the brahmin's case. Since ''revanche'' is ruled out, the danger in accepting presents is stronger. The brahmin has to be constantly on his guard against those patrons ''whose food is not to be eaten,'' ''from whom one should not accept presents'' *(anāśyānna, apratigṛhya)*. The highest brahmin is a *śrotriya,* one learned in the Veda *(śruti),* who does not accept gifts.[62]

It is easy to see that the well-known relationship of the brahmin ''chaplain,'' the *purohita,* and his royal patron is extremely dangerous to the brahmin's purity, and to his hierarchical position. This is clearly shown by the story of the purohita Vṛśa Jāna and his patron king, Tryaruṇa.[63] Once when the king was driving his chariot, he killed by accident a brahmin boy. His purohita Vṛśa has to shoulder the guilt of killing the brahmin boy: ''Under thy chaplainship has such an (untoward) thing happened to me,'' as the *Pañcaviṃśa Brāhmaṇa* has the king say to his purohita. Of course, the classical ritual knows how to deal with death. By means of the *vārśa* melody, Vṛśa is able to restore the boy to life. But the story makes clear that the purohita's function is to deal with evil, which would otherwise befall his patron, in the same way as the brahmin, whose original function is not to redress the ritual fault, but ''to heal the sacrifice,'' i.e., to take over the burden of death.

Thus we can understand that ''the food of the king takes away the brahmin's lustre *(tejas),*'' while the same goes for the royal gifts.[64] Service with a king is even ruled out for the proper brahmin. For the learned brahmin, the king is as great an abomination as ten brothels or even as the keeper of ten thousand slaughter houses.[65] It is not surprising, then, that the purohita's position is highly ambiguous. He precedes the king but the brahminical texts often evince contempt for him.[66] It is interesting that the epic, dealing with various types of brahmins according to their occupations, does not consider the sacrificial officiant *(ṛtvij)* and the purohita real brahmins *(vikarmastha);* they are equal to kṣatriyas *(kṣatrasama).*[67] Also *Manu* 12. 46 brackets the purohita together with the king and the kṣatriya and with those who engage in verbal contests *(vādayuddhapradhānāḥ).*[68] That is, the purohita cannot be a proper brahmin because he is stuck in the sphere of antithetical relations where he has to exchange his purity for the impurity of his patron.

In fact the brahmin when serving a patron must either relapse into the ancient system of exchange and reversal or become one with his patron. The latter solution, however, tends to render his relations with a patron outside the brahmin caste all but impossible. Such relations of maximal closeness are only viable within his own caste, and even then he has to be careful: he should only eat at the sacrificial ceremony of a yajamāna who is a śrotriya.[69] Conversely, the yajamāna has to be equally careful as to whom he invites.[70] Insofar as the śrauta ceremonies are still performed at the present day, it is only among brahmins, almost as a secret ritual, and non-brahmins are rigorously kept at a distance.

It stands to reason that the highest place in the hierarchy of sacrifices is taken up by the sacrifice ''without dakṣiṇā,'' according to *Gopatha Brāhmaṇa* 1. 5. 7. Such sacrifices are the *sattras* of the classical ritual. In the satrra only brahmins participate. They unite their sacrificial fires and thus are actually assimilated with each other and are fused into one single unit. Each of them is at the same time yajamāna and officiant, and consequently, dakṣiṇās are neither given nor received. It is clear, however, that in this way the brahmin and his ritual were limited to the point where they shut themselves out from the wider community. Priestly functions are more often than not fulfilled by non-brahmin castes, for instance, by the potter, or castes have their own ritual functionaries. The *Arthaśāstra* says that the brahmin need not participate in village festivals. He tends to be a distant onlooker.[71]

But apart from the antithetical relations which characterized the preclassical ritual and the assimilating relations of the classical system, the individualization of ritual thinking led up to a third possibility.

## *10*

The development of brahminical theory, set off by the individualization of the ritual, did not stop at the point where the host-guest, protagonist-antagonist complementarity was fused into the single unit of yajamāna and officiants. It had to advance to its logical conclusion, that is, the interiorization of the ritual, which makes the officiants' services superfluous.[72] In fact, the classical doctrine of ritual has already concentrated the ritual in the person of the single yajamāna. His prototype is the cosmic man, Prajāpati, who is at the same time the primordial sacrificer, victim, and officiant. Thus the classical doctrine implies—as we have already seen—that the yajamāna, through the knowledge of the equivalences, becomes the integral cosmos, realizing in himself, and thereby mastering, the cosmic alternation of life and death.

The interiorization of the ritual is made fully explicit in *Bṛhad-Āraṇyaka-Upaniṣad* 1. 4. 17 in the description of the completeness of the self *(ātman)*, which is at the same time the completeness, the self-sufficiency, of the one who "knows thus": "(Thus is) his completeness *(kṛtsnatā)*: mind *(manas)* is his self; voice his wife; breath *(prāṇa)* his offspring; the eye his human property because through the eye he becomes aware of it; the ear his divine (property) because he hears it with the ear; the self is his act, because he acts with the self. This is the fivefold sacrifice; fivefold is the victim, fivefold is man, fivefold is all this. All this he obtains, who knows thus." Thus one who "knows" the equivalences based on the number five resumes in himself the universe and performs in himself and by himself the sacrifice without any outside intervention.

It would seem to me that here we touch the principle of world renunciation, the emergence of which has been of crucial importance in the development of Indian religious thinking.[73] The renouncer can turn his back on the world because he is emancipated from the relations which govern it. He is a world unto himself, or rather, he has resumed the oppositions of the world in himself; there is no duality for him anymore.[74] "He sees himself (or, the self) in all creatures and all creatures in himself (or, in the self)."[75] He has resumed the sacrificial fires in himself,[76] and so he is able to perform the ritual in himself and by himself. Thus it is said of the renouncer: "After the *ādhāna,* the solemn installation of the (interior) fires, the five (sacrificial) fires are contained in the sacrificer: his prāṇa is the gārhapatya fire, his apāna the southern fire, his vyāna the āhavaniya, his udāna and samāna the sabhya and āvasathya fires; he offers only in the self." Our text calls this the *ātmayajña,*[77] the sacrifice in the self, an internal, mental sacrifice *(mānasa yajña),* which according to *Manu* 2. 85 is a thousand times more efficacious than the normal ritual.

## *11*

It is often thought that the institution of renunciation emerged as a protest against brahminical orthodoxy or that it originated in non-brahminical or even non-Aryan circles.[78] The theory of the four āśramas, or stages of life, would then have been an attempt at legitimizing the renunciatory modes of life and drawing them within the orbit of brahminical orthodoxy. There is of course full scope for recognizing the influence of extraneous beliefs and practices, for instance, in the matter of various forms of ascetism. But the important point is that these influences do not seem to have made a decisive irruption in the development of religious thought. They seem rather to have fitted themselves into the orthogenetic, internal development of Vedic thought. Or one might say that these extraneous beliefs and practices were not in principle dissimilar from those that obtained among the adherents of the preclassical ritual.

The ritual is usually thought of as belonging to the sphere of the householder, but it is possible to find traces of the other modes of life in the classical theory as well. The four āśramas divide themselves neatly in two parts: life in the world as a householder *(gṛhastha)* and life outside the world, either as a Vedic student *(brahmacārin),* as a forest dweller *(vānaprastha),* or as a roaming mendicant *(pravrājaka, saṃnyāsin)*. The solidarity of the various modes of life outside the world seems to be borne out by the possibility of passing immediately from the brahmacārin's to the other modes of life outside the world without living first as a householder. These modes of life outside the world correspond to the stages through which the sacrificer has to pass. The brahmacārin corresponds to the dīkṣita; not only are their observances and dress similar, but the connection between brahmacārin and vrātya and between vrātya and dīkṣita suggests that they were originally variants of the same basic type.[79]

As to the modes of the life in the forest and the life of the mendicant, the ritual texts contain some interesting information. At the *abhijit* and the *viśvajit* sacrifices, the sacrifier spends all his possessions in dakṣiṇās or he gives a thousand cows, which is tantamount to giving all, as *Kauṣītaki Brāhmaṇa* 25. 14 declares. The number thousand being fairly ubiquitous as the number of dakṣiṇās to be given at various types of sacrifices, we may assume that the idea of giving one's all, either symbolically or in reality, in dakṣiṇās, underlies much of the śrauta ritual. Having given away his possessions, the sacrificer then retires with his wife, in a kind of renewed dīkṣā, to the forest. According to the prescription in the *Jaiminīya Brāhmaṇa,* this period lasts twelve days.[80] During three days, he and his wife live on roots and fruits they collect in the forest; then they stay for three days in a tribal *(niṣāda)* settlement; next they resort for three days to alien people *(jana),* explained as either a vaiśya or a rival *(bhrātṛvya)*;[81] and the last three days they stay with their own relatives *(sajana),* explained as a kṣatriya. In this way, the sacrificer obtains the various types of food associated with his hosts and in the end becomes (re)established in śrī, good fortune.

In these rules we can recognize a perhaps not too distant reflection of the preclassical alternating pattern: the sacrificer offers the sacrificial banquet and presents to the others; then he regains what he has spent by resorting to the forest and going as a guest to other people to be entertained in his turn. Having thus recouped strength, he finally returns home, possibly to start on a new cycle. A similar alternation seems to have been the basis of the vrātya ritual, which even in its normalized classical form shows a markedly agonistic character. Perhaps we can even recognize this pattern in the epics, in the vicissitudes of the Pāṇḍavas and of Rāma. The fortunes of the Pāṇḍavas especially alternate between royal court and forest, and the joints of the cycle, the points where the reversals take place, are marked by large-scale contests. It would seem to me that here perhaps lies also the origin of the well-known figure of the exiled *(aparuddha)* king, who turns up in the ritual texts with disconcerting frequency.[82] In this connection, it is interesting that it is said that one should renounce the world in times of distress, when overcome by old age or when vanquished by the enemy.[83]

In the course of development, the two poles of life in the world and life in the forest have been dissociated. This dissociation is part of the general evolution of the ritual outlined above. The ancient cycle of exchange and reversal has been broken up, the participating parties have been separated, and the sacrificer has been left alone on the place of sacrifice. By the same token, the cycle of alternating sacrifices to which the parties invited each other has been broken. The sacrifice no longer derives its value from its place in a cyclical concatenation, but each sacrifice has a value of its own. Sacrifices have even become independent of the time cycle, having lost in many cases the periodicity of performance and the connection with a particular season.

In the same way, the cycle of the modes of life alternating between the community and the forest—which was no other than the cycle of the reciprocal prestations—has been cut in two. Consequently, the renouncer cannot return anymore to his previous state as the viśvajit sacrificer did. Where there was cyclical alternation, brahminical theory has substituted a rectilineal succession. The transition can be illustrated by what the ritual texts teach about a sacrifice similar to the viśvajit and abhijit, the *sarvamedha*. At this ceremony, the sacrificer should give in dakṣiṇās all he has conquered, and having resumed the fires in himself, he should betake himself to the forest.[84] After the sarvamedha, however, the sacrificer does not return anymore.

## 12

The point I want to stress is that the institution of renunciation is already implied in classical ritual thinking. The difference between classical ritualism and renunciation seems to be a matter rather of degree than of principle. The principle is the individualization of the ritual, which could not but lead to its interiorization. Renunciation is therefore not necessarily anti-brahminical. Moreover, it should also be taken into consideration that interiorization meant the real fusion into one person of patron and officiant. Consequently, it not only emancipated the patron from the bond with the officiants, it also set the brahmin free.

Thus there seems to be a close relationship between ritualistic and renunciatory thought and practice. Mention has already been made of the prāṇāgnihotra and the mental sacrifice; we may also think, for instance, of the meditation on ātman, which is spoken of in terms of the agnicayana ritual, or the yogic breath exercises, which are put on a par with the pravargya ceremony,[85] while *Manu* recommends that the parivrājaka constantly recite sacrificial texts.[86] The question that occupies religious thought does not appear to concern the affirmation or rejection of sacrifice, but rather what is the true sacrifice, the latter being, of course, the interiorized sacrifice. Nor does the question turn on brahmin superiority or its rejection, but on the point of who is the true brahmin. On these points, both orthodox and heterodox thinkers seem to agree to a great extent.

Thus, for instance, the *Uttarajjhāyā* of the Jaina Canon contains two stories where a Jaina monk remonstrates with a group of brahmins engaged in a sacrifice on the wrongfulness of their behavior.[87] The interesting point is that the monk does not condemn the institution of sacrifice as such; on the contrary, he exhorts the brahmins to perform the true sacrifice—that is, the renunciatory way of life of the monk—and he declares that the true brahmin is the monk. In the same way the Buddhist *Kūṭadanta Sutta* (*Dīgha Nikāya* 5) gives a hierarchy of sacrifices, the highest sacrifices being the way of life of the monk and final emancipation.

One might be inclined to view this and similar instances where renunciation is spoken of in terms of sacrifice as a merely propagandistic device. But this seems hardly tenable when we consider that similar ideas obtain on the side of brahminical orthodoxy. Here too, the real brahmin is not the officiating priest or purohita, but the brahmin who keeps aloof from occupations that would enclose him in the web of relations and tie him to the others. The true brahmin is the renouncer or the individualized sacrificer.

This is borne out by the passage quoted above, where the ṛtvij and the purohita are said to be equal to kṣatriyas (*Mbh* 12. 76). Here the real brahmin appears under two forms: *brahmasama* and *devasama*. The brahmasama brahmin possesses knowledge—knowledge to be taken in the Upaniṣadic sense, knowledge of the equivalences. He has the proper characteristics—i.e., according to Nīlakaṇṭha, serenity, restraint, ascesis, purity and the like—and he looks impartially on all *(vidyālakṣaṇasaṃpannāḥ sarvatra samadarśiṇaḥ)*. The devasama brahmin is equipped with knowledge of the Vedic texts and is engaged in his own works—that is, apparently, the performance of Vedic ritual on his own, since the ṛtvij is not included in this category. The brahmasama brahmin represents the *jñānamārga,* "the path of knowledge," the devasama brahmin the *karmamārga,* "the path of works," but both live in the individualized sphere characterized by renunciatory values.[88]

The ideal brahmin should not follow, for the sake of subsistence, "the way of the world" *(lokavṛtta)* as *Manu* 4. 11 enjoins. In fact, the ideal brahmin is the renouncer. Thus *Manu* 4. 7 gives a hierarchy of brahmins according to the stores of grain they possess, the smaller the store the higher the brahmin; the highest brahmin has no provisions even for the next day. Having no provisions is exactly the rule presribed for the renouncer, as Gautama's *Dharmasūtra* 3.11 has it. In general, when we look for the characteristics of the ideal brahmin, we notice throughout the emphasis on renunciatory attitudes: He speaks truth, does not injure life, controls his senses, restrains passion and anger; for him the world is equal to his self, he studies and teaches, sacrifices and officiates, he gives (but apparently does not receive);[89] he is a brahmacārin,[90] he guards the four gates of his body, he has no upper-garment, does not sleep on a couch, he is equally pleased in all the opposites and does not need the others; he knows the course of all creatures, he does not cause danger to the creatures nor do they cause danger to him, he is the self of all creatures.[91]

It would seem to me that it is the renunciatory ideology that opens a way for the brahmin to enter into relation with the world without losing his purity. Having emancipated himself from the world, the renouncer can from his sphere of independence reenter into relation with the world, where he now enjoys unequalled prestige. Indeed, the renouncer can, and to the present day often does, exert considerable influence on the sphere of worldly life. The secret of his ascendency over life-in-the-world seems to lie in his impartiality. He is no longer a party to the affairs of the world because he is independent from it. "He who sees the self through the self in all beings, becomes equal-minded toward all *(sarvasamatām etya)* and attains the highest state";[92] "he sees the same in all" *(sarvatra samadarśana).*[93] As we have seen, he has resumed the opposites in himself and has identified himself with the cosmos. He is by himself the whole world, or, as the epic has it: "He who by himself fills as it were the empty space, through whom the void is crowded with people, the gods consider a brahmin."[94] Thus, on reentering into relations with the world, he is safeguarded, in theory at least, against its corrupting impact. He is then in the world but not of it—on condition of maintaining under all circumstances his total disinterestedness.

In the same way, the brahmin—that is, of course, the ideal brahmin—though rigidly separate from the world, can entertain relations with it. It is significant that at the śrāddha one should neither invite a friend nor an enemy—apparently a reference to the agonistic pattern of ritual—but an impartial *(madhyastha)* brahmin.[95] It is also recommended that he should be neither a teacher nor an officiating priest,[96] as is in keeping with the individualization of the ritual in general. Such a brahmin, who remains outside and above the oppositional relations, is not touched by impurity. He can accept food and gifts without accepting at the same time the impurity, as the purohita or the ṛtvij has to do. Of particular importance here is the motif of "knowledge." The brahmin invited to the śrāddha must be entirely devoted to it.[97] In general, the importance of knowledge in accepting gifts is stressed. It would seem to me that this knowledge refers to the knowledge of the equivalences through which the brahmin realizes his cosmic identification. By virtue of this knowledge, "evil does not overcome him, he overcomes all evil; evil does not burn him, he burns all evil," as the *Bṛhad-Āraṇyaka* says of the true brahmin.[98] *Manu* 3. 187 speaks of the knowledge of the rules for accepting gifts, but even so it is not to be lost sight of that these rules also contain a rite through which the donee identifies himself with the cosmic man Prajāpati.[99]

Thus being self-contained and independent, the true brahmin does not take part in the pure-impure complementarity and exchange. His purity is not dependent on his partners, it is absolute. On this basis he can dispense religious merit by accepting food and presents without staking his purity. But the condition is that he holds on to his independence and does not engage himself in the world. As a specialist of religious merit, he can be called a priest. But in this sense, he can only be a priest by virtue of renunciation. Thus the preeminence of the brahmin is not based on his priesthood, but on his being the exponent of the values of renunciation.[100]

The position of the brahmin is, therefore, as precarious as it is eminent. His monopoly of Vedic knowledge should enable him to hold this position without falling for the temptation either of worldly involvement or of total abandonment. But in the end, it is all by himself that he must bridge the gap that separates renunciation from the householder's world. The brahmin, then, is the exemplar of the irresolvable tension that is at the heart of Indian civilization.

# 3 The Case of the Severed Head

## *1*

In abler hands, the present study could have resulted in a mystery story. On the other hand, one might perhaps expect a full-scale treatment of the symbolism of the severed head. However, neither treatment is attempted here. Rather it is intended to unearth from under the weighty mass of imagery a clue to the tangible realities that seem to underly it.

The Vedic śrauta ritual presents a highly rationalized system of abstract symbols expressing the relations governing the cosmos and purporting thereby to enable the specialized operator, "who knows thus," to manipulate the universe, or rather to make his own universe.[1] This system finds its clearest expression in the arrangement of recitation and "laud" *(śastra* and *stotra);* their effectiveness does not depend on the content of the verses recited and sung, but on their abstract numerical arrangement. In other words, the ritual is divorced from the world of concrete reality. In the śrauta ritual, man strikes out on his own, free from ties with friend and foe, creating his own abstract universe. Leaving his friends behind and overcoming his foes, he obtains heaven all to himself. The divorce from reality does, however, involve him in contradiction. He remains of necessity tied to the concrete world, which he wants to control from the abstract ritual plane.

It stands to reason that the ritual must bear the imprint of this contradiction between abstract symbol and concrete reality. The foe is overcome by abstract means, without being bodily present; in fact, he cannot possibly have a standing on the place of sacrifice. Nevertheless, it is sometimes enjoined that he should be remunerated—without even being present—by a

This essay first appeared in slightly different form in *Wiener Zeitschrift für die Kunde Süd- und Ostasiens* 11 (1967): 22–43. Reprinted by permission.

gift *(dakṣiṇā);*[2] how this is to be effected is not stated. Contradictions such as these, where the system breaks, offer a chance to come nearer to the relation between abstract system and reality as well as to the development of the ritual. A case in point is that of the severed head.

## 2

The brāhmaṇa discussions on the details of the ritual system contain many references to the "head of the sacrifice," its being severed, the outflowing essence, and especially its being restored. It will be clear that the severing and restoration of the head in the language of the ritual system can only be an abstract expression. At first, though, one would be inclined to think of the head of the sacrificial victim. But it is exactly here that the abstract nature of the expression stands out clearest. There cannot be any question of the victim's head being referred to; the victim is explicitly not beheaded; it is even forbidden to make offerings of the victim's head.[3]

Thus we find that standard elements and acts of the ritual are referred to as the head of the sacrifice, their installation or performance signifying the severing or restoration of the head. The sacrificial cake is called the head, the potsherds on which it is baked representing the skull bones.[4] Similarly treated are the offering fire *(āhavanīya);*[5] the second *āghāra* libation preceding the main offerings;[6] the guest offering for Soma;[7] the *havirdhāna* hut where the Soma beverage is prepared and stored;[8] the ukthya Soma sacrifice, which has three more stotra-śastra rounds than the basic Soma sacrifice;[9] the *āsvina* Soma cup, the Aśvins' reward for restoring the sacrifice's head;[10] the *vaśā* cow, representing the essence flowing away when the head of the sacrifice is cut off, so that the vaśā sacrifice after the Soma sacrifice signifies the restoration of the head;[11] the *vaṣaṭ* call cutting off the head of the gāyatrī meter, the outflowing essence becoming sacrificial animals;[12] the *gharma* or *mahāvīra* milkpot, central element in the pravargya ceremony, which is explained as the joining of the head to the sacrifice.[13]

Incongruous though this random collection, which could easily be expanded, may seem, the connecting idea is clear. The sacrifice is a cosmos which is violently broken up in order to be put together again. This is in accordance with the cyclical conception of the universe underlying the ritual literature—the constantly alternating movement between the two poles of disintegration and reintegration, death and birth, nether world and upper world[14]—an idea which found its clearest systematic expression in the building of the fire altar, conceived as the restoration of the disintegrated cosmic man. The pivotal point, however, is that death and disintegration have been eliminated. Abstraction enabled the ritualists—and this is the rationale and the achievement of the ritual system—to do away with the reality of death.[15] Death has been rationalized away.

### 3

Before going into the relation between abstract system and reality, it may be worthwhile first to explore the meaning of the "head of the sacrifice." In the *Ṛgveda,* the head in expressions like the "head of the universe," "the head of the bull or of the cow," seems to indicate an invisible and mysterious place where the essence, especially of Agni and Soma, is hidden.[16] The head is associated with and contains a treasure or a secret that is the essence of the universe. Everything depends on obtaining the head, and the gods have to contend for its possession. This idea is graphically expressed in the myths of Namuci, Dadhyañc, Makha, and Viśvarūpa, often mentioned in the ritual texts in explanation of the "head of the sacrifice." They all have in common that their heads are or contain the priceless treasure. Without belonging unequivocally to the asuras, the rivals of the gods—they seem to be intermediary figures between the two parties of devas and asuras, in a position to grant their favor to either of them—they try to withhold the treasure from Indra and the devas.[17]

Though these myths are only partially known to us in the form of unconnected elements, it is clear that the head is the main point of interest.[18] By cutting off Namuci's head, Indra, with the help of the Aśvins, wins (or wins back) the fermented *sūrā* beverage. Dadhyañc similarly keeps the secret of a cultic beverage, the *madhu,*[19] which he teaches to the Aśvins by means of a horse head. Another element is that Indra searches for Dadhyañc's head with which he finally crushes the asuras. Makha, whose name in the ritual literature is synonymous with sacrifice, is the holder of the head of the sacrifice par excellence. On his flight from the gods from whom he tries to withhold the preeminence or fame *(śrī, yaśas)* of sacrifice, he rests his head on his bow; the bow springing upward severs his head. Indra thus obtains the preeminence. Viśvarūpa is equally a representation of sacrifice; with his three heads he consumes the Soma, the sūrā, and the sacrificial cakes, thus possessing in his three heads the whole of sacrifice. Indra therefore cuts off the three heads (or has them cut off).[20]

In these myths, there is still another element which should retain our attention. The cosmic essence is not with the sacrificing gods; they have to obtain it elsewhere, violently breaking up the primordeal unity of the cosmos. The point I want to stress is that this act is placed in the context of an agonistic festival. *Ṛgveda* 10. 131. 4–5 tells us that Indra and the Aśvins drank together with Namuci. Makha's name became synonymous with the systematized, nonagonistic sacrifice from which the rival has been excluded. It is characteristic, however, that the ritual myth makes him participate with the gods in a contest for preeminence; preeminence comes first to Makha, who wanting to withhold it from the gods, flees, bringing about the result we saw.[21] Similarly in Viśvarūpa's case, sacrifice and violent contest are combined. In the myth of Dadhyañc, there is no mention of a festival but only of a teacher-pupil relation, the Aśvins inducing Dadhyañc to teach them the secret *madhuvidyā,* the knowledge of the honey beverage, which is mythologically synonymous with his horse head. The secret knowledge they obtain seems also to involve the knowledge of severing and restoring the head—they cut off Dadhyañc's head to replace it with the horse head and vice versa.[22] Equipped with this knowledge, they are able to restore the head to the sacrifice for the benefit of the gods, obtaining a share in the Soma as their reward.[23] Thus the element of festival, though not directly connected with the way in which the Aśvins obtained Dadhyañc's secret, is not completely absent. Moreover, it would seem that the teaching of the secret of the *madhu* is mythologically equivalent to a madhu revelry.[24] Neither is the notion of contest absent, though it is again dissociated. Dadhyañc himself is a great asura-slayer according to *Jaiminīya Brāhmana* 3. 64: At the mere sight of him the asuras fall prostrate, and, characteristically, have to pay with their heads *(taṃ ha sma yāvanto 'surāḥ parāpaśyanti te ha sma tad eva viśīrṣāṇāś śerate);* by means of his bones Indra produces the same effect.[25] It would seem that it is not Dadhyañc at the center of the ritual, but the asuras, whose heads are severed. Moreover, the place where the head is found, Saryaṇāvat, is connected with Kurukṣetra, the scene of the battles of devas and asuras, Kauravas and Pāṇḍavas, as well as the place of sacrifice of the gods.

## *4*

Thus, the head is with others. In order to obtain it, one has to go to an agonistic festival to contend for it. The basic pattern of these festivals is dualistic, in principle involving two parties: hosts and guests. This pattern is also manifest, albeit reinterpreted, in the systematized śrauta ritual, which, as Thieme noted, is of the nature of a stylized banquet.[26] The classical systematized ritual ignores, of course, the aspect of rivalry since the rival has been eliminated from the ritual, though it is abundantly attested in ritual mythology, as we saw.[27] But outside the śrauta ritual, in the rules pertaining to the reception of a guest, we can discern what was involved in the host-guest relation. The host must offer a cow to the guest. This in itself shows that the *arghya* ceremony is not a casual affair but the occasion of a festival at which a great number of people are regaled, especially brahmins, as is expressly mentioned. It is the guest who has to give the order for killing the cow and preparing the meat. Though he need not be the actual slaughterer, he takes, by his order, the responsibility for the killing of the animal upon himself.[28] Though this is not explicitly stated—in the language of the systematized ritual this would obviously be impossible—I do not think we can be far amiss in surmising that it is in this way that the guest obtains "the head of the sacrifice."

Elements of the mythology involved do contain indications to this effect. Indra and the Aśvins apparently are guests of Namuci, with whom they partake of the cultic beverage. Makha is himself the sacrifice or the sacrificial substance; in this he is in the same position as the sacrificer,[29] who as a host must furnish the "head." Viśvarūpa, though clearly standing for the sacrifice, does not seem to be himself a sacrificer in this connection; in *Taittirīya Saṃhitā* 2. 5. 1. 1, he is characterized as an intermediary between the two parties of devas and asuras, sister's son of the asuras and purohita to the devas, openly promising their part of the sacrifice to the gods and secretly to the asuras. In the sequel to the episode of his cutting off the three heads, Indra clearly is a guest, albeit an uninvited one. Viśvarūpa's father, Tvaṣṭṛ, refuses to invite Indra, who then forcibly takes his part of the Soma. Tvaṣṭṛ then pours his Soma in the fire, thus engendering Vṛtra, who, enclosing Agni and Soma, is again a representation of sacrifice; in the end Indra entices Agni and Soma to leave Vrtra and join him, after which Vṛtra is slain.[30] Thus finally, Indra as guest obtains the sacrifice. Dadhyañc also is an intermediary figure between devas and asuras. As already mentioned, the occasion at which his secret is obtained seems equivalent to a drinking revelry at which the Aśvins are the guests, as in the case of Namuci. It is perhaps not just an arbitrary expression when the *Jaiminīya Brāhmaṇa,* as we saw, tells us that the asuras in their contest with Dadhyañc and Indra fall down headless; it could, in my opinion, very well mean that they lose their heads to the gods.

In this connection, it is interesting that the *Vādhūla-sūtra* tells us of a king of the Kurus who possessed the "knowledge of the heads of the victims" (used at the building of the fire altar, to be discussed below).[31] The brahmins of the Kurupancālas want to obtain this knowledge; one of them therefore goes to the king and asks to be taught the secret knowledge. Having heard his wish, the king states that indeed Agni has given him the knowledge of the head and in the same breath engages the brahmin to officiate for him. Now the interesting point is that the way to obtain "the knowledge of the victims' heads" is to go to the sacrifice of the one who possesses it. It would seem that here we have the dualistic pattern of exchange between host and guest couched in terms of the systematized standard ritual, where the guests and rivals are replaced by officiating priests.

## 5

Our brief and necessarily sketchy survey of these myths, broken down under the headings of the role of the head, agonistic festival, and host-guest relations, points to an ultimately coherent dualistic pattern. In this pattern, the two complementary opposites are the devas and the asuras, bound together in a permanent contest for a third, intermediary element, the "head of the sacrifice."[32] The "head" attached to one party creates a gap on the other side.[33] The gap must be filled by violently severing and reconquering the "head." Equilibrium can only reside in a permanently renewed contest in which the two sides exchange the head. There is no final victor, since the conqueror will again need the other party to rid himself of the death and destruction he caused. When Indra severs the head of Namuci, it rolls after him, loudly accusing him, as *Taittrirīya Brāhmaṇa* 1. 7. 1. 7 has it. The contest has to be followed by a revanche in unending cyclical repetition.

It was to break this deadlock that the classical system seems to have been developed. By excluding the rival, the need for actual death and destruction was eliminated from the ritual. The cyclical exchange between the two parties was broken and everything brought under the single denominator of the sacrificer. The single sacrificer incorporates alone the whole universe, articulating by himself the cosmic process, like his prototype Prajāpati, who is at the same time sacrificer, victim, and recipient of the sacrifice. If Makha and his like represent the agonistic festival, Prajāpati is the personification of the systematized ritual. The contradiction between system and reality is obvious if we consider that the abstract ritual has to be explained by a mythology which stresses violence. The violence excluded from the ritual is relegated to mythology. The ritual can only picture the restoration; its counterpart, destruction, can only be expressed mythologically.[34]

It seems characteristic that this contradiction stands out clearest in one of the achievements of the system, the building of the fire altar *(agnicayana),* viewed as Prajāpati's restoration.[35] This impressive ritual contains at the same time a glaring contradiction. Even though the ritual exclusively stresses the restoration of the primordeal unity of Prajāpati, the "head" is a pivotal element. Indeed, in the first of the five brick layers of the fire altar, in its center, five real skulls must be placed, a human skull in the middle, and west, east, south, and north of it respectively skulls of a horse, a bull, a ram, and a he-goat. The first question that arises is: How were these heads obtained? The answer seems obvious; they must be the heads of victims immolated at a sacrifice, and a human sacrifice at that. Therefore Rönnow, in his precited article, draws the conclusion that the agnicayana originally involved human sacrifice. However, the matter is more complex than that. Even apart from the question of human sacrifice, a sacrifice at which the heads of the victims are severed is completely irregular and cannot very well be made to fit the classical system. Obviously the system breaks here.

## 6

Let us have a look at the texts; how did the ritualists react to this situation? To begin with, the White Yajurveda starts out taking the boldest and seemingly simplest line.[36] The five "animals," including the human victim, are simply immolated according to the systematized standard ritual of the animal sacrifice. In terms of the standard ritual, this means only that an additional rule is given regarding the severing of the heads, since this has not been taught in the previous parts of the text. ''Having placed a grass blade on the necks he takes the heads,'' which takes place after taking out the omentum,[37] when the victim has already been consecrated and killed in the normal way, by suffocation. Apparently the human victim gets the benefit of being killed in a separate shed. ''On paper'' the appearances of the ritual system are saved, since the delicate matter is couched in the normalized terms of the standard ritual. Actually the texts are not so confident as it would appear.

The form of the system may have been saved, but the content continues to trouble the ritualist. Therefore the inverse solution is attempted: giving up the form and being free as to the content. The alternative is, then, to obtain the heads anyhow, either real ones or counterfeit ones of gold or clay, without performing an animal sacrifice.[38] But this alternative is again rejected in strong terms by the *Śatapatha Brāhmaṇa;* the real heads would not be ritually consecrated and the counterfeit ones would be false. No heads without sacrifice, and sacrifice means systematized standard sacrifice. Thus one has to fall back on the five sacrificial victims. *Śatapatha* 6. 2. 1. 39, however, states that this fivefold sacrifice was only the old way, and even goes so far in its historical concern as to mention the last sacrificer to perform it, Śyāparṇa Sāyakāyana, although we may doubt whether he really performed the sacrifice in its systematized form.[39] The text goes on to explain that nowadays only one animal is sacrificed, either a he-goat for Prajāpati or one for Vāyu Niyutvat. The head is apparently not severed, and the purity of the systematized animal sacrifice is saved. But this leaves open the problem of the heads which cannot be obtained ritually. Whichever way one turns, one ends in a stalemate, and *Śatapatha* 6. 2. 2. 15 can only state the three alternatives—''Whichever way may suit him, either those five animals, or the he-goat for Prajāpati, or the one for Vāyu Niyutvat (let him perform that)''—leaving the solution of the intractible problem to the inventiveness of the sacrificer and his officiants.

The Black Yajurveda is less uniformly systematized than the White and is therefore less concerned with solving the problem in terms of the system. It must, however, take essentially the same position.[40] Here again we find the same alternatives. The important difference is the treatment of the human head, to which we shall presently return. The number five is completed by the addition of an extra he-goat for Prajāpati, which obviously is meant to take the place of the human victim.[41] The Black Yajurveda thus offers two alternatives: the five animals, the sacrifice being either systematically concluded with all five or with the Prajāpati he-goat while the four other animals are ''freed'' *(utsṛjati),* i.e., let out of the sacrificial context, and beheaded;[42] or, instead of the five animals, a single he-goat for Vāyu Niyutvat. In the latter case, the altar is built with only the head of the Vāyu victim.

So actually nothing is solved here either, the problem is left in the air, except by Baudhāyana, the most systematic and at the same time the most explicit authority. He does not try to slur over the problem, but simply and clearly shows that here we have two different conceptions of the ritual. There is no attempt at forging a unitary solution—which we saw is unfeasible—but the two rituals are simply made to run side by side. On the one hand, there is the sacrifice of the Vāyu he-goat, completely in accordance with the classical system, without the head being severed. On the other hand, the nonsystematized ritual, which stands outside the pale of the classical system and which therefore is only briefly but clearly indicated: "They play dice, they cook a bull, a ram, and a he-goat".[43] If we leave for a moment the horse's head, like the human one, aside, it is this dicing and banquet revelry that delivers the heads. At the beginning of the Vāyu sacrifice, one of the officiants, the pratiprasthāṭr, is ordered to go outside and fetch the heads,[44] thus establishing the necessary connection between the two rituals.

The words in which Baudhāyana indicates the deviant ritual, few though they are, are highly suggestive of an agonistic ritual. The dicing hardly needs comment in this connection, its agonistic character is self-evident. The verb *pacati,* "to cook," does not belong to the standard ritual vocabulary, *śrapayati* being preferentially used. It does however occur, apart from the *Ṛgveda,* for example, in the *Aśvamedha* hymns 1. 162–63, in connection with the vrātyas, whose ritual presents another breaking point in the system and who are known for their unorthodox aggressive behavior and raiding habits.[45] Thus Baudhāyana, enumerating the equivalences of the vrātya acts to the standard ritual, states: "The goat that they snatch away and cook is their animal (sacrifice)."[46]

Here at last, in juxtaposition to the standard ritual, the agonistic festival which the other texts try to rationalize away emerges. When we now turn to the human and the horse's head we shall be able to determine its nature.

## 7

We saw that the White Yajurveda makes short shrift of the human victim. Though the brāhmaṇa texts of the Black Yajurveda are silent about its provenance, its sūtras present a nonstandard but, as it would seem, more authentic solution. The human head should be the head of a kṣatriya *(rājanya)* or a vaiśya killed by an arrow or by lightning.[47] Seemingly the problem is solved. But how is such a head to be obtained? One hardly expects a prospective sacrificer to wait till some rājanya or vaiśya obligingly has himself killed by lightning or by an arrow. Nor does it seem likely that one actually went round searching for such casualties, which would moreover imply desecration of the ashes, unless, of course, the fire altar is interpreted as a funerary tumulus for a high-ranking kinsman. Though the connection with the funerary tumulus is obvious and deserves further investigation, the indications point in another direction.

Baudhāyana is again the most helpful. According to him,[48] the human head is the head of a vaiśya who has fallen in battle; the same rule obtains for the horse's head. Now it seems clear that to obtain such heads, there is actually no way round going into battle oneself and fighting for it. In passing, one may recall the Homeric fights for the body of the fallen hero. In other words, the human head is the head of an enemy conquered in battle. It stands to reason that this can not be said explicitly in the language of the systematized ritual. Nevertheless, this is exactly what the texts do say, but, by disjoining the elements of the procedure, they have, one might say, taken the sting out of it. If we rejoin the elements, the complete picture emerges again.

For this purpose, we must turn to another component of the fire altar, the *ukhā,* "fire pot," in which the fire is to be carried during the year preceding the actual building of the brick construction. This ukhā, which is identical with the milk pot used in the pravargya ritual, is also a form of the "head of the sacrifice" or the head of Prājapati.[49] Thus the *Kāṭhaka* says that when Prajāpati carried the fire in the ukhā, his head "rolled off"; then the gods exerted themselves with his head and finally restored the head under the form of the ukhā.[50] Finally when the fire altar is built, the human head is put in the ukhā in the center of the first layer.[51]

Before the ukhā can be formed and baked, one must fetch the clay.[52] One may expect, considering the symbolic value of the ukhā, that this will involve an elaborate ceremonial. A solemn procession, led by a horse and a donkey (which will carry the clay), starts out toward the loam pit while mantras are recited. Which persons, apart from the sacrificer and the adhvaryu officiant, take part in the procession is not specified, but they are referred to in the plural. The lack of specification and the use of the plural in such a case is somewhat out of the common for the ritual sūtras and should put us on our guard. If we look further into the matter it appears that it is not just a solemn procession.

Thus *Maitrāyaṇī Saṃhitā,* speaking about the horse, tells us that "in the beginning the gods by means of the horse conquered their dominion; the going with the horse serves for conquest".[53] Further, when they have reached the loam pit or the place where the materials have previously been put ready—the rationalized ritual wants to be free from the contingencies of place and time and organizes its own universe—the adhvaryu, while reciting mantras encouraging it to drive away the enemies and to find Agni, makes the horse step forward; then he strokes its back while reciting the next mantra, which ends in "trample on the fighters," adding: "The enemies should be down, stand like Indra the Vṛtra killer conquering waters and fields".[54] The intention is made explicit by the injunction that at this point the sacrificer should think of his enemy. What is presented as a solemn procession seems rather to be characterized as a raid, or a battle to conquer "waters and fields."

## *8*

This might still be viewed as hyperbole. We have not yet met the enemy in person; he is only "thought of" and overcome abstractly. He does, however, emerge from abstract limbo at another point during the procession to and from the loam pit. In case, it is said, an enemy is met on the way, he is addressed with the following words: "In the way of the Angirases we are going to fetch Agni hidden in the mud, Agni Purīṣya" *(agníṃ purīṣyàm aṅgirasvád ácchemaḥ).* At last the enemy has reported in person for ceremonial duty. That this is not just a matter of meeting him by chance but an essential element in the ritual is shown by the fact that even in case the enemy does not oblige, the mantra must be uttered while "indicating" him, possibly by uttering his name or pointing in the direction where he is supposed to reside.[55]

But why this solemn announcement about the purpose of the procession? The mention of the Angirases may contain a clue; it seems to refer to their role in helping Indra to break open the Vala Cave and conquer the cows. In the same way, the mantra states, the procession goes out to fetch Agni. If I am right, this can explain the statement that by this mantra the enemy is robbed of his force;[56] that is, in plain language, the enemy is robbed of his possessions, albeit in a painlessly abstract way. But the hard facts of reality do not allow themselves to be abstracted away; they keep breaking to the surface.

It is again Baudhāyana who is clearest on this point. The texts prescribe the worship of Agni at an anthill on the way to the loam pit with the words "We shall carry Agni hidden in the mud," adding a mantra honoring Agni as the sun discerning the world at daybreak.[57] Now, instead of having an enemy materialize out of the blue or having him indicated, Baudhāyana has a vaiśya posted south of this anthill to guard it *(tāṃ dakṣiṇato gopāyann āste).* The processionists circumambulate him (moving sunwise); the vaiśya then asks (or rather challenges), "Men, what are you going to fetch?" *(puruṣāḥ kim acchetha);* the others answer with the solemn announcement, which according to the other texts is addressed to the enemy. In other words, the vaiśya is the enemy on guard at the anthill, blocking the way to the loam pit where the materials for the ukhā, the treasured head of the sacrifice, are to be found.[58]

We are now in a position to reconstruct the picture by simply putting together the two disjoined elements: the vaiśya guarding the treasure and the vaiśya fallen in battle whose head is taken. It may be recalled that elsewhere vaiśya and rival are also put on a par. At the vājapeya, the sacrificer has to contend—though in a strongly ritualized, that is, in a harmless, way—in a chariot race with vaiśyas.[59] *Jaiminīya Brāhmaṇa* 1. 183 equally puts vaiśya and enemy *(bhrātṛvya)* on a par. This passage is particularly interesting in that it deals with the sacrificer who has offered up all his possessions and then must recuperate. This he does by going to the enemy, that is, as we may surmise, to the enemy's festival.

The elements of the dismembered picture are all present, only the connecting link, the real contest, has been eliminated. It had to be, because it was exactly at this point that the ritualists had to break out of the deadlock of ever-renewed violent contest.

## *9*

Still one more question remains to be answered. Why is it an anthill the vaiśya has to guard? Of course, one may point at its symbolic value; the ants are connected with the subterraneous waters—they are said to be able to find water—and at the same time the anthill is connected with the hidden Agni or the sun, as evidenced by the worship it receives on the way to the loam pit.[60] It is one of the materials used in making the fire places, and it is also used for the gharma or mahāvīra pot in the pravargya ceremony. But these considerations do not yet help us in establishing a connection with the underlying reality which could explain why the anthill should provide the scene for the encounter with the rival.

The answer is implied in the ritual pertaining to the human head, as given in the Black Yajurveda. When the head of the fallen rājanya or vaiśya is cut off, an anthill with seven holes is put in its place.[61] Symbolically, the head and the anthill are identical, and this can explain why the contest for the head is located at the anthill. At the same time, the connection between the anthill and the loam pit becomes clear; the anthill is the head, and the trunk is represented by the clay from the loam pit in which, according to some texts, the trunks of the animals have been thrown previously.

Though the head is of course the prize trophy, it stands to reason that the contest with the rival vaiśya also involves the loam pit, where Agni Purīṣya is to be obtained. Indeed the *Baudhāyana Śrautasūria's* list of ritual controversies records that according to Baudhāyana himself the encounter should not take place at the anthill but at the loam pit, the opinion recorded in the main text being Śālīki's.[62] The scene of the contest is, then, the place from where the clay is to be taken. We must therefore shift our attention from the anthill and the contest for it to the clay.

The clay, referred to throughout as *purīṣa,* is rich in symbolic values.

Putting it briefly, the purīṣa is the subterraneous abode of the decomposed Agni (or the sacrifice), which is brought forth again from its womb, the loam pit or, in the standard ritual, the cātvāla pit on the ritual emplacement. The meaning, symbolic ramifications, and derivation are, however, far from being clear and require a special investigation beyond the scope of this essay.[63] There is, however, one feature that can point to a connection with the underlying realities with which we are concerned. Purīṣa is persistently connected with cattle, and the adjective *purīṣya* is declared to mean *paśavya,* pertaining to cattle.[64] In one passage purīṣa is identified with *goṣṭha,* the cattle corral.[65] Also interesting is the prescription that the sacrificer who wishes to obtain cattle should cover the place where the offerings are set down *(vedi)* with purīṣa, which he has taken from elsewhere,[66] possibly with somebody who possesses *śrī,* prosperity, and whom people for that reason call purīṣya, as *Śatapatha* 2. 1. 1. 7 tells us.

Here I think we hit the rock bottom of reality. The vaiśya or rival does not so much guard an anthill or a loam pit, however weighty their symbolic value, but his own head, his cattle, and his fields.[67] When he pays for it with his head, he offers up his cattle at the same time. This is also expressed in the symbolic language of the ritual. Thus, for instance, the ukthya Soma sacrifice is considered as the head of the sacrifice and at the same time as cattle; Vṛtra, threatened by Indra, tries to appease him: "He gave him the sacrifice, cattle, the ukthya." A parallel passage calls this "the head of the sacrifice".[68]

The antagonist is not just an enemy, he is related to the conquering party in a dualistic pattern. This is shown, for instance, in the rājasūya, where the sacrificer, in a ritualized raid, conquers the cattle of his relative.[69] Under these circumstances, the dividing line between agonistic festival and all-out fight must have been a very thin one, if it existed at all. Whether ceremonially contending for the treasure contained in the "head of the sacrifice" or plainly fighting each other for the resources of day-to-day life—cattle, pastures, and water—the two parties, like the Pāṇḍavas and the Kauravas in the great epic, needed each other for the agonistic exchange in which life could only be rewon out of the other's death.

## *10*

We have come to the end of our search for the severed head. That it had to be a long-winded one is a measure of the ancient ritualists' achievement; their ritual science was devised in order to eliminate the agonistic exchange of the "head of the sacrifice."

Of course, one is entitled to speak with Rönnow of human sacrifice, belonging to a "pre-Vedic," "asuric" religion. It is not my intention to go into the correctness of this terminology. The question I am concerned with is that of the relation between the two conceptions of sacrifice. Briefly, then, it would seem to me that the "Vedic brahmanic" conception originated orthogenetically in the agonistic festival. Rather than "asuric," the latter might be called "daivāsura".[70] Rationalizing away the agonistic element which locked the two parties together, the ritualists were able to break the dualistic pattern of cyclical exchange and make the sacrificer independent from rivalry and cooperation with the others.

That this was an orthogenetic development is shown by the fact that the śrauta ritual is built up with the disconnected elements of the dualistic pattern which were restructured in a "monistic" system. Piecing together the elements, we can, to a reasonable extent, reconstruct the ancient pattern. It would, I think, be possible to deal with the whole śrauta corpus from this point of view; the endless variety of the śrauta ritual could possibly be reduced to a single cyclically recurring pattern, in which the disconnected elements would fall back into their original place. This paper may serve to illustrate the original pattern as well as the way in which the Vedic ritualists broke up this pattern and "recycled" its disjoined elements. A further example can show how the rejoined ritual still reveals the original cycle that turned on the winning of "the head of the sacrifice."

In the śrauta ritual, the prestigious horse sacrifice is preceded by the building of the brick fire altar, on which the sacrifice is to be performed. In the *Taittirīya Saṃhitā,* the mantras for the horse sacrifice are inserted in a seemingly irregular way in the exposition of the fire altar. Now it is obvious that the agnicayana not only precedes the horse sacrifice, it is in its turn preceded by a "horse sacrifice" which must deliver the horse's head for the altar. Further, the clay-fetching raid recalls the roaming of the horse before the sacrifice. This can, in my opinion, explain the lack of a separate brāhmaṇa for the horse sacrifice in the Black Yajurveda; it is already covered by the cayana brāhmaṇa, especially by the parts that deal with the clay and the heads. We have here the disconnected elements of the original cyclical pattern that was broken up into single sacrifices. Where the Taittirīyakas still indicate the original unity, the Maitrāyaṇīyas and the Kāṭhakas have completely separated the mantras for the horse sacrifice.

We can put the relation between the two concepts of sacrifice in diachronic terms: orthogenetic development of the classical ritual from the preclassical pattern. More important, however, is the synchronic relation. The traces of the preclassical pattern are not just fossilized survivals. The preclassical pattern did not cease to exist. The classical system had to take into account the "preclassical" pattern, which continued to govern reality. Thus *Mānava Śrautasūtra* 11. 1. 4, dealing with the ritual for the acceptance of gifts, gives a mantra for accepting, of all things, a (victim's) head. The mantra *(candrāya tvā),* not recorded in the saṃhitās, does not look particularly ancient. It does not seem a survival but rather an accommodation, however contradictory, of actual religious practice, where more often than not the victim's head is severed and given away.[71]

The ritualists' enterprise was a bold attempt at forcing a way out into outer-worldly freedom and life untainted by death and destruction. They could not revolutionize the hard facts of reality, nor did they try. They tried instead to create a separate world, the ideally ordered world of rationalized sacrifice. Obviously the two spheres are irredeemably contradictory; the important point, however, is that in this way the ideal of freedom and life without death could be stated clearly and held out as a promise to man. Henceforth reality had to be formulated and justified with reference to this ideal.

I think here we touch the basic terms of the contradiction between "brahmanic" thought and unreformed reality, as when the Gandhian ideal of nonviolence was unavoidably attended by actual violence. It is this interaction between the two contradictory poles that is the pivot of Indian civilization, past and present.

# 4 The Flood Story in Vedic Ritual

## *1*

The flood story, like all myth, is not just an edifying or comforting tale for homiletic purposes. Perhaps we should even say that myth is not the place to look for any comfort or edification. It is concerned with the incompatible, the insoluble, with conflict and disorder. The only comfort myth can offer is to provide us with the words, the terms, the "code" for grasping, mentally and verbally, the perplexities of the human condition. This is no mean thing, but it is not a definitive answer to the problem of existence. Thus it may be too simplistic to see the flood story only as a fable of a new beginning, a cosmogony establishing a new and better order of life. This is, of course, an important aspect of the story. But underneath is the awesome intrusion of chaos and destruction. Even when the flood is interpreted as a cleansing or purification necessitated by the sinful disorder of the world,[1] the overriding motif is the havoc and violence of the catastrophe. In the oldest Indian versions of the flood story, no reason is given at all for the catastrophe and there is no question of any cleansing. This is the more remarkable since the oldest versions of the story occur in the context of ritualistic exposition where purity and purification are constantly recurring features. One would expect the flood to fit in smoothly with the concern for purity, but no connection is made. It is reported as a catastrophe without explanation. The central theme is the intractable antithesis of continuity and violent break, of order and the irruption of chaos. It is, in other words, a threatening story.

## *2*

Let us first look at the flood story as it is told in the *Śatapatha Brāhmaṇa*.[2] A small fish comes accidentally between the hands of Manu—always a par-

This essay is based on a paper read at the Fourteenth Congress of the International Association for the History of Religions, Winnipeg, August, 1980.

agon of ritualistic correctness—who has properly started the day with his morning ablutions. The small fish pleads with Manu to save him from the rapacious other fishes and offers in return to save Manu's life. Unruffled rather than unbelieving, Manu asks from what mortal danger the fish will save him and is told of the coming flood. Manu's next question is how he should save the fish. He is instructed to transvase it during the successive stages of its growth from a water pot to a tank, from there to the river Ganges, and finally, when full-grown, to the ocean. This accomplished, the now mighty fish tells Manu before setting out into the ocean when the flood will occur and instructs him to build a ship. The fish promises to return and to guide Manu through the flood.

So it happens. The fish has Manu tie the ship to the horn on its head and draws him safely across to the northern mountain. There Manu is told to moor the ship to a tree and to descend gradually after the retreating waters. The text then states laconically: "The flood had swept away all creatures, only Manu was left." Indeed, Manu is left with the problem of how to set life into motion again, for he did not take with him aboard the ship (as in the later Indian versions of the story) the seed of all manner of life.[3] This is not fortuitous. The restoration of life has to be brought about by the ritual. And so Manu, "desirous of offspring," engages in "worship and austerities" and makes an offering of milk products—ghee, sour milk, whey, and curds—in the retreating waters. In a year's time, there arises from this offering a resplendent woman, in whose footstep ghee gathers.

Here the story brings in another theme: the woman encounters the gods Mitra and Varuṇa, who want to claim her as theirs. She tells them, however, that she is Manu's daughter. The two gods nevertheless claim the right to a share *(apitva)* in her. The text then drops this theme again, only telling us that the woman either acknowledges or rejects the claim on her and passes by them to go to Manu. When asked by Manu who she is, she explains that, having arisen from his offering in the waters, she is his daughter. By employing her in the middle part of the sacrifice, she tells him, he will become rich in offspring and cattle. And so, "worshipping and exerting himself with her," as the text ambiguously puts it, Manu generates through her the human race and obtains all the blessings he wished for. The text then rounds off the story with its punchline: "This woman is the same as *Iḍā*—that is, the deified sacrificial food—and whosoever knowing this performs the sacrificial ritual with the *iḍā* thereby propogates, like Manu, the human race and obtains all blessings." Thus the main point of the flood story in the *Śatapatha Brāhmaṇa* is the deft interweaving of sacrifice and procreation in the figure of the woman who is at the same time the Iḍā invoked in the middle of the sacrificial ritual.[4] Moreover, the obvious incest motif—otherwise prominent in cosmogony, as in the case of Prajāpati and his daughter—is deemphasized or even avoided.

## 3

Although the purpose of the flood story is ostensibly found in the Iḍā ceremony of the sacrificial ritual, the linkage between flood and Iḍā is not as obvious as the text wants to make it. The story clearly falls into two independent parts, the flood on the one hand, the goddess Iḍā on the other. At the hinge between the two parts, we have already noticed some uneasiness, namely, where Mitra and Varuṇa intervene but immediately and inconclusively drop out of the story. More important, however, is the fact that the *Śatapatha Brāhmaṇa* is alone in bringing in the flood story at this point. The other brāhmaṇa texts give a different account of Iḍā, where Mitra and Varuṇa do indeed play an important part but where there is no mention of a cosmic flood. Conversely, the only other mention of the flood—a short reference in the *Kāṭhaka Saṃhitā*[5]—puts it in a different context and has nothing to say about Iḍā. Here too Manu, only survivor of the flood, makes an offering somewhat resembling the one in the *Śatapatha's* story: "With that (offering) he performed the sacrifice," this text tells us, "with that (offering) he spread out *(aprathata),* with that (offering) he went to this plenitude" *(imaṃ bhūmānam agacchat).* Although the image of spreading out the plenitude (or the earth's plenitude) could conceivably be linked, or rather conflated, with the Iḍā theme, it belongs to a different context, namely the cosmogonic scenario of the demiurge spreading out and fastening the earth that has emerged from or floats on the primeval waters.[6] The theme of the primeval waters and the *instabilis terra* blends easily enough with that of the flood, but the ghee-filled footprint, characteristic of Iḍā, has little of anything to do with either the floating earth or the flood.

But perhaps the flood story, apart from introducing Iḍā, is meant to account in its own right for the ritual. There is a telling parallelism: as a new world arises from the devastation of the deluge, so new life is created out of the destruction of sacrifice. Moreover, as the primeval waters are the basic element in the diluvial cosmogony, so water is prominent in the ritual. Thus the Soma sacrifice begins and ends with a bath. In connection with the final bath *(avabhṛtha),* it is stated that the ocean is the womb *(yoni)* of the sacrifice. At the avabhṛtha, it is said, "One makes the sacrifice go (back) to its own womb".[7] The sacrifice, then, arises from the waters and cyclically returns to its aquatic birthplace. One is tempted to think of Manu's fish, which comes out of the waters and finally, when full-grown, is brought back to the ocean, as an image of the sacrifice. Similarly, there is the recurrent theme of the sacrifice or of the sacrificial fire fleeing from service to gods and men and taking refuge in the waters, only to be found and brought back again.[8]

## 4

Particularly interesting for our purpose is the way this theme is used in a Vādhūla text and the part fishes play in it.[9] The gods want to rearrange the universe so that those representing the elements of fire, sun, wind, and waters can take up their residences in the spaces proper to each of them. To that end, they seek to perform a sacrifice, but they are in doubt as to the ways and means of this sacrifice. Agni, the Fire, offers to have himself immolated as a sacrifice *(medha)* to himself. However, when he is immolated, *medha* (sacrifice) and *asu* (life) escape. The sacrifice is then repeated by immolating again the escaped and recaptured medha part.[10] Each time, the double residue of medha and asu escapes taking the form of particular living things. In this way, a double series of life forms emerges through the sacrifice, the medha forms being immolated, while the asu ones—apparently unfit for sacrifice—are left alone. Finally the last medha residue, in the form of rice and barley, escapes, hides in the waters, and is swallowed by two fishes, the rice by a *rohita* fish and the barley by a fish called *caṣa*. The two fishes clearly represent sacrifice. Not only are they equated with the sacrificial substance they have swallowed, but they are also said to carry on their heads emblematic implements of vegetal sacrifice: the rohita fish bears a mortar and pestle, the caṣa a winnowing basket. When the gods finally catch them, the fishes—or rather, the two sacrificial substances, rice and barley—explain that if they are immolated, the sacrifice will be as small as they are themselves. First the gods should allow them to multiply. When the gods ask how this should be brought about, they are given the plough and instructed about agriculture. Only after the rice and the barley have grown and multiplied, do the gods successfully complete their sacrifice for the rearrangement of the universe.

The Vādhūla text summarized here provides an abundance of interesting leads: sacrifice as cosmogony; the interplay of the two basic elements of fire and water; the creative as well as the threatening, destructive aspect of sacrifice; the residual essence of sacrifice that through its flight under different guises establishes the diversity and plenitude of life; and finally the founding of agriculture together with vegetal sacrifice. For our purpose, the main interest attaches to a comparison of the two fishes with the one in the flood story. Thus the caṣa fish of Vādhūla immediately recalls the *jhaṣa* in the flood story.[11] More important, in both cases life is represented by the fish. In Vādhūla's text, it is the life-giving essence of sacrifice that is carried by the two fishes. In the flood story, we also see that life and its dynamics are represented by the fish, for on Manu's ark, life is entirely in abeyance. As we saw, not even the seeds of life have been taken on board. All life and action are in the waters with the fish who safely carries Manu across them. Similarly, in both stories the fish must grow or multiply. In Vādhūla's account, this entails the founding of agriculture and the growth and multiplication of rice and barley. In the flood story, great attention is given to Manu's efforts to have the fish grow to an enormous size, exceeding even the capacity of the Ganges.

Here still another point suggests itself. One easily imagines that the release of a sea monster, like Manu's full-grown *jhaṣa,* would by itself be sufficient to unleash the flood. Or, in other words, the growth of the fish seems tantamount to the swelling of the waters that ends in the catastrophal deluge. Indeed, the flood story begins with an insignificant amount of washing water brought to Manu in the morning with the equally harmless fish in it. At the turning point, both waters and fish have developed to monstrous proportions. The life force contained in the fish and in the waters is ambivalent. When fully developed, it brings both destruction and salvation. This seems to be anticipated in the beginning of the story when the little fish refers to the internecine rapaciousness of the fishes. The motif of life's ambivalence does not come out so clearly in Vādhūla's account. There more attention is given to the violence of sacrifice, which causes its essence to flee. But it seems significant that the two fishes swallow and do not want to give up the life-giving essence of sacrifice. Only by exercising their power as well as their wits are the gods able to catch them and force them to give up their secret.

Finally, the fishes have in both cases striking excrescences on their heads. In Vādhūla's story, the two fishes carry sacrificial implements on their heads, manifesting thereby their sacrificial identity. In the case of Manu's fish, there is no clear-cut reference to sacrifice. It has, however, been suggested that the horn, to which Manu's boat is tied, may represent the sacrificial pole *(yūpa).*[12] If so, the fish in the flood story can be seen not only as the life force active in the waters, but can also represent sacrifice. Whether we are justified in equating the horn with the yūpa or not is perhaps not so important as the point that the flood story seems to fit in with the course of the sacrificial ritual in yet another respect. I refer to the *avabhṛtha.* There, as already mentioned, the sacrifice is brought back to its birth place, the waters, as is Manu's fish. Manu's offering in the waters also seems to parallel the offering in the avabhṛtha water *(avabhṛtheṣṭi).*[13] Perhaps we may even go further. After the final ritual bath, there is yet another sacrifice, that of a cow, to Mitra and Varuṇa,[14] starting as it were a new sacrificial cycle. Would it be possible to connect the latter sacrifice with the intervention of Mitra and Varuṇa after the flood in Manu's story?

### 5

The flood story, then, when compared with Vādhūla's account of the sacrifice's origins, appears rich in ritual symbolism. However, the comparison also shows that the flood story proper—that is, the first part ending with Manu's descent from the northern mountain—is strangely lacking in direct references to sacrificial ritual. While Vādhūla's account from beginning to end turns on sacrifice, the flood story proper does not even allude to it. It is only against the general backdrop of the association of sacrifice with the waters—as, for instance, in the fairly common identification of sacrifice and waters[15]—that the connection with the ritual seems to impose itself. Once one starts looking for connecting points, one does indeed find many leads. But, even so, the story as told in the *Śatapatha Brāhmaṇa* does not follow up any of the possible leads. It steers clear of the ritual and its terminology. Only in the second part of the story, when Iḍā arises from Manu's offering in the waters, is the connection with the ritual made. But, as we already observed, the hinge between the two parts looks curiously factitious. The waters in which Manu makes his offering are, strictly speaking, no longer those of the flood. The flood has retreated and Manu has completed his descent from the mountain. The fish that instructed Manu on all manner of detail has nothing to say about offerings. And when Iḍā finally comes out of the waters, Manu does not even recognize her at first. The only connection between the flood and Iḍā is, in fact, a somewhat spurious *post hoc ergo propter hoc*. The flood story looks like an erratic addition, interrupting rather than strengthening the course of ritual exposition. The question then is: Why was the story of the deluge inserted at all? Perhaps a short investigation of the Iḍā ceremony may give us a clue.

### 6

Iḍā is invoked by the hotṛ priest in the middle of the sacrificial ritual after the main oblations in the fire.[16] The adhvaryu priest cuts off some small slices, called iḍā, of the offering substance, which are eaten by the sacrificer and his priests. The ceremony stands for the ritual meal at which the participants share the iḍā, the sacrificial food. The Iḍā, then, is the life-sustaining substance that is released by sacrifice to be enjoyed by the participants. In this connection, it may be mentioned that the Iḍā ceremony also is the time for bringing up and distributing the *dakṣiṇās,* or gifts, to the priests—another form of the life-sustaining substance.[17] After the destructive part of the sacrifice, signified by offering up the burnt oblation in the fire, life is set in motion again and distributed in the tangible form of food and gifts. In this way, we can easily understand that after the devastation of the flood, Iḍā is essential for the renewal of life. But if this explains the function of Iḍā after the flood, it does not justify that her appearance should be preceded by a flood. Perhaps one should not ask such questions in mythology. But the fact is that, apart from the *Śatapatha Brāhmaṇa,* the texts have no need for the flood to explain Iḍā's appearance.

The *Taittirīya Saṃhitā* gives the following account:

> Manu was looking for (a proper place) of the earth for sacrifice; he then found (a spot with) spilled ghee. He said, "Who is able to produce this at the sacrifice also?" Mitra and Varuṇa answered, "It is the cow, we are able to produce (her)." They then set the cow in motion; wherever she stepped, from there ghee was pressed out. Therefore she (i.e., Iḍā) is called ghee-footed *(ghṛtapadī);* that is her origin.[18]

In the first place Mitra and Varuṇa—in contradistinction to the *Śatapatha* version—here come into their own as the prime movers of Iḍā.[19] But the main point is the ghee-dripping foot or footprint of the divine Iḍā cow. This spot, the *iḍás* or *íḍāyās padá,* is said to be the best spot, the top or the navel of the earth, in other words, the creative center of the world. There Agni, the offering fire and primordial hotṛ priest, has his seat or birthplace.[20] Not surprisingly, Iḍā is both the mother and the daughter of Agni.[21] Her footprint is the primeval place of sacrifice and as such is associated with Manu, prototype of the sacrificer and progenitor of the human race. This, it would seem, gives Iḍā and her rite a firmer, more cogent ritual charter than the loosely connected flood story. But we still have to look further into the connection of the ghee-filled footprint, characteristic of Iḍā, with the sacrificial meal.

## *7*

The clearest ritual manifestation of the footprint is not in the Iḍā ceremony, but in the rite of the "seventh step" of the Soma cow, that is, the cow that will function as the barter price at the purchase of the Soma stalks.[22] After a piece of gold—representative of the fire—has been put on the step, ghee is poured on it. Then the sand of the footprint is taken up and divided in three parts; two parts are thrown on the hearths of the gārhapatya and āhavanīya fires and the third is given to the sacrificer's wife. The mantras that accompany this rite call the Soma cow Iḍā and refer to her seventh step as "the head of the earth," "the sacrificial spot of the earth," and "Iḍā's footprint filled with ghee." Interestingly, the Soma cow is also called dakṣiṇā.[23] As I have argued elsewhere, the Soma cow and the dakṣiṇā are related to each other as the two poles of the cyclical regeneration process of the goods of life, which starts with the Soma cow and its seventh step and reaches its acme at the distribution of food and gifts.[24]

The Iḍā cow, then, covers the whole of the sacrificial process. We may add that the *maitrāvaruṇī* cow sacrificed at the end of the Soma ritual, after the final bath, seems also to be connected with the Iḍā cow. This maitrāvaruṇī cow is a *vaśā,* that is, a cow that has become barren after having had a calf. This reminds us of the (exhausted) womb that remained after Prajāpati's creation, or rather release, of the different kinds of beings out of himself. As the *Maitrāyaṇi Saṃhitā* says, "The womb that was left over became the cow; she is 'womb' *(yoni)* by name",[25] Further on in the same text, the Iḍā cow is said to have been fashioned by Mitra and Varuṇa out of an *indigesta moles* produced by the gods. The different kinds of beings exploit her and finally, when she is completely exhausted, reject her. Prajāpati, however, takes pity on her and grants her the ghee-dripping foot—in other words, he restores her and makes her inexhaustible.[26] This tale of maltreatment, exhaustion, and restoration together with the apparent connection with the cow of Mitra and Varuṇa seems to suggest that Iḍā is not only the Soma cow, the dakṣiṇā cow and possibly also the maitrāvaruṇī vaśā, but also the sacrificial victim in general, whose meat is shared and eaten at the sacrificial meal. Strangely, however, no explicit connection is made. The nearest we get to this point is when the Iḍā and dakṣiṇā cows are equated, but no direct link is given as regards the vaśā cow immolated for Mitra and Varuṇa.

Nevertheless, there are several indications that the Iḍā cow is the immolated victim. The mantras addressed to the victim when it is led up to the sacrificial pole are also addressed to the Soma cow.[27] As we saw, Iḍā and the Soma cow are intimately connected with each other. If, then, the Soma cow can be linked with the immolated victim, the link will include the Iḍā cow too. Now Iḍā is Manu's daughter as well as his wife, and ritual mythology has it that Manu's obsessive ritual correctness did not even stop at immolating his own wife. In most versions, Manu's wife is saved by divine intervention, but the *Śatapatha* laconically describes her immolation.[28] In this respect—as in others—Iḍā recalls the goddess Śrī, Prosperity, who comes forth from the exhausted Prajāpati. The gods want to kill and rob her. But Prajāpati humanely objects that one does not kill a woman; one takes everything from her but leaves her alive. The gods then do just that, leaving her much like the exploited and rejected Iḍā.[29] This sorry tale is meant to explain a particular sacrifice, the *mitravindeṣṭi*. It suggests that the gods share Śrī among each other at a sacrificial meal—as the participants in any sacrifice share in the iḍā. But, as we saw, the critical point of the immolation is eliminated by Prajāpati's intervention.

## *8*

Now communal meals are hardly tolerated in the solemn *(śrauta)* ritual. The perfectly anodyne Iḍā ceremony is the last vestige of the sacrificial meal, and even it is not taken in common anymore. But where the meal survives, there is an abundance of cow's meat, as in the sacrifice for the "householder" *(gṛhamedhin)* Maruts.[30] A similar case is the rite for establishing the sacred fires *(agnyādhāna)*, where the participants gamble for the parts of a cow.[31] That such cows are the tangible substance of the Iḍā may by now seem fairly obvious, notwithstanding the reticence of the texts. But there is one instance where they almost seem to give away the game. This is in the rite of the Soma cow's seventh step. When a line is drawn round the ghee-filled footprint with a view to taking it up, the accompanying mantra says: "Here I cut the neck of the evil spirit, here I cut the neck of him who hates us and whom we have".[32] The ghee-mixed dust of the footprint is equated with cattle, and therefore this rite is supposed to make the sacrificer rich in cattle. If we further consider that just before, when the ghee libation was made, the spot of the footprint was called "the head of the goddess Aditi" and "head of the earth," we can hardly avoid anymore the idea of a killing or immolation of cattle, that is, of cattle belonging to one's rival or enemy. Appositely, the next mantra claims, "With us be wealth."

So not only is the Iḍā cow subjected to violence and immolation before she can perform her beneficial life-giving function at the sacrificial meal, she is also the object of agonistic proceedings between rival parties. This seems to be confirmed by a curious passage of the *Maitrāyaṇī Saṃhitā*.[33] The gods were, as usual, in conflict with their rivals, the asuras. The goddess Aditi was then with the gods; her counterpart, the otherwise unknown Kustā, with the asuras. The gods planned to cut off Kustā's head if they won. The asuras had the same in mind for Aditi in case of their victory. As we expect, the gods won and decapitated the asuras' Kustā. The text tells us that therefore, in the house of a victorious conqueror, Kustā, in the form of a cow captured from the rival party, is killed. The interesting point is that this passage, together with other no less agonistic ones, occurs in that part of the *Maitrāyaṇī Saṃhitā* called "the names of the cow" *(gonāmika)*, which is an extensive treatment of the Iḍā rite.

## *9*

Behind the Iḍā ceremony, then, there lurks the ugly specter of violent conflict, such as the one between gods and asuras, for the goods of life that must be immolated before they can be enjoyed at an abundant communal meal or distributed as gifts.[34] From this perspective, we can see why the Iḍā ceremony is considered to be a violent "rending apart," a "breaking asunder" of the sacrifice.[35] But the puzzling fact is that of all this, of conflict, violence, immolation, and communal meal—in short, of the potlatch scenario suggested by several mythological and ritual features—nothing remains in the actual Iḍā ceremony. It is a perfectly peaceful and harmless affair.

Even the sacrificial meal, though clearly suggested by the standard phrase in the ritual rules, "they eat the iḍā," has been reduced to an almost unrecognizable minimum. The small slices forming the tangible Iḍā are not even eaten in community. Insofar as there is a communal meal of the sacrificial food, it is removed from the place of sacrifice and can take place only when the ritual is over. We can now understand why. The meal was intimately connected with intense rivalry and violence. The central drive behind the development of the śrauta ritual as we know it was, however, to exclude all violence and conflict.

The ritualists achieved this by excluding the other party from the sacrificial arena. Though the rival comes in for frequent mention, even to the point of obsession, he is nowhere is sight anymore. The gods and asuras still had their regular battles on the place of sacrifice. By contrast, the śrauta sacrificer, but for the company of his priestly experts, is alone in the sacrificial arena. And alone he strikes out on his own into a transcendent sphere, unhampered by allies and bypassing his enemies. But then the old explanations of Iḍā had to go, because as well as her life-giving qualities, they stressed the violence and conflict involved.

It would seem that here we may find the reason for the insertion of the flood story in the *Śatapatha Brāhmaṇa,* a younger text steeped in the new ritual doctrine. We may then also understand why the violence and devastation of the flood are in the *Śatapath's* telling not only deemphasized but also, insofar as they are implied, totally unconnected with the ritual. For if there were a connection, the destructive violence of the flood would be a recurrent feature of the ever-repeated pattern of the ritual, as, for instance, would be the case if the avabhṛtha were explicitly associated with the deluge, or the maitrāvaruṇī vaśā with the Iḍā cow. The flood story describes a once-and-for-all intrusion of chaos, out of which arises the permanent order of the ritual.

## *10*

The story of the deluge holds the origins of the ritual. As is proper for the flood story, it founds the new dispensation of the śrauta ritual, putting its critical central part, the sacrificial meal, on a new footing. But even so, the Iḍā ceremony continues to be viewed as a breach, a tearing apart. Our texts suggest that this refers to the intrusion of an alien element into the ultramundane śrauta ritual, namely, the eating of the meal, which properly belongs not to the śrauta ritual but to the *pākayajña* of the worldly domestic ritual.[36] But at the same time, it clearly serves as a reminder of the paradox that the life-giving ritual is intimately connected with life's opposite, with death and destruction. Manu's unworldly ritual perfection is utterly meritorious, but it is barren. The tale of the fish confronts him with the internecine vitality of life in the depths of the waters. After this vitality has reached its destructive acme in the deluge, life, recreated and expanded through Iḍā has to admit the breaking asunder, the rending apart of Iḍā. In order to perpetuate life, the new ritual order of the universe established after the flood must still concede a place, however surreptitiously, to evil and destruction.

# 5 The Origin of the Nāstika

## *1*

It is obvious that the term *nāstika,* one who says "there is not," derives from the statement that is considered typical of him. Thus Manu's commentator Medhātiti (ad. 3. 150; 8. 309) characterizes the nāstika as one who, rejecting transcendence and the transcendental effectiveness of sacrifice, states: *nāsti dattaṃ, nāsti hutaṃ, nāsti paralokaḥ,* "There is no (value in) the gift, there is no (value) in the fire offering, there is no other world." This leads us to a further point. The term *nāstika* seems to imply also the context in which it is made, namely, the *(vi)vāda,* the disputation, where the nāstika confronts and competes with his opponent, the *āstika*. This is the situation known from the early expositions on vāda, for instance, the one preserved in the *Caraka Saṃhitā,* which exemplifies the vāda in these words: *ekasya pakṣaḥ punarbhavo 'stīti, nāstīty aparasya,* "One holds that there is rebirth, the other that there is none" (3. 8. 28). The point I want to stress is that in Caraka's example, there does not seem to be any question of a heterodox doctrine. In fact, the doctrinal content of the counterthesis *(pratiṣṭhāpanā)* seems to be nil. The negative statement is made simply and only for the sake of disputation, not in order to assert a particular doctrine.

This is not to deny that the terms *nāstika* and *nāstikya* can and do denote a particular teaching, or rather a variety of different teachings, which, for short, may be called materialist. What I want to draw attention to is that these cover on the one hand specific doctrines, on the other hand a role, a party in the game of disputation free from any specific doctrinal content, both parties being bound by the rules of the game that unites them, not by any doctrine that separates them.

This essay first appeared in slightly different form in *Wiener Zeitschrift für die Kunde Süd- und Ostasiens* 12–13 (1968–69): 171–85. Reprinted by permission.

Anyone interested in the actual content of ancient India's materialist doctrines should at this point stop reading. The purpose of the present paper is a short excursion in the meaning and history of the art of controversy, which through the vāda rules ultimately led to the development of Nyāya.[1] I shall therefore unrepentingly regress from the clarity of philosophy to the murky realm of mythology and ritual, from the specificity of doctrine to the diffuseness of agonistic dualism—for, if I am not mistaken, we may hope to find there some indications, not only regarding the nāstika's ancestry, but perhaps also regarding the place of the doctrinal nāstika in Indian tradition, as distinct from the simple controversialist. The way will lead us back to the Vedic ritual, beyond its classical form to the stage where the contest, verbal or otherwise, was still in the full sense a matter of life and death, not a means to assert and prove a specific doctrine, but the way to win the goods of life from the fangs of death.[2]

## 2

In this connection the *brahmodya*—the verbal contest in which the *bráhman,* the force holding the universe together, is at stake—should have pride of place. Here we can observe the development from contest to doctrine. We may conveniently start from Renou's classic analysis of the brahmodya.[3] Renou found that the classical brahmodya is "l'aboutissement (peut-être dégradé) de l'énigme essentielle du védisme ancien."The essence of its preclassical form would seem to have been an exchange of enigmatic "formulations." The question of the challenger is couched in terms of a well-turned enigma to which his opponent should react, not with a clear-cut, unambiguous solution, but with an equally enigmatic rejoinder, till one of the parties is reduced to silence[4] or till the strongest, well aware of his strength, enforces silence by withdrawing.[5]

The solution of the enigma, the bráhman itself, is not explicitly stated. It remains hidden in the antithetical relation between the elements of the enigma. For instance, the brahmodya hymn *Ṛgveda Saṃhitá*. 1. 164 consists of a series of antithetical formulations without the antithesis being resolved. Thus in verse 6 it is asked: "What is the One in the form of the unborn that keeps apart these six spaces?"[6] This question is not answered by a clear-cut definition of the unborn one, such an answer is not even called for. The point at stake here is the often recurring problem of the one and the multiple. The "solution" of the problem is contained in the antithetical relation of the unborn one and the six that it keeps apart. Since the solution is in a way already given, no explanatory answer is called for, but an equally or even more aptly antithetical rejoinder showing that one has "seen" or "found" the crucial relation is required. Thus verse 10 has recourse to similar terms for "encoding" the solution to the problem in an even more ingenious way: "Upholding the six mothers and the six fathers, the One stands upright not being wearied by them".[7] In this way, the central relation is ever further circumscribed by increasingly ingenious formulations, without a final definition being given. Even in the one case in this hymn where a question is followed by a direct answer, the answer is no less enigmatic than the question, couched as it is in antithetical terms. The question, "I ask you the farthest limit of the earth, I ask you the navel of the world, I ask you the seed of the stallion, I ask you the highest place of speech,"[8] has to be answered by an equally enigmatic formulation of the relations between the elements: "This *vedi* is the farthest limit of the earth, this sacrifice is the navel of the world, this soma is the seed of the stallion, this *brahmán* is the highest extension of speech."[9]

The point here is not the one-to-one identification of the separate cosmical elements of the question with the sacrificial ones in the rejoinder, but rather the antithetical relations governing both sets of elements. The opposites, farthest limit and energizing center, coincide as do the *vedi,* the place where the offerings are placed, and the creative activity of sacrifice. The seed of the stallion is the soma, but the point is that the soma is "killed" (pressed) to deliver its juice, as the stallion has been,[10] thus doubling and thereby heightening the expression of the mysterious life-death relationship.[11] To put it briefly, question and rejoinder here turn on the mysterious *coincidentia oppositorum,* which is finally clinched by the statement "I, this *brahmán* (i.e., speaker of *bráhman*) am the highest extension of speech," which for all its assertiveness offers no more explicit explanation.[12]

Thus the bráhman or, in Renou's apt phrase, the "énergie connective comprimée en énigmes," which keeps the cosmos from disintegrating or restores it, resides in the antithetical formulation, not in the explicit definition of the connection, the *bandhu,* which remains essentially enigmatic. This "énergie"is heightened by the two parties, who by their exchange of enigmatic challenges and rejoinders enact the antithesis. Its substance is not enunciation, but silence — the silence, as Renou observes, of the officiant called *brahmán,* who also brings the brahmodya of the horse sacrifice to its end. The culminating point is the moment of truth, when silence prevails between the partners.[13]

## *3*

This pattern still shows to advantage in the classical brahmodyas in the tenth and eleventh books of the *Śatapatha Brāhmaṇa*. Although often, but not always, explicit solutions are given, we can still observe here the crucial significance of silence as the culminating or turning point. The solution, if given, is placed after the silence in a different context, to wit, in a teacher-pupil relationship. In fact, where we expect discussion to be decided by objective, impersonal argument, the actual solution in the ancient verbal contest is a purely subjective, personal one. Actually this is what we should expect, as the problem is in a way acted out by the contestants. Thus we saw in the aśvamedha brahmodya that the prevailing party concludes the contest by simply asserting himself: "I, the brahmán (or, who have proved myself to be a brahmán), am the highest extension of speech." The respondent, finally, assured of his authority, gives himself as the embodied solution, the personified bráhman.[14] Perhaps such subjective solutions are nearer to our own everyday reality than our ideology prepares us to admit, as anybody with any experience of meetings may have had occasion to realize. Anyway, the brahmodyas of *Śatapatha* 10 and 11 are characteristically concluded by the prevailing party asserting himself and imposing silence; the dénouement is again a personal, subjective one. By the stereotype act of offering firewood, the loser becomes his conqueror's pupil, or *brahmacārin,* the alternative being death for one who "questions beyond this point" *(atipṛcchati),* as happened to Śākalya at the outcome of his contest with Yājñavalkya.[15]

In these passages we can, however, observe the transition from the preclassical sphere, where truth and order are subjectively dependent on the antithetical relations of the partners, to the classical clarity of the objective truth of doctrine and the objective order of ritual procedure. On the one hand, the moment of silence still has its full impact as culminating and turning point in the essentially personal relations; on the other, however, these ritualistic brahmodyas function as mere hulls for the imparting of specific teachings about cosmos and ritual. They are in some cases described as taking place at a sacrifice offered by a particular So-and-So, but one would look in vain for their places in the universalized classical ritual. They deal with specific points of ritual, but they are no longer part of it. The *brahmavādin* is no longer a versatile manipulator of words, but a ritual "scientist." Similarly, the elaborate brahmodya which has kept its place in the aśvamedha ritual, though preserving its quality of enigma, is no longer a real contest, the parts being unalterably fixed.

At this point the development bifurcates. On one hand, the brahmodya discussion of the ritual, which is now often called *mīmāṃsā,* methodical reflection,[16] serves to settle a point of ritual procedure. We are here on the threshold of classical Mīmāṃṣā. On the other hand, this same development has broken up the antithetical relations—indeed, as I have argued elsewhere, the impulse for the elaboration of the classical ritual was provided precisely by the aspiration to transcend these antithetical relations.[17] Taking away the antithetical relation meant that the poles of the relation came apart; they must either remain apart or they must be completely identified with each other. In this way, the partners who acted out their antithetical relation are completely separated as single sacrificers, each alone being identified with the cosmos, or they are amalgamated into a single body (of sacrificer and officiants) performing the ritual in unison. The latter is the case of the *sattra,* the sacrificial "session" where the participants are at the same time sacrificer and officiant. In the same way, the antithetical enigma is resolved by identification. Thus the brahmodya disputations on the ritual in the *Śatapatha Brāhmaṇa* lead straight on, as Renou has shown, to the Upaniṣads and from there to Vedānta.[18]

## *4*

This transition can be further illustrated by the so-called Four-Hotṛ, or *caturhotṛ,* formulas.[19] As they are given in the tests, they are straight identifications of officiants and elements of the ritual with gods and other cosmic entities. These explicit identifications, about which there is not much mystery, which generally are rather predictable in view of similar far from hidden identifications, and which moreover are learned by rote, are nevertheless called "the hidden bráhman of the gods".[20]

The original meaning still seems to be present in the ritual of the last day of the ten-day period at the end of the year-long sacrificial session. At the conclusion of this day, a brahmodya is prescribed.[21] Originally, of course, this was a battle of wits, and the simple rule that a brahmodya contest was to be held on this day at the end of the year was sufficient. In the classical ritual, however, this had to be fixed in form and content. One of the solutions was to have the participants sit around their leader, the *gṛhapati,* and each in his turn ask him fixed questions with regard to the Ten, Four, Five, Six and Seven Hotṛs (*daśahotāraḥ, caturhotāraḥ, pañcahotāraḥ, ṣaḍḍhotāraḥ* and *saptahotāraḥ):* "When the Ten Hotṛs held a sacrificial session, by which gṛhapati did they succeed?" Answer of the gṛhapati: "By Prajāpati as gṛhapati they succeeded, through him they created offspring," etc. Here we see the caturhotṛ formulas in the form of a dialogue instead of the classical single identificatory formula. The point actually at stake seems to be not so much identifying the gṛhapati of the different groups of mythical Hotṛs as establishing the relation of the one gṛhapati and the multiple (Ten, Four, Five, Six, Seven) Hotṛs—the crucial relation that brings about the cosmogonical result. Finally, we can observe here that the crucial relation is, as it were, acted out by the participants, the Hotṛs, on the one hand, and the gṛhapati (who names each time his mythical counterpart) on the other.[22]

Another solution was simply to have the hotṛ priest alone recite the caturhotṛ formulas in their unified classical form. Finally, according to some authorities, the brahmodya is subsumed in the immediately preceding *mānasa* liturgy, performed in mind only, preserving (and maximizing) from the verbal contest only the element of silence.

Here we have, I think, the whole development: from contest,[23] involving the formulation and enacting of the antithetical relation, to rigorously fixed liturgy and identificatory statement, to the final internalization of the whole procedure by the single, unopposed sacrificer.

## 5

All this may seem quite remote from the nāstika. Nevertheless, it is here, in the agonistic conception of sacrifice and especially in the verbal contest, that we may find his origin. We have to turn first to a particular form of the verbal contest: the reviling of sacrifice and its mythical representative, Prajāpati. This reviling takes place at the *mahāvrata* Soma festival at the end of the year-long sacrifice. This festival, otherwise a normal Soma sacrifice, is marked by the insertion of a number of contests in the midday service of the Soma liturgy: a chariot race, an arrow shooting, a tug of war (or wrestling match) between an ārya and a śūdra for a hide representing the sun, the exchange of verbal obscenities between a man and a woman who later copulate. It preserves, in other words, the elements of an orgiastic festival. In this context the *Pañcaviṃśa Brāhmaṇa* places the action of a "praiser" (*abhigara*), who eulogizes the participants, and a "reviler" (*apagara*), who blames them.[24]

Though the brāhmaṇa texts consider the blame to refer to faults in the execution of the liturgy and ritual procedure, the reviler's utterances refer to acts of violence.[25] Violence is not a peculiarity of the mahāvrata. In fact, sacrifice generally turns on the act of violence, on death, by which its opposite, life, is to be won. Since the classical ritual was based on the break-up of the antithesis (the essential antithesis being life-death), it had to stress life and eliminate death (or at least eliminate it from the place of sacrifice). Actual, violent death was replaced, as I have argued elsewhere, by the nonviolent ritual error, to be avoided or expiated in a "technical" way.[26] What is of interest to us is that the antithesis of life and death, albeit under the guise of ritual correctness and error, is not only verbalized, but acted out by the two parties, as in the case of the brahmodya.

Though no conclusion to the praising-reviling contest is given, we can infer it from an analogy in a passage of the *Śatapatha Brāhmaṇa*. There Śaulvāyana, serving as adhvaryu officiant with Ayasthūṇa and his cosacrificers, deprecates their sacrifice. Ayasthūṇa answers by blaming Śaulvāyana's handling of the sacrificial spoons. Characteristically, the conclusion is that Śaulvāyana becomes his opponent's pupil.[27]

Of course, the simple abuse and the equally artless praise are a far cry from the sophistication of the verbal contest. But the case of Śaulvāyana and Ayasthūṇa illustrates how the verbal contest developed into the discussion of ritualistic detail. The transition to ritualistic discussion of procedure and to the correction of ritual mistakes can be seen in the rules for "declaring" ritual errors on the last day of the ten-day period, which immediately precedes the mahāvrata festival. Though there are set procedures for correcting ritual errors in general, "declaring" them seems to be a distinguishing feature of this day. This "declaration" is to be made by a "declarer" (*vivaktṛ*) in the form of an improvised anuṣṭubh verse, that is, either by reciting an anuṣṭubh verse and then reciting the passage where the error occurred, or more ingeniously, by fashioning the erroneous passage into an anuṣṭubh. Thus the "declaration" resembles nothing so much as a contest in verbal skill between two parties enacting the crucial life-death antithesis.[28]

### 6

The adversary role of the vivaktṛ's pointing out of errors is clearly related to other contest-like episodes which also belong to the last day of the ten-day period. On that day Prajāpati, the mythical personification of sacrifice, is to be ceremonially reviled. Though this abuse, which consists either in verses mentioning the bad things he created or relating the well-known tale of Prajāpati's primordial incest, is not given as a dialogue, it follows immediatley on, or is even a part of, the brahmodya at the end of the tenth day.[29] The mystery of origins, resulting in both good and evil, and especially when these origins are cast in the controversial mold of the primordial incest, would seem to be a fitting theme of the brahmodya.[30]

Now Prajāpati is the representative of the classical nondualistic, nonagonistic conception of sacrifice, and it stands to reason that he can hardly be the subject of a verbal contest and that consequently the blame is not put in dialogue form. It is rather with Indra, in a sense Prajāpati's predecessor as the divinity presiding over the sacrifice, that we expect this to be the case; not so much because of the warlike sound and fury of his exploits, which have perhaps been overstressed, as because of his essentially ambiguous nature. Because of his violent cosmogonic exploits, he is not only praised, but, like the mahāvrata sacrificers, he is strongly abused. Thus he is blamed for his violence by an inauspicious "voice" (*aślīlā vāc*) accusing him of brahmin-slaying (*brahmahatyā*).[31] These acts of violence even are the subject of a contest, as recorded by the *Aitareya Brāhmaṇa*.[32] King Viśvantara Sauṣadmana performs a sacrifice from which the Śyāparṇas are excluded; the latter nevertheless sit down in the sacrificial enclosure; the king then gives orders to remove these "perpetrators of evil deeds, speakers of impure language."[33] Then the Śyāparṇas, boasting of their prowess in winning the Soma drink, appoint one of them, Rāma Mārgaveya, as their champion. Rāma, claiming to be one who knows "thus",[34] challenges the king, who asks contemptuously: "What is it that you know, you second-rate brahmin (*brahmabandhu*)?" Rāma then recounts Indra's acts of violence leading to his exclusion from the Soma drink, an exclusion shared to the present day by his human counterpart, the kṣatriya. The point here is that the Soma drink belongs by right to the brahmin Śyāparṇas, whereas the king, who tries to withhold it from them, should be excluded. The debate then develops into an exposition by Rāma on the sacrificial food proper to each of the four varṇas and is concluded by the gift of a thousand cows by the king to the brahmin Rāma Mārgaveya and the reinstatement of the Śyāparṇas at the sacrifice.

Though the episode is obviously remodelled so as to fit the classical non-dualistic conception of sacrifice,[35] the original pattern seems perfectly clear. The pivotal point is a sacrificial contest for the goods of life (the Soma drink, which the two parties dispute in a debate on the primordial act of violence).[36] The Śyāparnas, "of bad work (and) evil speech," using the account of Indra's misdeeds as a ploy for blaming the king, challenge his right to the Soma drink. They closely resemble the vituperating reviler at the mahāvrata, except for the learning they exhibit in the debate.

## 7

Not only is Indra abused, in some *Ṛgveda* passages his very existence seems to be doubted and even denied.[37] Thus we read in *Ṛgveda* 2. 12. 5 "about whom they ask, 'Where is he?' the dread one. And they say about him, 'he is not.' He takes away the goods of the lord like (a gambler) the dice. Trust him; he, O men, is Indra."[38] On the words "he is not," Geldner confidently notes in his translation "die Nāstikas".[39] Though apparently we touch here on the classical nāstika's ancestry, it is highly unlikely that this is the expression of a doctrine. It would seem that this and similar expressions of doubt have to be seen in the light of the verbal contest, especially the contest with the "reviler."[40]

The reviler, of course, does not reject sacrifice as a matter of abstract doctrine, otherwise his participation would be inexplicable. What he does reject is his opponent's sacrifice. His is not a religious doctrine but a ritual role in the contest for the goods of life, which calls for his wholehearted participation in the hope of reversing the roles. In the same way, it would seem, we must view the negation of and the disparaging doubts about Indra. In fact, it is not Indra's existence that is denied; on the contrary, the nay-sayer tries to deny his opponent Indra's presence and help.

The point at stake seems to be Indra's ambiguous nature, and it is in this connection perhaps not irrelevant that he is sometimes called *brahmán*.[41] He seems to be absent, or even hidden, most of the time. On the question of where Indra is, the poet answers that he has secretly espied his place.[42] Indra must be summoned and activated in order to manifest himself. In the next verse, the poet triumphantly announces to those "who know and who do not know": "Here drives the bountiful in full armor".[43] The way to activate

Indra seems to be by questions and answers, working up toward his decisive manifestation. Thus he is called upon to decide the question by declaring whether the power, the *vīrya* (of his former deeds) is now his or whether it is not.[44] Similarly, *Ṛgveda* 6. 27 starts with questions about Indra's achievements (answer: "The being [*sat*] is his [achievement]"); then addresses Indra directly "We do not now perceive your greatness. . . . your Indra power [*indriya*] has not shown itself"; and announces, finally "Now this your indriya has become manifest."[45]

Indra, as is well known, manifests himself in battle and contest, but his manifestation is ambiguous. His appearance means victory to the party on whose side he will throw his weight, but it spells doom to the other party. Both parties activate him and contend for his help in "rival invocations" (*vihava*),[46] trying to deny each other Indra's effective presence. This is the situation known in the classical ritual—where of course it is considered faulty procedure—as *saṃsava*, sacrificial rivalry: "The two (parties) who press (the Soma) together do so with a view to (obtaining) Indra; the pressing stones, being the teeth of Prajāpati-sacrifice, devour one of the two parties".[47]

In this context, I think, the negation of Indra has its proper place. That is, initially Indra is not present with either of the contending parties; the rival invocations activate him and (when his manifestation is imminent) the one tries to deny the other his presence.[48] This would seem to be the case in *Ṛgveda* 8. 100. 3, where the parties are exhorted: "Bring forward the praise, competing for the prize, a true one for Indra if there is truth. 'Indra is not,' says the other, 'Who has seen him? Whom shall we praise?' " Then, in the next verse, Indra manifests himself: "Here I am, O singer, look at me here."[49] The same situation suggests itself in *Ṛgveda* 2. 12, where verse 5 records the question, "Where is he," and the negation, "He is not" (or, "He is not here"). Verse 8 clarifies the situation: "Whom the two battle lines, engaging each other, invoke, vying with each other, both the parties here and yonder—the two standing on the same chariot invoke him separately—he, O men, is Indra."[50]

## 8

These passages suggest a rudimentary scenario, question-answer, affirmation-denial, possibly further heightened by vituperation and finally subsiding when Indra manifests himself with one of the two contending parties (meaning that one of the parties has subdued the other). This pattern seems still to subsist in the classical ritual, where the consecrated sacrificer, often identified with Indra, may be said to act Indra's part, going from concealment to resplendent manifestation. He is symbolically reduced to the embryonic state and speaks, if at all, only in veiled language. He recalls somewhat the *śreṣṭhin* who silently presides over the banquet while the participants strive to know his silent voice (*vāc*).[51] In fact, the sacrificer is the counterpart of the brahman officiant, with whom he originally exchanges his role.[52] It stands to reason that in the nonagonistic ritual no ill should be spoken of him, his evil (*aślīla, pāpman*) should not be mentioned; but the fact that he is considered to be possessed of evil is sufficiently significant. Though the blame, the mention of evil, will in any case have been reserved for a certain (probably advanced) stage of the proceedings—the reviling at the mahāvrata takes place in the midday service—it seems unlikely that the sacrificer would originally have escaped the lot of his prototypes, Indra and Prajāpati. Finally, at the culminating point of the ritual he manifests himself, is proclaimed brahmán, and distributes the dakṣiṇā wealth.[53]

This is elaborately enacted in the rājasūya. The king, seated on his throne and surrounded by the four chief officiants and the office bearers, addresses each of the priests: "O brahmán. To which the priests answer: "Thou, O king, art brahmán."[54] The scene recalls exactly the brahmodya in the caturhotṛ formulas at the end of the last day of the ten-day period.[55] Though we find here no "reviler" or vituperative utterances,[56] the idea of contest—chariot race, cattle raid, game of dice—is not very far away.

Moreover, truth and nontruth seem originally to have been involved in personal form at the king's unction and enthronement. One of the king's office bearers is the *pālāgala*, the "messenger," who is explained as *anṛtadūta*, "nontruth messenger." His counterpart is the *satyadūta*, the "truth messenger," who brings the message of the king's unction (that is, of his manifestation, his birth) to the rival kings (*pratirājan*) and exhorts them to put faith in the king (*śraddhā*).[57] This rite is explained by a reference to the contest of devas and asuras. Depositing truth (*vācaḥ satyam*) with the Aśvins and Pūṣan, the devas conquer the asuras by untruth (*anṛta*). The original idea would seem to be that the two functionaries, *anṛtadūta* and *satyadūta*, represent the two opposite champions, the negator and the affirmer. The king is born out of the antithetical relation between satya and anṛta. Arising out of embryonic limbo and combining in his person both satya and anṛta, he manifests himself as the personified solution of the antithesis, like his prototype Indra.

## 9

When we now try to piece together the scraps of information delivered by the texts, they appear to converge in a coherent picture of the verbal contest—question and rejoinder, praising and reviling, affirmation and denial—all turning on the essential enigma of being and nonbeing, life and death. The enigma cannot be objectively solved, it can only be circumscribed in antithetical formulations and acted out by the contending parties who, like "two on the same chariot," are bound together by the contest.

In fact, an objective solution is not aimed at. The pivotal concern is the antithetical complementarity. What the kavis, in the words of Ṛgveda 10. 129. 4, found was not objective truth or absolute being (*sat*), separate from nontruth, nonbeing (*asat*), but the connection between the two opposites, the *sáto bándhum ásati*. The antithesis is not an abstract problem to be solved once and for all. It is a concrete contest between opposite parties. In the same way as life and death, being and nonbeing, the parties are locked together in agonistic complementarity. Consequently, the contest must ever be renewed. No objective solution is strived for, but an ever-alternating, personal outcome.

The point where development sets in is the impulse toward transcendence, a reaching out toward absolute life beyond the alternation of life and death. This means cutting the Gordian knot of complementary antithesis, resulting in the atomization of the world. The unity of the world has to be realized either by arranging the disconnected elements in discontinuous series or by bringing them under the same denominator through identification. Instead of antithetical connection, *bandhu* now means identification.

Truth and nontruth are no longer bound up with the parties in the contest who act out their mutual relation. Instead they have been freed and absolutized. That is, abstract doctrine and individual belief are born. The superior contestant's assertion of himself as the brahman is transformed into the doctrine of the ātman-brahman identification. The rules of the contest, the vāda manual, yield their place to the rules of abstract proof.[58] By the same token, the reviling antagonist is cut loose from the praising protagonist. The complementary ritual roles make place for mutually exclusive doctrines. It is no longer a question of denying a particular person's (or group's) sacrifice, but of denying the abstract institution of sacrifice. The doctrine of sacrifice is either true or false.

It is at this point that the classical nāstika makes his appearance, as does the orthodox ritualist. The utter acerbity of their relations signifies the fact that they are no longer bound together in a complementary pattern. The initial point is, however, the breakthrough out of mutual dependence in the contest for the goods of life. Both ritualist and nāstika reject karman in the sense of the (sacrificial) "work" of agonistic exchange between two parties. What divides them is the truth or falsehood of the doctrine of individual karman regulated by transcendent Vedic injunction. In the essential point, man's freedom to transcend his condition of bondage, both find themselves on the same side. But neither can realize both freedom and transcendence. The ritualist (and his āstika progeny), in order to safeguard man's transcendence, subjects his freedom to transcendent injunction. The nāstika, on the other hand, surrenders transcendence in favor of man's freedom.

# 6 Vedic Sacrifice and Transcendence

## 1

Sacrifice and transcendence are closely related to each other. Regardless of its bewildering variety and the many questions it raises, the purpose of sacrifice is clear. It mediates between the human and the transcendent world. Sacrifice, therefore, takes up a pivotal place in religion, not least in Christianity. It is precisely this central importance of sacrifice that can mislead us when we come to consider Indian religious thought.

Now sacrifice is indeed a conspicuous theme in Indian religious and social thought. The Veda, the revealed knowledge, focuses almost exclusively on sacrifice, while the universal order, the *dharma*, is said to rest on or even to be contained in the sacred lore of Vedic sacrifice.[1] It is thus tempting to view Hinduism in terms of sacrifice, which seems to promise us a unifying theme to organize the confusing richness of Hindu religious thought and practice. In a stimulating essay, Madeleine Biardeau has taken just this approach.[2] Even though no longer purely Vedic, sacrifice is singled out as the organizing principle of religion and society. In this way, Professor Biardeau aims at establishing a unitary picture of Hinduism in all its variety, integrally based on and unified by the concept of sacrifice. The idea is undoubtedly persuasive. Yet caution is in order. It is certainly important to try to overcome the atomizing tendencies to which the bewildering variety of phenomena that go under the single name of Hinduism seems to condemn our studies. The attempt to strike out toward a more coherent picture is to be welcomed, but it is questionable whether the concept of sacrifice offers the right angle of vision.

It cannot be gainsaid that the Veda takes up an exceptional place in Hin-

This is a translation of "Vedisches Opfer und Transzendenz," which first appeared in *Transzendenzerfahrung*, edited by Gerhard Oberhammer (Vienna, 1978), 28–44.

duism. This is true even today. It would otherwise be hard to account for the vivid interest, devotion, and controversy aroused by the recent performance of a complicated Vedic sacrifice in the tradional style of the Nambudiri brahmins of Central Kerala.[3] More important, the "language" and terminology of sacrifice appear to have known a far-reaching influence and diffusion. Thus the recitation of Vedic texts is itself considered a sacrifice (*yajña*), namely, a *brahmayajña*.[4] The brahmin who takes his food can do so as a sacrificial offering in the internal "fires" of the breaths (*prāṇāgnihotra*)[5]. The king or warrior is allowed to look on his worldly and not always very devout activities as a life-long sacrificial session (*sattra*), which entitles him to claim purity and immunity in the exercise of his duties.[6] Similarly, the patron, or "boss," is in many Indian languages known as *jajmān*, that is, *yajamāna*, "sacrificer." Even the renouncer's texts, which have no use for the actual practice of sacrifice, are replete with the sacrificial idiom. It is clear that the idea of sacrifice has been very much generalized. But should this also be taken to mean, as Professor Biardeau says, that "l'action rituelle, sans cesse répétée, est le modèle même de toute action, et que le sacrifice, mode de communication de la terre avec le ciel, en est le centre"?[7] Or is it only a generalized way of expression which has irretrievably blurred the precise outlines and content of sacrifice?[8] Put differently, does all talk of sacrifice in reality amount to "de la poussière védique"?[9]

The question is not without importance. For, if Professor Biardeau is right and the Hindu's life and thought are governed by the ritual order of sacrifice, then Hinduism, notwithstanding its notorious variety, is contained in an all but monolithic structure. But this means that the Hindu would be constrained to live under the rule of an unforgiving ritual order. More than that, the ritual order, geared as it is to sacrifice, brings with it a constant nearness of the transcendent. A life in unremitting proximity to the transcendent, though perhaps not unthinkable, is exceptional. It is hard to imagine a society based on these premises.

## 2

There are many indications that we shall not be able to understand Hinduism and its view of the transcendent in this way. Take, for example, the plain fact that although the Veda enjoys supramundane, transcendent authority, its painfully detailed system of ritual injunctions lacks all relationship to the reality it is ostensibly meant to govern. The dharma's total dependence on the Veda is clearly a pious fiction. In some respects, the two are even incompatible. This is the case in the tangled matter of animal sacrifice, enjoined in Vedic ritual but against the dharma's rule of *ahiṃsā*, which prohibits the taking of any life. The dharma texts can only deal with the Vedic injunction by setting it apart in a separate autonomous sphere of its own;

animal sacrifice is strictly limited to its appropriate place, time, and purpose within the extrasocial confines of Vedic ritual.[10]

The solution is reasonable enough, but, at the same time, it makes the gap between Veda and dharma all the more glaring. The problem of Vedic animal sacrifice remains a sensitive point of controversy. Yet the fiction of dharma being entirely founded on the Veda is a necessary one, for otherwise the dharma would be cut off from its source of ultimate authority. Here, then, we see a significant fault line, and it may not be fortuitous that we see it precisely in the matter of sacrifice. We shall therefore have to proceed with caution if we want to investigate the place of sacrifice—and especially of Vedic sacrifice—in Indian thought.

First, however, a general remark on sacrifice is in order. In spite of many efforts, there does not seem to be a satisfactory theory explaining this phenomenon.[11] This is perhaps to be expected. At least it is in keeping with the problem sacrifice presents to the participants themselves. The communication between this and the yonder world by way of sacrifice (or otherwise) always remains a problem that defies attempts at a definitive solution. The point that most of all hampers our understanding is the unavoidable interlacing of sacrifice and gift.

Now the theory of the gift has been clarified by anthropology and especially by Marcel Mauss's classic study.[12] The three interconnected duties of giving, receiving, and reciprocating are well understood. As analyzed by Mauss, the gift establishes the solidarity of givers and receivers and brings about a constant circulation, which maintains a dynamic and manipulable equilibrium. Since sacrifice is also concerned with gifts (offerings), it is tempting to explain sacrifice in the same way as the gift. Hence the unsatisfactory and often criticized *do-ut-des* explanation in its variously trivial, magical, or learned versions. Of course, the do-ut-des idea is not totally wrong, for it is a matter of no mean import for man to inveigle the transcendent powers, whose impact he can not avoid in any case, into a manipulable equilibrium of gift and reciprocity. Man will seek, if not to direct unilaterally, at least to arrange his relations to the transcendent in an orderly, predictable manner. But he also knows that this enterprise is ultimately doomed to fail. The constraint to reciprocate loses its power when confronted with the absolute power of the transcendent. Not even the obligation to accept man's gifts holds good for the gods, as we know from the classical story of Polycrates' ring. The desperate attempt of the all-too-fortunate ruler of Samos to restore the equilibrium through the sacrifice of his invaluable ring fails. The gods reject his sacrifice, and the sacrificer finds a miserable end. The transcendent cannot be contained by any compact or arrangement, and man knows it.

The transcendent does not submit to any system, to any order but its own. In its unpredictability, it is full of terror for man, as the theophany of the

*Bhagavadgītā*—to take just one example—shows us. It only knows its own absolute order and as such is a deeply disturbing power that ever threatens to overthrow all humanly conceivable order. Sacrifice, therefore, like all endeavors to come in touch with the transcendent, is an awesome and terrifying venture. It goes far beyond the bounds of gift and reciprocity, of solidarity and participation. This stands out clearly in the fact that sacrifice always involves the destruction, through fire or otherwise, of part of the sacrificial offering, be it ever so minimal a part. In this respect, sacrifice is decisively different from the gift, which remains at man's disposal and will return by way of reciprocity. This element of destruction tells us that something dangerous is at stake in sacrifice.

## 3

Yet, when we turn to the Vedic conception of sacrifice, it is striking to notice that it is regularly connected with unbroken universal order. The cosmogonic Puruṣa hymn, *Ṛgveda* 10. 90, tells us that the gods sacrificed and dismembered the cosmic man (*púruṣa*), establishing thereby the world and its order. "These were the first institutions".[13] Even though the world is founded on the destructive violence of sacrifice, the sacrificial order is nonetheless viewed as the rigidly stable order of the universe established by the gods. The rules of sacrifice are the world's "first institutions." Viewed in this way, sacrifice is the supreme means to found and maintain universal order. "All this here follows sacrifice".[14]

Perhaps this motif has been overemphasized, if not hackneyed, at the expense of other themes, such as the overcoming of death—that is, gaining access to transcendence—but it is all the same striking that sacrifice has come to be represented in our texts as the fail-safe, risk-free mechanism that will automatically deliver the goods of life. Clearly this is the result of a peculiar development, one that took out the sting of death and absolutized the capacity of sacrifice for establishing order. But even so, the awareness of sacrificial violence and destruction was preserved.

For all the mechanistic security of the classical conception of sacrifice, the original danger and insecurity still shine through the cracks, as it were, of the professed risk-free system. Thus we are told, albeit metaphorically, of the dangers of "the wilderness of sacrifice".[15] Elsewhere the awareness of terror and mortal danger is more clearly felt, as, for instance, in the story of Śunaḥśepa, which is to be recited at royal consecrations. King Hariścandra desperately seeks to obtain a son. Finally, through rigid ascetism, he moves the god Varuṇa to grant him a son, but his wish is granted only on the contradictory condition that he sacrifice this son to the deity. The story takes a fortunate turn: the king finds a young brahmin, Śunaḥśepa, as a substitute for his son. The substitute victim manages by means of his mantras—that is, through his expertise in sacrificial lore—miraculously to release himself as well as the king and his son. But this is not the end of the story. After his sacrificial experience, Śunaḥśepa must again find a place in the human world. To that end, he is adopted by the brahmin Viśvāmitra. The adoption, however, creates a rift between the sons of Viśvāmitra, one party siding with their father, the others rebelling against his authority. The evil of death is in this way transferred and shifted to another area—significantly, the area of brahminhood—without there being a definitive solution.[16] The problem of sacrifice and death cannot be solved; it can only be shifted round. But what the story clearly shows is the terror and contradictoriness of the confrontation with the transcendent in sacrifice.

In a different legend, and in direct connection with the sacrificial regulations, the theme of mortal danger is given still clearer expression. The passage where this legend is recorded deals with the ritualistic question of the proper time or occasion for concluding a long-lasting sacrificial session (*sattra*).[17] The times or occasions are when the participants have reached a place called Plakṣa Prāsravaṇa—probably representing the middle of the world[18]—when the cows they have taken with them have increased tenfold, or, conversely, when they have lost all their property, or, finally, when their leader dies. At first sight, this list of occasions for ending the sattra looks rather puzzling. On further consideration, however, the connecting idea becomes clear: the sacrifice is an all-or-nothing enterprise; it ends either in success or in failure, in triumphantly enriched life or in loss and death. The outcome is unpredictable. But the essential ambivalence of sacrifice goes still further, for even death and failure can still turn into a sign of ultimate triumph. This is what the story embedded in the rules for the sattra's termination tells us. A group of sacrificers under their leader (*gṛhapati*) Sthūra, "the stout one," are engaged in a sattra. While performing the sacrifice, they are surrounded by a hostile band, defeated, and plundered. Sthūra is killed in the affray. The pitiful survivors sit in mourning round the body of their slain leader. Then comes the unexpected reversal. One of the mourners, the *dhruvagopa*, or guardian of the Soma, has a vision of the slain Sthūra passing along the place of sacrifice to the offering fire at the eastern end, going upward from there, and entering heaven. The dhruvagopa then calls out to the others: "Do not lament, he whom you are lamenting has gone upward from the hearth of the offering fire and entered heaven." And so, out of their loss and defeat, Sthūra's followers gain praise and honor.[19]

The striking point of this rather trite story is that the final success is not brought about, as we would expect, by the orderly performance and conclusion of the sacrifice, but, on the contrary, by the drastic disturbance and overthrow of the proceedings. It would seem that here death and destruction breaking out of the ritual structure are not so much a fatal disturbance as they are the essence of the sacrifice itself. Only by submitting to the mortal perils of sacrifice can one hope to find access to the transcendent. Yet there is no glorification of heroic death. The cry "Viva la muerte" has no place in the liturgy. One simply tries somehow to come through and to reach the goal in spite of all the risks. It is not a matter of egregious bravery and even less of superior sacrificial knowledge. We are even told that Sthūra's companions were a rather miserable band (*pāpagrāmatarā iva hi tataḥ purāsuḥ*). There is no question of their redeeming themselves by seeking death in battle. When misfortune hits them, this does not mean that their path *per aspera* will automatically lead them *ad astra*. By itself, Sthūra's death on the place of sacrifice is just a lusterless misfortune. It is only the unexpected revelation of his entering heaven that brings ultimate redemption. Till then, the final outcome remains uncertain.

One might, of course, object that the story of Sthūra and his companions is a marginal episode that has nothing much to do with sacrifice and only by accident found its way into the explanations of the ritual. However, we are told in the same context that the gods act in exactly the same way among each other. When the Maruts are engaged in a sattra, the gods Indra and Agni set upon and plunder them.[20] Moreover, there is a similar instance of a sacrificer who is killed on his place of sacrifice. Significantly, the misdeed is perpetrated by *ajinavāsinaḥ*, "people clad in antelope skins".[21] The antelope skin is the typical attribute of the consecrated sacrificer (*dīkṣita*). If I am right, this means that attacks and disturbances are not accidental intrusions, but belong to the sacrificial scenario. The attackers and the attacked are both consecrated and are engaged in the same sacrificial action, in the same way as the gods Indra and Agni are closely connected with the Marut gods whom they attack. The Sthūra legend, then, is not fortuitously introduced but is intrinsically related to sacrifice. Battle and catastrophe belong to the essence of sacrifice, as we can still see in many passages of the epic, the *Mahābhārata*. Not only do we find many instances of battle and sacrifice being equated,[22] but also it would seem that the terrifying sacrificial battle, pitting against each other two parties that are as close as brothers, was the model or prototype of the great epic. It overthrows the order and continuity of the world. And so tradition situates the catastrophe of the *Mahābhārata* war at the end of a world era, on the breach line of time.[23]

## 4

The catastrophic conception of sacrifice we have encountered above is not characteristically Indian. It is equally known in other religions. For our purpose, however, it is more important that the agonistic and violent conception of sacrifice, though never forgotten, is not a fundamental or central theme in Indian religious thought (as opposed to folklore or popular religion). Even though it can still be recognized in the *Mahābhārata* with comparative ease, it is hardly the epic's leading motive. Rather, the main theme has shifted to the dharma's being fatally endangered by the sinful war between brothers. Typically, the destructive war is brought about by the sacrifice of the royal consecration. Here the original pattern is still recognizable, but the *Mahābhārata* is predominantly critical of agonistic sacrifice and its catastrophal consequences. It is predicted at the beginning that the sacrifice of the royal consecration will lead to the destruction of the whole warrior race.[24] Sacrifice in the epic is a fatal doom, not a just and ultimately promising enterprise. The epic raises the numinous ambivalence of sacrifice to an unbearable pitch. Its sacrifice is a sacrifice to end all sacrifices.

In the epic, sacrifice has in fact already been overcome. As we saw, it belongs to the preceding world era, the *dvāparayuga*, which ends in the self-defeating paroxysm of the *Mahābhārata* war. In the following era, our present *kaliyuga*, animal sacrifice belongs to the *kalivarjya* institutions, which should not be put into practice in the kaliyuga. The men of our era are no longer deemed strong enough to cope with the heady excitement and terror of sacrifice.[25] In the dvāpara era, sacrifice was the foremost meritorious work, but in our age it has been replaced by the gift.[26]

Sacrifice in its original agonistic sense, however, has not simply been rejected. Instead it has been fundamentally changed in form and content. What we know as Vedic sacrifice is not sacrifice *tout court*, to be put on a par with its normal, popular practice as we find it to the present day in India and elsewhere. To illustrate the difference, we may briefly look at the immolation of the victim, the point of maximal tension in sacrifice. Usually the victim is immolated by cutting off the head. This was originally also the case in Vedic sacrifice (or rather, in its preclassical predecessor), but the Vedic ritual texts expressly reject this procedure. Instead they prescribe that the victim be killed by suffocation outside the sacrificial enclosure proper.[27]

Vedic sacrifice, as it has been elaborated and systematized by the ritualists, has been resolutely turned away from its origins and from popular practices as well. It has been made into a fully technical and harmless procedure. Violence, death, and destruction are mentioned with a frequency that borders on the obsessive—for instance, the slaying of the Vṛtra dragon in the Soma ritual—but the ritual has no room for such violently heroic proceedings. There is no antagonist anymore, the dragon was slain long ago, and mortal peril has been replaced by the concept of the technical error in the performance of the ritual—an error that is to be repaired by equally technical means.

Clearly a bifurcation has taken place. The intellectualized and systematized Vedic ritual, which has reduced sacrifice to the point where its very name is a source of misunderstanding, has been set apart in lonely eminence as the *śruti*, the revealed injunction. As such, it has no common ground with the world, with its concerns and sacrifices. But for the same reason, one keeps referring back to it, as we noticed, in language and terminology, in the same way that the dharma has to invoke the ultimate authority of the śruti with which it has no real connection anymore. The connection between the peasant *jajmān* and the Vedic *yajamāna* is at best a flimsy one. Nor can the Vedic ritual provide the jajmān with a model for the management of his affairs or even for his sacrifice. But the intention to relate life to ritual somehow is all the more serious, for otherwise there is no source of ultimate authority and legitimation.

## 5

Vedic ritual, as transcendent injunction, can only be devoted to the maintenance of a static, unchanging order of the universe. At least, that is what the texts keep telling us. It should keep up a constant, uninterrupted circulation between men and gods, earth and heaven. The burnt offering goes upward to heaven whence it comes down again in the form of beneficial rain.[28] It is all unbroken order based on automatic reciprocity. But within this order, there is no room anymore for the unpredictable working of the transcendent. It is then not surprising that in post-Vedic Hinduism the gods are no longer considered to be transcendent. They are, like their human counterparts, caught within the same *saṃsāra*, the same closed circulatory system.

On further consideration, however, we find that Vedic ritual in fact undermines its own claim to be the absolute universal order. In the first place, one can, of course, never be completely sure that one has not unwittingly committed an error in the ritual proceedings, which, if unrepaired, will irretrievably impair the ritual order. Thus there is always an element of uncertainty. Fittingly, the uncertainty about ritual error can be shown to be a transformation of the old uncertainty about the outcome of the sacrificial catastrophe.[29]

No less important is another point. The ritual, according to its own statements, is obviously of great importance to the life of the community and to the universe at large. Nonetheless, its performance is left to the decision of a single individual. One would expect that such a weighty matter would be a collective concern, involving the support and participation of the whole community. However, communal or collective rituals are absent from the Vedic *corpus rituale*. They are even rejected.[30] The yajamāna, assisted only by his brahmin experts, performs the ritual alone, at his own cost and for his own benefit. There is clearly an unresolved tension here between universal order and individual enterprise. That this tension is not resolved should not be understood as a marginal defect. Rather, it bears witness to the seriousness and honesty that somehow resists the temptation to solve the insoluble by sleight of hand.

Vedic ritual, then, can neither offer a viable model for man's life and activity in the world nor do justice to the transcendent. It can only propose an absolute order, which is, however, undermined from within and restricted to the place and time of the ritual's execution. In the final analysis, the Vedic śrauta ritual has to and does in fact acknowledge defeat. But how then should the orthodox Hindu relate to the transcendent when the Vedic sacrifice fails him?

## *6*

At this point, it may be useful to summarize briefly the nature and development of Vedic sacrifice by taking as an example a particular sacrificial ritual. This example is the *agnihotra*, which is both the simplest and the most widespread Vedic ritual.[31] It has, moreover, the advantage that it came to epitomize Vedic sacrifice and thus offered a starting point for ritualistic speculations that found their way into the Upaniṣads. In many respects, the agnihotra is the hub of Vedic ritualism.

Insofar as we know it from its rules, it is a simple and, all told, a rather dull affair, conspicuous only by its unremitting repetitiousness. Every day, in the early morning and at sunset, a portion of boiled milk is offered in the fire and the rest drunk by the sacrificer or, if he has engaged the ritual services of a brahmin, by the latter. Although milk is the normal offering substance, other food or drink can be used—rice or other vegetal preparations, the Soma beverage, and even meat. We have here the basic paradigm of Vedic sacrifice in its simplest form: on the one hand, the cult of the fire involving the sacrifice of a little bit of food or drink; on the other hand, the meal or, albeit reduced to the barest minimum, the solemn banquet.

Because of its connection with the rising and setting of the sun, the agnihotra has usually been explained as a magical operation meant to support and maintain the sun on its regular daily course.[32] The essential point of the ritual—to which the obvious solar connection seems to be subservient—appears, however, to be a different one, namely, the neutralization or desacralization of food so as to make it free for consumption. The materials for his food do not belong to man by right; it is, in other words, something inviolable or sacred. As a passage on the agnihotra says, "food belongs to the gods."[33] And even of the gods it is said that those among them who ate without sacrificing a bit of the food in the fire disappeared.[34] Appropriation and preparation of food are a violation of the sacred. The ritual texts are perfectly clear on the point that grinding, pressing, cooking, and boiling constitute acts of killing the same as the killing of an animal.[35] Later texts also speak about kitchen utensils as so many slaughter houses.[36]

The need for food forces man to enter into violent contact with the sacred and to expose himself to the ominous consequences of his transgression. He can only neutralize these risks by giving up again what he has gained by his transgression—as King Hariścandra had to give up his son obtained from the deity—or, at least, by abandoning a token part of the food by pouring it in the fire. Otherwise he will, as in Bhṛgu's vision of the underworld,[37] be killed in his turn by the killed. In this way, we can understand why the agnihotra is viewed as an expiation for the evil committed in the house and that all food is seen as the remainder left from the fire offering.[38] In the same line, we also understand why the agnihotra is said to make the sacrificer overcome death and to lead him to immortality.[39] Without the fire offering he would himself fall prey to death because of the violation and killing he had to perpetrate to obtain his food.

This numinous and threatening background forms a striking contrast to the total harmlessness of the agnihotra. The insecure interaction of transgression and retribution, of killing and being killed, has been replaced by the steady alternation of the sun's rising and setting, of day and night, and by the circulation between heaven and earth. The ritualistic control of alternation and circulation should enable the sacrificer to rise above them and so to overcome death. The unsettling interplay with the sacred has been eliminated. What is specifically lacking is the element of contest and battle, the fight for the goods of life that we have come to recognize as the essential uncertainty of sacrifice. Instead, the exclusive emphasis is on mechanistic certainty.

However, on further consideration, the element of violent conflict cannot be totally eliminated. How else is it possible to find a statement, albeit an isolated one, that equates the innocuous agnihotra with a weapon, a *vajra*, which the sacrificer hurls at his enemy?[40] At first sight, it is hard to see what exactly this means. It can be clarified, though, if we connect it with an even more curious passage, which comes under the heading of the possible errors and mishaps in the execution of the ritual. Among these errors, we find the somewhat surprising case that a chariot or cart passes between the sacrificer's fireplaces in the ritual enclosure.[41] Such an event would obviously constitute a most serious disturbance of the ritual. One wonders, however, how such a traffic accident could occur. It should be easy to avoid driving through the ritual enclosure, unless, of course—and that is the point—one expressly does so with evil intent. The case is analogous to the fate that befell Sthūra and his followers when they were set upon and defeated on their place of sacrifice. Similarly, we are often told of the asuras' invading the gods' place of sacrifice. In other words, the traffic accident is no accident at all, but a reflection of the ancient sacrificial battle, which has been transformed into a ritual error.

Significantly, the correction for this "error" is the same as the one prescribed when someone passes with his sacrificial fires through someone else's ritual enclosure. Apparently the two cases—crossing with a vehicle or with one's fires—are one and the same. Such a "mishap" can hardly be explained otherwise than in terms of agonistic procedures between two competing groups of sacrificers within the compass of the same sacrifice. It is then hardly surprising that a sacrificer's death in foreign parts requires the same expiatory rite.[42] As we have seen, violent conflict and death were the essence of sacrifice. In this way, we can understand why the serene and harmless agnihotra can still be identified with a vajra hurled at the enemy.

## 7

The elimination of death and catastrophe from the ritual does not seem to have been a gradual and cumulative process of erosion but a conscious reform. Its aim was to control the perils of the quest for transcendence. That the reformers were well aware of the issue comes out clearly in the mythical story of the sacrificial contest between the Lord of Life, Prajāpati, and his opponent Death—a story that may be considered the "charter myth" of Vedic ritualism.[43] The decisive point is Prajāpati's "seeing" the equivalence of the elements of his sacrifice with those of his opponent's sacrifice. Prajāpati is thereby enabled to integrate the rival sacrifice and to overcome Death. "Since then," the *Jaiminīya Brāhmaṇa* proudly concludes, "there is no sacrificial contest anymore; the sacrifice is one, Prajāpati is the sacrifice." Conflict and the rival, Death, have been eliminated.

Identification based on equivalences of cosmic and ritual elements is indeed the premier intellectual tool of the Vedic "science" of ritual. It enabled the ritualists to construe a closed mechanistic universe to be controlled and directed by the ritual. Uncertainty and catastrophe were replaced by the fail-safe certainty of ritualism. But the price of excluding uncertainty was internal contradiction. The ritualistic system breaks down on the insuperable obstacle of the transcendent.

The agnihotra illustrates how the elimination of conflict and catastrophe resulted in the internal contradiction of Vedic ritualism. This has already come out in the remarkable fact that the kṣatriya—the king and warrior who as the upholder of the dharma is the ideal sacrificer—is, according to the rules, excluded from the agnihotra. He cannot perform the agnihotra himself, and the brahmin is forbidden to perform it for him. The kṣatriya, so we are told, perpetrates many impure acts, eats impure food, he kills and plunders.[44] The ritualists have, of course, tried to remove this contradiction, but the result is a further deepening of the problem. Since the kṣatriya cannot perform the agnihotra or have it performed for him, he must instead feed brahmins. In this way, he still makes the required offerings, not in the fire, but in the brahmin.

The solution is based on separating the priestly office at the sacrifice from the eating of the sacrificer's food. However, both acts, officiating and eating, are two sides of the same function. The brahmin cannot officiate for a sacrificer whose food he cannot eat.[45] Conversely, if he does accept the sacrificer's food, it is hard to see how he can refuse to officiate for him on the grounds of the sacrificer's impurity. The kṣatriya's impurity is in both cases equally prohibitive. So the problem is further complicated, and therefore we find yet another attempt at solving it. The exclusion of the kṣatriya is waived if he has shown his ritual devotion by performing the Soma sacrifice. But how can the impure kṣatriya be able to perform the complicated and weighty Soma ritual, for which he will have to engage not just one but sixteen or seventeen brahmin officiants, when he is already excluded from the simple agnihotra? Not surprisingly, this is left unexplained and the problem remains as refractory as before.

How did the problem arise in the first place? The kṣatriya's impurity is not a very convincing ground for his exclusion, for, as we saw, it does not exclude him from the Soma ritual. The interesting point is that the reference to the kṣatriya as a Soma sacrificer appears to hold the key to the origin of the contradiction. This requires a short excursus on the Soma ritual: Some time before the actual Soma sacrifice, when the Soma beverage will be prepared, offered in the fire, and drunk, the sacrificer undergoes the consecration (*dīkṣā*). The consecrated *dīkṣita* starts on a begging tour that should help him to collect the necessities for the sacrifice (*saniyācana*). Although this begging tour is a rather marginal and perfectly harmless rite, its original character is easily recognizable. The dīkṣita sets out as a warrior on a war or racing chariot.[46] Clearly, the original purpose of this pomp and circumstance is to obtain the goods for sacrifice at the sacrificial contests organized by others or perhaps, less ceremonially, by way of a razzia. We have already come across such warrior dīkṣitas, and we could notice that the dividing line between razzia and sacrificial contest is disconcertingly thin, if there is one at all. It is this keenness on prize and plunder that marks the dīkṣita—like the kṣatriya—as impure.[47] It is only afterward, when his warrior prowess has won him the property—especially cattle—needed for sacrifice, that he can set himself up as a liberal host and sacrificer. Incidentally, he is then of course entitled to the agnihotra.

Originally, then, there was a cycle consisting of two opposite phases: on the one hand that of the consecrated warrior, on the other hand that of the munificent sacrificer.[48] The pivot and connecting point of this, in more than one sense, vicious circle was the sacrificial contest with its uncertain outcome. This cyclical course of sacrifice can be genetically connected with the mechanistically conceived circulation between heaven and earth propounded by ritualistic theory. But the ritual is of an entirely different nature. It removed the catastrophic turning point and thereby excluded the transcendent. The old cycle, deprived of its dynamic center, collapsed. The two opposite phases "imploded" into the now vacant center. The aggressively acquisitive dīkṣita fell into the same place as the peacefully munificent yajamāna. The kṣatriya warrior must therefore at the same time act as a peaceful sacrificer. By the same token, the brahmin should be able to officiate for the kṣatriya and to accept his food and gifts, notwithstanding his impurity. Hence the contradiction of the rules that exclude the kṣatriya from the agnihotra and yet allow him to act as yajamāna at the Soma sacrifice. These rules that were once perfectly understandable in their original context result in an insoluble contradiction now that the two opposite phases have come to coincide.

The ancient alternating cycle left room for the transcendent in its catastrophic center at the cost of an awesome uncertainty. The mechanistic system of ritual excluded the catastrophe, but it too had to pay for its achievement. Catastrophe was replaced by contradiction. This was the only way in which the ritual system could account for the insoluble problem of the transcendent.

## *8*

The ultimate breakdown of ritualism is, however, not the last word. This is illustrated again by the agnihotra, namely, by its last manifestation, the *prāṇāgnihotra*, or sacrifice in the internal fires of the breaths. In plain fact, it is a meal surrounded by some simple ritual acts and mantras.[49] But its significance is far weightier than it appears. The idea of numinosity and transgression involved in the production, preparation, and eating of food make the connection with sacrifice a natural one. The special importance of the prāṇāgnihotra is the fusion and concentration of both meal and sacrifice in the single person of the sacrificer. It emancipates the sacrificer from society. In sovereign independence from the surrounding world, he performs his sacrifice, which is at the same time his meal.

The starting point for the prāṇāgnihotra may again be found with the dīkṣita. As we saw, the dīkṣita is not yet qualified to act as a sacrificer and patron. He must still win the goods to be spent in sacrifice and gifts. In the meantime, he should, by virtue of his vow (*vrata*), nourish himself only with boiled milk—a restriction that is apparently so characteristic that the dīkṣita's milk diet is simply known as vrata. The interesting point is that this vrata is expressly mentioned as the replacement of the agnihotra, which he is not yet entitled to perform as a sacrificer.[50] The dīkṣita is a prāṇāgnihotra sacrificer *avant la lettre*. As the dīkṣita sets out from the community, so the prāṇāgnihotra emancipates himself from society. The difference is that the dīkṣita hopes to return to society, and the prāṇāgnihotra perpetuates the distance from society. In the daily prāṇāgnihotra, the practitioner performs the food sacrifice without any outside help or reciprocity. In this way, it allows him to stay in society while maintaining his independence from it.

It is, of course, easy to see that this construction hides a new contradiction. In simple terms, how should the single individual obviate the practical need for dependence on or cooperation with others in the production of food? The prāṇāgnihotra contradicts the reality of the relationships that of necessity govern the social world. But, then, contradiction is the sign of the transcendent.

## 9

The utter reduction of sacrifice in the prāṇāgnihotra is the end station of Vedic ritualism. All oppositions—dīkṣita and sacrificer, giver and recipient, world and transcendence—have been drawn together and fused in the single sacrificer. In the mythical language of Prajāpati's victory over Death, the sacrifice is now "one." Dualistic sacrifice has become monistic ritualism. It does not communicate or connect anymore but, by means of identification, posits the unification of opposite poles in the individual. This also means that the ritual has withdrawn into splendid isolation and requires its adherent to view himself as equally withdrawn. The prāṇāgnihotra is then either a meaningless complication of daily life, unthinkingly accepted, or a contradictory sign of transcendence. The important point is that out of the awesome violence of sacrifice a new and unique view of the transcendent has been won. It urges man to emancipate himself from his mundane bonds and to realize the transcendent exclusively by himself and in himself.

At this point, not sacrifice and ritual, but knowledge—the knowledge of the self—holds the center of the stage. This knowledge had already announced itself when it enabled Prajāpati to resolve all antitheses and to integrate into himself his opponent, Death. In the "one who knows," all opposites coincide and become one. The ritual of sacrifice therefore cannot be the pivotal moment in Indian thought, for it has been overcome and superseded by knowledge.[51] This is what gives knowledge in the form of the Veda its transcendent authority. Therefore, too, this knowledge is cut off from the world over which it holds ultimate authority but to which, for the same reason, it cannot relate.

In the final analysis, not even the knowledge of the self can be the pivotal moment, for then it would have to stand in the world and thereby lose its transcendent absoluteness. There is no mediation. There is only contradiction. There, in the contradictory tension between world-denying self-realization and worldly piety is the dynamic center. In the perplexity of contradiction, man must wrestle with the transcendent. The outcome remains uncertain. Man's quest for the transcendent is first and last a desperate leap into the unknown.

# 7 Ritual, Revelation, and the Axial Age

## *1*

It may seem at best idiosyncratic to connect ritualism with so dramatic a concept as Karl Jaspers's Axial Age. When ritualism, moreover, is hallowed by the antiquity and authority of the Veda, it would seem to be the very antithesis of anything revolutionary. Ritual is generally supposed to have gone on for ages past, and in the case of Vedic ritual, it goes on unchanged even in our time. Though subject to internal development, it has shown itself strangely impervious to the changes in its physical, social, intellectual, and religious surroundings, all of which would, moreover, seem to militate against its very survival. To make the case against Vedic ritual even worse, it is credited with the power to bring about all that one desires—health, progeny, wealth. It is, in other words, thoroughly magical and clearly at odds with all that the Axial Age stands for.

Among the Vedic scriptures only the Upaniṣads are viewed as evidence of a decisive turning point, but only insofar as they, though rooted in ritual thought, are seen to go beyond and to supersede Vedic ritualism. Our attention is thus focused on the suggestive similarities as well as on the divergences of Upaṇisadic and early Buddhist thought.[1]

Obviously, Buddhism is an imcomparably more presentable candidate for the axial breakthrough. It shares with the Upaniṣads the doctrinal concern with *karman,* transmigration, world renunciation, and final release; but its purely ethical karman doctrine untrammeled by ritual or magical reminiscences, the rational clarity of its stand on transmigration and salvation impress the observer as a decisive advance. Its rejection of the Veda, moreover, gives Buddhism the character of a radically new beginning. No less

This essay is based on a paper read at the Conference on the Origins of the Axial Age and Its Diversity, Bad Homburg, 4–8 January 1983.

important in this respect is the impact it had on the mundane order through the intimate connection with the Maurya Empire, which arose with other new empires at the end of the Axial Age. Giving the empire a new ethical legitimation, Buddhism owes to empire the realization of its universalistic claim. Even though the Maurya Empire lasted only for a relatively short time, the pattern for a new type of universalistic imperial order, based on the intimate connection of the ruler and the monastic establishment, the *sangha,* was set.[2]

The Veda, on the other hand, though ostensibly addressing itself to man and his mundane interests, kept out of such involvement with the world and its powers. True, its ritual does contain prestigious ceremonies that are explicitly meant for the consecration of kings and emperors, but when performing such ceremonies, the royal celebrant is just a sacrificer (*yajamāna*) like any commoner.[3] Conversely, the legal authors do not even prescribe these ceremonies for sanctioning the ruler's power. Although they were often used to enhance the standing of the ruler by documenting his access to the Veda as a proper *kṣatriya*, the Vedic ceremonies by themselves did not turn a mere ruler into a king or emperor.

Vedic ritualism, then—even when taking its Upaṇisadic extension into account—does not appear to present a prima facie case for the axial breakthrough. Its indecisive position vis-à-vis the world, as well as the restriction of its access, gives it a marginal place that seems to deny any such contention from the start. In postaxial Hinduism the Veda, and even more its ritual, is for all its high prestige controversial, that is, if it is not just treated as an idol that only rates a bow in passing, as Louis Renou has graphically put it.[4] The classical proposition that the whole of the dharma rests on or is already contained in the Veda is a pious axiom that vanishes into thin air as soon as one tries to pin down their supposedly intimate connection.[5] In one point at least, Veda and dharma are disturbingly at odds with each other. The very attempts to harmonize Vedic animal sacrifice with the dharma's ideal requirement of *ahiṃsā*, or at least to give sacrifice a secure place of its own, show that the relationship of Veda and dharma is a highly problematic one.

But this contradictory valuation, running from transcendent elevation through indifference to outright rejection, should put us on our guard. On one hand, from the beginning, the Veda has not lacked in controversy. On the other hand, its extensive body of texts has been preserved in all its intricacy with unique faithfulness, which is all the more remarkable when one considers India's otherwise rather cavalier fashion of managing its textual heritage. Both the controversy surrounding it and and the care spent on its preservation place the Veda in a class by itself. They may be considered as typical symptoms of the documents left by the Axial Age.

The contention of the present paper, therefore, is that Vedic ritualism—

no less than Buddhism or other "heterodox" sects—does indeed represent in its own and powerful manner the axial breakthrough. Notwithstanding the problems of textual chronology—the ritual texts in the version before us may be later than is commonly assumed—it may well reflect the primary breakthrough.

## *2*

At this point we should recall that the Veda is viewed as ultramundane, suprahuman (*apauruṣeya*) truth, in short as "revelation." The claim to being revealed truth is in no way an unusual one for Hindu scriptures, which are as a rule considered to have been taught or recited by the Godhead to the sage, who then handed down the revealed teaching through the teacher-pupil chain. In the case of the Veda, however, the matter is subtly different. The Veda is *śruti*, "hearing," and as such is sharply differentiated from *smṛti*, "remembrance," especially from the dharma texts. The term *śruti*, however, requires some comment. It implies oral transmission by the teacher to the pupil, who learns the text by rote. In this respect, the situation is not much different from that of the smṛti. However, this is not the way the texts tell us the śruti was originally received. They were not "heard" from the Godhead but "found" and, especially, "seen" by the ecstatic seers, the *ṛṣis*. In contradistinction to the smṛti, which is received and transmitted through the teacher-pupil chain, there is a sharp break between the vision of the revelation and its transmission by "hearing," *śruti*. That the Veda nevertheless goes under the name of *śruti* suggests that the age of the ecstatic seers is over and the revelation complete.[6] The only thing that remained to be done was the painfully precise transmission of the revealed knowledge by hearing and learning it by rote. From then on, the Veda became a fixed and bounded body of texts, like the scriptures of Buddhists or Jains.

The point to be retained is the break between the revelatory vision of the seers and the śruti that purports to be the content of their vision. Though one readily understands that the seers' vision is the source of the ritual formulas (*mantra*), it is hard to accept the notion that the ecstatic visions should be equally concerned with ritualistic minutiae, for the corpus of texts which form the śruti is concerned with the systematic elaboration of the utterly complicated ritual. Or, as an authoritative text has it, "Veda means *mantra* and *brāhmaṇa*",[7] that is, ritual formula and exposition of the liturgical rules. There is, then, a decisive gap between the revelatory vision and its ritualistic substance. It is in this gap—and not in the preceding age of the seers—that the axial turning point is situated. This turning point does not lead to the exploitation of the revelation but is aimed at overcoming it. It replaces vision and revelation with something entirely different, namely, the rational order of ritualism that by itself constitutes ultimate truth and leaves no room for anything so unsettling as revelatory vision.

At first sight, this may suggest a retreat from the transcendent breakthrough and its creativity and a movement toward ritualistic routinization.[8] It could even be easily construed as a backsliding into a world of myth and magic. Such an appreciation would indeed be in line with the usual evaluation of Vedic ritual thought, which is at best qualified, in Hermann Oldenberg's words, as "vorwissenschaftliche Wissenschaft."[9] While this qualification acknowledges a rationalistic impulse, Vedic ritualism is generally considered the hallmark of the magic-bound Hindu world.[10] It cannot be denied that the Veda and its brahmin carriers gave much ground for such views. But even when we concede to these views their part of truth, the question is whether it can be the whole truth. For it leaves us with the obstinate problem of an ancient ritualism that has been kept alive and in exceptional esteem till the present day but that is and has always been at odds with the Hindu world and its values. We shall therefore have to look into the ritualistic content of the śruti.

## 3

The central concept of the śruti is sacrifice (*yajña*). It is the primordial act of creation and establishes the order of the universe. In the enigmatically involute words of the *Ṛgveda*, which defy interpretation, it is said that "the gods sacrificed the sacrifice with the sacrifice, these were the primordial ordinances."[11] In this way, the text tells us, the gods found their place in heaven and thereby set the rules for men's activity. Starting from this mythic statement, one is tempted to view sacrifice as the organizing principle of the Hindu world order.[12] But it is exactly here that the problem stands out clearest.

Essential to sacrifice is the immolatory act of violence and destruction. Even if the element of death is minimized, it remains a violent attempt at gaining access to the other world. At this point, as already mentioned, sacrifice collided with the Hindu value of *ahiṃsā*. The euphemisms for expressing the act of immolation—such as *saṃjñapana*, "making (the victim) consent"—highlight the utter gravity of the sacrificial enterprise. Rather than establishing and guaranteeing order, sacrifice overthrows order by the violent irruption of the sacred. The place of sacrifice is a battleground where one must risk life and goods in the uncertain hope of winning access to the other world. Thus the gods fought their rivals, the asuras, on the place of sacrifice, and so must man. Kurukṣetra, the epic battlefield of the *Mahābhārata*, is the gods' place of sacrifice. The ritual brāhmaṇa texts abound in references to their violently agonistic procedures. But, significantly, these brief, lemma-like statements are not considered to have a founding authority. Not being by themselves authoritative rules for the execution of the ritual, they are qualified as *arthavāda*, nonauthoritative explanation.[13] They are the scattered and fossilized remnants of a lost and discredited world.

This world was the world of the heroic age that the Indian epic, like Hesiod, places in the breach that divides our present world age from its predecessor—a mythic reminiscence, as it were, of an authentic axial crisis. Its warriors were constrained again and again to risk their all in the agonizing sacrificial contest. On one hand, the invitation to sacrifice is a challenge that the warrior cannot afford to refuse on pain of losing his honor.[14] On the other hand, not being invited is a grave insult that may compel one to force his way in and challenge the host of the sacrificial festival.[15] Better still than in the flat and dry allusions of the brāhmaṇa tests, the tragic predicament of the warrior ethos comes out in the epic, for example, when Yuddhiṣṭhira, who wants to renounce the insensate violence, is reminded that he is bound to stake again "the material sacrifice" (*dravyamayo yajñaḥ*) he has won in renewed sacrificial battle. For this, he is told, is the ever-lasting way of existence, the great "ten-chariot road" (*dāśarathaḥ panthā*).[16]

Therefore the gods too are said to drive about on their chariots while their opponents, the asuras, stay at home. And it is through their wheeled drive that they obtain the revelatory vision of the sacrificial "work" *(karman)*.[17] The statement is, as usual, short and undramatic. The "vision" in this context is, of course, nothing more exciting than ritual procedure. But however devoid of drama, it is nonetheless highly suggestive of a previous and totally different state of affairs. The interesting point is, however, not the hint at the violent warrior ethos, but the fact that this was the condition for the revelatory vision.

If we look for what may have been the original context and content of such visions, there is another instance, where, again in the flattest possible manner, the story of a band of warriors is told.[18] They are attacked and plundered on their place of sacrifice—which is also their camp—apparently by a similar warrior band. Their leader is among the slain, but while the survivors sit in mourning around his remains, one of them has the clear and sudden vision of the slain leader walking along the place of sacrifice to the offering fire at the eastern end and then upward, entering heaven. Here, it would seem, we see the full scenario in abridged and demythologized form: the sacrificial encampment and battleground, risk, defeat, death, and finally the redeeming vision of the hoped for but till the last uncertain access to heaven. At the same time, this explains how the heroic age where these visions were at home came to its end. As Hesiod explains, the heroic race was destroyed by "evil war, some of the heroes before the city of Thebes fighting over the animals of Oedipus and others brought across the sea to Troy because of fair-haired Helen".[19]

If nothing else, the self-defeating violence to which the warrior was in honor bound time and again to expose his life and goods—even if we discount the hypertrophical elaboration in the epic—could not but call forth a radical reaction. The result was the decisive turning point where the warrior's sacrifice was replaced with the brahmin's ritualism, which rules out conflict and marginalizes violence. In fact, we are told as much by a brāhmaṇa passage, in which Prajāpati, the Lord of Life, after an age-long sacrificial struggle defeats and subjects his rival, Death, by the abstract means of the new ritualism. Since then, the text triumphantly declares, there is no sacrificial struggle any more.[20]

## 4

The striking feature of Vedic ritualism is its unmythical, rational, and individualistic character. The mythical presence of gods and ancestors has evaporated to mere names. Their deeds no longer form the authoritative foundation of the ritual that now finds its authority in itself, in the comprehensive system of rules ordering the limited set of standardized liturgical elements—acts, formulas, recitations, and chants.

The character of this ritualism comes out with particular clarity in the way it transformed the visionary truth of the *brahman,* the mysterious inner "connection" that holds together the universe.[21] By its nature, the cosmic truth could only be expressed in the enigmatic formulations that did not explain the brahman but contained it in the silent hollow of the unresolved riddle. The contest in which the parties fought each other with visionary enigmatic formulas formed an essential part of the sacrificial scenario. It was a momentous and hazardous struggle where the contestants risked their lives, and the winning contestant showed himself to hold the visionary truth of the cosmic enigma. But, as we saw, Prajāpati's victory over Death put an end to all this. The contest for the brahman only survives in a few *brahmodyas,* ritualized exchanges of fixed riddle formulas learnt by heart.[22] "L'énigme essentielle du Veda"[23] has been replaced by the rationalized brahman that consists in cut-and-dried identifications of disparate elements of the divine and human worlds with those of the ritual. Indeed, identification, based on qualitative and numerical equivalence *(saṃpad, saṃkhyānam),* is said to have given Prajāpati his decisive victory. It is the premier intellectual tool for organizing the disjointed universe in the perfect order of the ritual. Even though the sheer weight of intricate detail requires the services of technical experts, the priestly *ṛtvijaḥ,* the system of liturgical elements and identifications is clear in itself. It has no place for mystery or enigma and, above all, it can be systematically taught and learned.

But the important achievement of the ritual system and indeed its purpose was that it took away ultimate legitimation from the violent and destructive contest for the goods of life and access to heaven. When the ritual does require the immolation of an animal victim, it is no longer decapitated at the sacrificial stake but bloodlessly suffocated in a separate shed outside the ritual area. Violence and death have been replaced with the ritual mistake to be corrected by ritual means.[24] The sacrificial battleground has been turned into a serene and perfectly ordered ritual emplacement. There, freed from the ties and contingencies of the world, the yajamāna strikes out in his own universe through the artifice of the ritual. But this artificial universe, for all its systematic control of even the smallest detail, is brittle and ephemeral. The price it must pay for the perfection of its order is divorce from the world. It can only be realized outside society and for the limited duration of the ritual. At the end the ritual emplacement is abandoned,[25] and the yajamāna goes home again to his place in society, "as the one he was before."

There is, then, a complete break between the social world and the world of the Vedic śruti. The bridge between this and yonder world that sacrifice was meant to be has been broken down. The ritual that took its place could only be transcendence itself—or nothing at all. Therefore it cannot be obligatory. It is left to the individual's choice whether he subjects himself to the ritual's transcendent law or not. If he does, it has no direct, visible bearing on his mundane life. Insofar as it has an impact, it is through the intermediary of an impersonal transcendent mechanism, namely the ritual's invisible or previously nonexistent faculty *(adṛṣṭa, apūrva)* that in an unknown way will bring about the intended result (say, wealth or progeny). This is not, however, a mystical or magical faculty but is simply inexplicable as the ritual itself, being transcendent, is inexplicable.

## 5

The rise of Vedic ritualism broke the coherence of the world and produced an irreparable rift which closely resembles Max Weber's postulate of the *Entzauberung,* or disenchantment of the world.[26] The tragic world of the warrior's sacrifice was certainly no Arcadia, but at least god and man were at one in the internecine strife for the goods of life. Even though the pitch of violence was raised to the breaking point, it was still one world held together by the nexus of sacrifice. Life and death were not irreconcilable but complementary, success and defeat not decisive but reversible, good and evil not absolute but ambivalent. Nothing is definitive and everything is liable to recall at the next round of sacrifice. In the epic, Bali, the defeated king of the asuras, can still tell the victorious god Indra that at the next turn there will again be the renewal of the battle between gods and asuras, "when the sun will be standing still in the middle." Indra, however, retorts that such a day will never arrive since the sun's course has been permanently fixed, the world definitively ordered.[27] The ever-renewed sacrificial hour of truth has lost its power to give meaning and coherence to the world. Instead, the world has been definitively split between the transcendent order of ritual and the unreformed sphere of social life.

However, this did not lead to the disenchantment of the world postulated by Weber. The social world was in no way divested of its mythical and magical meaning and values. It did not become a world where everything just "is" or "happens" but has no "meaning" anymore.[28] Such a world, denuded of meaning and therefore desperately looking to the transcendent sphere for a new and, this time, rational order and meaning, did not arise. What happened was that ultimate value and legitimation, as it was realized and activated in the warrior's sacrifice, was taken out of the mundane sphere. Henceforth, ultimate legitimation could only come from the transcendent ritual that took the place of sacrifice. For that reason, the whole of the dharma had to rest on or even had to be contained in the śruti—a necessary fiction, but a fiction all the same—for the śruti is patently devoid of use or meaning for the world's affairs and it is so as a matter of principle. Closed upon itself, it has no meaning other than the self-contained rationality of its system. Even if it may be supposed to offer an exhaustive pattern for life regulated by the law of ritual, it is for the life of the single yajamāna who chooses to spend his life in ritual and can afford to do so.

True, we do find statements in the ritual texts that claim a total cosmic effect for the śruti, for instance, that the sun will not rise without the daily performance of the *agnihotra,* the milk offering in the fire.[29] This is, of course, in line with the ritualistic technique of identification, which equalizes the elements of the macro- and microcosmos with those of the ritual. The ritual can in this way be viewed as the central mechanism of an ideally ordered universe. Such statements are, however, obviously arthavāda and therefore lack ultimate authority, even though it would be wrong to ascribe them simply to priestly self-importance. They follow logically from the system of identification. The point, however, is that if the ritual is an essential condition for the maintenance of the universe, it is contradictory that its faithful performance is left to the decision of the single individual. But, as we already saw, the cosmic import is just arthavāda in praise of the agnihotra. That is, in the final analysis, Vedic ritualism rejects its rich potential for magical meaning.

It was not the world that was "disenchanted" but the ritual, when it was stripped of the numinous meaning of sacrifice. Though the word "sacrifice" *(yajña)* suggests continuity, it is significant that the technical term for the central act of offering is *tyāga,* "abandoning" or "renouncing," which implies a free, nonobligatory and nonbinding gift without social tension or strife.[30] "This to the god N.N., not to me," as the oblation formula has it. Indeed, in the theory of the four world ages, sacrifice is too much for our fallen and spineless times. Its place has been taken by the gift, *dāna.*[31]

The result is two separate and fundamentally incompatible worlds: on the one hand, the break-away transcendence of rationally systematized but meaningless ritualism; on the other hand, an unreformed social world of conflict and ambivalence. Here, in the social world, all things are interconnected. It is a world that does not lack in numinous and magical meaning, but it knows itself to be cut off from ultimate value and legitimation and its arrangements to be contingent and reversible.

## *6*

These two worlds have to exist together and must work out their mutual accommodation, even though their essential incompatibility makes all accommodation precarious. There is, of course, the temptation to exploit the magic potential of Vedic ritualism for worldly uses. Its brahmin experts could easily turn into magicians and demonstrably often did so. But we have seen already that this possibility is in the last resort rejected and the brahmin is forbidden to put his Vedic expertise at the service of worldly interests. The ideal brahmin, like the Veda, stands apart from the world and cultivates the Veda by himself. The world, on the other hand, could not remain unaffected. The brahmin's standing apart illustrates how the world was impaired by the withdrawal of ultimate value and legitimation. The king and the web of power relations he represents especially stand in need of the brahmin's legitimizing services. But it is exactly the king who is singled out as the one whom the brahmin should utterly shun.[32] The situation is the more contradictory for the fact that subsistence and survival may force the brahmin to turn to the king for support.

The point is that Vedic ritualism, by outlawing conflict and violence, not only makes kingship questionable but also aims at dissolving the ties of exchange and interdependence that constitute the social arena. To that end, it set the yajāmana apart and isolated him on his ritual emplacement. Therefore too, it not only isolated the brahmin, but also required the whole of society to observe absolute dividing lines, namely, those between the *varṇas*. The fact that the numberless castes *(jāti)* are viewed as the outcome of inter-varṇa marriages breaching the dividing lines vitally impaired the caste order. Caste society—like any other society—cannot do without exchange and interdependence, but at the same time, it is required to honor the principle of varṇa-like separation. In short, the strictly ultramundane divisiveness and individualism of the śruti threatens the world's vital relationships with disintegration. Hence the tension and controversy surrounding the Veda. They are the more dynamic for being irresolvable.

The unresolved tension not only affected the social world. Vedic ritualism was also pried open to give way to other but never definitive solutions. It could either follow out the line of otherworldly individualism or it could turn back to the world in an attempt to encompass it. Indeed, both roads were followed.

The first path led to the evaporated ritualism of the "offering in the internal fires of the breaths" *(prāṇāgnihotra),* that is, en clair: eating, ritualized by means of a few simple mantras and mouth rinsing.[33] However pale this may seem to be, it is more than just a bow in the direction of a hollow and outlived tradition. It is a ritual purified of the last vestiges of violence and death and solely geared to the maintenance of life. Above all, it marks the individualism of the eater. Alone and withdrawn into himself, he follows the injunction of "sacrifice" in sovereign independence from the world. And this brings us straightaway to the brahminic renouncer, who is no different from the ideal brahmin. Both stand apart and have no truck with the world. That the individualism implied in this type of ritualism is a palpable fiction makes the tension all the more poignant.

Second, the attempt to encompass the world is well illustrated by the reinstitution in the prestigious agnicayana ritual of a wheeled vehicle for carrying the fire that eventually will be installed on the elaborately constructed fire altar. This rite of carrying the fire clearly harks back to the raiding and transhuming treks of warrior bands carrying their fire and belongings with them—the backdrop of heroic sacrifice, so frequently referred to in arthavāda passages but eliminated from the ritual and replaced with purely liturgical elements. In this case too, the setting out on the trek and the unyoking at the resting places were replaced by taking up the fire in its pot, making three steps, and putting it down again as well as by a particular recitation, the *vātsapra* hymn. There was, then, no need anymore even for mimicking the trek. Generally the texts are content to leave it at that. However, this is exactly what a comparatively late and highly systematized text, the *Śatapatha Brāhmaṇa,* objects to. After discussing the case, our text enjoins the performance of both the abstract ritual and the actual driving about of the fire on a cart. The reason given for this doubling of the procedure is significant. The abstract symbolization is said to be the divine form, the actual driving, the human form. By performing both, one makes the ritual "whole and entire" and encompasses both the transcendent and the human world.[34] The logic is compelling and deeply sincere, but, again, it is no more than arthavāda. The result is an amplification of the ritual as such. But the ritualistic injunction of an aimless "driving about" can only mimic an archaic reality, not give it new life and meaning. The intended encompassment cannot be validly achieved.

So either way, we end in a stalemate. The chasm between transcendent ritualism and mundane reality remains unbridgeable. The world, once unified in the agonal violence of sacrifice, has been irreversibly broken. Society is left unhinged. Its arrangements are permanently undermined by the withdrawal of ultimate legitimation, which in the final analysis requires no less than the dissolution of society. By the same token, the source of ultimate legitimation itself cannot escape doubt and controversy.

## *7*

If the Vedic scriptures reflect the axial breakthrough, the question of the historical conditions which led to it imposes itself. The question is the more pressing for the unexplained parrellelism and simultaneity of the phenomenon in different areas of the ancient world. The answer must be disappointing at best. As Jaspers has already warned us, it is a historical mystery that the progress of research can only amplify but not solve.[35] If, however, we do not immediately expect to find valid causes but only try to fill in some of the historical backdrop, we can take advantage of frequent and telling indications scattered throughout the Vedic ritual texts. These indications seem to center on the transhuming and cattle-raiding warriors and the violence of their sacrificial encounters as they desperately strove for a way out of *aṃhas,* the narrows of want and insecurity. It seems safe to surmise—as indeed we have—that the self-defeating violence of giving and receiving death must have brought on a crisis. But we can only see this in the effect it had of eliminating conflict, violence, and destruction from the sacrificial ritual. The actual historical circumstances of an axial crisis escape us.

The general picture of ancient Indo-Aryan society suggested by our texts is that of a world constantly on the move in a relentless push toward the east. This eastward move is a stereotype of the ritual texts, as in the legend of the ritual fire's triumphant progress from the Sarasvatī River in the west to the River Sadānīra in the east finally to be settled even beyond that border.[36] It is symbolically expressed in the extension of the ritual emplacement to the east and the bringing over of the fire to its new hearth at the eastern end of the extended emplacement. This is even clearer in the processional rituals *(yātsattra),* in which the whole emplacement is each day moved further east. A more balanced and realistic view of the historical process, however, seems to be contained in a passage relating the activities of the ancient Kuru-Pancālas over the year. In the cool season, they set out toward the east, settled there temporarily at different places, forcibly took hold of the winter crop, fed their men and animals, and finally, at the end of the hot season, returned to the west again where they stayed during the rainy season and worked their own fields.[37]

The pattern, then, seems to have been a yearly circuit of transhumance and raiding, starting from permanent agricultural settlements and returning there again for the agricultural operations of the monsoon crop. It seems plausible that the eastward movements of the Vedic Aryans should be viewed in these terms, as a gradual extension of these centers and their circuits into the eastern "frontier areas." That this implied a growing density of agricultural settlements—as is also suggested by the Kuru-Pancālas' seasonal movement to settled areas—seems equally plausible. This may be indicated also by the shift in meaning of the world *grāma* from "trekking warrior band" to settled "village" in the later ritual texts. In these texts, fairly densely settled tracts with contiguous villages are, if not the standard, at least the ideal of peaceful conditions.[38] But this is as far as the Vedic ritual texts will allow us to go. We may surmise that sedentarization and expansion of settled agriculture played a role in the rise of Vedic ritualism, but our texts have nothing to say about this, let alone about the urban world of trade, commerce, and courts found in early Buddhist texts. Instead, the ritual texts keep the imagery of the trekking warrior who is forever yoking his horses to set out again to lord it over the *kṣemya,* the stay-at-home sedentary people.[39] In this archaic world, the brahmin is not yet the priestly expert, but a warrior who is proclaimed a *brāhmaṇa* at his consecration *(dīkṣā)* and who sets out on a chariot, even though the ritual no longer has use for chariots or wide-ranging movements.

Nevertheless, mention of the chariot is interesting. In the first place, it recalls the emergence of the mobile *Streitwagenvölker* and their breaking into the old world at the end of the second millennium B.C. Their climactic appearance is the only possible explanation—which Jaspers, following Alfred Weber, cites but finally rejects—for the otherwise inexplicable simultaneity of the Axial Age in areas as far apart as China and the Eastern Mediterranean. Indeed, our text show an enduring fascination with the war and racing chariot to the point where the whole of the ritual is identified with it.[40] But—and this is the second point—the chariot itself is clearly a thing of the past. Its use and technique are no longer clearly understood by the ritualists. The ritual, which is now stationary and confined to the narrow limits of its emplacement, has symbolized the chariot away. Having lost its reality, the chariot has gained a grandiose afterlife in ritualistic imagination.

The ritual texts, then, are not concerned with the real world which surrounds them. The historical realities they refer to are those of a hallowed heroic past that the ritual meant to overcome and to replace with its own perfectly ordered world. Our texts therefore will not tell us about the historical conditions of the Axial Age. But they do tell us what, in their perspective, triggered the axial movement, namely the self-destructive violence of the warrior's sacrifice, whose emblem was the chariot. Though it lived on in the imagination of the epic, agonistic sacrifice was deprived of its value and legitimacy by the ritualists' achievement. This enables us to understand why the ritual texts faithfully preserved the fossilized but telling remnants of the heroic world they rejected, while neglecting their own actual surroundings. The conspicuous neglect of the latter therefore need not by itself prove an early date for our texts. The reason for their archaic nature is that the *śrauta* ritual was created out of the dismembered ruins of the warrior's sacrifice and therefore remained tied to its disembodied memory.

### *8*

There is an interesting parallel as well as a contrast with the axial breakthrough in ancient Iran. Working under the same or at least under comparable conditions and with essentially the same dismembered material, the outcome was an entirely different one. Both civilizations rejected the cyclical violence and destructiveness of the warrior's circuit between settlement and trekking camp. But while Vedic ritualism started from the menacing mobility of the trekking warrior and chariot fighter, which it transformed into the stasis of the single *yajamāna's* ritual, the Zarathustrian reform took its stand at the other end of the circuit, in the settled community on which it built its ideal ethical order.[41]

Vedic ritualism exalts the gods who "drove about on wheels" while their rivals, the asuras, stayed at home in their lordly halls and lost out. With Zarathustrianism, however, it is the supreme asura who holds ultimate truth against the demoniacally destructive devas. Their cyclic conflict is not eliminated but elevated to the height of a battle betwen Good and Evil. Zarathustra's ethical dualism aimed at reforming the world; Vedic ritualism, in contrast, taking its cue from the ancient heroes, turned away from the world and in the last resort aimed at its dissolution. Both, however, irreversibly broke open the old world of violence and sacrifice.

### *9*

In the sacrificial arena, man had again and again to risk all in the contest for the ultimate truth that held the world together—a truth that could only be expressed in the paradoxical language of the seer's *brahman*. With the removal of the sacrificial nexus of meaning, the paradoxical tension of the personal brahma vision collapsed into the flatly impersonal *brāhmaṇa,* or identification of disconnected elements. Connective myth gave way to divisive doctrine. The demise of the central nexus left a great rift but for the same reason invited ever new attempts at bridging the unbridgeable.

In Jaspers words: "Auch die Achsenzeit ist gescheitert. Es ging weiter"—relentlessly and indefinitely.[42]

# 8 The Conundrum of the King's Authority

## *1*

Nowhere is the problematic character of kingship clearer than in the Indian case. At first sight, though, it is taken very much for granted and other possibilities are hardly considered. The so-called republics of ancient India receive only marginal attention in the texts. The interest they have aroused seems to owe more to the temptation of looking for ancient precedents of modern ideas than to their intrinsic importance. What is more important is that, as will become clear further on, the difference between these republican oligarchies and monarchies—even though Kauṭilya contrasts the first with his ideal monarchic state—is a matter of degree rather than of principle. The relevant divide is another one than the difference between monarchy and republic.[1]

The problematic character of kingship stands out clearly when we consider the lack of a consistent theory. The reason for this lack is not that kings and kingship were so much taken for granted that any theoretical speculation would have been otiose. On the contrary, the texts expound on this subject to the point of tedium, if not obsession. But all this does not deliver a unified view of kingship. Taken together the different statements agree on one point, namely, that kings are somehow necessary for the protection of the people through the maintenance of the moral order or *dharma*. But beyond that point, we meet, even within the same text, with a disconcerting variety of views. Now it may be theoretically possible to try to harmonize these diverging statements by interpreting and reinterpreting them as the classical Indian commentators have done. However, they have come up with different solutions. Or, failing that, we may string out the statements that seem the most refractory to us, as well as the ancient commentators' efforts

Reprinted with minor revisions from *Kingship and Authority in South Asia,* edited by J. F. Richards (Madison, 1978), 1–27.

on a chronological scale, so as to make the divergent statements into points on a line of development. This has often been done, and the results have provided us with interesting surveys of the textual evidence,[2] but all this effort does not detract from the fact that the sources do contain the most diverse views. Rather than to try to make up for the apparent lack of a consistent theory, we stay nearer to the intentions of our sources if we view their fulsomeness and inconsistency as evidence of their struggle with a real but intractable problem that was too important to gloss over.

## *2*

The texts are unanimous in assigning the protection of the people and the maintenance of the order of the world or even of the whole universe to the king. He is then easily exalted to be the world order itself, dharma incarnate,[3] or at the very least, equal to ten wise men learned in the Veda.[4] So whatever the king does is the norm[5] and all dharma is subsumed in the *rājadharma*.[6] A kingless country therefore comes to ruin, and one should not settle in such a place.[7] But on the other hand, the king—not just the unrighteous king, but the king in general—is roundly abominated. That instead of being exalted as the benign protector of his people he is simply the "eater" of the people who devours everything he can lay hands on is already a cliché in the Vedic prose texts.[8] Later texts enlarge upon this point by stating, for instance, that ten slaughterhouses equal one oil press, ten oil presses one tavern, ten taverns one brothel, finally giving the ultimate prize for wickedness to the king, who is as evil as ten brothels; or the king is put on a par with a butcher who keeps a hundred thousand slaughterhouses.[9] It is then hardly surprising to find him mentioned together with other calamities like floods, fires, and thieves.[10]

It is, of course, possible to explain these diametrically opposed views as the two sides of the same coin. This does not mean, to put it in a down-to-earth way, that there will always have been more bad kings than good, let alone ideal ones, for the texts will not let us off so easily. Although they obviously know the difference and exploit it to show their ideal king to advantage, their condemning statements more often than not refer simply to kings in general. It is clearly not simply a question of good kings who further prosperity and evil ones who are destructive. For even that epitome of royal unrighteousness, the legendary King Vena, who out of greed and arrogance banned gift and sacrifice and thereby virtually nullified the dharma, seems still to have been indispensable to the commonweal. The holy men who rightly put him to death—or rather immolated him—are to their embarrassment confronted with waste and ruin, this being the unintended result of their depriving the world of its king, however unrighteous he may have been.[11] So the beneficial aspect is not completely absent from the reign of even the proverbially wicked Vena, and it is probably not fortuitous that he is honorably mentioned in the *Ṛgveda* as a liberal patron.[12]

### 3

It is tempting to explain the conflicting views as the ambivalence that naturally goes with the awe-inspiring numinosity of kingship. Thus the king is likened to a fire which, when approached carelessly, burns not only the single transgressor, as a normal fire would, but destroys his whole family together with his cattle and other properties.[13] The restrictions on the consecrated *(abhiṣikta)* king,[14] which in fact make him a sacred person—or, more precisely, a consecrated sacrificer *(dīkṣita)*—point in the same direction, as does the *Atharvaveda* when it says that the king protects the realm by *brahmacarya* and *tapas,*[15] that is, by the ascetic practices that are proper to the dīkṣita.

The apparent numinosity is further supported by the notion of the king's divinity—a topic on which the texts are wont to expatiate. Thus the king is generally said to be made up of parts of different gods.[16] Even an infant king is not to be disregarded, "for he is a great deity in human form".[17] And Bhīṣma, when asked by the puzzled Yudhiṣṭhira why it is that one man who is no different from other mortals in birth, death, and general appearance stands over all other men, answers straightforwardly that the only reason is the king's divine quality.[18] Since the gods were not only the recipients, but, according to an oft-quoted *Ṛgveda* verse, also the primordial celebrants of the sacrifice,[19] it is not surprising that we find the king as the principal celebrant at the great festivals. His dīkṣita-like quality, which we already noted, fits perfectly in this pattern. In fact, the king's activity is often equated with a life-long sacrifice, and the purāṇic royal rituals give a complete tableau of the king's functions.[20] These rituals would leave the king no time for anything else, if indeed he would ever be able to finish all the ritual cycles and cycles within cycles.

So it seems that when we start from the sacrality of kingship, the different pieces fall into a consistent pattern. The king is thus primarily a religious figure: divinity as well as chief celebrant. Even his power of punishment is not a purely secular one, for, as Robert Lingat argues, the king when inflicting punishment equally fulfills the priestly function of purifying the evildoer.[21] We may even tie in the legendary Vena, who not unlike the sacrificial king par excellence, Soma, is ritually immolated by the holy men. In this way, we could construct a complete sacral complex where the king—like Prajāpati, the Lord of the Universe—is a sacrificer, victim, and divine recipient of the sacrifice all in one.[22]

Yet all this, to which many points could still be added—like the king's responsibility for rainfall—remains essentially a construction. The religious aspect of kingship cannot be denied. All the parts seem to be available, but the texts do not try to put them together. They remain isolated and disparate pieces of evidence spread over different contexts. What is lacking is a consistent overall scheme that would give substance to a consolidated theory of sacral kingship. As it is, however, kingship remains, even theoretically, suspended between sacrality and secularity, divinity and mortal humanity, legitimate authority and arbitrary power, dharma and adharma.

### *4*

We know, of course, what the reason for this undecided state of affairs is, namely, that it is not the king but the brahmin who, according to the classical conception, holds the key to ultimate value and therefore to legitimacy and authority. The theory of sacrifice, as it was developed in the Vedic prose texts has no place for the king as such, let alone for a sacral, divine, or priestly one. He is at best a sacrificer *(yajamāna)* with the same status as any commoner sacrificer. Strictly speaking, he cannot even be that, for the brahmin should refrain from officiating for him.[23] It is significant that the Vedic *rājasūya,* though ostensibly meant for the royal investiture, is not by most dharma commentators understood to be the decisive sacrament *(saṃskāra)* that legitimates the king.[24]

The critical point is that the classical theory of sacrifice has resolutely and as a matter of principle turned its back on society. Why this is so will concern us further on. At this point, it may suffice to note that the king as such has no *locus standi* on the place of sacrifice, which is also spatially segregated from the life of the community.[25] Whatever may have been the original meaning of the proclamation formula at the rājasūya—"This is your king, O Bharatas, Soma is our, the brahmins', king"[26]—the commentators invariably take it to mean that brahmins are set apart from the king's power, and conversely, that the king is excluded from the brahmin's ritual domain. Although Indo-European comparison shows that the Latin cognate of the Indian *rājan,* the *rex,* does have religious connotations,[27] it is important to note that the word *rājan* can be applied to any man of substance without any thought of sacrality.[28]

But the final blow to a consistent theory of sacral kingship is delivered by the dharma commentators, who clearly indicate that whoever holds the de-facto power is king, irrespective of his legitimacy or, rather, lack of it. Not even the requirement that he at least be a kṣatriya is upheld.[29] And even this does not give rise to a consistently areligious theory of power pure and simple. For, whatever the claims of artha, dharma disturbingly keeps hovering over it and even Kauṭilya's notorious *Arthaśastra* does not break with the dharmaśāstra in order to formulate an independent *raison d'état.*[30] So here too the theoretical foundation of kingship remains in suspense. This does not mean that there can be no effective kings—in fact there were obviously many capable and effective ones—but it does mean that kingship as an institution has no authority and legitimacy of its own. It is dependent on the uneasy relationship between king and brahmin. Or, as the texts put it, the *brahman* can stand on its own, the *kṣatra,* however, cannot and depends on the brahman.[31]

Now it may be argued that the unique phenomenon of the brahmin, whose monopoly of the source of authority and legitimation leaves the king with mere power and effectively bars kingship from developing its full potential as the central regulating force, makes the Indian case a very special one. The problematic character of kingship would then be an exclusively Indian phenomenon. It cannot be denied that the Indian case cannot be put on a par with other cases of a division between spiritual authority and temporal power such as the problem of church and state in Western Europe or the one of *sulṭānat* and *'imāmat* in the Muslim world. This is not the place to go into the details of these other situations, nor is the present writer qualified to do so. But the essential difference would seem to be that in the Christian as well as the Islamic world, both spiritual authority and temporal power have to be realized in the single sphere of society. India, on the other hand, recognizes a second, independent human sphere, namely, the renunciatory life that turns its back on the social world. It is in the sphere of world renunciation that the brahmin and the ultimate authority he stands for belong. Society and its king have no claim on him beyond what he is willing to concede and he can—ideally, he even should—withdraw from society. In the Indian case, the two forces do not compete for priority within one single sphere. On the contrary, the spiritual one simply opts out, leaving the other to cope for itself as best it can.[32]

The Indian case therefore is indeed a special one, but this does not mean that the problem of kingship is peculiar to Indian civilization. In fact, I intend to argue that the problem is a general one and that the specifically Indian king-brahmin "model" is what Indian civilization has developed to formulate this general problem. It may therefore be appropriate first to look at the general aspect of the problem, as it is presented by the Indian material, and next inquire how the specifically Indian "model" came to be formulated.

## 5

It is a stereotyped phrase that the king is "the maker of the age" and that is depends on him whether the age is the *kṛta, tretā, dvāpara,* or *kali* age.[33] These terms, however, cannot be dissociated from the dicing game, which we also see the king play in the rājasūya, and it is hard to miss the implication that kingship is in more than one way a gamble. Now this gambling may be considered an agonistic divinatory rite at the opening of a new age or era—a gambling for the future, as it were—and so would fit perfectly in a theory of sacral kingship. But the essential point is the fact that the outcome does not depend solely on the king, for the game and its outcome are equally if not predominantly determined by the other participants, variously given as representatives of the four varṇas, household functionaries, or relatives.[34] In fact, some rājasūya texts seem to suggest that the king does not even take an active part in the game.[35] At any rate, he is not at all a free agent but part of a web of intersecting relationships that hem him in on all sides. The same impression is conveyed by those brāhmaṇa passages which make the kṣatriya dependent on the people *(viś)*. Thus the king is said to need the people's consent, to be "propped up on both sides" by the people and to be capable of showing strength only through the people.[36] That this dependence is, of course, mutual does not alter the fact that the king is tied up in a closely meshed web.

This is, of course, a far cry from the idea of the powerful king "who makes his own age." But it would be erroneous to view the shift in emphasis from the dependent king in the ritual to the unrestricted "maker of the age" as the result of historical development, for the same picture of the king's confinement in a network of actors emerges from the classical doctrine of the "circle of kings." This circle is constituted by the "conquering king" *(vijigīṣu)*, his enemy, the power adjacent to both, and the outside power; each of these four "elements" *(prakṛti)* again has an ally and an ally's ally. That makes twelve "elements" to start with. Then we have to add for each of these "king elements" five further "elements"—minister, land-cum-people *(janapada)*, fortified place, treasure, and army—so that the total comes to seventy-two.[37]

Now, although the "circle" is seen from the single point of view of the would-be conqueror, it is clear that he is just one of the seventy-two "elements." Each of the first twelve can in his turn be a vijigīṣu, none being at the top or even in the center. In fact, the whole exposition turns on the pivotal question of how to husband one's resources in such a way that one may attain the central position in the "hub" of the "circle of elements".[38] Moreover, as Hartmut Scharfe has shown, the terminology shows a conflation of two schemes, a concentric one and a dualistic rectilineal one in which the would-be conqueror faces his rival while their allies and enemies interlock at their backs.[39] In the latter scheme, there cannot even be a single central position, since the center is held by two chief contestants. In order to achieve whatever predominance is attainable, one has to move with utmost caution on the same level as all the other "elements"—not only the twelve "king elements"—each of which is a power in its own right. This, incidentally, makes short shrift of the notion of states with a modicum of centralization and entertaining "interstate relations." It also means that the difference between "monarchy" and "republic," already alluded to, cannot be a very significant one. The circle doctrine is a schematic representation of a universe made up of various interlocking forces, where the king has to stake himself in an ever-continuing gamble with his like as well as with other forces.

Now this certainly is not a specifically Indian problem. It means that power and resources are diffused throughout the whole system to such an extent that the king is hard put to find and manage the means that would give him sufficient leverage to lift himself, in a sort of Münchhausen act, above the level of the competing forces, or even to attain a central position among them. It is not even sure that if some "element" were to emerge that "element" would be the king. Indian history can provide many examples of the opposite. Yet we see that even in those cases, the successful pretender will either assume the royal title himself or will rule under the nominal authority of a pensioner king—as, indeed, the East India Company did for about a century. Here, then, lies the heart of the problem. Somehow kingship, in whatever way it may have been obtained, implies legitimacy and authority, but a consistent theory clarifying this pivotal issue is lacking.

Not only for this power is the king dependent on others but also, and more important, for his authority. Even apart from the classical king-brahmin formula, this is made clear in a number of ways. Thus the king shares equally in his subjects' spiritual merits as well as their demerits.[40] "Le salut du roi," as Robert Lingat concludes, "dépend de ses sujets comme le salut des sujets dépend du roi."[41] This is certainly a perfectly valid way of putting it, but it does mean that the king has no independent moral standing and therefore no legitimacy or authority independent from the "elements" of the realm, of which he is but one. His authority is not fixed but suspended somewhere in the middle, at the intersection of the relationships that make up the realm. In the same way, the king is bound to consult in all matters his counsellors, drawn from various groups and not necessarily his own retainers.[42] True, after ascertaining their opinion, he should reach a decision himself, but he should not push his luck too far by a show of independence, for "kings depend on their counsellors as cattle do on rain, husbands on their wives, and brahmins on the Veda".[43] In the same vein, the *Aitareya Brāhmaṇa* speaks about the "kingmakers" *(rājakartṛ)* who arrange for the acclamation, failing which the king is devoid of strength.[44] Similarly, the pseudoetymology that derives the word *rājan* from *rañjayati,* "to gladden, make happy" (namely, his people), whatever its religio-magic connotations, does not speak for the king's independent authority. All this mutuality and interdependence may seem touchingly harmonious, but the verso side is clearly that where this harmonic relationship is impaired or lacking the king can simply be killed.[45]

### *6*

In Indian terms, the crux of the authority problem is the king's standing in the matter of dharma. Notwithstanding the tall claims made in behalf of the king's being dharma incarnate, it is made perfectly clear that in matters of dharma—that is, in practically every aspect of his activity—he has no autonomy whatsoever and, instead of leading, must follow. Even in the case of customs and usages which are contrary to dharma, he has no authority to intervene.[46] That he should not intervene in customary law, even if contrary to dharma, of a conquered population may be considered simply a pragmatic policy,[47] but the same goes for his own subjects, even for those who reject the Veda, which is considered to be the *fons et origo* of all dharma.[48] What is more, it is enjoined that the king should consider all customs of the virtuous twice-born—that is, practically, the dharma—as law only if these customs are not contrary to the usages of land, family, or caste![49] The dharma is beyond the king's grasp and his relationship with it is at best an uneasy one. It is, of course, his foremost duty to protect the dharma. But then what is dharma if it can encompass even contrary customs and usages? Or, as one text puts it, "Dharma and Adharma do not go about saying: here we are; nor do gods, gandharvas, or manes say: this is dharma, that is adharma".[50] So there is nothing for it but to define dharma as that "which wise twice-born men praise".[51] Now it is not uncommon that kings have no authority to interfere with established customs and rights, whether written or not. Thus, for instance, it is significant that in a medieval Latin play it is the Antichrist who is made to say when he mounts the throne: "I will abolish the old laws and dictate new ones".[52] But it would seem that it is only in India that the king's lack of authority emerges with such clarity.

Yet there are, as we have seen, strong countervailing statements. Apart from hyperbole, it is flatly stated that no one should transgress the dharma decreed by the king.[53] We even find that in case of dispute, the royal edict *(rājaśāsana)* is given priority over dharma.[54] We can readily understand why such statements are necessary. Just because of its undefined nature and its lack of institutional moorings, the dharma is in dire need of a point of support that can provide the modicum of power necessary for its maintenance. An abstract category of wise or holy men *(śiṣṭa, sādhu, āpta)* obviously lacks the power and organization for the effective maintenance of dharma. It is only the king who can and therefore should provide the power and organization required, even if it can only be a bare minimum. But this makes the dilemma of kingship no less insoluble. The king must all the time perform a precarious balancing act between forcefully proclaiming his own writ to be dharma and, on the other hand, following unassumingly what his subjects tell him to be dharma.

It is no matter for surprise, then, that the legendary accounts of the origin of kingship are wrought with equivocation and near-failure. Thus Bhīṣma, while answering Yudhiṣṭhira's perplexed question on the nature of kingship, relates that notwithstanding the intervention of Viṣṇu, who created the first king as his "mental son," kingship in fact all but failed.[55] Indeed, the first three kings wanted no part of it and opted out by renouncing the world. Only with the fourth, does kingship get a fair chance, but then passion and greed also start their corrupting work, culminating in the notorious King Vena. It is only with the seventh in line, Pṛthu, produced by the holy men out of the immolated body of his father, that the ideal king enters on the scene. There, as far as our text is concerned, the line ends, for going beyond this point could only spoil the ideal.[56] Leaving aside for the moment the ideal case of Pṛthu, Bhīṣma's account clearly expresses the king's dilemma. Either he safeguards his righteousness by retiring from the world, as the first three kings did, or he submits himself to the yoke of worldly unrighteousness and falls prey to greed and passion, as happened to the next three kings. The first alternative obviously makes nonsense of kingship, the second obliterates the claim to authority. When we finally reach the ideal King Pṛthu, there still is a fatal flaw. He can only give protection, justice, and plenty by confessing his utterly feeble grasp of dharma and having himself led in all matters by the brahmins. Since he must promise the brahmins exemption from all punishment, the arbitrariness of the king is replaced by the absolutism of the brahmin. This flaw is already present in Pṛthu's origin. Although he was properly produced from the immolated body of his father, this immolation was no less a breach in the functioning of dharma. For by this act, as already mentioned, the brahmin seers reduced the world to the adharmic chaos of kinglessness—a point that the legend explicity stresses. So even the Pṛthu story's idealization of the king-brahmin formula does not solve the problem.

The same problem is expressed in a different way in the so-called contract theory of kingship also taught by Bhīṣma.[57] At the entreaty of the people, who feel fatally threatened by anarchy, the supreme deity appoints the patriarch Manu to be king. But here again the appointee, fearing the cruelty of the task and the sins of man, fights clear of the royal function. Only after a covenant has been made with the people, which guarantees the king a share in the people's material resources as well as an even bigger share in the merit of their righteous acts, does Manu agree to be their king. After what has been said about the interdependence of king and people, the idea of a covenant or contract is not very surprising. The striking point here is, however, the stipulation that Manu does not share in the demerit of his subjects' evil deeds. This stipulation—contrary to the idea referred to above of the king's share in and responsibility for both merit and demerit—does set the king free from the oppressive material and moral bonds with the people, but it is hardly fair. The trouble is that once the king is no longer affected by the world's evil ways, he is freed from responsibility for them. It is then hard to see why he should bother to correct the wrongs of the world. He virtually withdraws from the world, like the first three kings in the previous account, the difference being that the latter at least took the full consequence of their withdrawal and renounced all claims to their subjects' material and moral resources. So Manu's covenant does not offer a solution either; rather, it offers another formulation of the same problems.

So much is clear, the king cannot derive his authority from the community, for within the community he is himself subject to the community's dharma as well as its adharma, and, as we saw, the two are difficult to define. So authority has to be looked for outside the community. The king has to belong to the community, but at the same time he must stand outside so as to guarantee his authority.

## *7*

That the dilemma of kingship does not admit of a definitive solution is after all not very surprising, nor does this seem to be an exclusively Indian phenomenon. The pertinent question, however, is, In what way did Indian, or more precisely, "Sanskritic" thought—as distinct from the sometimes successful but always dubious compromise of historical reality—deal with the intractable aporia? For an answer to this question, it may be appropriate to look at the Vedic ritual texts, especially those that deal with the royal rites. They are useful not only because of their unique extensiveness and authoritativeness—whatever their practical value—but also because they demonstrate that the ritual, however mindlessly performed, is based on penetrating thought. Ritual cannot escape the fundamental problem but must somehow express it in well-defined acts. Ritual, in other words, should make the insoluble at least acceptable without glossing it over. Putting it plainly, the ritual cannot simply put the king on his throne and leave the matter there. The rājasūya, for instance, is far from being so restricted; it is in fact an all but endless series of cycles stretching over a number of years. When it ends, the end seems to be rather arbitrary, and indeed the king has then again to start upon yet another ritual, the sauṭrāmaṇī, not to mention others. This unremitting series of beginnings and re-beginnings indicates that the ritual is not simply a question of unction, or rather aspersion, and enthronization. There are, to be sure, abbreviated forms such as the consecratory aspersion *(abhiṣeka)* of the *Aitareya Brāhmaṇa,* but the same text also knows the *punarabhiṣeka,* or repeated consecration, which curiously is mentioned even before the abhiṣeka proper.[58] Here we can already notice that the royal consecration is not performed once and for all but is in fact an unending cycle. As we shall see, this cycle enables the ritual to give full weight to the dilemma of kingship and to handle it effectively.

As we have seen, the dilemma is that the king has to be both part of the community and external to it. Now Indian civilization offers a basic paradigm, used in many contexts, for such an opposition, namely, the opposition between the settled agricultural community *(grāma)* and the alien outside sphere of the jungle *(araṇya)*. This opposition obviously has a directly practical and historical importance.[59] It does not only imply that the settled community should all the time be on its guard against the dangers that threaten it from the alien jungle world, but also that the two spheres complement each other in a number of ways. The settled community needs the jungle for grazing ground; as a source of new land, man power, and forest products; as a link between settled areas; and finally as a refuge. The jungle and its "tribal" inhabitants, on the other hand, look to the settled areas as a source of agricultural produce, cattle, and other riches as well as for employment, either in a military capacity or as agricultural labor. In other words, grāma and araṇya are complementary. Their constant latent or open conflict does not militate against their complementarity, but on the contrary, bears out its importance.

The dilemma of kingship can then be expressed in terms of this basic paradigm: the king must belong to the grāma, but his authority must be based in the alien sphere of araṇya. Thus, for instance, the god Dharma—the divine representative of ultimate authority—reveals himself, after imposing an ordeal, to his son Yudhiṣṭhira in the jungle.[60] Generally speaking, there is abundant evidence of the king's special relationship with the jungle—a relationship that is clearly related to transcendent authority.[61] The necessary complementarity of the two spheres can then be ritually expressed as alternating phases in a cycle connecting the two opposites. Since the opposition as well as the complementarity is there all the time and cannot be overcome, the cycle has to go on forever. In its simplest form, the grāma-araṇya cycle is expressed in the dictum: "In the *grāma* one undertakes the consecration, in the *araṇya* one sacrifices".[62] We must now try to determine how this cycle is worked out in the case of the royal rites.

## *8*

A first look at the royal ritual of rājasūya and abhiṣeka gives the impression of a rather garbled scenario. In the first place, it is overgrown with a confusing cumulation of all sorts of rites which make it difficult to discern the central moments. To some extent, it is possible to overcome this difficulty by paying attention to the "boxing device" of the ritual, which tends to embed an important episode in the middle of another rite or cumulation of rites, such as offerings of ghee, cake, animal, and soma. This is prominently the case of the unction, which stands out as a pivotal point in the ritual. But then there appear to be at least three possible "boxes," as is shown by the three moments in the ritual where the proclamation (or acclamation), which goes with the unction, occurs.[63] Another important episode is the enthronization. It would seem logical that unction and enthronization should be closely connected with each other.[64] This is indeed the case in the *Aitareya Brāhmaṇa,* where the king receives the unction while seated on the throne. However, in the rājasūya, the unction is not only separated from the enthronization by a considerable interval but also precedes it.

This state of affairs does not look very promising, and some have even concluded that it is impossible to obtain a clear picture of the proceedings.[65] Indeed, when we start from a preconceived idea of what kings and kingship should be like and assume that the royal ritual should be a single once-and-for-all accession to the throne, we can only conclude that the brahmanic ritual has garbled the matter beyond recognition. If, however, we accept that kingship is an open problem and that the ritual tries to handle the problem by means of a cyclical succession of opposite phases, the garbled pieces fall into an intelligible pattern.

## *9*

The ritual cycle, as we saw, should connect community and outside world as two phases. When we now look again at the rājasūya, we notice that not only unction and enthronization are separated but, more importantly, that the interval is taken up by an interesting rite, the chariot drive. This rite is clearly marked as a symbolic war expedition by the fact that the king has to shoot arrows in the direction of a kṣatriya posted at the far end of the chariot course. According to one version, this seemingly harmless event even appears as a ritualized cattle raid.[66] In other words, after the unction the king should go abroad on a raiding expedition. Then, after his triumphant return, he mounts the throne and the cycle is closed. That the unction is followed by an expedition into the outside world does not seem to be accidental. It tallies perfectly with the overall scheme of the Soma ritual where the sacrificer undergoes the dīkṣā in the grāma, as the dictum quoted above has it, and then departs. In fact, the royal unction is nothing but a prestigious, complicated version of the dīkṣa—or, rather, the other way round. The dīkṣa is the generalized and simplified, not to say "democratized," form of the abhiṣeka, putting on a par the royal and the commoner sacrificer.[67] Also the dīkṣita's collecting of charitable gifts for the purpose of sacrifice *(saniyācana),* although reduced to the innocuous format of religious begging, still bears a distinct relationship to the chariot raid. If we consider that, according to Manu, the necessities for the sacrifice may be taken by force, if not willingly given, the saniyācana reveals its not so innocuous nature.[68]

The interpretation of the sequence unction, war or raiding expedition, enthronization as a cycle connecting grāma and araṇya receives further corroboration from the fact that it is again encompassed in a greater cycle of the rājasūya along the same lines. This greater cycle is marked by the unction and haircutting Soma festivals. Unction and haircutting are here what dīkṣā and final bath *(avabhṛtha)* are in the normalized Soma sacrifice. During the intervening period, the anointed is, like the dīkṣitā, subjected to a number of restrictions, such as the interdiction of shaving and haircutting, of treading upon the earth without wearing shoes, of cleaning his teeth, and, significantly, of the duty to accept battle when challenged. For our purpose, the interesting point is that the interval between the unction and haircutting festivals is filled out with a symbolic expedition abroad. First there is the series of ten offerings for which the fires are each time removed further to the north or east, the so-called *saṃsṛp* offerings. In this way, different stages on the road of the expedition are marked. Then follows a sacrifice featuring the drinking of soma by a hundred brahmins *(daśapeya)*—the idea probably being the solemnizing of a bond or covenant.[69] The next set of offerings—significantly called offerings of the yokings or harnessings *(prayujāṃ havīṃṣi)*—explicitly symbolize another expedition, for these offerings are explained by the account of how the Kurus and Pañcālas of old went every year in the cool season on a raiding expedition toward the east and returned at the end of the hot season.[70] The cycle is then finally closed by the haircutting solemnity.

In this connection, two further points are worth mentioning. First, the prayujāṃ havīṃṣi as evidenced by the explanatory account are not only a setting out but equally a coming back again. Accordingly, the time for the haircutting is set on the full-moon day of the month Jyaiṣṭha or Aṣāḍha, that is, at the end of the hot season. The second point is that, although this is not specified in the context of the rājasūya, in another consecratory Soma sacrifice, the *rājābhiṣeka,* where we find the same haircutting rite with the same set of special mantras again, the rite is connected with an enthronization, the king being seated on a throne during the ceremony.[71] So the greater cycle parallels exactly its shorter counterpart, unction–chariot drive–enthronization. The same pattern is shown in Baudhāyana's version of the *vājapeya,* where a chariot race is the central feature, preceded by an unction and followed by the "ascent to heaven" (i.e., climbing the sacrificial post) and the enthronization.[72]

## *10*

But the pattern does not only involve cycles encompassed by other cycles such as those we have just observed. It also repeats itself in an unending sequence, and this means that the enthronization should again be followed by another abhiṣeka, another departure, and so forth. This indeed appears to have been the case. Thus Baudhāyana's version of the vājapeya offers, as we saw, the sequence unction, chariot race, enthronization, but Āpastamba's version starts with the race, which, as expected, is followed by the enthronization and finally the unction, which is administered on the throne.[73] Baudhāyana and Āpastamba have, one might say, cut the cyclical concatenation in different places, but it is still the same cycle. This is not all. Although the vājapeya—like all śrauta sacrifices—is given as a single limited stretch of rites bounded by the standard beginning and end of the normal Soma sacrifice, the texts cannot completely disregard its cyclical follow-up. Therefore the vājapeya must again be followed by another consecratory Soma sacrifice, the *bṛhaspatisava*.[74] Now it is not made clear what exactly the ritual of the bṛhaspatisava is, but it is at least remarkable that the vājapeya itself is called a bṛhaspatisava.[75] No less interesting is what appears to be the occupation of the sacrificer during the interval between vājapeya and bṛhaspatisava: he leads the life of a warrior, for, as one text puts it, having performed the bṛhaspatisava, he should abandon the "warrior's way of life".[76] This is corroborated by another text, which enjoins that the vājapeya sacrificer should lead a warrior's life, and the same text says about the purpose of the bṛhaspatisava: "Whom they put at their head should henceforth lead a friendly life amongst them," that is, give up his warrior habits.[77] We have come to expect that the warrior phase of going abroad is followed by an enthronization after the triumphant return. Indeed, though the ritual specifics of the bṛhaspatisava that follows the vājapeya and the warrior phase are not clarified, there is at least one text that gives an elaborate description in which throne and enthronization figure prominently.[78]

In connection with the bṛhaspatisava sequel to the vājapeya, a further particular may be mentioned. This sequel is also called *pratyavarohaṇīya*, "alighting," the point being that the vājapeya sacrificer should not get down, alight, in honor of anybody until he has performed the "alighting" ritual. The injunction not to get down obviously belongs to his proud warrior status. He must accept battle—and, if necessary, die—as is also demanded of him during the interval between the unction and haircutting festivities in the rājasūya, but on no account should he get down and thereby show himself to be the lesser man. The curious point is, however, that the punctilio implied here is not so much the king's affair as that of the warrior. Only when the vājapeya sacrificer has freed himself from the rigid warrior etiquette through the "alighting" ceremony, can he settle down again, mount the throne, and "henceforth lead a friendly disposed life." The "alighting," then, seems to refer primarily to alighting from the chariot, signifying the return to the settled community from the warrior's life in the outside world. Or, as one text puts it, "He who performs the vājapeya goes away from this world: they run a race, he climbs the sacrificial pole. If he would not perform the 'alighting,' he would ascend to yonder world, but he would waste himself. . . . By performing the 'alighting' he gains a firm base in this world, does not come to harm and obtains his full span of life. By means of these offerings he comes back from that world which he has conquered through the vājapeya."[79]

In the meantime, it will have become clear that the difference between the rājasūya of the *Yajurveda* and the abhiṣeka in the *Aitareya Brāhmaṇa* is not a result of confusion but of the way in which the cycle was cut. The *Aitareya Brāhmaṇa* begins with the enthronization, which is followed by the unction. But there the matter does not end, for, as we have seen, after the unction the king goes abroad on a war or raiding expedition. This is also clearly indicated in the *Aitareya Brāhmaṇa*. After the punarabhiṣeka, the king not only makes three steps to the north—which is a symbol of departure and conquest—but the text follows this up with instructions and explanations regarding battle rites.[80] Still clearer is the case of the *aindramahābhiṣeka* in the same text, where a list is given of kings who performed this ceremony, went out on conquest, and on their return performed another consecratory sacrifice, namely, the horse sacrifice.[81]

## 11

It would be tedious to continue this demonstration, which could in fact be extended throughout the śrauta ritual. But one more point is interesting for our purpose. This point concerns the king's *daṇḍa,* or staff. In the classical dharma texts, the daṇḍa is the primordial and exclusive symbol of the king's capacity to punish. Daṇḍa has even come to mean punishment itself and as such is identified with dharma. Now we know the daṇḍa, though not in the later sense, from the Vedic ritual as the typical attribute of the consecrated sacrificer, which is handed to him after the dīkṣa bath, that is, at the time when he is supposed to set out on his expedition.[82] In this context, it represents Voice, who took refuge in the trees, that is, in the jungle. But without Voice, it is said, no prowess *(vīrya)* can be shown.

It would seem, then, that the dīkṣita's daṇḍa represents the voice of superior authority, which has to be found outside, in the forest—the daṇḍa being significantly addressed as "lord of the forest" *(vanaspati)*. On a more mundane level, it is a weapon as well—to enforce authority—and is equated with the *vajra*.[83] Not unlike the scepter, it seems originally to have been the typical equipment of one who goes abroad.[84] Thus the daṇḍa also belongs to the paraphernalia of the wandering and fighting *vrātya*.[85] This also may explain why in the cyclical pattern of the ritual the daṇḍa is not acquired once and for all, but has to be transmitted after the wandering phase, at the beginning of the sacrifice proper, to the brahmin who acts as the *maitrāvaruṇa* officiant, called in this connection leader of the sacrificial priests.[86] Although the daṇḍa is not specifically mentioned in the context of the royal unction, where its place seems to be taken by a bow and arrows, it is interesting to see it turn up unexpectedly again at the end of the rājasūya. There the daṇḍa, together with the shoes (which prevented the consecrated king from coming into direct contact with the earth) and a dry skin bag, is sent to the rival kings *(pratirājānaḥ).*[87] Presumably, this may originally have meant that it was now their turn to take up the burden of the wandering warrior's life. The point I want to stress, however, is that the daṇḍa, the archetypal symbol of kingship and maintenance of the dharma, is when we first meet it the typical attribute of the warrior's life abroad. That is, authority and its symbol are situated outside the community. They can only be put into contact with the community by means of the alternating cycle.

## *12*

At first sight, the paradigm of cyclical alternation between the complementary phases of grāma and araṇya may appear as an elegant solution to the conundrum of the king's authority. On further consideration, however, it is clearly far from satisfactory, for it makes authority the sport of fortune in the unending circulatory game. Instead of wielding the daṇḍa over the community, the king has on his return to pass it on to another who then has to set out, if the king does not start again on another wandering phase himself. In fact, it makes effective kingship illusory. But that is not all, for we cannot overlook the risk and mortal danger involved in the aggressive conventions of the warrior phase.

The jeopardy to which kingship is subject is curiously but no less clearly expressed by the recurring notion of the disintegrating effect that the unction is supposed to have on the anointed. The rājasūya is also known as *varuṇasava,* or consecration of Varuṇa.[88] The rājasūya sacrificer enacts the role of this sovereign god. But in the same context, it is said that the unction takes away the god's as well as his human epigone's strength, causing them, like humpty-dumpty, to fall apart. The king's unction is at the same time his undoing, and he must be put together again by the *samsṛp* offerings. In other words, he must, as we saw, go out into the wilds to recuperate the strength that has left him.[89]

Quite apart from the mythological motif of Varuna's disintegration, the ambivalence and danger of the royal ritual and specifically of the rājasūya is in a different but no less telling way documented in the epics. Now the epics—both the *Mahābhārata* and the *Rāmāyaṇa*—show exactly the same paradigm of cyclical alternation between grāma and araṇya. Both the Pāndavas and Rāma are forced to leave throne and realm and go out on a life of adventure in the wilds and return only after they have successfully come out of a long series of dangerous battles and ordeals. In both cases, the departure is connected with the abhiṣeka. Rāma is cheated out of his already arranged unction. In the *Mahābhārata,* Yudhiṣṭhira, the leader of the Pāṇḍava brothers, has the rājasūya performed but is then also cheated out of his realm in a game of dice forced upon him by his opponent, Duryodhana. Though the dicing game follows Yudhiṣṭhira's rājasūya, it does so without interval, and comparison with the ritual texts makes clear that it actually belongs to the rājasūya. It is not surprising, then, that the rājasūya is considered in the epics to be particularly dangerous. When the deceased father of the Pāṇḍavas has his wish that Yudhiṣṭhira perform the rājasūya transmitted by the sage Nārada, the latter takes the opportunity to point out the dangers of this royal ritual, which will lead to the destruction of the kṣatriyas in the great Mahābhārata war—an idea that is later repeated by the sage Vyāsa, as well as on other occasions.[90] So the rājasūya is directly linked to the tragic war, or rather, we might say that the war is part and parcel of the rājasūya cycle. We saw already that the *Aitareya Brāhmaṇa* has the abhiṣeka followed by war and conquest, after which another consecratory sacrifice, the horse sacrifice, is performed. Similarly, the Pāṇḍavas as well as Rāma perform on their triumphant return the aśvamedha, which in the case of the *Mahābhārata* is given as an expiation for the catastrophal bloodshed.[91]

## *13*

So the cyclical paradigm, far from offering a solution, is wrought with constant risk and the threat of violent breakdown. It called, in other words, for a thorough reform on the basis of a new orientation. That such a reform did indeed take place is indicated by the restructuring of the ritual. Although the original pattern of endless cyclical alternation can with relative ease be reconstructed from the texts,[92] this is no longer the meaning of the ritual. On the contrary, it is cut up in single rectilineal stretches of rites with clear-cut beginnings and ends. As we saw, this was the reason for the seemingly confused order of the relevant consecratory rites, the original cycles having been cut at different points. The restructuring, which cut up and destroyed the cyclical concatenation was, of course, not a frivolous undertaking. It was pointedly and systematically done. The purpose was to break out of the endless cycle by establishing a new conception of the transcendent, and thereby of authority.[93]

As long as settled agricultural communities were limited in number and restricted in their resources, while wide expanses were left open, the alternation of settled life with nomadic raiding and transhuming expeditions to supplement meager resources may have been a reasonably effective proposition. However, with the growth and spread of settled agriculture, a different type of organization and a new conception of authority would have been needed. At any rate, the ritual reform gave a new answer to the problem of authority. The cyclical pattern of alternation between grāma and araṇya did manage to keep up the contact between this and the other world, between settled community and authority transcending it, but at a price of violence and insecurity. Authority and the settled life dependent on it remained all the time contingent on the uncertain outcome of the cycle of violence. We can readily understand the criticism which even the *Mahābhārata,* though still clearly showing the original cyclical pattern and even recommending death while facing the enemy as the "sacrifice of battle",[94] has Bhīṣma, himself a warrior-sage, level against war. Even victory in battle, Bhīṣma convincingly argues, is simply an evil.[95] The same idea seems to underlie the ritual reform, which as we have it in the texts, rules out violence and battle, reducing the last remnants of agonistic rites such as the chariot drive to innocuous, strictly ritualized affairs. In order to achieve this, it broke the cycle of violence. And by breaking the cycle, it opened the way to free authority and make it unassailably transcendent.

However, the price for establishing transcendent authority was again a heavy one. Authority was still located outside the community, in araṇya, but by the breaking of the cycle that connected grāma and araṇya, it was irretrievably cut off from the social world. Absolute, transcendent authority therefore could not benefit society's premier agent, the king. It became instead vested in the Veda, which was fixed and codified as the eternal, not man-made, and therefore indisputable knowledge of the ritual. But the Vedic śrauta ritual has no relation to society anymore. Its performance is situated outside society, its reward is in itself and its result the metaphysical *apūrva* ("what was not there before") of the *mīmāṃsā* theorists without any social relevance. The price for the Veda's transcendent authority was that society and king were barred from its operation.

## *14*

How, then, could the newly won concept of authority be put to work in society? Here the classical king-brahmin formula comes into its own. A short digression may elucidate the meaning and origin of this formula. Originally, in the cyclical scheme, king and brahmin do not seem to have belonged to separate, mutually exclusive groups. On the contrary, at the unction festival of the rājasūya, the king—like any dīkṣita—is proclaimed to be a brahmin. That is, when he is about to go out into the wilds, he exchanges his royal quality for that of a brahmin. In other words, kingship and brahminhood are qualities that are exchanged in accordance with the cyclical paradigm.[96] In this way, we can also understand that, conversely, a brahmin—namely, the *adhvaryu* priest—takes over the royal function from the king at the beginning of the *aśvamedha,* when the expedition with the sacrificial horse is to begin.[97]

It may at first sight cause some surprise that the brahmin should be associated with the violent raiding and transhuming phase. Indeed, from the classical point of view this is forbidden, except in case of dire need. Nevertheless, the disconcerting figure of the *ātatāyin,* or aggressive brahmin ("with bow drawn"), still turns up regularly in the classical dharma texts when they deal with the question of whether such a brahmin may be slain in contravention of the brahmin's general immunity. This brahmin is not thought to be utterly depraved and forgetful of his duties, for it is considered possible that he is at the same time an austere and learned Veda scholar.[98] It seems clear that we have here a remnant of the original situation where we meet the warrior-brahmin. This warrior-brahmin we know as the *vrātya,* later to be deprecated but in the *Atharvaveda* a highly respected figure.[99]

The wilderness was not only the extrasocial sphere of the warrior and his violent way of life. It was equally the sphere of esoteric knowledge, which is the substance of ultimate authority. To this knowledge the term *brahman* refers. The two—violent contest and esoteric knowledge—are intimately connected. The brahman seems, in fact, to have been originally the winning enigmatic "truth formulation" in a verbal contest, the *brahmodya.*[100] Though seemingly a peaceful pastime, the violence involved in it should not be underrated, for, as the oldest Upaniṣads tell us, the unsuccessful contestant might have to pay for his imprudence with his life. After all, what was at stake was no less than the mastery of the cosmic enigma. To qualify for such contests, one had to go out into the wilderness and commend oneself as a pupil to a teacher in order to obtain the esoteric knowledge from him. Thus we are told of one Hrtsvāśaya Āllakeya, known equally as a king, who went out as a dīkṣita and while wandering abroad found a teacher who was willing to impart to him the "knowledge of the year." This knowledge, it is said, made it possible for Hṛtsvāśaya to reach "the end of the year" safely or, in other words, to pass unharmed through the full cycle—no small prize indeed, when we consider the danger involved.[101] This procedure—going abroad, commending oneself as a pupil, and obtaining the esoteric knowledge—is explicitly given as a general one for a *rājanyabandhu,* that is, a nobelman.

One more detail of this procedure is noteworthy: when commending himself, the would-be pupil should offer his teacher a *sāmūlājina* (possibly a sort of carpet), a jewel, and a golden ornament. These items are elsewhere called the king's ornaments *(rājñaḥ pariṣkāra).*[102] The meaning seems to be clear: in accordance with the cyclically alternating pattern, king and teacher exchange their qualities, the king becoming a *brahmacārin,* the teacher receiving the royal ornaments.

## 15

It was, however, exactly this cyclical exchange of qualities that was intentionally broken up by the ritual reformers. King and brahmin were definitely separated and made into two mutually exclusive categories. But this meant that the king's access to esoteric knowledge and the authority based on it was irrevocably cut off. Ultimate authority was not the exclusive domain of the brahmin, who held the monopoly of the Veda. The king—like any mortal—can force his way to the new transcendence by renouncing the world, like the first three kings in Bhīsma's account of the origin of kingship; but in that case, there is no longer a way back to a triumphant return, for he has then irrevocably given up status and realm. The king, therefore, desparately needs the brahmin to sanction his power by linking it to the brahmin's authority. The greater the king's power, the more he needs the brahmin. This, then, is the classical Indian formulation of the problem of authority.

However, the achievement of transcendent authority, epochal as it was, was in a way a Pyrrhic victory, for in order to safeguard the transcendence of authority, the brahmin, though equally in need of the king's favors for his subsistence, was not allowed to serve the king and lend him his own authority, but had to keep himself free from worldly entanglements and especially from being entangled in the king's affairs. Royal power and brahmanic authority were irredeemably divorced. This explains why, as we have seen, there is no consistent theory of kingship: there cannot be one. The conflicting necessities of the cooperation between the king and brahmin on the one hand and of their rigorous separation on the other demonstrate the irreducible character of the problem. Though this problem is not the sole property of India, it may be reckoned to be one of the achievements of Indian thought to have formulated in such exemplary fashion the ultimately insoluble conundrum of authority.

# 9 Kauṭilya and the Ancient Indian State

## 1

It is only natural that national claims and aspirations should look for justification to history. The finality and immutability of the past offers the fixed points of reference for justifying or rejecting the conditions and aspirations of the present. The rediscovery of Kauṭilya's *Arthaśāstra* therefore could hardly avoid making a considerable impression. Here at last the Indian intellectual found full and incontrovertible proof of the superior maturity of Indian political thought. No more grand, misty "spirituality," but hard-headed pragmatism. Of course, this momentous text did not offer a ready-made model for the modern state as envisaged by nationalists. But that hardly is the point. Nationalist thinking remained no less wedded to Western political theory. But this alien matter had somehow to be anchored in Indian civilization; it had to be translated and justified in terms congenial to Indian history. It is here, I think, that Kauṭilya's *Arthaśāstra* made its most effective contribution. It offered a point de repère that enabled the political theorist to relate Western concepts and theories to elements of Indian tradition. In other words, what presented itself as alien theory could be shown to be after all not so overwhelmingly alien, and national identity could be vindicated by referring to the hallowed past.

Though these concerns are perfectly valid and even laudable, they have a serious drawback. The past may be immutable, but not so the view we have of the past. The search for legitimation forces the past to answer the needs of the present and prevents the facts from speaking for themselves. Clearly our understanding of Kauṭilya's text was to suffer from the effort to translate the needs of the present in terms of the past. One may deplore that a lot was lost in translation, but it is only fair to observe that at least equal and cer-

This essay first appeared in slightly different form in *Wiener Zeitschrift für die Kunde Süd- und Ostasiens* 15 (1971): 5–22. Reprinted by permission.

tainly more harmful confusion resulted from similar concerns with, for instance, the ancient Germanic or the medieval state.

No plea for the self-evident need for scholarly objectivity can gainsay the fact that our view of the past does fulfill this necessary function of self-understanding and justification. But at the same time, there should be room for attention to the past irrespective of its possible uses or misuses in the present. This means the patient and sometimes fruitless task of listening to facts and documents for their own sake, without burdening them with our contemporary concerns. Not infrequently, they then appear of their own accord to be not all that remote from our problems.

It is on this side that the case of the *Arthaśāstra* is still largely open. Though the philological study of the text has made significant progress,[1] we are, I feel, still very much in the dark about the purpose, the raison d'être of the work, or more succinctly: What is the problem that it tries to answer?

## 2

It seems hardly likely that Kauṭilya's purpose was to fill some pressing need for a practical manual of statecraft and administration. If such a need was felt, the text certainly does not answer it. Its teaching on administration is either too detailed or too vague to be of much practical use, the tricks prescribed for the secret agents are actually rather elementary, and generally there is too much of the obvious to make its study worthwhile for the practitioner. Thus the second book deals at considerable length with a long list of administrative departments but significantly leaves out the important point of how these departments tie in with each other and with the whole of the administrative machinery. Specifically, the text leaves its student in the dark about who is responsible to whom. Delegation, chains of command, and reporting are conspicuous by their absence. It is even possible to be in doubt as to whether the important official called *samāhartṛ* is a provincial "collector" or the chief administrative officer of the state as a whole in the manner of a dīwān.[2]

Moreover, the notion of the *Arthaśāstra's* eminent practicability has already been effectively ridiculed by Daṇḍin's picture of a king who has mastered the science of the text and while listening in accordance with its prescripts to daily statements of payments and receipts is robbed of twice the amount by his clever bureaucrats.[3] Even Kauṭilya has to admit that in spite of the financial controls he teaches, the officials' peculation can be as little ascertained as the amount of water drunk by fishes.[4] And his most pratical advice in the matter would seem to be when he winds up the discussion on auditing by stating that the king should overlook minor offences and be content with even a small revenue.[5]

All this, however, does not mean that the text can be written off as a pedantic exercise in irrelevance. It purports to be—and has been valued as—a serious treatise on "acquiring and managing the earth".[6] It is based on methodical inquiry, that is on *ānvīkṣikī,* which according to Kauṭilya's definition investigates by means of methodical reasoning *(hetubhir ānvīkṣamāṇā)* Vedic lore, so as to decide what is right or wrong; economics as to gain and loss; and politics as to appropriate and inappropriate courses of action.[7] To underline this scientific intent, the text claims that its composition is ruled by the thirty-two devices of exposition and argumentation *(tantrayukti),* which are enumerated, defined, and exemplified from the text in the last part of the book. This emphasis on scientific method and on the tantrayuktis gives us, I think, a clue as to the meaning and purpose of the *Arthaśāstra*.

Now science and scientific method in the classical Indian context should not, of course, be taken in our usual empiricist sense emphasizing precise observation and experiment. They center on debate that should lead to the right decision. Similarly, the *Arthaśāstra* wants to be primarily, not a straightforward manual of government and administration, but a guide for methodical argumentation and the proper handling of discussion on questions of statecraft. Viewed in this way, the seemingly pedantic enumerations and definitions fall into their proper places as aids toward articulate debate. Equally, the many discussions on the reasoned opinions of other teachers seem to be models of argumentation and discussion rather than refutations of previous views.[8]

It is here, I think, that we have to look for the practical value of the *Arthaśāstra*. If we think of the importance of *mantra,* the consilium of king and councillors, it is easy to see that the art of argumentation and discussion is not a purely academic concern but a matter of extremely practical importance. The interesting point is that whereas administration usually was in the hands of specialized castes or, rather, families of brahmins, kāyasths, and the like who naturally tended to guard their expertise in arguing and deciding administrative business so as to be indispensable to their masters, the matter is here thrown wide open, and the master is invited to acquire the special skills of argumentation and debate that are the brahmin's, not the kṣatriya's, birthright and raison d'être.

## 3

It has been asserted that the *Arthaśāstra* is first and foremost concerned with matters of practical administration and that it has little to say on theoretical issues such as the origin and nature of the state.[9] The practical aspects are certainly prominent, but primarily in the sense that practical politics depends on objective discussion. The *Arthaśāstra's* concern is with the terminology, arguments, and method that should articulate debate and help in reaching appropriate decisions. This should warn us against relying too confidently on it for our knowledge of the realities of ancient Indian political life. Perhaps its greatest importance for us lies in the field of theory, for the *Arthaśāstra* seems to be based on and permeated with a particular conception of state and kingship.

Now, if we are looking for a sacral theory of kingship, its origin and nature, we are bound to be disappointed. Kauṭilya does know such theories, but he treats them with characteristic disdain. Thus some secret agents should refer to such theories while their colleagues maintain that the king is simply an oppressor devoid of virtue; the reactions of the public to these altercations will then provide something of an opinion poll.[10] These apparently popular theories are not refuted, they are simply left to subsist on their own, popular level, where they may even have some usefulness. But as a source of legitimation, they are completely indifferent to Kauṭilya. In fact it would seem that Kauṭilya would prefer his king to break away from the sacrality or divinity of kingship as a basis of the state.

Now, as Gonda puts it, "In India the divinity of kings, however small their domain, has always been accepted by the masses,"[11] and Kauṭilya recognizes this. But we should be clear as to what sacral kingship means in the Indian context. The sacral or divine king does not derive his authority from a transcendent principle, but from the community itself. As the chief organizer and celebrant of communal festivals, he symbolizes its essential unity. He is, as it were, the nodal point where the relationships of cooperation and rivalry that make up the community and that are ritually expressed in communal festivals come together. But by the same token, he remains enclosed in the web of personal relationships that constitute the community. This position is felicitously expressed in a brāhmaṇa text when it calls the king the "embryo" *(garbha)* of the *viś,* the common people.[12] In all his activities, he remains dependent on the community. He does not transcend it.[13]

It is this situation, where the king is no more than a primus inter pares, that the *Arthśāstra* wants to remedy. The ideal Kauṭilyan king has an authority and a legitimation not derived from the community but all his own, for here the king's basic qualification is not his sacrality or divinity, but the *indriyajaya,* the victory over the senses,[14] which sets him free from worldly interests. In this way, he becomes the worthy counterpart of the ideal brahmin, who is equally detached from worldly concerns.

It is interesting that the attainment of indriyajaya is said to be based on training in the sciences, first among them *ānvīkṣikī,* methodical inquiry. This means that the unpredictable pulls and pushes of personal relationships that hem in the king and his power of decision should be replaced, not by arbitrary despotism, but by objective methods of reasoning and decision making. What is at stake is no less than the founding of a state transcending the limitations of the tribal clan monarchy or oligarchy.

It would seem that this is the central issue of the *Arthaśāstra*. At the same time, however, this issue presents an insoluble dilemma. The king has to win his independence of action at the price of renouncing worldly interests, for it is the renunciatory value of indriyajaya that enables him truly to transcend the community. But what can then motivate the king, whose hard-won conquest of the senses has placed him above worldly interests, to acquire and increase his worldly power, in brief to act as a *vijigīṣu,* a conquerer?

## 4

Notwithstanding the obvious dilemma presented by Kauṭilya's conception of the king—detached from worldly interests and yet striving for power—it might still have been possible to develop on this basis a viable supratribal state and a modicum of rationalization. But in order to realize such a set-up, it would be necessary to mobilize and concentrate a substantial part of the resources in the hands of the king, so as to give him a decisive measure of power and independence from his social environment, where otherwise he has to remain only a primus inter pares. The mobilization and administration of resources again requires an equally independent bureaucracy, working with objective methods. Indeed, the second book of the *Arthaśāstra* does deal with such a bureaucracy. But here the formidable difficulties come out clearest. I referred already to Kauṭilya's somewhat dispirited sayings about the near-impossibility of controlling peculation in the treasury. In fact, the impressive bureaucracy seems more of a machinery for the diffusion of resources than for their pooling and husbanding.

In these circumstances, one will of course look with some expectation to the crucial question of financial control and audit. Kauṭilya does indeed give a detailed description of the accounts and audit office, the *akṣapaṭala*. The rules for auditing suggest a thoroughly detailed investigation, in Breloer's words "ein regelrechter Abrechnungsprozess".[15] All officers should assemble on the full-moon day of the month of Āṣāḍha, at the end of the hot season, with sealed accounts and with balances to be paid in the treasury. They are confined and forbidden to speak with each other. Fines are prescribed for those coming late or without their account books. Not only the small bureaucrats but also the highest officers, the *mahāmātras,* are involved. All in all, it must have been an impressive gathering.[16]

The essential question, however, is: Which body or which persons form the auditing authority? For proper auditing implies that there should be an impartial agency watching over the procedure and responsible for the verdict. It would seem that Scharfe shows us the right way. According to his carefully researched translation, the crucial passage runs as follows. The mahāmātras should unanimously proclaim who has proceeded correctly. He who puts himself apart (i.e., breaks the unanimity) or talks untruth should pay in full the highest fine.[17] Scharfe concludes convincingly that the mahāmātras are the judges in the auditing process.[18] One is reminded of the twelfth-century English Exchequer, which was simply the curia regis sitting for the regulation of matters of finance.[19]

Now this circumstance has consequences into which Scharfe does not go, but which decisively impair the concept of objective bureaucratic procedures. First, there is the strong emphasis on unanimity—a unanimity that is even enforced with heavy fines. It is difficult to understand the need for this, since the decisive factor in acquitting the accountable officer is in his written accounts, not in the unanimity of the judges. More serious is the fact that the mahāmātras are themselves interested parties, even though the officers whose accounts are to be audited may be lower in rank. They can hardly be considered to constitute an impartial agency. We have only to think of a mahāmātra like the samāhartṛ to realize what abuses this could imply. Enforced unanimity obviously would only worsen the situation.

The most serious point, however, is that we are not told how the mahāmātras themselves render their accounts.[20] Even if one wants to avoid the argumentum e silentio, the reticence on this important point cannot be overlooked. If, then, the mahāmātras on the one hand are the judges in the auditing process and on the other hand do not render their own accounts in any clearly prescribed way, they are more like a body of cosharers with the king than regular bureaucrats. The elaborate bureaucratic procedure, thought out to ensure the king's independence of action, comes to nought, and the king is once again no more than a primus inter pares.

## 5

The obvious unevenness of a bureaucratic auditing process based on written accounts and the curious position of the mahāmātras bring us to another question. From where did Kauṭilya take the idea of an impressive gathering in the month of Āṣāḍha? Here again Scharfe seems to point in the right direction when he suggests a possible connection with the Vedic *varuṇapraghāsa* sacrifice, which also takes place on the full-moon day of Āṣāḍha or of Śrāvaṇa, at any rate, right before the onset of the monsoon.[21]

Although this sacrifice, which incidentally forms part, together with the other seasonal sacrifices, of the royal ritual *(rājasūya),* is not presented in the ritual texts as a collective festival—like other śrauta sacrifices it is described as strictly a single-sacrificer affair—it is not difficult to read between the lines its origin in a collective ceremony, as is the case with the śrauta sacrifice in general.[22] In other words, behind Kauṭilya's auditing process lies a festive tribal gathering.

Viewed in this light, the strong emphasis on unanimity comes into its own. It is reminiscent of the traditional pañcāyat and similar gatherings, where we also find this stress on unanimity and consensus as a corollary of the strife and factionalism characteristic of the little community. Unanimity and consensus have their proper place in the tribal order, with its diffusion of power and authority. In the bureaucratic order, where power and authority are clearly articulated and decisions have to be made in a rationalized way, they can only be of marginal importance, as seems to be the case in Kauṭilya's auditing process. This means that Kauṭilya wants to realize a bureaucratic order, but is held back by the tribal order, which wrecks his intentions.

In order to arrive at a fuller understanding of Kauṭilya's problem and its context, we must first try to find out more about the nature of the festival that seems to lie at the root of the auditing process. In this way, we may be able to understand what opening the festival offered for the intended transformation into a bureaucratic procedure.

In the first place, when we take the description of the varuṇapraghāsa as our guide,[23] this festival is essentially concerned with guilt and atonement. No doubt any sacrifice involves guilt and expiation, be it only on account of the immolation involved, but here they are the central issue. As the *Maitrāyaṇī* and *Kāṭhaka Saṃhitā*s tell it, Prajāpati created the beings through the *vaiśvadeva* seasonal sacrifice that is performed at the end of the cool season four months earlier, but they were seized by poverty and anxiety *(aṃhas),* or rather by Varuṇa.[24] The express purpose of the varuṇapraghāsa is the release from Varuṇa's bonds, and this motive recurs in the brāhmaṇa explanations of all the sacrifice's distinctive features. As the brāhmaṇas put it: "As little guilt *(enas)* as there is in a child just born, so little guilt is there in him who performs the varuṇapraghāsa sacrifice".[25]

The motive of atonement is also made prominent in the curious role assigned to the sacrificer's wife. She is led up by the pratiprasthātṛ officiant from her usual place at the back of the sacrificial emplacement behind the gārhapatya hearth and bluntly asked who her paramour is, or even worse, how many paramours she has.[26] She is expected to state truthfully the name of her paramour, who is then cursed to be seized by Varuṇa. It would, of course, be unwarranted to take this confession rite as evidence for ancient Indian habits and morality. The main point is the reversal that turns untruth *(anṛta)* into truth *(ṛta, satya)* and transfers untruth to the rival, who is seized by Varuṇa.

That this rite should have the sacrificer's wife as its focus can perhaps be explained by the ambivalent position of women in the exclusively patrilineal brahminical system. In the context of the system's stress on the identification of father and son, woman's role is all but excluded. She passes out of her own family, and she cannot be fully integrated in the family into which she marries except as the passive means that enables the father to be reborn as his own son, without propagating herself.[27] She has to remain an element of insecurity between the two lineages which, through her, establish or maintain connubium. In this way, we can understand why in the *Maitrāyaṇī* and *Kāṭhaka Saṃhitā*s woman is roundly identified with untruth, as against sacrifice, which is truth. In fact, it is not so much the infidelity of woman that seems to be at stake here as it is the ambivalent relationship between the two families or clans whose connubial alliance is represented by woman, for if she would not tell the truth, it is not she who is to suffer but a relative of hers.[28]

### *6*

The consideration of the wife's "act of truth" brings us to a further point: the ritual of atonement is played out by two parties that are linked by connubial alliance—an alliance that involves both cooperation and strife. The ambivalence of this relationship is also expressed elsewhere. Thus evil *(pāpman)* is to be taken away from the aśvamedha sacrificer by affinal relatives, the son of a younger sister of the sacrificer's father and the son of a younger sister of his mother.[29] In the same vein, it is prayed that the rival *(sapatna)* may be subjugated like the daughter-inlaw.[30] In the varuṇapraghāsa, this idea receives expression in the unusual feature of two *vedis,* "altars," each with its own offering fire—the main northern one served by the adhvaryu, and the southern smaller one served by his assistant, the pratiprasthātṛ.[31] The northern vedi is said to be the sacrificer's own, whereas the southern one belongs to his rival *(bhrātṛvya);*[32] or the northern vedi is the *yoni,* the birthplace, of the "eaters," and the other the yoni of those that are to be "eaten";[33] or again, the northern one is connected with Varuṇa, with spiritual and temporal dominion *(brahman* and *kṣatra),* the southern one with the Maruts or the people *(viś).*[34]

So rival, viś, and Maruts are put on a par through their common connection with the southern vedi. And it is of course this southern vedi that serves the purpose of the disposal of untruth *(anṛta)* and Varuṇa's bonds. Thus the milk dish for the Maruts and the dishes made of barley groats *(karambhapātrāṇi)*—the latter a distinctive feature of this sacrifice—are placed on the sourthern vedi and offered in the southern fire, as against the milk dish for Varuṇa and the other offerings that are placed on the northern vedi and offered in the northern fire. The offerings in the sourthern fire signify the disposal of anṛta and Varuṇa's bonds as well as the subjugation of the opponent, the recalcitrant viś, or the Maruts.[35]

In this conflict between the two parties in the sacrifice, the sacrificer's wife plays a central part. She is first, when she is led up by the pratiprasthātṛ, associated with the Maruts, for while leading her up, he invokes the Maruts and makes her recite the same mantra.[36] It would seem that the Maruts and the southern fire represent her own relatives, whose connubial link with the sacrificer's party she embodies. The resolution of the conflict therefore centers on her as well as her husband. Having been led up and made to confess, she and the sacrificer together make the offering of the karambhapātrāṇi in the southern fire. While the sacrificer alone recites the invitatory stanza invoking Indra and the Maruts, the two together recite the offering verse: "What sin *(enas)* we have committed in the community or in the jungle, in the gathering *(sabhā)* or in ourselves *(indriye)* against the śūdra or the ārya, whatever sin we have committed against anybody's right, of that sin you are the expiation, *svāhā*."[37] Thus not only the wife has been in the wrong, for both sacrificer and wife must atone together, but it is only through her cooperation that the conflict can be resolved and harmony restored.[38] Marital union, pairing *(mithuna)*, is said to be essential for release from Varuṇa's bonds.[39]

## 7

So far we have seen that the festival's pivotal issue is atonement and that this is worked out in a conflict and its resolution between two parties that seem to be linked with each other through connubium. But before we can round off the picture, one more question remains to be answered. What is the sin, the guilt, that has to be expiated? In a way the guilt seems to lie in the strife between the two parties. When Prajāpati created the *prajāḥ*, "the beings," through the preceding seasonal sacrifice, they treated him with disdain and left him. Prajāpati, becoming Varuṇa, seized them;[40] alternately, it is said that, when created, they or Prajāpati's sacrifice were attacked by the Maruts.[41] Here it would seem that guilt indeed lies in strife, for it is difficult to see why the prajāḥ should have to expiate the aggressiveness of the Maruts. Unless, of course, as seems quite probable, the prajāḥ and the Maruts are actually the same; the prajāḥ fall out with Prajāpati, and the Maruts are said to rob Prajāpati's sacrificial viands. Both prajāḥ and Maruts seem equally guilty,[42] and both are in the position of viś. The nature of the original sin is, however, explained in clearer terms by the *Śatapatha:* when created, the prajāḥ ate Varuṇa's barleycorn, and because of that Varuṇa seized them.[43]

It seems to be possible to translate these mythological statements about disobedience, strife, and the eating of Varuṇa's barley into terms of social reality. After the vaiśvadeva festival, at the end of the cold season when the harvest reaped in autumn after the monsoon was exhausted, people had to leave their homesteads in search of food and pastures, this food being mainly the winter crop of barley. That is, the appropriated "Varuna's barley." As the *Kāṭhaka Saṃhitā* explains: "Varuṇa is the cold season, therefore these two (barley and the *śamī* tree) do not wither in the cold season."[44] Now a precious text gives us exactly this picture when it describes the cycle of activities round the year of the Kurupañcālas: in the cold season they start out toward the east; there they seize the barley crop, feed their men and animals, and finally, at the end of the hot season before the onset of the monsoon, they return to the west to work their fields and harvest the monsoon crop.[45] So the year is divided in two parts with contrasting patterns of conduct: the time starting from the end of the hot season that one spends at home in the settled community to work one's fields and the time of the year, starting with the cool season, that is marked by transhumance, forays in search of food, and razzias. This latter half of the year, the lean season, is characterized by violence and conflict, as against the quiet and peaceful season of the settled community. In short, it is the season of the vrātya expeditions and of the aggressiveness and disobedience of the *praghāsya,* or greedy, Maruts.[46]

Viewed in this light, the nature of the guilt and expiation here is clear. The varuṇapraghāsa, or rather, the festival that lies at its root, signifies the turning point between the season of violent strife and the season of settled life and harmony. The people that have gone out to lead an irregular life outside the settled community are now reintegrated into the community and brought again under the sway of its norms.

## *8*

Our brief survey of the nature of the festival that closes the raiding season—atonement for the evil of violent strife and restoration of harmony—seems to offer a perfect opening for the transformation into the bureaucratic *règlement des comptes* intended by Kauṭilya. In both, there is an opposition between two parties whose conflict is resolved.[47] In this connection, it may be worthwhile to look more closely at the *akṣapaṭala,* the records and audit hall, or more literally, the hall of *akṣas*. These akṣas can be easily explained as counters used in the computation, although this is not made explicit. However, there seems to be more behind it.

Kauṭilya's akṣapaṭala is situated in the southeast part of the royal residence.[48] It is perhaps no mere coincidence that the *Āpastamba Dharmasūtra* also places a *sabhā,* "meeting hall," to the south of the royal residence and that in this sabhā we find a sacrificial fire and a place for dicing.[49] This dicing hall would seem to be the sphere of activity of a special officer, the *akṣarakṣitṛ,* the keeper of the dice, whom we encounter in the purāṇic rajadharma texts among the king's retainers *(sahāya)* and who recalls the *akṣāvāpa,* one of the "jewel bearers" *(ratnin)* in the rājasūya.[50] Though the akṣarakṣitṛ is clearly connected with dicing, his qualifications suggest a bureaucrat concerned with accounts: he should know income and expenditure, the productivity of the land, and the tasks of the king's servants.[51] Here the royal game of dice with its ritual associations shades over almost imperceptibly into the bureaucratic process of accounting and auditing. Almost, for though both the puraṇic rājadharma texts and Kauṭilya seem consciously to gloss over the difference, this should not deceive us. Obviously there is a world of difference between the sacral king and his tribal assembly, where wealth, power, and prestige are periodically redistributed through contests, verbal and otherwise, including dicing games, and the bureaucratic state with its objective methods of administration and decision making.

Thus, in the royal game of dice that forms part of the rājasūya, we see the king take part on an equal footing with the other players, and it is significant that the stake of the game—a cow or a dish of food *(odana)*—is divided in differential share among the participants.[52] It is a matter of redistribution of resources, diametrically opposed to bureaucratic management. In this context, the king clearly does not transcend the community. He is ritually "reborn" through the agonistic interaction of his equals.[53] This idea of the king's ritual "birth" figures largely throughout the whole royal ritual, he is "born," as already mentioned, as the garbha of the viś. And this idea fits in perfectly with the conception of the community as being made up of connubial relations.[54] He is, as it were, the nexus and issue of these bonds, and it is not surprising that connubium, as we saw, takes up an important place in the atonement and reintegration festival.

## *9*

From this perspective we can, I think, readily understand the mahāmātrās' role as cosharers or holders of differential rights in the realm, among whom the king is but a primus inter pares. Indeed, Kauṭilya seems to concede as much when he deals with succession at the death of the king. In case there is no obvious successor, an *amātya,* a minister or household officer, should present a likely pretendent to the assembled mahāmātras, saying: "This one is a trust with you, consider his father, his quality, and noble birth and that of yourselves; he is but the standard, you are the masters".[55] Obviously this is a stratagem to obtain the consent of the assembly, but in order to be effective, this flattering statement about the status of the mahāmātras should have a firm basis in the accepted norms. We have, therefore, to conclude that the mahāmātras are not far from being *svāminaḥ,* masters of the realm. They closely resemble in this respect the ratnins in the rājasūya, who are said to be "the givers and takers of kingdom."[56]

Considering the realities of socioeconomic life, this could hardly have been otherwise. For the crux of the matter is the problem of free resources.

These had to be found in the agricultural productivity of the kingdom. Now the king, whatever the legal theory, was not in practice the exclusive owner of the soil. In fact, it would be misleading to think of exclusive individual ownership in our sense at all. Rather, the situation should be viewed as one where the members of the community hold differential rights in the productivity of the same lands. This is clearly demonstrated by the traditional "division of the grain heap" at harvest time, our of which the king's share had to come.[57] This was a most intricate system of shares and deductions both from the standing and from the harvested crop. The complexity was enhanced by the use of both proportions and absolute measures. The details varied from place to place, but the procedure was easy to handle for the local participants, because the shares were allotted while going along and no aggregate data were required. By the same token, however, it is hardly possible to reduce the king's—or any other's—share to a manageable numerical formula, a problem that haunted the British as well as the pre-British land revenue administration.

The traditional system clearly expresses that the king's rights in the soil are inextricably enmeshed with those of the other members of the community. It certainly was an equitable system in that each received a share according to his place in the community, but it did not leave the king much freedom for mobilizing resources. He would have to upset the delicate balance forcibly—a thing that he could only manage safely if he had already concentrated sufficient power in his hands to face the consequences of serious disturbances. Kauṭilya shows himself keenly aware of this when he advises the king, as we saw, to be content with even a small revenue.

The problem is further complicated in that this land system implies a low degree of monetization. In order to realize a modicum of centralized power, the king would have to remunerate his officers in the neutral medium of cash and to concentrate the superior rights in the soil (and the political rights that go with it) in his own hands. Or, in other words, he would have to transform the body of cosharers, of "givers and takers of the realm," into a corps of salaried officers. Indeed, Kauṭilya does give us pay scales for the different grades of mahāmātras. However, as it was, the king had to remain content with the diffusion of rights throughout the community, or at least throughout the ranks of the mahāmātras—a circumstance that Kauṭilya apparently acknowledges. The pay scales therefore seem a simplified conventional formula for status differences rather than real salaries.

The only means for the king to achieve control seems to be all-embracing espionage. But how to pay and control the agents? In fact, the king is reduced to operating the system of personal relationships from within, as a participant in it, by balancing the different factions that jealously watch each other. Not only does the king have to spy on his officers, but everybody has to spy on everybody else. Pervasive watching and spying may well be the truth behind Kauṭilya's presentation of espionage as an independent means of control in the hands of the king alone. It is typically a factional system in which the king represents no more than one faction among many others. The only way to stay on top is for the king to play the factions against each other and to have them keep each other in check. Thus Kauṭilya recommends that the administrative departments be headed, not by one, but by many officers.[58] In the same way, he advises that there be more than one commander in the garrisons, so that out of fear for each other they will abstain from entering into deals with the enemy.[59] Under the circumstances, this certainly is a sound policy, but it can hardly contribute toward bureaucratic efficiency of government and administration.

Briefly then, whichever way we look, in practice the essence of the system remains diffusion of power and scattering of resources.

## *10*

Rounding off these considerations of Kauṭilya's conception of the state, we can now perceive the well-nigh insurmountable difficulty that he found in his way. He wants to achieve a universalistic bureaucratic state, but he is forced to work within the context of a particularistic "tribal" system that effectively withholds the means needed to achieve the goal to the extent that he has to take the radical step of imagining his ideal, independently and rationally acting king as completely cut off from his social environment.

His strategy for dealing with the intractable gap between practice and theory is not to destroy the existing tribal order and to replace it with the order of the centralized bureaucratic state—as we saw, this would anyhow be hard to do. We noted already how the *Arthaśāstra* and other texts glossed over the chasm between the two orders. They take a concept or an institution from the tribal order and present it in terms of the opposite order. This is not just wishful thinking; it is realistic in that it shows how the old may change into the new, transforming existing institutions. But there is no intention to force the change. Rather than destroy the existing forms, Kauṭilya prefers to cumulate the old and the new without forcing a decision. He offers a different, ideal orientation point for the transformation of the state but remains in tune with the redistributive system based on the interdependence of the participants and geared to the immediate equitable diffusion of resources. It is this combination that seems to govern India to the present day. Modern India does have its competent planners and top bureaucrats, but, as in Kauṭilya's day, the modern mahāmātras—the chief ministers of the states and other regional leaders—bargain on an equal footing with the central authorities for the distribution of power and resources.

# 10 Power, Priesthood, and Authority

## 1

The triad of the title forms a closely knit whole. Power, in order to be legitimate, must be sanctioned by authority, and authority in its turn must be validated by priesthood, which provides the channel to the divine or transcendent source of authority. The problem is how this bill should be filled. The divine or transcendent source of authority is, by definition, beyond man's reach. This leaves two functions to be filled, power and priesthood. There are many ways in which these two functions can be intertwined or separated, collapsed into one, the priest-king, or diffused throughout the community. Indian tradition, however, offers a clear and, to all appearances, self-evident bipolar pattern, namely, that of *kṣatra* and *brahman* or, in terms of their representatives, king and brahmin. Their relationship is well known, but perhaps not so well understood. The pair of king and brahmin stands for temporal power and spiritual authority. That the brahmin's spiritual authority stands above the king's temporal power is hardly surprising. It has, however, weighty consequences. How is the preeminent holder of spiritual authority to serve the temporal power of the king? The brahmin's preeminence bars him from being the king's servant. Or, conversely, how is the king to acknowledge the superiority of the brahmin, which impairs or even threatens to invalidate royal power?

The problem has often been seen as the outcome of a historical struggle in which the brainy brahmins would have bested their illiterate kṣatriya masters in an all-embracing *Kulturkampf*. Here I should at once mention the views of Louis Dumont, who has placed the problem in its proper perspective. Rejecting the conjectural historical struggle for preeminence as an explanation, Dumont proposed to look at the problematic relation between

This is an expanded version of an essay that first appeared in *Tradition and Politics in South Asia*, edited by R. J. Moore (Vikas, 1979).

king and brahmin "as a necessary institution." "In approximate, Western, terms the situation results from the distinction between spiritual and temporal being carried out in an absolute fashion."[1]

The king-brahmin formula takes care of power and authority, distinguished from each other "in an absolute fashion." However, it is exactly with this absolute distinction that the problem lies. The formula leaves the middle terms, the mediating function of the priesthood, vacant. Understandably Dumont, following time-honored practice, views the brahmin as a priest and uses the two words interchangeably. But, as we saw, it is logically inconsistent for the brahmin to be both preeminent and a priest. As a priest in the service of king and community, he would derive his position from them and so jeopardize his claim to represent ultramundane authority. Indeed, the texts are perfectly clear on the point that he should not be a priest and especially not the king's priest.[2] Yet it is equally obvious that power and authority should complement each other and that king and brahmin therefore must cooperate.

The absolute distinction between power and authority or between their representatives, king and brahmin, involves a fundamental contradiction, which should not be explained away but made central to the argument. The well-known tales of the struggle between king and brahmin—for example, when the earth has to be returned to the care of the kṣatriyas after they have been completely defeated by that curious combination of warrior and brahmin, Paraśurāma—do not relate historical events; they give expression to the contradictory relationship. It is on this contradiction that I want to focus the discussion of power and authority.

The ambiguity of the king-brahmin relationship is expressed in the words of the *Bṛhad-Āraṇyaka-Upaniṣad* 1. 4. 11, where the kṣatra is said to have emanated from the brahman as the latter's foremost form: "Therefore nothing transcends the kṣatra; therefore the brahmin sits below the kṣatriya at the royal consecration *(rājasūya);* he bestows this honor only on the kṣatra. But the brahman is the womb of the kṣatra; therefore, though he attains the highest status, he finally rests on the brahman, his own womb; if he (the kṣatriya) hurts him (the brahmin), he hurts his origin; in the same way as when attacking a superior, he is worsted." I think this contradictory statement, which alternately makes the king or the brahmin supreme only to deprive each again of his supremacy, sums up the problem of the dual dominium.

## 2

In order to place the problem in its context, we should look more closely at the conceptual framework of the ancient Indian state. I think we should dismiss the deceptive appearances of a centralized unity held together by a bureaucracy reaching down from the king to the people at large. This certainly seems to be the ideal presented by the *Arthaśāstra,* but its reticence on chains of command and reporting suggests otherwise. Indeed, we find an almost pathetic stress on the necessity of officials' trustworthiness and a concomitant all-pervading spy system, which can only block administrative action and in the end reduce it to chaos. Moreover, it is clear that the realization of a centralized bureaucratic set-up requires objective conditions, such as a high degree of monetization, which would make it possible to separate the functions of government from rights in the soil. As it was, the ruler was mostly forced, like his feudal Western counterpart, to parcel out clusters of his own superior rights. Thus, for instance, Gupta inscriptions seem to suggest that many nominal officials were rather like feudal lords, whose official charges depended less on the ruler's orders than on their own landed power. After all, even France's ancien régime was hardly capable of the centralized bureaucratic control it attempted to achieve.

Nor should we think of a clearly defined territorial state, internally coherent and closed to the outside. Already the fact that the well-known seven elements, which according to the *Arthaśāstra* form the realm, include the ally indicates the open-endedness of the state. It is equally significant that territory is not included as a separate item. The term *janapada* (or, in some texts, *rāṣṭra)* means the undifferentiated whole of people-cum-territory, in the same way as the French "pays" or the German "Land."[3]

I think we should interpret the situation as one where membership of the polity, to a greater or lesser degree, is not primarily defined by residence in a specific well-defined territory, but rather the reverse: differential rights in a territory arise from personal ties of kinship and dependency. Outsiders may be admitted, even welcomed, but their admittance has to be legitimized in terms of personalities or even kinship.[4] The state, then, is based on a network of personal relations in which rights in the soil are subsumed. This means that power and authority are situated at the crossroads, so to say, of the personal relations which make up the polity. Power is dispersed. If there is a king, he can only be the living expression of the balance of these relationships and their opposing pulls and pushes, which tie him down and prevent his acting on his own. His authority does not transcend the community by divine right or otherwise. At best he is a primus inter pares.[5] In this respect, cooperation with the brahmin imposes itself.

## *3*

Let me try to illustrate the king's position by a consideration of the *ratnins,* the "jewel holders," "the givers and takers of kingship," in the royal consecration ritual *(rājasūya).*[6] They have been taken to constitute a sort of bureaucracy, and the ceremony connected with them, the ratnin offerings, to indicate a significant advance in administrative organization.[7] However, as far as I can see, the texts do not indicate anything of the kind. At best the ratnins may be considered household officials, who, of course, according to the needs of the moment, may be entrusted with all sorts of charges not covered by their designations. In fact, the commentators' inventiveness is hard put to explain these designations in terms of specific charges. More significantly, the underlying pattern seems to be connected, not with a rationalized model of the state, but with cognate and affinal kinship.

The eleven or twelve ratnins take up residence in a half-circle around the place of sacrifice. The king, taking his sacrificial fire with him, visits each ratnin in his residence, where a sacrifice is performed with materials provided by the ratnin. At the end of the whole series of visits (or alternatively, after each visit), the king performs a sacrifice at the central place.[8] This reciprocal pattern of prestation and counterprestation—we should recall that the underlying model of the Vedic sacrifice in general is that of the generous reception offered to the guest—is indicative of the reciprocal ties binding king and ratnins. The ritual idiom of the ratnin offerings clearly covers the mutual acts of allegiance between each ratnin and the king, who by his return sacrifice makes himself the nodal point of all relationships.

If we now look at the mixed group of ratnins, the kinship character can be discerned. First, there are the two or three consorts of the king who represent in a direct way his affinal links with the people, whose "husband" he is sometimes said to be. A similar relationship obtained in the case of brahmin (or the *purohita,* the royal "chaplain") and king. Notwithstanding the later strictures against the brahmin's bonds with the king, the brahmin could not be left out from the circle of the ratnins. As we already saw in the *Bṛhad-Āraṇyaka* passage, the brahmin represents in the rājasūya the "womb" or origin of kingship, which explains his presence among the ratnins. His part, like that of the royal wives, falls in line with affinal relations. In the same way, the relation between the king and his purohita is represented as a marriage-like bond. It may also be recalled that this relationship has its counterpart in the king's acting as bride-giver to the officiating brahmins at the horse sacrifice—this being, in my opinion, the original meaning of the prescript that the king should give his wives to the chief officiants. More generally, the Soma sacrificer can by way of dakṣinā give his daughter in marriage to one of the officiants. Next come the *senānī,* or army leader, and the *rājanya* or *rājan*. The senānī seems to represent the cognate kin, to wit, the king's brother.[9] Possibly the rājanya or rājan is also a cognate.[10] He seems to correspond to the *bhrātṛvya,* the paternal cousin and rival, who at first sight, somewhat surprisingly, is one of the four anointers—a point to which we shall have to return.

The brahmin, senānī, rājan (or rājanya), and the consorts form the first group in this and similar lists.[11] The distinctive feature of the second group is that they form pairs: *sūta-grāmaṇī, kṣattṛ-saṃgrahītṛ, akṣavāpa-govikarta,* and (with the Maitrāyaṇīyas) the *takṣa-rathakāra* pair.[12] As the ritual texts never tire of explaining, pairs mean pairing. That this is equally the case here appears also from a similar group we encounter elsewhere, namely, the twelve "kingdom-bearing" *(rāṣṭrabhṛt)* oblations on the completed fire altar. These twelve oblations are offered in six rounds of two each, one to a male, the other to a female deity. The series is rounded off by a thirteenth oblation on a chariot, whereby the sacrificer is made to encompass the six couples.[13] The parellelism with the ratnins as regards name, numerical arrangement, and intention is obvious. Moreover, the rāṣṭrabhṛt oblations are also associated with an unction. I think we shall not be far amiss when we interpret the ratnin and rāṣṭrabhṛt pairs as a representation of two moieties connected by the king who, as the third, is "born" from and dependent on their connubium.

This two-three scheme may also be at the root of the first group, but here another, related numerical principle seems to have disturbed the arrangement, to wit, the four-five scheme, used in the horse sacrifice to organize a similar set of personages. There we find four groups of guardians designated as ratnins[14] round the royal horse which represents the king, to wit, *rājaputras, ugras* (or *rājanyas*), *sūta-grāmaṇīs,* and *kṣattṛ-saṃgrahītṛs.* Furthermore, four royal consorts prepare the horse for immolation. Each of them is accompanied by a group of attendants, who are the female counterparts of the horse's guardians. These female attendants act again as partners of the four brahmin officiants in the exchange of obscenities which further the sham copulation of the chief consort and the immolated horse.[15] This numerical arrangement is also clearly expressed in the unction ceremony of the rājasūya. The king, in the center, is anointed by four officiants standing round him in the four quarters; interestingly, these anointers are an affine *(janya-mitra)* in the east, the brahman officiant in the south, a vaiśya in the west, and the already mentioned rival cousin *(bhrātṛvya)* in the north. Here again we find kinship as a basic principle of organization.[16]

It is interesting that the scheme of the four varṇas, though at first sight an obvious principle of classification, does not enter the picture of the ratnins. Only the *Śatapatha* half-heartedly tries to introduce the four varṇa scheme. Nor does it play a significant role elsewhere in the rājasūya, except in the dicing ceremony, where, according to some texts, the four players represent the four varṇas; but other texts mention, instead of them, kinsmen or sūta-grāmaṇī and kṣattṛ-saṃgrahītṛ as participants in the game.[17] The fourfold scheme here would seem to be a different, earlier conception of the four classical varṇas. The four parties are not varṇas in the classical sense of rigidly separated "castes" shunning intermarriage, but on the contrary, marriage classes, whose essential unity is expressed by a circulative marriage system. It is interesting that the *sūta,* the *kṣattṛ,* and the *ugra* are in the dharma literature considered as the offspring of "mixed" marriages, and as the texts state, after a number of such marriages, the fifth generation returns to the original varṇa.[18]

In short, the rājasūya in general and the ratnin ceremony in particular do not present the picture of a "state" in our sense, but of a clan system based on connubium.

## 4

The analysis of the ratnins shows that kingship is constituted by the network of personal relations; it cannot transcend it. Indeed at least one school includes the king himself—namely the *rājan* mentioned above—in the list of the ratnins. The basic paradigm of the network seems to be kinship and connubium spanning the whole quadripartite community. The king is only a primus inter pares who, even when consecrated, needs the concurrence of the ratnins for making a land grant to the brahman officiant.[19]

Hierarchy in the classical brahminic sense hardly comes into the picture. But this does not imply an egalitarian system. On the contrary, as is already perfectly clear from the status difference between the consorts and the ratnin categories with whom they are associated, we can discern two, three, or four hierarchical tiers. The interesting point is that hierarchy does not imply the absolute separation of the hierarchical groups, as in the classical varṇa theory. The hierarchy finds expression in kinship and marriage, like differences between older and younger, between the offspring of different wives, or between bride-givers and bride-takers. But here we come up against a difficulty. Hierarchy based on circulative connubium (or "generalized exchange") turns on a contradiction. As Lévi-Strauss observed about the Kachin, "L'échange généralisé suppose l'égalité et il est source d'inégalité".[20] This contradictory situation is reflected among the Kachin in two opposed orders: the aristocratic *gumsa* order and the egalitarian *gumlao* order, analyzed by Leach.[21] Though shifts from one order to the other are represented in local history as the result of historical events, it appears from the analysis that the two orders are actually complementary. Alone each is unstable and incomplete, tending to shift into the other. A comparable situation has been analyzed for Minangkabau by de Josselin de Jong. There the aristocratic adat Katumanggungan and the egalitarian adat Parapatih exist side by side, while the followers of both orders can be considered as two opposing "phratries" (respectively, Bodi-Tjaniago and Koto-Piliang).[22] Though the two phratries are each conventionally associated with a particular territory, while the third territory, that of the king, holds them symbolically together, the two adats are in fact "fairly evenly scattered over all Minangkabau".[23]

It would seem that the complementarity of the two orders also underlies the opposition of monarchy and "republic" in ancient India.[24] But not only in ancient India, for the same opposition between the aristocratic and democratic orders seems to underlie present-day communities. We may cite Dumont's exemplary study of a Kallar community as an example. The Kallar sum up their unity in a conventional numerical formula: four chiefs *(tevar),* eight provinces *(nādu),* twenty-four secondary villages *(upagrāma).* One of the four chiefs, sometimes styled rāja, is the highest in rank. The other three (or four, since some informants enumerate five chiefly lineages), considered as "ministers," characteristically derive their prestige in descending order from connubial relations with the first lineage. But at the same time, all members of the community are styled *tevar,* chief. As Dumont aptly observes: "la notion de chef en tant que transcendante au groupe n'existe pas".[25] Under these circumstances, the decline of the first chiefly lineage into near obscurity is perfectly understandable even without the intervention of external factors. At any rate, it would seem that the case of the Kallar illustrates the interplay of the hierarchic or "aristocratic" and the egalitarian or "democratic" principles.

Although the two orders are in the classical Indian texts represented as separate systems—monarchy as against "republic"—in actual fact the difference is rather a matter or degree, since each of the two, as we saw, is ambiguous. On one hand, the egalitarian order needs must lead to differences of rank. The king, on the other hand, cannot be an autocrat; his position remains embedded in the constituent relations of the community, whose unity he should represent. Power and authority are therefore not exclusively the king's; they are diffused throughout the community. In this connection, it seems significant that, for instance, in the Minangkabau example there is not one king but three *radjo,* each having a third part of the seat of kingship, Pagarrujueng, as his residence. This and similar forms of multiple kingship can best be interpreted, not in terms of differentiation of specific, well-defined functions—this seems to be a later and a particularly modern development—but in the sense of a basic diffusion of power and authority.

The principle of multiple kingship can already be noticed in the Vedic texts. Thus the *Taittirīya Saṃhitā* says that the two kings of the gods, Agni and Soma, are honored in the sacrifice in the midst of the gods in order, as the text explains, to keep the gods apart.[26] This statement recalls the two-three scheme discussed above. Indeed the parallel passage in the *Śatapatha* mentions Indra as the third god. This text then makes the interesting point that these three gods and the other gods reciprocally participate in each other so that "the gods came in a threefold way to consist of one 'deity' "; "he who knows thus becomes singly the chief of his people".[27] Thus the single king or chief can only be so on account of reciprocal relations with his people. But, so as to take away, as it were, any illusion about the privileged position of the king as the connecting third, the text then continues paradoxically with the statement: "Twofold in truth is this, there is no third",[28] thus stressing the essential ambiguity of the situation.

## 5

So far the analysis has led us to the conclusion that both power and authority, whether in the egalitarian or in the aristocratic order, are dispersed. They are enclosed in the network of personal relations. Their exercise is therefore bound up with the fluctuations of these relations and with the corresponding shifts in the actual distribution of power. The difficulty this involves is clearly reflected in Kauṭilya's advice on the number of councillors the king should have. If only two, they may combine against the king or they may fight each other; in both cases they will ruin him. Kauṭilya's advice therefore is for the king to have three or four councillors—recalling the four-five scheme we noticed with the first group of ratnins—but he concedes that even then disastrous combinations or divisions are still possible.[29] In fact, there appears to be no definitive solution. The problem is that the exercise of power and authority is beset with factional strife. In other words, it would seem that the state is not based on harmony but on conflict; not on the horizontally layered order of varṇa, but on the shifting vertical lines of faction.

Multiple kingship and diffusion of power and authority have as their corollary pervasive conflict, which takes care of their periodical rearticulation. The temporal order, then, turns on the institutionalization of conflict, not on its elimination. What this entailed can still be seen in the original pattern that underlies the Vedic śrauta ritual. Its central institution was the periodic sacrificial contest, which was no less violent for being ceremonial.[30] Not surprisingly, it is especially in the rituals connected with kingship (rājasūya, vājapeya, horse sacrifice) that the contest has left its clearest traces, in the form of chariot races, mock cattle raids, games of dice, and verbal contests. It is not without interest that, as we saw, many of the ratnins in the rājasūya are connected with chariot racing and fighting. But agonistic features and myths run through the whole corpus of ritual texts. Thus, notwithstanding the exclusive stress on the single sacrificer, his enemy, the *dviṣat* or the rival cousin *(bhrātṛvya)* is well-nigh ubiquitous in the ritual explanations, even though he has no locus standi on the place of sacrifice anymore and is dealt with in abstracto. Occasionally, however, he does still emerge from the limbo of abstraction and so we even saw him take part in the unction ceremony of the royal consecration. Generally the ritual texts do not tire of referring to the continuously recurring battles between the gods and their rivals, the asuras. This agonistic pattern is brought to a high level of all-embracing destructiveness in the epic war of the *Mahābhārata,* which has been called by Marcel Mauss "l'histoire d'un gigantesque potlatch." It is significant that this war between the Pāṇḍavas and their cousins, the Kurus, was set off by the rājasūya sacrifice of the Pāṇḍāva leader, Yuddhiṣṭhira.

The outcome of the contest was never fixed once and for all. When Yuddhiṣṭhira as a result of his victory has won the earth and, disgusted by the internecine violence, wants to renounce the world, he is sternly exhorted to stake again in further rounds of violent sacrificial contests the "material sacrifice" *(dravyamayo yajñaḥ)*. It is therefore no matter for surprise that the rājasūya, though ostensibly meant to be a once-and-for-all consecration of the new king, appears in fact to be based on a yearly recurring festival, as is already clear from the fact that it consists of a long series of sacrifices stretched out over a couple of years. Wealth and with it power and authority must periodically be staked again so as to be redistributed anew. The king is not consecrated for his whole lifetime, but has to submit himself time and again to the sacrificial contest. This would seem to be the background for the frequent mention of the "exiled king" *(aparuddho rājā)*, who must win back his position in yet another sacrifice, as also the epic heroes had to do after their exile. These few but telling indications may illustrate that the diffusion of power and authority found its sanctioning and organizing principles in the sacrificial contest.

It might be objected that the nexus of the sacrificial contest belongs to the mythic imagination of Veda and epic and has no direct bearing on the realities of realm and kingship. However, the same pattern of diffusion and institutionalized conflict is illustrated and elaborated in "secular" fashion in the ancient Indian lore of statecraft, the *Arthaśāstra* of Kauṭilya. I am referring to the sixth book, which deals with the so-called circle of kings *(maṇḍalayoni)*.[31] Kingship and realm consist of seven constituents *(prakṛti):* king, minister, country, fort, treasury, army, and ally. I mentioned already the inclusion of the ally, which shows that the modern conception of the unambiguously bounded territorial state does not apply. Kauṭilya's realm is open-ended and tied in with other such realms. This open-endedness goes even further, for immediately after the seventh constituent, the text discusses the enemy as an unnumbered eighth constituent.[32] The analysis continues, enumerating the kings that constitute the circle. In the first place, there is the would-be conquering king, the *vijigīṣu,* who is taken as the center. He has his ally and the ally of his ally. The enemy is, of course, similarly constituted, and so are the neutral king *(madhyama)* and the uninvolved one *(udāsina),* each with his ally and ally's ally. We then get a "circle" of twelve kings, each with his five other prakṛtis, which makes a total of seventy-two constituents organized in overlapping groupings.[33]

The total "circle" can perhaps best be viewed as a schematization of a continually shifting and unstable factional system. The *Arthaśāstra's* intention is, of course, to let the conqueror-king win through to universal dominion, but even then he would still be tied down by the crisscross of factional relationships that constitute the total polity of the "circle of kings." The ambivalence of the conqueror-king's position—on the one hand pretending to universal rule, on the other hand tied down by the diffusion of power and authority throughout the "circle"—comes out even clearer when we consider that the maṇḍala configuration is based on two different, in fact incompatible, principles that have been conflated in the seemingly unitary scheme, namely, a concentric and a linear principle. The concentric principle places the conqueror-king in the "hub of the wheel," surrounded by rings of enemies and allies. The linear principle, on the other hand, does not have one conqueror-king in the center; instead the center is formed by two kings, the conqueror and his enemy, with the various allies and rivals aligned behind each of the two, the conqueror's ally being placed at the back of the enemy and so on.[34] In the first case, the conqueror forms the center, supported by his allies and subduing his rivals; the second configuration is a dualistic scheme which continually pits the conqueror against his rival in never-ending conflict (if it ended, the whole configuration would collapse). Where the concentric scheme still seems to leave open the possibility of the conqueror's eventual universal rule, the linear alignment definitely precludes that eventuality. But in neither case does the king rise above the maṇḍala; his position remains dependent on the changing outcome of the perennial contest.

## *6*

The diffusion of power and authority with the ever-renewed sacrificial contest as the mediating and organizing institution would seem to call for a clearly defined priesthood to manage the central institution. In this connection, one will of course immediately think of the brahmin, who is indeed in charge of the Veda and its ritual and owes his preeminence to this charge.

However, brahmin as a specialized and closed class, or rather "estate," in the sense of the first of the four varṇas, is a late construct and certainly does not belong to the context of the agonistic sacrifice. In general, the *brahmán* or *brāhmaṇa* has no clear counterpart in the old-Iranian evidence but is a specifically Indian development. The brahmán in the Vedic texts is the bearer or representative of the impersonal *bráhman*. Perhaps the best and most comprehensive paraphrase of the latter term is the one given by Renou: "énergie connective comprimée en énigmes." Its context is the verbal contest, the *brahmodya,* where the contestants fight each other with enigmatic formulations—not solutions—of the cosmic riddle that they have "seen" or "found." The contestant who finally manages to reduce the others to silence vindicates himself as the *brahmán* par excellence.[35] But this also means that the quality of being a brahman is open and dependent on the outcome of the periodically renewed contest in the same way that power and authority are.

In the royal consecration,there is an episode where the king, after unction and enthronement, is addressed as *brahmán*. This episode looks very much like a reduced version of the brahmodya scenario. Seated on the throne, symbolically the center of the universe, the king calls out to each of the four chief officiants sitting around him to the four quarters, "O brahman." The addressed officiant answers, "Thou, O king, art brahman," each adding an identification of the king to one of the four deities, Savitṛ, Indra, Mitra, and Varuṇa.[36] Though there is no enigma here but only straightforward identification, it seems clear that the king is made to stand out as the cosmic connection holding the universe together. The little ceremony signifies the dispersal and the concentration of the "connection" by the king.

It is in this sense that we can interpret the later statements about the divinity and the sacral character of kingship. Thus according to *Manu,* the king does not represent a one and only king of the gods; there are eight of them who coalesce in the human king.[37] These eight gods recall the eight human magnates or "heroes" *(vīra)* who in a ritual text are said to support kingship. Such statements mean that the king is seen as the connecting link of the manyfold (in this case eightfold), dispersed kingship. The sacrality or divinity of the king resides in his connectiveness. But this leaves little room for an independent and closed priestly class, for the main sacral function is already occupied by the king.

There are, of course, priestly functions in the sacrifice, but originally these did not require a professional priesthood. This is illustrated by the *sattra,* the sacrificial session (lasting twelve days or longer) in which a number of sacrificers join together and divide among themselves the various priestly functions without there being any question of the participants having to belong to a priestly class. Rather, it would seem that the sacrifice was primarily a concern of warriors competing for the goods of life—material as well as spiritual—in all manner of contests, not in the last place the verbal contest. As we saw, the decisive point in the contest is the inspired "vision" of the cosmic enigma expressed in the victorious riddle formulation. But this vision does not seem to be the monopoly of a priestly class.

One may, however, think of a specific professional priestly figure—the *purohita* (the one "placed before"), the king's (or magnate's) "chaplain." But here again it would seem that originally his was not a purely priestly function, but was associated with warriorlike activities. The purohitas were charioteers. "In previous times," we are told, "the purohitas used to serve the kings as their chariot drivers",[38] the king himself being the chariot fighter. This is certainly not an unimportant function, and its priestly content is clear from the fact that the charioteer in the epic combines this function with that of a bard, as appears from the word *sūta,* which carries both meanings. One is reminded here of Kṛṣṇa's position as the charioteer of the royal warrior Arjuna, who reveals to his master the ultimate truth of the *Bhagavadgītā*. But for all that, it is a subservient role, supporting, not creating, the sacrality of the king's connectiveness, which is expressed in his being proclaimed the brahman par excellence.

The purohita's role as a charioteer reminds us once more that the central position of sacrality depended on the changing outcome of the ever-renewed sacrificial contest. As power and authority are subject to dispersal, concentration at the outcome of the periodic contest, and redispersal, so also is the priesthood dispersed. This situation still seems to be reflected in the diffusion of priestly functions throughout local communities, where we may see potters, barbers, washermen, and others acting in priestly capacities at particular occasions, while in some cases, members or branches of families function as sacrificial priests for their cognate and affinal relatives. Nor is it exceptional to see the king at great state occasions as the chief celebrant and sacrificial patron of festivals on which the general well-being depends. In all this, we can still recognize the original basic pattern of the diffusion of power, authority, and priesthood regulated by the institution of sacrifice.

## *7*

All this, however, is remote from the strict separation of power and authority where we started our discussion. In fact, it is its very opposite. Coming together in the nexus of the sacrificial contest, power and authority as well as priesthood are inextricably interwoven. The ever-repeated contest decided who should occupy the central position of connective sacrality—till the next challenge.

Here we may find the origin of the legendary stories of the recurring conflict between kṣatriyas and brahmins. Louis Dumont, as already mentioned, saw in these stories the expression of the strained and conflictive relationship between king and brahmin which he analyzed as "a necessary institution."[39] We can now recognize that these stories of conflict indeed reflect a necessary and central institution, namely, the sacrificial contest. However, we also see that these stories cover a contradiction. Though perfectly consistent with their original background where power, authority and priesthood are inextricably interwoven in the sacrificial contest, the legendary conflicts refer explicitly to kṣatriyas and brahmins, not as interchangeable positions, but as distinct and separate groups in the sense of the classical varṇas. They are indeed so distinct and separate that there cannot be any common ground between the two for fighting their battles. A definitive split has occurred between the power of the kṣatriya and the brahmin's authority. The brahmin should not venture into the kṣatriya's realm to try to wrest the control of the earth from him, nor should the king pretend to the brahmin's authority. As we saw, the contradiciton comes out starkly in the story of Paraśurāma, who conquers the earth and defeats the kṣatriyas, for in the end, the warrior-brahmin must return the earth to the control of the kṣatriyas he has so utterly devastated.

There are, then, two incompatible and competing patterns. The one interweaves, the other separates power and authority, while neither offers a distinct, autonomous place to the priesthood, which either is integrated in the king's connective sacrality or disappears in the gap between royal power and brahminical authority. How should we explain this dual pattern? More specifically, how did the split between power and authority come about—a split that nothing in the originally unitary situation seemed to presage? The answer can be found in the Vedic ritual texts, which reflect a fundamental reorientation of the institution of sacrifice that resembles nothing so much as an "axial breakthrough".[40]

The ritual texts allow us to reconstruct with comparative ease and clarity the original, preclassical pattern we have discussed. The actual presence of death in sacrificial contests gave access to the ultramundane world of gods and ancestors and thereby sanctified the outcome. Bringing together the human and divine worlds in the sacral nexus of the sacrificial contest, it was a unified pattern. But the pattern was essentially unstable and threatened to collapse through the constant danger of destructive violence. It was at this point that the breakthrough was made. This was done by excluding the rival from the place of sacrifice. In mythological terms, it was the final victory of the Lord of Life and divine representative of sacrifice, Prajāpati, over his rival, Death—a victory that definitively ended the sacrificial contest.[41] By the exclusion of the rival party, contest and violence were banned from the place of sacrifice. The uncertain outcome of the sacrificial battle was replaced by the certainty of the strict and exhaustive order of ritualism. Henceforth the single sacrificer stood outside society in a perfectly ordered ritual universe which was exclusively his own. The sacrifice was desocialized and individualized.

In this way, a unique view of a perfect order transcending the conflictive order of society was won. But for the same reason this order of ritualism was irreversibly cut off from society. Where once there was the connective nexus of the sacrificial contest there was now a void. The sacrifice was separated from the social world and offered no scope for a priesthood to fill the void. It could no longer function as the channel of ultimate authority. Worldly power and ultimate authority were broken apart. The center gone, the king's social world and the brahmin's ritualistic order came to stand in unmediated opposition to each other.

## *8*

It may be objected that the Vedic śrauta ritual provides sacrificial ceremonies that are ostensibly an effective link between the king's order and the order of the brahmin. In the first place, there is the rājasūya, consisting of a series of sacrificial rituals during which the king is anointed or, rather, profusely showered with the consecratory waters *(abhiṣeka)*. There are, moreover, other royal rituals as well, including the prestigious horse sacrifice, the aśvamedha. However, these royal rituals are just modifications of the extrasocial, individualized Soma sacrifice and equally require that their single sacrificer, even though a king, stand outside the social world. The Soma ritual has no place for the community. The ratnins have no part in it, but are accommodated in a separate series of non-Soma offerings, each of which has again the form of an individualized, single-sacrificer ritual. There is no common ground between the ritual universe and the social world.

Still one might be tempted to view the episode where the royal sacrificer is acclaimed *brahmán* as the decisive junction of the temporal and the transcendent. But in the first place, not only the king but also the commoner is proclaimed a *brāhmaṇa,* a representative of the *bráhman,* at his consecration for the Soma sacrifice *(dīkṣā).* The king's brahman proclamation fails to distinguish him from his subject, and this brings us back again to the diffusion of power and authority. More serious, indeed decisive, is another point. Though the proclamation originally conferred connective sacrality in this and the other world on the king, it can now, in the reformed, "postaxial" ritual, only have meaning within the strictly limited time and place of the ritual. After its conclusion, about to leave the ritual enclosure, the sacrificer, whether king or commoner, returns to his normal, unchanged self in society: "Here I am just the one I am," as he has to declare in his concluding mantra.[42] Nothing has changed.

Under these circumstances, it is not surprising that the dharma authors do not seem to attach practical value to the rājasūya. Though they require a brahmanic sacrament *(brāhmaḥ saṃskāraḥ),* there is no agreement as to what this ceremony should be.[43] It may even be no more than the *upanayana,* which opens the period of pupilage with the teacher and so gives the king access to the Veda but which is also required for all "twice-born" commoners. Again it does not distinguish the king from, say, the vaiśya. In fact, the ritual texts themselves appear to concede the point that the rājasūya does not make the king. "A king who desires to win heaven should perform the rājasūya",[44] that is, he is already a king. His desire for heaven is a strictly individual matter that has no bearing on his royal function.

Whatever the śrauta ritual may achieve for the strictly personal gratification of the king, it can not confer its authority on him. Nor can there be a priesthood to bridge the gap. The king, like any other sacrificer, can of course engage brahmin experts to officiate in his sacrifices, but the king's link with this priesthood does not extend beyond the sphere of the ritual's strictly limited time and place. More important, however, is the individualization of sacrifice, which makes the brahmin's participation in a patron's, and especially in the king's, sacrifice intensely questionable. Even if the close relationship between patron and officiant lasts only for the duration of the ritual—but the rājasūya, for one, spans a couple of years—the brahmin has to accept the food and gifts of his patron during that period. The sharp dividing line between the ritual universe and the social world tends to be blurred, if not obliterated, and the brahmin's authority to be fatally impaired by involvement in worldly relationships. In this respect, we can readily understand that the sacrificial gifts to the officiants are viewed as a "salary" *(vetana)* for a well-defined, specific service. Once the salary is paid, the relationship is ended and, in theory at least, there are no further personal bonds of obligation and reciprocity.[45] Nonetheless, the distinction may easily turn out to be too sophisticated, and the texts have harsh things to say about the brahmin who serves the king.[46] Such service cannot, of course, be ruled out, be it only for the fact that the brahmin cannot live on his spiritual authority alone. But insofar as he is allowed to serve the kṣatriya, he loses his brahmanic value and becomes the kṣatriya's equal *(kṣatrasama),* even if he serves in the specifically brahmin capacity of an *ṛtvij,* an officiant, in the śrauta ritual. The position of the king's purohita, in what is an enduring and close relationship, can therefore only be an utterly ambiguous one. He precedes the king but is at the same time held in contempt. No wonder the king's confidant and jester in the Sanskrit theater, the *vidūṣaka,* is typically a brahmin.

Ironically, the king who has successfully enticed the brahmin to serve him only obtains an empty husk, for the brahmin then loses his special quality that was the reason to engage him and becomes equal to a kṣatriya. The truth is that the ideal brahmin should cultivate the Veda and its ritual by himself, in himself, and for himself. The ideal brahmin, like the ideal sacrificer, is a renouncer. Only in this way can the hard-won view of the transcendent that was gained out of the violence of the ancient sacrificial battle be saved from corruption by the world's powers and conflicts. The sacrificial battle for the transcendent is over, leaving worldly power without authority, transcendent authority without power, and ruling out priesthood as a mediator.

## *9*

It was not the brahmin who by some obscure stratagem wrested sacrality and priesthood from the king. It was the other way round. Not the king, but the brahmin was emptied of magic and sacrality. The brahmin was "desacralized," and the burden of connective sacrality came to rest all the more heavily on the king. This sacrality weighs him down and enmeshes him in the constricting web of conflictive relationships. It cannot raise him to a level of authority transcending society. Even when the Hindu king is viewed as a god, it should be remembered that the gods do not transcend the world of *saṃsāra*. They are like humans, only more so. The king's sacrality does confer on him a measure of authority to the extent that he fulfills the connective function amid the relationships that constitute society. But for the same reason, his authority lacks ultimate validity. It is not derived from a transcendent source but is rooted in worldly relationships. The king's sacrality is the exact opposite of transcendence. Access to the transcendent and the ultimate authority it bestows are the exclusive prerogative of the brahmin, but only so long as he keeps free from worldly involvement.

The king's connective sacrality is incompatible with the brahmin's separative authority. For the king and the brahmin to meet each other, it would be necessary that the brahmin, instead of stepping down from his ultramundane stand, steps up to a level from which he can enter the king's world of pervasive conflict without being affected by it. That is, the brahmin must be absolutely disinterested. This is indeed the image of the ideal brahmin. But it is hard to see how such a paradoxical stance could be realized and maintained in actual practice. It would, in fact, require a similarly detached king, who would rise above the restrictive bonds of personal relationships. This quality is recommended by the *Arthaśāstra* where it stresses the need for "victory over the senses" *(indriyajaya)*—a victory won, not by means of magic, but through science and discipline *(vidyā, vinaya)*.[47] Kauṭilya's ideal is a rationalistic, impersonal, and detached kingship. But kingship based on the renunciatory virtue of indriyajaya would not need the brahmin's authority anymore. Although Kauṭilya reiterates the time-honored idea of the kṣatra fostered by the brahman,[48] he does not seem to have much use for the brahmin and his authority. For him the purohita is a learned magician, averting calamities and bringing about happy turns of events, but he is not a bearer of authority. More serious, however, is the fact that the king, by virtue of his renunciatory stance, would cut himself off from his field of activity in the middle of personal relationships and conflicting interests. It is significant that the discussion of the king's lofty detachment is concluded by stating the king's dependence on his associates *(sahāya)*. "One wheel alone does not turn."[49] Here we are back again where we started. Both the power and authority of the king remain entangled in the web of relationships with his associates, the cosharers in the realm.

## 10

Only under the absolute, universal rule of the dharma can temporal power and spiritual authority be fused. The dharma would then realize the revealed order of the Vedic śruti. In other words, the world would have to be transformed into an atomized universe made up of individual sacrificers, each singly submitting to the exhaustive and inflexible order of the śrauta ritual. But as we saw, such a seamlessly ordered universe can only be realized temporarily within the confines of the ritual enclosure. The universal rule of ritual over the world would mean the dissolution of society.

It is, however, possible to think of an approximate analogue. One example would be the Buddhist *sangha,* the community of monks individually following the strict ritualistic rule of monastic discipline. It only knows the impersonal authority of the Buddhist dharma. But for that reason, it can only endure in juxtaposition to the temporal power of the king, who must resolve the internal conflicts that the sangha itself has no power to decide, even though outside intervention compromises its integrity.[50]

The universal rule of dharma, whether Hindu or Buddhist, would withdraw from society, not only all authority, but all power as well, so as to vest them in each individual. This was the situation of mankind's mythic golden age, the *kṛtayuga*. But as the *Mahābhārata* tells us, it was exactly this situation which gave rise to confusion and conflict, for men only had the unmediated dharma, vested in each single individual, to maintain order and to protect each other.[51] Universal order succumbs to its inner contradiction. Depending entirely on the individual, it has no room for conflict, for there is no power and authority left for a mediating agency. Monolithic universality breaks down on its unacknowledged explosiveness.

The problem may not be much different from that of the modern polity of the nation-state. In order to save society from dissolving, the nation-state pretends to fuse the individual citizens, each singly subject to the rule of law, into a single monolithic unity. It represents a maximal concentration of both power and authority. Hence its inviolability. But it must then direct its inner conflict outward to other nation-states. The more strongly fusion and unity are stressed, the more explosive is the conflict. We know the catastrophic consequences.

The seemingly coherent and harmonious triad of power, priesthood, and authority owed its effectiveness to the sacrificial nexus of the contest. In other words, it required and gave sacral sanction to the unsettling violence of conflict. The "axial breakthrough," on the other hand, dissolved the agonistic nexus. It devalorized sacrality and denied conflict its ultimate legitimacy. Instead it posited the ideal of an absolute transcendent order that is, as a matter of principle, incapable of worldly realization. The triad collapsed under the pressure of the ideal into an irreversible dichotomy of worldly power and transcendent authority that cancelled the mediating capacity of priest or magician. The ensuing problem of power and authority is as insoluble as it is universal. Indian tradition, instead of trying to solve the problem, acknowledges its insolubility. Notwithstanding the deficiencies of the compromises it requires in day-to-day practice, recognition of the dichotomy may still be the most efficacious way to deal with the problem. At the very least, it leaves the future open.

# 11 Western Expansion, Indian Reaction: Mughal Empire and British Raj

## 1

Expansion and reaction: the coupling of the two concepts in a complementary pair seems obvious. In fact it is too obvious to be true. Expansion of Western, specifically British, control over the Indian subcontinent there certainly was—even though our understanding of this complex phenomenon is less than perfect. But what about its counterpart, the Indian reaction? One is even tempted to ask, Was there a reaction at all? Such a question flies in the face of the consecrated rhetoric that glibly speaks of the defense of traditional values, national identity, and the struggle for freedom. But then the same goes for the countervailing slogans of the white man's burden and the *mission civilisatrice*—not to mention the ambitious utterances of our latter-day development ideologists, which make the rhetoric of their colonial predecessors look rather pale and shame-faced.

The point is, of course, that all this rhetoric—whether of the old-fashioned colonial, the equally old-fashioned (though hardly out of fashion) nationalist, or the brand-new foreign-aid variety—will not help us to understand what has happened and is still happening. If we want to give substance to the theme of expansion and reaction, we shall have to interpret it in a radically different way. First of all, we shall have to avoid the obtrusive logic of the action-reaction type, which traps us into viewing the story of European involvement exclusively in terms of a clear-cut confrontation. Even when the swelling tide of nationalism produced the noncooperation and civil disobedience movements and the clashes of 1941, the confrontation kept a curious air of tepidity, which led one historian to speak of "a Dasehra duel between two hollow statues, locked in motionless and simulated com-

This essay appeared in slightly different form under the title "Was There an Indian Reaction: Western Expansion in Indian Perspective," in *Expansion and Reaction,* edited by H. L. Wesseling (Leiden, 1978), 31–58. Reprinted by permission.

bat."[1] It was only with the breaking away of the Muslims that "a real ferocity appeared—between Indian and Indian." Nor is this a pecularity of the Indo-British entanglement. Other cases of expansion—take for instance Islam or Buddhism—similarly refuse to respond to the action-reaction logic.

Admittedly the story is a complex and often contradictory one, which moreover ranges over a huge and diverse subcontinent. It seems, then, a natural step to take refuge in breaking up the all-too-global picture into probably endless series of areas, sectors, groups, and instances, where confrontation and reaction did occur in different ways and with different outcomes. No doubt such case studies contribute most valuable material for our understanding of the structures and processes involved. Moreover, it is clear that the two parties to the expansion-reaction game were far from being unified blocs. Even the British Indian government and its prestigious "steel frame," the Indian Civil Service, hardly resembled the powerfully monolithic juggernaut of popular imagination,[2] so that here too there is unlimited scope for fragmentation. The main trouble with this break-up, however interesting its results, is that it can only lead to ever further atomization, while a comprehensive view recedes more and more behind an impenetrable screen of monographs on unique situations and events—as indeed seems to happen too often in modern Indian historiography.

The fragmentation inherent in the expansion-reaction paradigm seems, however, to cover another, perhaps somewhat unexpected, but fundamental fact. Namely, that the aims, terms of reference, modes of operation, and organization of the parties involved had little if anything in common.[3] In other words, what we should like to construe as the complementary expansion-reaction pair takes place on two different and separate planes, in two distinct worlds, as it were. Their contacts and confrontations could only have an incidental and episodic character for lack of common ground. Even in those instances where it was actively pursued, the "dialogue" is more often than not a dialogue of deaf-mutes, or at least one of misunderstandings.

Does this mean that we have to resign ourselves to this atomization or, alternatively, that we have to fall into the trap of another fragmentation along the lines of Eurocentric, Indocentric, Sinocentric historiographies? I do not think that we have to submit to either of these unattractive alternatives. But first we should try to characterize the society where, since the second half of the eighteenth century, the expansion of British control took place.

## 2

The first thing that strikes us is—in contradistinction to, for example, China—the virtual absence of a long-established empire commanding active and unquestioning allegiance. There was, of course, the Mughal Empire. But what was the extent of its effectualness, what the reality covered by its prestigious name? It is not that its origin in conquest by Central-Asian warriors in any way impaired its acceptance and legitimacy, nor was its explicit Islamic character a serious impediment to acceptance by its largely non-Muslim subjects. In both respects, the Mughal Empire had old and venerable precedents in the Delhi Sultanate. The truth is that—again in contradistinction to China—no ruler, whether Hindu rājā or Muslim pādshāh, could have ultimate authority and legitimacy. For these belonged to the ideal brahmin, that is, to the ultramundane renouncer, and only on condition that he kept himself free from entanglement in society, so that the ruler was barred from access to the source of ultimate authority.[4] A comparable situation obtains in Islam where the separation of secular power and spiritual authority also keeps the ruler under a cloud of suspicion. Paradoxically, where no grave questions of the divine right of kings, the mandate of heaven, or similar transcendental concepts were directly involved, the position of the ruler was unproblematic. Whatever his origin or confession, he could be accepted with comparative ease and even enjoy a modicum of effective allegiance. So there never was a serious problem of the Mughal's legitimacy. Whatever legitimacy and authority were possible under these circumstances he certainly possessed. If we may attach any value to the reaction of an old man in a Rajput town, who, when told of the British departure from Delhi, ponderously supposed that in that case the Mughals would be back in power,[5] the legitimacy of Mughal rule vastly outlasted even the twilight of its declining presence.

The doubts about the Mughal Empire are in another area. The extant administrative documents, relatively few though they may be, conjure up a most impressive picture of a centralized bureaucratic empire, efficiently run on lines of adequate regulations.[6] No doubt, if more of the Mughal archives had been salvaged, or if more official documents come to light, this impression would only be further substantiated. However, even the most complete archives cannot tell the whole story. Perhaps we should even say that the greater their precision of focus and formulation, the less they will fit untidy reality. And so perhaps we should not be surprised that the empire appeared to observers as singularly ineffectual. Or, as the comment of an English factor has it, "every man honours the king, but no man obeys him".[7]

This inconsistency can, of course, be explained away by invoking an organic scheme of rise, decline, and fall that explains itself and only needs to be filled in with details. In this view, the Mughal empire had its day of youthful vigor in the sixteenth century under Akbar. Its middle age in the seventeenth century sees the beginning of decline—notwithstanding the fact that it reaches its greatest expansion at the end of the century—and old age is reached in the eighteenth century when the empire founders in chaos, its remnants salvaged by the incipient British-Indian Empire, which then starts on a new cycle of rise and fall. Such a view, however, does little to provide adequate reasons for the fatal decline of the once impressive imperial administration. The reason cannot be found in the personalities and capacities of the successive rulers, for the prime requisite of an adequate and well-established bureaucracy is that it withstand just such vagaries. Indeed, a good case can be made for the strength of Mughal administration even under the strains and stresses of Aurangzeb's Deccan campaigns (especially after 1689) and of his declining years.[8]

So the discussion centers, not on the nature of the empire, but on possible explanations for its decline and break-up. The doyen of Mughal studies, Sir Jadunath Sarkar, has given strength to the argument that the empire was fatally impaired by the break between Hindus and Muslims caused by Aurangzeb's religious policies.[9] Recently a variety of other explanations have been brought forward. Satish Chandra has pointed to the disruptive effect of intense factionalism over the allocation of increasingly scarce land assignments among the vastly increased service nobility.[10] Irfan Habib sees the decisive factor in the exploitation of assigned lands, leading to flight and finally rebellion by the oppressed peasantry.[11] J. F. Richards stresses Aurangzeb's decision to direct his efforts at subduing the Marathas instead of coming to a settlement with them so as to round off the Deccan conquests and integrate them, with the result that "the imperial administration and military machinery was stretched past its capacity".[12] Finally M. Athar Ali seeks to place the crisis of the Mughal Empire in a global context by contrasting the growing preponderance of Northwestern Europe with the economic stagnation of the Islamic empires, which in the last resort he ascribes to a cultural failure of the entire Islamic world.[13] The debate is certain to continue for some time to come,[14] but the divergence of even the most recent opinions seems to suggest that in the end we may have to admit defeat in the face of an inextricable tangle of interacting causes—a formula often intoned in such cases.

In the meantime, we might consider, albeit tentatively, whether we are asking the right question. Our perception of the Mughal breakdown is, of course, conditioned by our knowledge of what happened afterward, namely, the unforeseen takeover by the British. In other words, was the breakdown as absolute and irreversible as India's subsequent history has made it? Questions about what might have been are notoriously vacuous. We should not, however, forget that there was at least one other Islamic empire, the Ottoman, whose doom was already spelled out in gloomy terms in the beginning of the sixteenth century. All four pillars of the state—religion, justice, the council, and finance—are broken, and one wonders whether matters can continue in this way, a Dutch consul reported in 1626 from Aleppo.[15] Well, as we know with the inexorable certainty of hindsight, matters were to continue for another three hundred years, and it took a global conflagration to put an end to them. When such time spans are involved, we may wonder whether we should not look for the reasons of the remarkable resilience rather than for those of the decline. Both sets of reasons may be largely the same. Most, if not all, is in the eye of the beholder. In other words, what we perceive as a process of decline, relentlessly leading to an unavoidable and definitive fall, may well be, not a process, but a structure—and a remarkably durable one at that, allowing for dramatic ups and downs without an inevitable and irreversible collapse.

The Mughal Empire, it would seem, fits very well into the perspective of resilience and durability. Thus, J. F. Richards convincingly concludes that "the vector of change was always in the direction of centralized power exercised by an Islamic ruler . . . . Despite the extent and severity of revolts and disorder in the first half of the eighteenth century Muslim rulers and Muslim institutions retained a tenacious hold on power."[16] If this is the case, the question as to how the empire actually worked rather than how it declined and collapsed imposes itself.

### *3*

In the center of the stage were the Mughal and his retainers, the *mansabdārs,* whose primary function was the recruitment and maintenance of specified contingents of the Mughal heavy cavalry, the prescribed size of the contingent indicating the mansabdār's rank. These ranks, it should be noted, did not derive from a hierarchical command structure, but only represented a gradation of status. A military command structure was largely missing. This made for maximal flexibility, but it also meant that the Mughal was not comfortably situated at the apex of a vertical military hierarchy but had to move in a horizontal field of personal relationships with at least the higher-ranking mansabdārs or nobles—this possibly was the reason for the complicated rules of court etiquette, which stressed the otherwise less-than-absolute rulership of the Mughal. In other words, the central, or at least most conspicuous, organizational principle was that of an elaborate predatory war band with an ethos of martial panache and personal loyalty to the Mughal, proven on the battlefield and rewarded with heroic titles. Thus the Mughal primarily worked through a personal network of high-ranking retainers that was ideologically oriented toward conquest.

However, this was only part and perhaps not even the most important part of the picture. The actual base of the empire was clearly agrarian, which means that the central concern had to be the extraction of whatever agrarian surplus could be made available, for this had to pay for the mansabdārs and their troopers, either indirectly through salaries derived from the crown lands or directly through assignments of taxable land *(jāgīr).* So the main problem was not conquest but the extraction and management of the agrarian surplus from the tracts that could be controlled. This obviously called for intensive regulation and considerable bureaucratic effort. The mansabdārs, therefore, were not only warriors and courtiers, they had to be competent administrators as well, so as to be able to head the bureaucratic establishments at the center and in the provinces—not to mention the supervision of the management of their land assignments.

That there was indeed an impressive bureaucracy which administered the complicated regulation system is, as already mentioned, amply attested. However, even the best of military and administrative systems cannot by themselves produce the agrarian surplus that they need for their own maintenance. This meant that the imperial undertaking—apart from its being a "gamble on the monsoon"—essentially depended on the degree of cooperation that could be obtained from the local producers or, rather, from their leaders, the local men of substance. Over the centuries, a considerable store of mutual accommodation as well as of technical experience with assessment had been built up, but the yearly realization of the agrarian revenue always remained a precarious matter of what in each case the trade could bear.

Because of the insecure agrarian base, conquest remained a necessary complement to the management of the areas already under control, and as we saw, the central organization and ideology were in principle geared to that purpose. However, conquest—as distinct from mere raiding—not only meant a fairly heavy outlay in campaign costs, but also, and more important, the winning over of the local men who were in actual control of the agrarian resources in the areas to be conquered. This in turn meant that these new "subjects" had to be rewarded, preferably by integrating them into the mansabdār corps and giving them the corresponding salaries in cash or taxable land. Thus, for instance, the conquests in the Deccan resulted in the influx of a great number of Deccani notables into the higher mansabdār ranks.[17]

This investment in local influence was always a risky one. For whatever was to be added to the central resources in crown lands and the revenue to be derived from them was in fact largely preempted by the demand for salaries and assignments to pay the rising number of mansabdārs. In the case of the Deccan, the conquest conspicuously failed to produce the expected returns and even seems to have created a severe shortage of assignments. Even the newly won crown lands of Golconda, which were left relatively undisturbed by the Maratha inroads, could not remedy the pressing demand created by the expansion of the mansabdār corps.[18] In this way, the effects of direct military failure in open battle were less damaging than the risks of successful conquest—particularly since the Mughal heavy cavalry usually remained master of the battlefield till they were outdated by the firing power and organization of the sepoy battalions. The danger was in the aftermath of conquest.

So the empire remained precariously suspended between the opposite needs of careful husbanding of its resources and risky investment in conquest. But in order to put this dilemma in its proper context, two further points must be considered, namely, the role of trade and the problem of the frontier.

## 4

While there is no doubt that the main prop of the Mughal Empire was agriculture, it would seem that trade and finance as important, even pivotal, factors are left somewhat in the dark. The language of the official documents and the chronicles puts almost exclusive stress on the warrior-administrator with his troopers and clerks on the one hand and the peasant or ryot *(ra'īyat)* on the other, and nothing in between. The situation looks as if the administration was in direct contact with the peasant-producers who provided the sinews of war as well as of peace. Such a situation, where all manner of intermediaries are excluded and dealings are directly with each peasant separately seems indeed to have been the ideal, as it also was of the British administration.[19] And it stands to reason that the bureaucratic idiom was geared to this ideal. However, the various ways in which the sources insist on direct relations with the peasant—to the point of encouraging him to pay his revenue directly into the treasury, bypassing the revenue collectors[20]—suggest that actual practice will have been rather different. In fact, it could hardly have been otherwise.

The point is that at least from the thirteenth century onward, the revenue was assessed and paid in cash.[21] So the crux of the matter was the conversion of the extracted surplus into money. The relationship between warrior-administrator and peasant could therefore hardly be a direct one. In between the two was the cash nexus. Short of an enormous state trading organization—even with the help of modern facilities such ventures are beset with dismal failures—the administration was unable to handle the cash nexus by itself. The only possibility was to shift the burden of the problem to the peasant and let him cope as best he could with the conversion tangle.

Now "peasant" is a reputedly vague category—in fact, something of an abominable snowman of Indian history, ubiquitous but elusive. But so much is clear, the actual tiller or cultivator could hardly be called upon to make revenue payments in cash. The evidence is scanty, but what we know clearly indicates an utterly depressed condition of the country people.[22] As a Dutch observer noted about 1614, "When travelling through the country, I have often wondered whence so much money could be collected, for they live extremely poorly and meanly."[23] Even the growers of an important crop like indigo near the great center Agra were "constrained to sell to engrossers at very low prices for want of money to supply the needful."[24] The cultivator, then, appears to be generally unable to deal with the revenue demand by himself, nor can he have been an interesting target for the revenue authorities. So both "peasant" and administrator needed an intermediary class of financiers and merchants, such as the indigo engrossers, who had sufficient liquid capital at their disposal to handle the cash nexus. Although the sources have little but disparaging remarks to offer on merchants and moneylenders, it seems safe to infer that they actually were the pivot of the imperial enterprise.

That the sources nevertheless tend to ignore this class need not surprise us, since they stress the warrior-administrator's outlook and values. Generally speaking, the merchant is, from the point of view of agrarian society, a marginal figure, if he is not roundly deprecated as a dangerous interloper. Thus the ancient Indian book of statecraft, the *Arthaśāstra,* ranges the merchant with the "thieves known under other names" and describes him as a "thorn" in the body politic.[25] Possibly his pivotal importance made him even more suspect in the eyes of those who depended on him. On the other hand, the commercial class was far from being easily definable. The variety of its operations made it perfectly possible to classify the merchant and financier in other ways. His access to local or regional markets meant that his function was the marketing of the agrarian surplus. This enabled him to act as a source of credit and to "engage for the revenue." And this in turn was practically tantamount to land control. He could then quite naturally be labeled as a landholder, while conversely, the landholder had to have liquidity and credit at his disposal. Superior rights in land had by nature a commercial aspect, and we do indeed meet landholders of different denominations who at the same time had important commercial interests.[26] The fact, attested by sixteenth-century documents, that superior rights in land were a perfectly saleable commodity, also bears out the connection of landholding and commerce.[27]

By this route, the merchant and financier found his way into the bureaucracy to which he was anyhow indispensable. Tax collecting and "engaging for the revenue" look very much like the two faces of the same Janus—if indeed they were not identical—and we can readily understand the orders, which, as already noted, attempted to bypass the *'āmil,* or tax collector. As one mansabdār complained with characteristic literary flourish, "the boat of his jāgīr was floundering in the flood of misappropriations raised by his tempestuous 'āmils." And this was only a jāgīr; the vast imperial and provincial bureaucracy must have offered staggering opportunities to the "tempestuous." At any rate, whether tempestuous or not, the official tax collector needed to have the same financial expertise, knowledge of the district, and understanding of the market as the grain dealer and moneylender.

Even though the Mughals clearly strove to keep commercial interests and official administration apart, they badly needed the cooperation of these experts and they could hardly avoid recruiting them to the financial departments of their bureaucracy. Thus the repeated injunctions against the farming out of revenue rights seem to indicate that this was more of a practice than the sources want us to believe. Moreover, it is difficult to see how, for instance, the holders of land assignments *(jāgīrdār),* often posted at a great distance from their assigned lands, could manage them without leaving a great measure of freedom to their 'āmils. The question whether the actual arrangement was technically one of farming or not seems largely an academic one. In fact, the practice of farming out the collection of estate rents to groups of local financiers who provided for the management of the estate while being equally involved with the district administration through family connections seems to have remained a common practice in the nineteenth and even twentieth centuries.[28] We know the difficulties that the incipient English administration experienced on a far larger scale in the second half of the eighteenth century over the problem of divorcing commerce from administration.

So it cannot come as a surprise when on one hand we learn that local governors seem in practice to have been free to enter the market on their own initiative, while on the other hand, we see merchant community leaders in political roles, financing pretenders to imperial succession or negotiating political settlements. No less indicative are the fairly common instances of public authorities lending money to merchants and vice versa in the sixteenth and seventeenth centuries[29]—that is, long before the time of the empire's break-up. Nor was there a serious barrier preventing the merchant-financier from entering the ranks of the mansabdār nobility.[30] Even military roles came easily within his purview, since his operations would anyhow have acquainted him with the use of arms, both for the control of the revenue-paying estates and for providing protection to his transport.[31] The cash nexus made the combination of commercial and financial operations with land control on the one hand and official administrative, on occasion even military, functions on the other rather natural and unavoidable.

The point of all this is not, of course, to celebrate the period as one "of equal opportunities" and "careers open to talent." The essential point is that we should be wary of viewing the empire as a rigidly centralized and hierarchical bureaucratic structure rationally extracting and managing its agrarian resources. The Mughals certainly wanted it to be just that, but their imperial pyramid had to be built on the quicksands of personal networks with variously overlapping personnel and interests, which controlled the local and regional markets and thereby the surrounding agrarian tracts. It was these groups and networks that were in actual control of the sources of revenue on which the empire depended. Instead of controlling them from a commanding height, the Mughal, in order to get at the resources necessary for his survival, had to involve himself all the time in local affairs and had to stake his power in the ever-changing alignments of factions jostling for local and regional predominance. By the same token, local influence was free to encroach on the imperial center. The integrity of the whole was therefore in the intertwining and overlapping of interests competing for the distribution of power, rather than in the spectacular use of superior force, which moreover could all too easily lead to overextension. The system, then, was one of a "balancing of relative weakness," managed by conflict in which the Mughal could at best be a superior arbiter, arranging and rearranging the distribution of power by a judicious and sparing use of his resources.[32] Viewed in this perspective, the imposing pyramid of imperial power sags into a rather shapeless horizontal reality, formed by constantly shifting power configurations and governed by pervasive conflict.

## *5*

The resulting diffusion of power was not, however, mere confusion and chaos. The neat picture propounded by the sources, which opposes the peasant-producer and the warrior-administrator as the two poles of the empire, is broken in the middle by the operation of the cash nexus. But the same phenomenon can also offer us a vantage point for discerning a certain leading principle in the seemingly chaotic free-for-all. This principle would, as we saw, be hard to find in the formal administrative and military structure of the empire; rather, we find it in the movements of trade.

Though the imperial administration held on to an exhaustive organization of the total area claimed by the Mughal in nested territorial units—pargana, district, province—it would be misleading to view the empire as an integrated territorial whole, pushing its boundaries ever further into the subcontinent. Rather, we have to think of the empire in terms of strings of greater and smaller centers controlling their immediate hinterlands. These centers were the market towns, where the cash nexus found its natural solution. From these towns, the business communities could control the immediate agrarian hinterland, extract the marketable surplus, convert it into cash, and pay the revenue. These greater and smaller market centers did not exist in isolation. They were linked with each other by an extensive network of trade routes. In an ancient trading area like India, with its strategic position in the Indian Ocean and its overland connections with Western and Central Asia, important trade routes existed together with a well-developed system of long-distance transport and finance. "All nations bring coin and carry away commodities for the same; and this coin is buried in India and goeth out not," as an early English merchant succinctly put it.[33]

Rather than the actual control of vast territories, which anyhow had to be left to all manner of intermediaries, the leading principle of imperial power appears to have been the control of trade routes and the market towns along them. The emphasis on the protection of the roads and the principle that the officer in whose jurisdiction a robbery or theft had been committed had either to recover the stolen goods or pay compensation were obviously dictated by more than a simple concern for public order as an aim in itself.[34] The safety of the trade routes clearly was of vital importance to the empire. The remittances of revenue depended on the capacity of long-distance trade and finance for this essential service. The breaking away of provincial administrations and their becoming independent sultanates—as happened to the Delhi Sultanate—may well have been occasioned by severe imbalances in interregional commerce or the rerouting of trade rather than by purely military weakness. Conversely, the Mughal Empire's cohesion may have had the strength of interregional trade as its mainstay, since the revenue transmitted through the channels of interregional commerce was an important factor in financing this trade. That the Delhi Sultantate, like so many other Indian empires, had a history of repeated break-ups while the Mughal Empire did not would seem to be a tribute to the increased strength of interregional commerce, stimulated by the growth of overseas trade. The weakening of the Mughal Empire may, then, have been caused by the impossibility of controlling the sea lanes and forcing the seaborne trade to use the ports that it favored. The growing concentration on Calcutta in the eighteenth century, corresponding to a rerouting of trade and a falling-off of other trading areas, including the routes to Western and Central Asia, may have had more to do with the declining effectiveness of the empire than its military-administrative weakness.[35]

Admittedly, this line of reasoning raises more questions than this essay can even begin to answer. But it seems safe to assume that roads and their trade provided the basic framework of the empire. It was only through the intermediaries of the market towns along the trade routes that the cash nexus could be handled. This meant that the Mughal's effective power and authority—as distinct from mere ceremonial suzerainty to be invoked or disregarded at will—was virtually limited to the trading centers and their immediate hinterlands. As the Dutch Company merchant Pelsaert reported, the Mughal "is to be regarded as king of the plains and open roads only".[36] The expansion of the Mughal Empire was therefore as much a matter of extending control along the main routes as of developing lateral feeding roads and qasbahs in the further hinterlands.

By the same logic, the limited areas of effective control interconnected by the main and lateral roads left large interstices where the Mughal had to content himself with, at best, a nominal overlordship, leaving the management of affairs to the local *magnati et potentes*. That the latter were either recognized as tributary chiefs or, if they could not be made to agree to a tributary arrangement known as rebels and robbers was, of course, a fine but largely theoretical distinction. In practice, the personnel of both categories could and did change from one to the other with disconcerting ease.

Thus Pelsaert, after stating that the Mughal's rule only extended over the plains and open roads, continues: "for in many places you can travel only with a strong body of men or on payment of heavy tolls to rebels. The whole country is enclosed and broken up by many mountains and the people who live in, or beyond the mountains know nothing of any king or of Jahangir; they recognize only their rājās who are very numerous. Jahangir, whose name implies that he grasps the whole world, must therefore be regarded as ruling no more than half the dominions which he claims."

This would not have been so serious a limitation if the situation could have been stabilized in a durable manner. But, of course, that would have been too much to expect, and it stands to reason that the activities of the "rebels" in the interstitial areas were primarily directed at the trade routes, where sizable gains, ranging from simple plunder to regular transit dues, could be made.[37] Tolls and transit dues, though certainly an object of imperial regulation, were levied not only by "rebels," but also by tributary rājās and even imperial officers, whether authorized to do so or not. An instructive case is provided by the transit dues levied by the rājā of Dhaita—not a "rebel"—on the road from Surat to Burhanpur. When the English complained on the grounds of the exemption from transit dues granted to them by the emperor, they were made to understand that the emperor could not interfere. The interesting point is that this was not so much a matter of the rājā's autonomy as it was of the tributary arrangement, for, as the emperor somewhat lamely but understandably explained, it was out of the transit dues that the rājā paid his tribute.[38] Obviously, the empire was not a territorial unity, but this case shows the degree to which the emperor not only acquiesced in, but depended on, local situations and arrangements that went against the grain of imperial regulation. Quite apart from tributary rājās, there were also cases of villages forcibly exacting transit dues, even within a few miles of the imperial center, Agra. Even worse is reported by Pelsaert, who mentions the rājā of Rajpipla's forces pillaging up to and inside Surat. Nor were the immediate neighborhoods of even greater centers, such as Ahmadabad, Agra, Delhi, and Lahore, spared the inroads of "thieves and robbers," coming "in force by night and day like open enemies"[39]—all this in the twenties of the sixteenth century, that is, long before there was any question of an impending breakdown of the empire.

The point to be stressed is not the deficiencies of public order—the situation seems to have compared favorably with that in other areas, for instance, the Deccan sultanates—but that observers seem to have taken such disturbances as in the nature of things, as a fact of life. The basic structure, then, to which one had to adapt oneself, was the precarious balance of "regulation" tracts round the market towns and uncontrolled interstitial areas with their numerous rājās beyond the Mughal's effective grasp. Or, in Mughal terms, revenue paying, or *ra'īyatī,* areas as against the "rebellious" ones known as *mawās*.[40] Since the Mughal could not hope definitively to subdue the mawās, he had to settle for an uneasy and constantly changing balance of forces.

## 6

In this context, we can perhaps better understand the problems involved in the dual aim of conquest and careful management of already controlled areas. As already pointed out, the precariousness of the agrarian resource base often made conquest a likely or even unavoidable proposition. But we also saw that conquest could well turn into a self-defeating venture. The Mughals must have been perfectly aware of this risk. That they nevertheless gave prominence to conquest seems to have another reason. This is that there was not just an external frontier, which one could either choose to round off and secure or to push further out. The real frontier was a ragged and shifting internal one, dividing ra'īyatī and mawās. On the one hand, control of the main trade routes had to be followed through to their end. Stopping at a particular point, say half-way across the Deccan, would not only impair the use of the routes, which would then depend on what happened at the end beyond the empire's control, but, what is more important, uncontrolled forces would find sanctuary there and be able to interfere with traffic even on the Mughal side. On the other hand, with the extension of control along the trade routes, the interstitial areas grew *pari passu*. Both faces of the dilemma were amply demonstrated by Aurangzeb's experiences in conquering the Deccan, but by the same token, it seems doubtful whether he had much of a real choice between continuing his costly campaigns or limiting his efforts to the areas conquered earlier.[41]

The problem showed its sharpest edge in Aurangzeb's campaigns, but we may doubt whether this was simply a matter of foreign conquest that one could decide for or against as one saw fit. The problem was essentially the same as that of the inner frontier. The inner frontier was not, of course, a more-or-less fixed line but consisted of wide stretches of area weaving round the trade arteries. In these stretches, competing groups of warriors, traders, and landholders—categories which, as we saw, easily overlapped to the point of being indistinguishable—converged and struggled for control, sometimes coming dangerously near to the main centers. To understand the nature of these areas, it may be useful to recall the classical Indian opposition between the areas, or patches, of settled agriculture and the wastes surrounding them, each with its own way of life and institutions. While family and caste were at home in the agricultural village, the wastes were the home of the warrior and his war band. The two, though opposite and perpetually in conflict—latent or patent—with each other, were not mutually exclusive. People from the villages would join the warriors in the wastes, while the warrior and his retainers might either be called into the village for protection against other warriors or force their protection upon the village. Agriculturalists would try to extend their cultivation to the wastes, which they also needed for grazing their cattle, while warriors would strive for control of the settled areas and their productivity.[42] Most important, however, was the fact that the connections between the areas of settled agriculture and between them and the greater urban centers ran through the wastes.

Thus, for instance, an early Rajput chronicle of the great Rathor house relates how an ancestor, Vīrama, after joining two leading members of the inimical Johiyo clan, started a feud against his elder brother, was expelled, made attacks on the "imperial road," fought and dodged the troops of the sultan, and finally, combining again with his two Johiyo allies, "went and unyoked his carts at Vaderana. And the Johiyos gave Vīrama the fourth part (of the profits of) the road." Then, finding new allies through marriage, he "started to devastate the territory of the Johiyos and to seize the whole (profit of) the road," till Vīrama at last was killed with 140 of his men, as was the leading Johiyo, when the latter retaliated by devastating the villages controlled by Vīrama. And so the story of feuds, alliances, establishing and losing control over roads and villages, founding and attacking towns and principalities went on.[43] Though this particular episode relates to the fifteenth century, it may well epitomize the inner frontier under the Mughals.

As will be clear from its similarity with the small-scale situation of the village and the surrounding wastes, the inner frontier was ubiquitous. But it was, of course, weightiest around the main through routes, which attracted the greatest density of interested parties, especially bands of warriors, and a correspondingly high level of competition and conflict. These areas amounted in many cases to what might be called "frontier marches",[44] which included both revenue-paying regulation tracts around the market centers and uncontrolled areas in ever-changing balance. Now cultivation and regulation were extended, then again sedition took over, whole tracts reverting to mawās status and giving shelter to "malefactors" and "non-chiefs."

The only thing that the Mughals could do to reduce these inner marches to a modicum of order was to involve themselves in local affairs and stake their power in the ongoing tussle for local control—an activity that tallied particularly well with their origin and ideology of a war band. The time-honored and, in fact, only way to do this successfully was to make use of the pervasive conflict between the different participants and to enter into alliances with a number of them, so as to control the others. That is, in many ways they had to act, not so much as powerful overlords, although this was certainly their intention, but rather as partners in the affairs of the inner marches.

The pattern for these arrangements was set from the start by the Mughal-

Rajput alliance, which made the empire in effect a joint venture. This meant that the Mughals had to tie some of the great Rajput houses into their system by establishing asymmetric marriage alliances with them, which virtually made the Mughal into the highest ranking Rajput, and by giving them high mansabdār ranks with the corresponding remunerations and court privileges. This particular alliance was a notable success. But the arrangement had as its corollary that many of the important roads running south from the Delhi-Agra area had to be left in the control of Rajput chiefs.

The direct route between Surat and Agra via Ahmadabad, which ran through the territories of tributary Rajput chiefs, was so beset with dangers and exactions that usually the longer route via Burhanpur was preferred, although the latter was far from free of risks. Moreover, the rules of the game, namely, making use of and involving oneself in the existing factional alignments, implied that only a part of the Rajputs were effectively tied into the imperial system, while the Mughal had to content himself with, at best, tributary arrangements with the others. In fact, the situation was even more complicated, for factionalism did not stop at the level of the chiefs of the great Rajput houses. It was not unusual for their sons and relatives, when they felt they had been wronged, to ''take to the fields'' with their retainers and start harassing their chiefs till a settlement was reached.[45] The latter feature could, of course, work both against and in favor of the Mughals, but in order to exploit it, they had to involve themselves in these dissensions. What is worse, involvement meant that dissension could all too easily spread to the Mughal side as well. So the careful balance between the limited capacity to establish and keep up imperial regulation and the threatening forces of the mawās essentially depended on the exploitation of local dissension and making alliances with certain of the contenders—Rajputs, Marathas, and others, as the case might be.

The constant rearticulation of the balance demanded that the Mughals most of the time had to commit their forces in local situations, sometimes becoming submerged in them to the point where imperial officers were allied with ''rebels'' and vice-versa. The pervasiveness of the conflict of the inner frontier was such that they could often hardly do otherwise. Mawās areas were often, and on purpose, included in their jāgīrs. Since the forces of the imperial or provincial centers were either already engaged in particular campaigns or otherwise dispersed in local involvements, extra support was hard to get, so that the imperial officers, both in their jāgīrs and in their posts, were left to fend for themselves as best they could. They therefore had to adapt themselves to the ways of the ''marches.'' There they had to tussle cheek-by-jowl with their opposite numbers, known in the imperial idiom as ''malefactors,'' ''rebels,'' and ''non-chiefs'' or as landholders *(zamīndārs)* and officers if they had somehow obtained an imperial sanction.[46] In other words, imperial officers had to operate in the same way as those they purported to rule, intertwining their military and administrative functions with financial and landholding interests in a situation where imperial pretensions could easily become more of a burden than a support.

When viewed in this perspective, it seems somewhat superfluous to look for specific internal reasons to explain the decline and fall of the Mughal Empire. Even in its hey-day, it rested on a precarious balance of forces round the inner frontier. A breakdown was always just round the corner, but the system could just as well continue indefinitely. It was, moreover, precisely this fluidity that gave the Mughal Empire its remarkable resilience and durability, even under the pressure of overextension and adversity, for the working of the precarious balance and the corresponding diffusion of power meant that there was no single, readily definable point where the imperial system could be attacked and defeated. In fact it never was. It was simply overarched and finally replaced by a completely different dispensation.

## *7*

After this lengthy disquisition, it is time to return to the theme of expansion and reaction. But before we can speak about a reaction, or even before we can ask whether there was a clear-cut reaction at all, a few words must be said about the way expansion took place. In the first place, it is important to note that there was no strategic level or center where the expansionist forces could come to grips with the Mughal system in a decisive manner, even if they had wanted to do so. But except for a single and ill-prepared venture to start a diminutive empire of their own, the English, like their European competitors, did not want to do so. Instead they desperately tried to stick exclusively to their commercial role. When they were finally forced to give up this stance and started to intervene in India's politics, it was not because of the empire's weakness. Primarily it was a by-product of inter-European competition for control of the sea lanes. When this happened, the English had to combine their commercial operations with military activities and land control. In other words, the English—following the French lead—became partners in the classical game of the inner frontier, to the point where the Company Bahādūr obtained, as provincial dīwān, the revenue rights of Bengal, and Clive became a high-ranking imperial noble with a resounding Persian title. Although it presented the somewhat jarring picture of a mercantile company going into agrarian land control, and on a dangerously large scale at that, this type of expansion hardly called for an Indian reaction. On the contrary, it was the English who reacted by adapting, not without enthusiasm, to Indian ways and circumstances. The game was played on Indian terms, even though the English generally could call the shots.

However, after what has been said about the precarious balance that the inner frontier implied, it is clear that the English venture could all too easily lead to overextension and play havoc with the company's finances—as indeed happened during the first decade or so after Plassey. Essentially, the choices before the English were to involve themselves and their resources at the local level, to manipulate and arbitrate competition and conflict—as the Mughals had been forced to do—or to withdraw as far as possible from local conflict in order to pool and reserve the company's power and resources. Since the first course of action—especially in the form of illegal private trade by company servants using the company's power and privileges—had proved disastrous, it was the second that imposed itself. This found its clearest expression in the Permanent Settlement of 1793. Whatever this momentous decree may have done for the introduction of full private ownership of land protected by law, its main thrust was the reservation of British power and of the use of force, and it reflected the British refusal to get involved in local affairs. This meant that the state, now a public realm, was decisively set apart from the web of competing social forces, which were left to cope with their local situations, as many new-style landowners found to their grief.

It took, of course, a considerable time before the policy could be fully effective. For some time, the company still had its own frontier areas, such as the semi-independent Oudh kingdom, where British merchants and even official personnel, together with their Indian partners, continued to dabble profitably in trade and land control in the traditional way.[47] But compared with the Mughal system, the new dispensation was an unprecedented departure from tradition. Where the Mughals had been forced to involve themselves in local affairs and conflicts to the point of submergence, the English could extricate themselves from them and could even pay the price of leaving a possible surplus in the hands of the landholders. Such a step the Mughals would never have been able to take, not because of indiscriminate greed, but because the undrained surplus would have strengthened the forces of dissension and aggravated the pervasive problem of the inner frontier. The English, on the other hand, could afford to do this, since theirs was not an exclusively agrarian empire but a worldwide trading network with its power center safely outside India and soon to be backed by the industrial revolution.

Nevertheless, the British Indian regime was far from being a laissez-faire proposition. It had to and did pursue vigorous policies of pacification, regulation, education, and public works. Apart from that, even while following a policy of reservation and withdrawal, the government could not ignore Indian society. The British Raj, like any colonial regime, was perpetually pulled in opposite directions by the need to leave the ruled-over society alone and the equally pressing need to deal with it in an effective way.

However, not only the rules of the game, but the game itself had changed. One might say that the traditional game was the balance of the inner frontier, which demanded "horizontal" involvement and dispersion; the new one, on the other hand, involved an equally precarious balance, but now between "vertical" involvement and withdrawal. Or, more plainly, where the Mughal was concerned with nobles, chiefs, "malefactors," and "nonchiefs" in their comprehensive capacities as leaders of men controlling local networks, the British Indian government only recognized them as isolated individuals holding narrowly defined legal rights of land ownership. With the Mughals they had been little kings and partners in empire, in the eyes of the English they were simply landowners, albeit sometimes big ones. Even when the Great Rebellion of 1857—in fact, not a reaction, but a chaotic resurgence of the sprawling inner frontier—had dramatically demonstrated the need to give them special consideration, the English could do no better than to classify them arbitrarily as landholders whose estates paid 5,000 rupees and upward per year in land revenue, and the modern association that was meant to give substance to this category never really came to life.[48]

This, however, did in no way mean that Indian society was destroyed as the English, taken aback at their own innovative daring, were often prone to think. The fact is that their mode of operation, however striking a departure from tradition it was, precluded such drastic results. The new dispensation implied that in order to preserve itself from the run-away effects of involvement in society the government must refuse to work with influence networks and their leaders and only deal with categories and legal abstractions. The British Indian government could only view society in terms of census categories and of nested territorial units, from the revenue village upward—incidentally creating considerable misunderstanding about the concepts of caste and village. In other words, British rule was a thoroughly bureaucratic one—the ideal first of the Mughals, who had, however, been betrayed by circumstances.

Now bureaucracies may be utterly irritating and deeply disturbing, but they cannot by themselves change society. Although the British Indian government increasingly widened and deepened its dealings with Indian society, it only did so by reducing total situations to abstract models, which were amenable to impersonal rules and regulations. For instance, shifts of rights in land from indebted landlords to their creditors—a disturbing phenomenon to the administration, which feared that it might result in sedition and violence, or rather, more deeply, felt it to be a threat to its static view of society—led to the construction of agricultural castes so that legislation preventing alienation of land from one category to the other could be devised and applied. That such categories were not too well-founded in reality is, of course, clear from what we have already seen of the unavoidable interlocking of landholding, commerce, finance, and, as modern additions, journalism and law practice. Local society could, of course, find its way toward accommodation with the bureaucratic heaven and its less heavenly minions. But the important point is that government action was directed at specific, abstractly defined cases, not at the fluid, multidimensional web of relations that was the substance of society and was for the same reason studiously avoided by the administration. Actual influence networks could sometimes be destroyed by bureaucratic action, but then there were others to take their place without a change in the social system being effected. Thus, for instance, in a study of the social consequences of extensive land transfers in the Benares region, Bernard Cohn, answering the question, What happened to the dispossessed? concluded that "the overall answer may well be that nothing happened".[49] On the other hand, the bureaucratic grid and procedures may have added a new but hardly innovative way for fighting the old fights.[50]

It seems, then, that the respective modes of operation of the British Indian government and of Indian society were, not merely different, but worlds apart from each other. They could and did impinge on each other, the government by specifically directed actions and Indians by claiming government support. But they had their being in different worlds. Encounters remained incidental, limited to specific activities and only for the duration of the activity. For persistent contacts and a broadly based confrontation there was no room. And this may well be the reason for the impression of "a Dasehra duel between two hollow statues locked in motionless and simulated combat," life entering into the duel only when at last forces within Indian society itself came to grips with each other.

I would argue, then, that the episode of European expansion did not evoke a consistent and directly related reaction—except for the reception of yet another classical medium, the English language, in India's impressive range of literary idioms. Should we then resign ourselves to the mockingly hollow echoes of Forster's Malabar Caves? Although they might seem a fitting epitaph to the era of expansion, what actually happened proves otherwise.

## *8*

What happened is, briefly and prosaically, this. Instead of obtuse stagnation, or the equally popular notion of a vulnerable arcadia, Indian society showed once again its remarkable resilience. The public domain of the state had been taken out and set apart from society, but this set Indian society free to develop new potentialities. The withdrawal of power and resources which had fed and strengthened the interaction and overlap of society's innumerable local and regional segments meant at first that Indian society lost much of its diffuse but effective coherence. It became more parochial and fragmented even though the government covered all of the subcontinent. However, the corollary of the government's aloofness was that society was left with more resources than before, which, moreover, increased considerably over the nineteenth century, and these resources stimulated the development of new linkages.[51] The government, by creating channels for its actions and allocations, set certain cadres for these developments. The most conspicuous was the rigid hierarchy of territorial units. Present-day "regionalism" may owe as much to this circumstance as to India's variegated cultural history. But the government could not contain, let alone guide, these developments and was rather prone to panic when confronted with unforeseen results threatening to overflow the neat bureaucratic grid of units, categories, and rules.[52] The important question was, however, not whether the government could contain the growing impetus of new developments and supralocal linkages, but whether Indian society could devise the means to regulate itself on a wider scale than the local community. Briefly, the main problem was that of supralocal, universalistic authority, for authority on an all-India scale had been reserved by the government and was administered in bureaucratic fashion, impinging on but not guiding society.

Now universalistic authority transcending local society—or any actual society for that matter—had always been there in specifically Indian form in the person of the renouncer, who stood outside society and therefore was the ideal arbiter and consensus-maker.[53] When the increased possibilities and resources in society tended to uncontrollable growth and pervasive conflict passed far beyond local society, India naturally had to fall back on the institution and transcendent values of renunciation for guidance. It is hardly surprising, then, that when developments had gained momentum in the interbellum period, the acknowledged leader should have been a Gandhi, who saw himself and was acknowledged as a classical exemplar of renunciation—however enigmatic and contradictory the Gandhi phenomenon may have appeared, first of all to his own compatriots.

His achievement had little to do with his usual image as a not-too-decisive preacher and social worker. His aim was nothing less than the reorganization of Indian society on the universalistic basis of the renunciatory ideal. His spectacular noncooperation and civil disobedience actions were not so much directed against the British regime as they were aimed at national unity under the aegis of the renouncer's ultimate authority. This meant that national unity was to be realized by an ultramundane "renunciatory" society which required its adherents to give up en masse their state-supported positions and distinctions. For all its dramatic expressiveness, this was hardly a viable proposition. Nor could it aim at overthrowing the government. Insofar as it could be viewed as open rebellion, it could only be so in the way of a temporary *secessio in montem sacrum,* leaving state and government in their place and ready to arrive at a negotiated reconciliation—as time and again happened. It is therefore perhaps not fortuitous that Gandhi's actions had the same specificity as bureaucratic state action. As bureaucratic action was geared to apply specific rules, so Gandhi's actions were aimed at breaking specific rules, for instance, the government salt monopoly. But all the same, they remained within the overall conventions of the government. They were not meant to be formally "seditious," and the road to negotiated settlement was expressly left open.

Here, then, it would seem, was the real issue, namely, to develop a workable relationship between state and society. This could obviously not be achieved by the dramatic but ephemeral noncooperation and civil disobedience actions. What was needed was a lasting organizational framework for supralocal, national unity, a framework that could function as an effective counterpart to the state. To this end Gandhi reorganized the Indian National Congress in successive stages during the interbellum period, keeping it attuned to the devolutional reforms of the state.[54] Though this organizational work was totally unspectacular and therefore easily overlooked, it may well be that this was the field where Gandhi's leadership showed its most important and lasting results.

The Congress was not a movement, still less a party, but an all-India arena for handling the pervasive conflicts of particularistic society. It did not aim at eliminating particularism—an impossible task—but at accommodating it in a universalistic setting. While it accommodated conflict, it took care of national consensus as well. Now Congress had since its beginnings in the eighties of the last century laid great stress on producing unanimous resolutions, to the point of simply skipping important but controversial points. But consensus enforced by the renouncer's transcendent authority was altogether a different matter, as the concerned Indian parties found to their discomfort, for instance, in the heated controversy over the separate vote for untouchables, when Gandhi started on a fast unto death to force consensus. But even more important was the fact that Gandhi practically transferred his authority to the consensus-making center of the Congress, which during the last decade of the British regime came to be known by journalists as "the high command." With that, Gandhi's role virtually ended and he could be safely enshrined in India's mythology.

In this way, the dual system of postindependence Indian came into being. On the one hand, there is the government with its widespread professional and rigidly hierarchical bureaucracy administering impersonal laws and regulations; on the other hand, the essentially horizontal arena of Congress—the low degree of professionalization of its organization is significant—taking care of interest groups and their intensely personal conflicts, while at the same time handling national consensus. Though it was only developed in the interbellum period, it is strangely reminiscent of the horizontal, factional system of management by conflict that was both the bane and blessing of the Mughal dispensation. The dual structure was comparatively easy to maintain as long as the English were there and Congress was barred from the government apex. When Congress had to take over the central government, the precarious balance between state and society became intensely problematic.[55] The horizontal arena increasingly encroached on the vertical organization and process of government, whose bureaucracy had before independence already lost much of its celebrated "steel frame" character. It may well be that new formulas will have to be developed to handle the balance.[56]

The point I want to stress is that the new dimension added as a result of Western expansion enabled Indian society seriously to attempt, however partially and ephemerally, long-standing universalistic ideals that so far had been beyond its grasp, such as Gandhi's attempt to realize the old ideal of outerworldly harmony in the modern political terms of national unity. That ideals when brought to earth from the safety of their ultramundane heaven seldom make for happy endings is, of course, all too well known. Indeed, the story given here in brief is one of intense conflict and unpleasantness. The most dramatic chapter was the break between Hindus and Muslims. Whatever recent and future research on the train of events leading up to the partition catastrophe teaches us,[57] it seems clear that the specific form of universal authority propounded by a Gandhi could not be easily accepted by conscientious Muslims, who were also forced to restate in modern terms the implications of Islam for universalist authority. Whether the break was unavoidable or merely the result of a series of quirks and accidents is hardly a valid question. But the dramatic break does show that the introduction of universalistic ideals into reality is beset with unforeseen and explosive risks. Unhappily, these seem to be the price of reaching out for new horizons.

To conclude: the concept of a reaction to something alien can be better replaced by that of symbiosis—a symbiosis between old, established, particularistic, and comparatively risk-free modes of operation and organization on the one hand and the risky new dimension that promises the realization of equally old, established, universalistic ideals. The symbiosis is obviously an uneasy one, turning as it does on incompatibility. The essential point is, however, that it steadily grows and develops new forms. This symbiosis was brought about by Western expansion, which nevertheless did not and could not share in it. Not because it was Western, but because it would not involve itself in the problems of the relationships.

Does this mean that there is only scope for ethnocentric history? The answer would seem to be that the situation is not peculiar to former colonial countries. It is a worldwide problem that is usually and confusingly known as "modernization." It was and is experienced in Europe as in other parts of the world. Perhaps we may therefore expect that the comparative perspective will overcome the fragmented landscape of ethnocentricity.

# 12 Caste, Village, and Indian Society

## *1*

Who says India says caste, or so it seems. The first problem is, of course, what precisely one is saying when invoking caste and, second, whether this will give a sufficient basis for analyzing Indian society. If one considers that caste purports to an exhaustive ordering of Indian society in exclusive groups, the answer to the latter would indeed seem to be affirmative. If one further considers that caste should account for both the socioeconomic aspects of a society, such as division of labor, and the religious or ideological ones, it may seem superfluous to try and look elsewhere. Caste, then, in the eyes of the observer, is the hallmark of Indian society. However, this has not always been the case. Although particular features, especially restrictions regarding commensality, connubium, and means of subsistence, did not fail to draw the somewhat puzzled attention of foreign observers, the Portuguese word *caste* for a long time kept its general, nontechnical meaning, remaining interchangeable with words like "tribe," "race," or "nation."[1] It was only in the nineteenth century that it acquired its exclusive and specific meaning to the point where it even could be considered by some as an Indian word with a (spurious) Indian derivation.[2] It was only then that caste began to loom large, until it became in our century a shorthand expression for Indian society at large: Indian society is caste.

Clearly our systematic knowledge and understanding of the caste phenomenon has made significant advances since the last century, but there remains a nagging doubt. Has not the attention given to caste—so striking for the Western observer—somewhat narrowed our view? The point is that one can study the relevant Indian texts, as well as the voluminous data and secondary literature about caste, without having to recognize the overarching fact that we are dealing with a peasant society and economy and all that this entails. For that reason we turned to the study of the village. In the village,

This essay is based on a paper read at the Fourteenth World Congress of Sociology, Uppsala, July, 1978.

both caste and facts of peasant life should find their natural junction. Thus there appeared, especially in the fifties and sixties of this century, a flood of village monographs. However, these monographs seem in the main to reflect the dominant concern with caste rather than furthering our understanding of Indian peasant society. Moreover, the carefully constructed caste rankings more often than not are at variance with the actual relationships in the village, and the brahmins as such often do not fit in at all. Dominant castes are seen at ceremonial occasions to eat—that is, sitting in the same row—with their low-ranking servants. Members of other peasant castes in the same village keep to themselves and refuse to participate in these exchanges, breaking the unity and cohesiveness of the ranking order.[3] Apparently we have to recognize two different orders of facts that impinge on but refuse to be assimilated to each other. And so our understanding remains stuck between the twin poles of caste and the village that have come to monopolize our view of Indian society.

As with caste, the vogue of the village as a predominant focus of Indian sociology seems to be a product of the nineteenth century. It owes its rise to the pointed statements of influential and in many ways remarkable English administrators in the first decade of the last century. Here we encounter the romantic idealization of the village as a "little republic," all but completely self-sufficient, impervious to outside influence, and lasting "where nothing else lasts".[4] The theme has been reiterated ever since to an extent that borders on ritual incantation. In due time, it even became an emblem of the nationalist movement—the true India that lives in its villages—and the starting point of legislation formalizing village autonomy *(pancāyatī rāj)*. Ideologically, the notion of the "village community" with its suggestion of egalitarianism, primitive democracy, and pristine harmony has, of course, much to recommend itself, especially when set off against the hierarchic and undemocratic notions of caste. However, neither the vogue of village or caste seems to derive from any real Indian arrangement, but rather from the needs of the modern bureaucratic state as it was introduced at the beginning of the last century.

In contradistinction to the strongly personal and particularistic nature of the old regime, the new rule stressed a universally applicable system of rules and regulations. Where the old regime had been intimately involved with overlapping and shifting networks of various right holders, their dependants, and rivals to the point of being submerged in such networks, the new dispensation was calculated to create a distance between government and society.[5] Standard expressions like "falling upon the neck and importuning" the powerful for help—in spite of the obvious element of criticism—suggest a personal proximity that was unthinkable under the new dispensation. One simply does not "fall upon the neck" of the Rule of Law. Though this change did not alter Indian society, which indeed was very much left to its own devices, it did bring about a fundamentally different view of society; or rather, where no view of society as a separate, objective entity had existed before, there now developed an official view for the purpose of dealing with society from a distance. This official view was an exhaustive grid of narrowly defined categories covering the whole of society and enabling the state to apply its impersonal rules and regulations rationally.

This involved two things. In the first place, the whole of the territory had to be uniformly mapped out in neatly separated units, which could not take cognizance of the multidimensional and widely stretched out networks and interests. Here the concept of the village as an autonomous unit came into its own. The "little republic" marvellously filled and legitimized the bureaucratic need for a well-defined basic unit. This took care of territory. Second, the people had to be categorized and counted as well. The inescapably obvious answer to this was caste. Irrespective of the manifold and significant complications of intercaste relationships, the concept of caste was hardened by administration, law courts, and especially the census into a system of tight compartments, each stereotyped by its customs, beliefs, attitudes, means of subsistence, governing institutions, and other attributes. Like the "village republic," each caste came to be seen as a separate world complete in itself.

This dual pigeonholing effort had the added advantage of conceptually separating land and people under the two grids of village and caste. Instead of rights in land being subsumed in the relationships between people, land and people could now be separately dealt with. The link between them was to be provided by a new concept of a single-stranded connection between the individual owner and his exclusive property.

Thus it would seem that the dual focus of caste and village does not derive its predominance from the realities of Indian society, but primarily from the modus operandi of the modern state, which had to view these realities through a bureaucratic prism. This may also explain the hold of village and caste over our view of Indian society, for it was the modern state that everybody—colonial administrator, reformer, or nationalist politician—wanted. Whether one favored autocratic or democratic forms was hardly relevant. Once state and society were conceptually distanced from each other, the prismatic official view, dissolving reality into neatly defined entities, imposed itself. Even the social anthropologists, detached but naturally on the look-out for primary units and categories, had to follow suit, their main concern being how to unite the two foci.

This had another unfortunate consequence, namely, the notion of Indian immobilism and stagnation. Was not caste a religion-based and therefore unchangeable institution and was not the village perennial, lasting where nothing else lasts? It was precisely this quality of supposedly unchanging stability that had recommended caste and village to the bureaucracy. The obstinate "tradition" of caste and village was then no tradition at all, but a consequence of the modern state, which needed immutable basic entities for its own regulating purposes. Paradoxically, whenever the carefully devised construct ran aground on the realities of Indian society, which kept blurring, overflowing, and generally subverting the neat dividing lines in true Schweikian manner, the resulting confusion tended to be blamed on the benighted traditionality of caste and village attitudes. The dichotomy of state and society implied that leadership for change, development, and the millennium devolved on the state, which had precisely for this purpose developed its unchanging system of categories, institutions, and regulations.

## 2

All this, of course, does not mean that village and caste do not exist in reality. But if we want to obtain a clear view of Indian society, we will have to free ourselves from the dominant hold of the modern official definition of village and caste. One way of doing this is to look at the society before the introduction of the modern state. Although research on this point is still in the beginning stages, sufficient is known for us to try to discern some of the principles of Indian society undistorted by the overlay of the modern official view.[6] Here, then, we do find the village as the nucleus of agrarian production and taxation—the starting point of the Anglo-Indian notion of the all but autonomous and self-sufficient "little republic." But what is immediately apparent is precisely the lack of autonomy and proud self-sufficiency. The village appears embedded in a complicated and wide-stretched network of personal rights, holdings, and prestations that passes far beyond the village boundaries and makes the notion of village autarchy untenable.

This state of affairs seems to obtain from the time of a village's founding. An example is found in the report of an English official investigating at the time of the English takeover of the Western Deccan (1818) the administrative structure of the previous regime:

> In an old account of the village Wing (Vāngī) . . . it is stated that "during the management of the Nubeeyar of the Koolburga Sultanate there was neither a division of the fields nor of the bounds of the village, the plains being covered with grass and the occupation of the people the feeding of cattle, for which a fixed sum was exacted . . . . During the management of the Bureadus (Barīd Shāhīs of Bīdar, 1487–1609) and in the administration of the black and white Khojas (ministers) the village bounds were fixed, portions of land were given to particular persons, whose names were registered and a rent was established" and then there follows a list of their fields.[7]

This quotation suggests that, far from being a spontaneous, grass-roots move, the founding of villages is a large-scale operation of converting waste lands into arable. It does not involve only simple cultivators but powerful men of substance—such as the Khojas mentioned and other state officers—who have the means and influence to bring in the necessary people, divide the fields, and fix the boundaries. It is these men of substance who as de-facto sharers in the realm constitute the state. The process of state formation under the old regime—in this case under the Barīd Shāhī Sultanate of Bīdar—is the settling of villages by the powerful for turning waste into arable and appropriating the agricultural surplus. Fixing, allocating, and registering portions of land and their holders is therefore practically synonymous with "establishing a rent," as the quotation has it. This means that the state is directly involved in and dispersed throughout the countryside and its settled villages.[8] Conversely, the village appears at its outset to be shot through with all manner of outside interests that far transcend its boundaries and tie it into a widespread network of exploitative and distributional relationships, which cannot but reflect themselves in the inner organization of the village.[9]

In this connection, a related point should be noted. Not only are rights, tax shares, holdings, and even offices such as headmenships fractionized to an often extraordinary degree, but, as appears from the extant documentation, many of these fractional rights of diverse description are held by men of substance, who belong to the wider context and who secure in this way strategic footholds in a wide range of localities. The state—that is, the powerful men who constitute it—is in this way everywhere present and achieves the proximity that we already noticed and that the modern state can only view as next door to corruption. Indeed, the village can be described as a nexus of rights that, far from being closed toward outside powers and their agents, is "the institutionally permissive means" whereby these powers directly take part in its inner life and organization.[10]

There is still a persistent notion of the local headmen, who are fondly fabled to form the real and unchanging backbone of the old regime polity, safely cantoned in their "little republics" and turning their back to the wider polity beyond the limits of their jurisdictions. However, the people who really count clearly are not strictly local men, but those who accumulate widely dispersed fractional rights—(part-)headmanships, tax-free or taxed fields, tax shares, tolls—in a variety of localities. In fact, their power can be measured as much by the aggregate of rights as by the geographical extent of their dispersion. The corollary of this is that the rights and holdings of the powerful tend to intermingle to the point where these men are practically at each other's doorsteps in the localities, thus making the notion of the closed village community even more illusory (but giving the locals more room for maneuvering in and out of the village context). The local headman, by contrast, is small fry indeed, distinctly vulnerable and in danger of having sooner or later to sell part or whole of his headmanship to a more powerful man.

The interpenetration of rights and holdings is abundantly attested by the surviving documentation.[11] For our purpose, the conventional idiom in which these dealings are expressed is particularly interesting. The fact that the proceedings often boil down to a sale of rights under pressure of indebtedness and distress—or even, we may surmise, a measure of duress—is not veiled or glossed over, but it is embedded in a language that stresses "brotherhood": "As we are now two brothers in the office of muqaddamī (headmanship), you shall be the third brother and we will equally enjoy all the rights, privileges etc. of the office and perform the duties"; "he fell upon your neck begging of you to become his brother and received 200 rupees and a mare, for which he gave you his third share of the muqaddamī"; or again, "and of his third share he had given three parts to the above-mentioned Powar (a well-known powerful family), making him his brother." The purchase of a share in a hereditary right is not viewed as an incidental market activity but as establishing a permanent and comprehensive relationship of brotherhood. The sharing brotherhood also is the institutional form for resolving conflict, integrating the contending parties into a corporate unity and thus restoring the wholeness (instead of excluding one of the contenders): "Formerly you damaged and injured the muqaddamī; we now have made you our brother and so let it be."[12] Viewed in this way, the parcelling out of rights and even offices is not a matter of mere atomization, but the means for recombining the actors and restoring the wholeness of society inside and outside the village.

Another frequent and telling expression is that of "eating" a hereditary right: "For ages past our ancestors have eaten the muqaddamī of (the) village".[13] The metaphor is a classical and well-known one, especially with regard to rulers who have a natural right to "eat" their subjects, the rights of the husband over his wife, or the king's on the earth.[14] Here, however, the emphasis is on the exclusive and irrevocable nature of the connection between the holder of the right and its object. Through its "eating," the object or right is integrated with its holder.[15] The metaphor is full of meaning in Indian culture, where always much thought has been given to exchanges of food and the permissibility or otherwise of acceptance.[16]

In this connection, the distinction between sharing and exchange seems to be relevant. Sharing food and other goods among brothers is essentially different from exchange. The difference will be immediately evident when we consider that brothers do not as a rule exchange sisters and daughters (though they may share the same wife, as the Pāṇḍava brothers did). In sharing, nothing is passed from one partner to the other. Every sharer knows the dish, his part in it and when to dip in; there are no uncertainties and no further arrangements are necessary once the rules have been agreed upon.

The relationship is a permanently fixed and irreversible one. Relationships based on exchange, on the other hand, may be equally permanent, but there always is an element of built-in uncertainty and instability, for the exchange relationship is based on reciprocity. While the sharers ''eat'' their portions simultaneously so that there are no scores to be settled afterward, the reciprocity of exchange is based on settling the scores over time. At each turn, the partners in the exchange arrangement have to reverse their roles, the previous receivers acting as givers, and so the relationship is perpetuated through reversals. However, one never knows whether the other partner will be able and willing to honor his obligations when it is his turn to reciprocate. At each turn, there is the risk that the relationship will fail and break off. Nevertheless, exchange relationships have the advantage of being capable of indefinite extension to include new partners, while the sharing brotherhood is a formally fixed and exclusive grouping.

There is one pitfall here, that of associating both sharing and exchange with our notion of egalitarianism. The sharing brotherhood, because of the formal nature of its arrangements, is particularly expressive of the complications and ambiguities involved. On the one hand, the notion of brotherhood implies equality of shares. On the other hand, however, an elder brother clearly ranks higher than his younger brother. And so we hear of senior and junior shares. But even when the agreement entails equal shares, this does not necessarily mean that each brother holds just one share. Thus the lordly and powerful Sindhia of Gwalior holds six out of seven shares in the muqaddamī of village Jamgaon. This expresses unambiguously his obvious dominance. But there is a significant qualification. The formal arrangements made it possible to differentiate power and status,[17] leaving the ceremonial rights of precedence, defined in meticulous detail, to the elder (selling) ''brother.'' However powerful Sindhia obviously was, precedence went to his one-seventh ''brother''.[18] Similarly, the equally lordly and powerful Holkar had to pay two-and-a-half times the ordinary price of his share in the headmanship of village Vafgaon for the addition of seniority.[19] Obviously the old-regime brothers knew both the price and the value of everything. And so the institution of the sharing brotherhood managed to square the circle by fusing into one formula equality and inequality. The more informal arrangements of exchange essentially leave this matter open. The asymmetry of giving and receiving may be equalized over time by the working of reciprocity, or the relationship may turn out to be a distinctly asymmetrical one. In the latter case, the relationship will tend to be more stable because of the element of dominance involved.

In sum, then, Indian society, stripped of the modern state's overlay, is not characterized by exclusive social categories on the one hand and separate cohesive blocks of territory on the other, but by interpenetration as well as dispersion of diverse fractional rights and holdings. This fractional character of rights and holdings not only favors dispersion in widening circles, but equally and more importantly enables the right-holding actors of various descriptions to recombine the fractionized whole through inclusion and interpenetration. The formal instrument for this purpose is the sharing brotherhood—the genealogical formula is a special form of the brotherhood, not necessarily its origin. Being a sharing brother involves the least endangered permanent relationship and thereby the strongest title to the shared object. The formal nature of the initial agreement makes its rules enforceable: "We acknowledge that we had become amenable to the Sarkar (government authorities) by the opposition made to your enjoying the rights of the third share in the headman's office," as the document already quoted has it. And, at the same time, it facilitates the resolution of conflict by formally admitting rival claimants to the brotherhood according to a reallotment of the shares.

The brotherhood institution by itself, however, is not sufficient for the task of recombining and manipulating the fractionized whole. It is, as we saw, an exclusive, formally bounded grouping and therefore lacks the more informal and expansive, though less stable, capabilities of exchange and reciprocity. Thus exchange arrangements are needed in juxtaposition to the institution of brotherhood. Because of their more informal nature, they lend themselves less to documentation. But from all we know, we may suppose that the brotherhoods are afloat in a sea of exchange arrangements. Further on, we shall have occasion to come back to the latter.

### *3*

So far, and somewhat surprisingly, caste seems to be little in evidence. However, this is what we should have expected. As already noted, the facts of peasant society and those of caste belong to two different orders, each with its own orientation.[20] This insight we owe to the work of Louis Dumont, who has clarified the sharp ideological separation of power relations on the one hand and authority based on purity on the other.[21] Now the features of peasant society we have so far dealt with clearly belong to the realm of power and dominance, or, in classical terms, of the king. Caste, by contrast, exclusively refers to the value of purity. As a matter of principle, it lacks common ground with the world of power relations.[22] It therefore stands to reason that caste receives little attention in the context of power relations. But by the same token, we touch here on a sensitive and indeed pivotal problem—a problem not only for the observer but for the participants. How should the two orders—the royal order of power relations that pervades society and the equally pervasive caste order based on purity—which regulate the lives of the same people, be related to each other? Dumont's answer is "encompassment." The ultimate value of purity encompasses its opposite, the world of power "as the mantle of Our Lady of Mercy shelters sinners of every kind in its voluminous folds".[23] The encompassment is achieved through the hierarchy of purity which assigns to each part its place with reference to the whole and integrates them in a system of hierarchical interdependence. Power, then, is subordinated to the hierarchy of purity, as the king is hierarchically inferior to the brahmin.

But this does not solve the problem, for there still is the chasm between power and hierarchy. The final junction of the two is brought about at the "secondary" level of actual practice by "surreptitiously" assimilating power to the hierarchy of purity.[24] The fact that something surreptitious should be needed to achieve the junction of the two opposite orders shows, of course, that the problem remains wide open. Hierarchy "is obliged to close its eyes to this point on pain of destroying itself".[25] The problem cannot be solved, it can only be patched over. But the model of hierarchic interdependence tying together the whole with the encompassing value of purity has much to recommend itself since it seems to transcribe Indian attitudes and utterances.

Indeed, recent work on traditional caste literature from Bengal and Gujarat bears out the idea of hierarchic interdependence upheld by graded marriage and food exchanges.[26] "Rank is maintained through gift and acceptance," as one of the texts from Bengal has it.[27] Particularly interesting is that the exchanges upholding hierarchic interdependence are equated with "worship." This term apparently harks back to the hallowed Veda and the transcendent injunctions of Vedic sacrifice. "Thus the whole of caste and rank revolved around what we might call the symbols and ideology of vedic worship. . . . Vedic worship is the attribute often referred to as the relative degree of purity."[28] Society is thus integrated by graded access to the Veda through worshipping the next higher rank, only the brahmin having immediate access to the Veda. In short, Indian society is viewed as a sacrificial universe encompassed by the Veda.[29] In this connection, the word *jajmān,* used throughout India to refer to the patron or boss and derived from the technical term for the Vedic sacrificer *(yajamāna),* seems particularly relevant. Here, it would seem, we have a clear example of the assimilation of dominance by the value-based hierarchy represented by the Veda.

But however deftly the assimilation is achieved, the element of "surreptitiousness" becomes immediately evident when we are informed that "the exchanges of wealth and food on the occasion of tantric worship *(pūjā)* are often equated with vedic worship *(yajña),*" that "the mere offering of food to the gods is seen to be equivalent to vedic worship by the brahmin," and "that the leavings of the gods accepted by the brahmin and the leavings of the brahmin accepted by the (pure) śūdra come increasingly to be equated with the powerful coded substances of the Veda itself".[30] Not only is the connection with the Veda a pious fiction, but Vedic sacrifice in the classical form we know from the relevant texts is individualized to the extent of intentionally excluding social communication and interdependence. It does not arise from social relationships nor does it establish them beyond the restricted place and duration of its performance. It is resolutely extrasocial and typically is performed, if at all, outside the community.[31] This exclusiveness gives the Veda and its sacrifical injunctions their transcendent, absolute value, but by the same token, they are cut off from society. But the Veda, precisely because of its transcendent nature, is the repository of ultimate authority and legitimation. The wish, or rather the need, to assimilate social interdependence and exchange to "Vedic worship" stands to reason, but, as we saw, this can only be done "surreptitiously." This has nothing to do with dishonesty or hypocrisy. It is a desperate means of trying to deal with an insoluble problem—the problem of relating the ultramundane order of Veda and purity with the worldy realities of power and dominance.

## *4*

Now one may raise the question whether this was perceived as a problem by the participants. The answer is that it was. Thus hierarchic interdependence requires that the brahmin perform sacrifice for the king, who provides him with sustenance and protection by "worshipping" him with gifts. This relationship is a standard item. But here the problem of the two orders comes out sharply, as is well illustrated by a caste text from Gajarat, dealing with the Modh brahmins. The brahmins, even when entreated by the divine king Rāma, refuse to perform the sacrifice for him and to accept his largesse. The refusal can only be overcome by the supernatural intervention of the gods. But then new obstacles come in the way of the sacrifice: "All the signs were inauspicious, the fire would not take the oblation, the brahmins could not recite the sacred formulas, and the gods were not favorably inclined." Again supernatural intervention is invoked, and finally the sacrifice is successfully completed. Even so, some of the brahmins—significantly called Caturvedis, that is, those who possess all four Vedas—hold out and keep refusing the king's munificent gifts.[32] The point of the story is that, although the connection between the king's power and the brahmin's authority is indeed required, the exclusivism of the Veda and the brahmin's purity forbid him to enter into this relationship with the king. Ironically, the same texts that require the connection between king and brahmin threaten the brahmin who responds to the king's advances with losing the purity that was the reason for the king's seeking his association. The brahmin loses his superior status, and the king ends up with an empty shell.[33] The problem is deadlocked—or one compromises, as the situation requires, knowing full well that one does.

If we now return to the caste order as governed by hierarchic interdependence, we can easily see that caste in actual practice is the Indian model for ordering and formalizing the informal and inclusive relationships of asymmetrical exchange, whose widespread existence we already assumed. In this sense, we could say that caste complements the exclusive arrangements of the brotherhood. However, the point is that exchange and reciprocity are in no way the ideal. The ideal is precisely the opposite—to break the oppressive circularity of exchange and reciprocity. This is clear from the classical Indian theory of the gift. The gift should be a "free" one, that is, a gift that does not result in any obligation and therefore is without reciprocity. As was already noticed with surprise by Marcel Mauss: "Il faut convenir que sur le sujet principal de notre démonstration, l'obligation de rendre, nous avons trouvé peu de faits dans le droit hindou . . . Même le plus clair consiste dans la règle, qui l'interdit".[34] Though Mauss had no use for this rule in his essay on the gift, the fact is full of significance. It means that exchange and reciprocity are rejected. This may explain why the asymmetrical exchanges of caste are couched in terms of disinterested "worship," "service," or "duty". Equally it may help us to understand the emphasis given to "brotherhood," for, as we saw, sharing among "brothers" does not involve reciprocity and so is ideologically incontrovertible. It can therefore even bring together adherents of different religions and members of different castes.

So far, we have spoken of caste as a single, coherent system. But it is striking that, where we have only a single word, caste, India has at least two terms: the well-known set of four *varṇas* and the numerous *jātis*. The question then is how the jātis are related to the varṇas. The answer is obvious: through mixed unions. But here is the catch. Such unions represent the abomination of *varnasaṃkara,* the confusion of the varṇa order, which is based on strict separation of the varṇas. The interesting point is that the jātis came about through exchange in its weightiest form, namely, marriage. The jātis stand for asymmetrical exchange relationships, and that is exactly what is rejected by the varṇa theory. Here we come up against the same problem as before. The varṇa order and the jāti order are each other's opposites. Hierarchical interdependence upheld by "worshipful" and disinterested exchange may mask the pivotal problem, but it will not solve it.

## 5

Where does this leave us? The institution that stands out clearest is, not caste or village, but the sharing brotherhood. While jāti is obliged to derive a surreptitious legitimacy from its irreconcilable opposite, varṇa, the brotherhood is ideologically neutral and therefore can safely raise its ensign. On the other hand, the brotherhood institution is by its nature strictly limited in its capacity to order society. But its formal sharing arrangements point at and exemplify a different order that is directly relevant to peasant society, namely, a jural order of rights. It is this order to which old-regime documents refer and which enables them to bypass the dubious order of jāti and varṇa. While jāti expresses—and varṇa denies—hierarchical exchange and interdependence, the jural order speaks of rights that are independently "eaten" and are free of obligation and reciprocity. Thus at harvest time, the "division of the grain heap" among the participants—including the king and the brahmin as well as the untouchable—may be, and usually is, interpreted in the sense of hierarchical exchange and interdependence.[35] To the participants, however, it seems to signify something else, namely, the realization of well-defined, independent, and inalienable rights in the soil and its productivity. These rights may be shared among brothers, or they may be differentially divided among unequal participants, as at the "division of the grain heap," but the essential point is that this is not viewed as a matter of gifts and obligations but of rights and shares.[36]

Even though these rights obviously imply the rendering of certain services or other prestations, there is no direct relationship between the right or share on the one hand and, on the other, the nature or amount of the counterprestation.[37] Or one might say that right and duty are not clearly separated and balanced but are inextricably interwoven in the sense that one has a "right" to serve (including, of course, the perquisites of the service)—in contradistinction to either a contractual relationship specifically balancing service and payment or a comprehensive bond between unequal partners. The background of this conception of rights is not contract, even less purity, but honor or "propriety." For our purpose, the point to retain is that these differential rights are viewed as independent properties defining the particular "propriety" of their various holders. The ultimate integration of these rights and of their holders is based, not on the bonds of hierarchical exchange and interdependence, but on the fact that the differentially distributed rights and shares rest on the same good, the soil's productivity.[38]

Here we get away from "caste" as the one and only mold of Indian society. What we tend to view exclusively as the equivocal bonds of hierarchical exchange can be and are handled by the participants in terms of shared or differential rights. The brotherhood, then, is not only afloat in a sea of exchange arrangements, as we surmised in a first approximation, but equally and more importantly, it is anchored in the jural order of rights and shares.

## *6*

There is then no single principle for ordering and integrating society. This, far from obstructing change and fostering stagnation, gave the ancient regime a flexibility and adaptiveness that, paradoxically, offered ample scope for instituting the modern state. However, what the modern state needed was not flexibility but fixed, unambiguously defined entities. For this purpose, it had to do away with ambiguities and polarities. The equivocations of jāti and varṇa were replaced by the unitary concept of "caste," which interprets jāti in the sense of varṇa. The village also had to be redefined as a closed, self-sufficient unit, to the exclusion of the wide-ranging web of dispersed and interspersed interests. In other words, the modern state took away, or drove under ground, society's flexibility, suggesting instead an image of motionless stagnation.

The first and pivotal point that offered itself as an opening for the operation of the modern state was the jural order of rights and shares. But in order to stabilize itself, the modern state had to withdraw from society, that is, it had to lift its right to a part of the "grain heap" out of the overall order of differential and shared rights. Instead of being the holder of a differential right among other such right holders—albeit the single most important one—it had to levy its revenues under a title of a different nature, whether that of a rent or a tax. But if the state was not to slide back into the order of differential rights and so become again an integral part of society, another concept of property was needed, namely, the single-stranded tie between the owner and his land and the exclusion of other holders of rights in the same land.[39]

In this way, the nexus of land and the rights in it held by various people could be untied, land and people separated, the taxable fields mapped out, and the taxpaying owners isolated. But this does not mean that the modern state succeeded where the old dispensation failed in definitively ordering and integrating society. The modern state breaks down society into separate, clearly bounded entities. But how, after this operation, all the king's men should put Humpty-Dumpty together again is largely left to society and its diffuse modus operandi—sometimes to the considerable discomfort of the state. This obviously creates a new and often explosive tension between the forces dividing society and society's tendency to seep through, overflow, or subvert the dividing lines. This situation is indeed a new one. The interesting point is that both the old and the new dispensation are not, as a matter of principle, geared to social integration and collective identity.

Here we touch the inner springs of Indian civilization. Its heart is not with society and its integrative pressures. It devalorizes society and disregards power. The ideal is not hierarchical interdependence but the individual break with society. The ultimate value is release from the world. And this cannot be realized in a hierarchical way, but only by the abrupt break of renunciation. Indian society and its ideal are separated by a chasm and cannot be united. Nor are they intended to be united. The chasm is intentional. Therefore all attempts, whether by the observer or the participant, at joining together the two orders in their different forms—king and brahmin, power and authority, jāti and varṇa, "worship" and Veda, society and its rejection—are doomed to failure. Above the Indian world, rejecting and at the same time informing it, the renouncer stands out as the exemplar of ultimate value and authority.

# 13 Caste and Karma: Max Weber's Analysis of Caste

## *1*

Apart from its obvious place in Max Weber's study of Hinduism, caste, though fairly often mentioned, does not appear to be a central concern in his thought. Weber, it would seem, is mainly interested in caste as a particular, even extreme case of the closed estate *(Stand)* as different from *Klasse*. The distinctive element that turns *Stand* into its extreme form, caste, is that it is underwritten by the ritual sanction of pollution.[1] With Louis Dumont, we may note in passing how Weber on this basis achieves a remarkable junction of hierarchy, ethnicity, and division of labor.[2] In an imaginative tour de force, he pulls together disparate notions on the nature and origin of caste in a succinct, logically coherent formula. In Weber's view, the caste phenomenon comes down to "eine umgreifende Vergesellschaftung die ethnisch geschiedenen Gemeinschaften zu einem spezifischen politischen Gemeinschaftshandeln zusammenschliesst".[3] This formula may count as a school example of Weber's particular use of the concepts of *Gemeinschaft* and *Gesellschaft*.[4]

For Weber, however, the point is the difference between the situation where ethnic groups, such as Jews and Gypsies in Europe, are tolerated, sometimes even privileged, because of their particular economic function and so are juxtaposed to a political society and the caste order that joins together the ethnic communities in a hierarchy of honor to create a political society in the common interest. The formula has been criticized for attempting to do too much, namely, connecting the hierarchical view of society with the exceptional situation of minority communities through the intermediary of the supposedly racial origins of caste.[5] Its advantage, however, is that it keeps caste within the bounds of a comparative discourse.[6] But

This essay will appear in slightly different form in *Max Weber's Studien über Hinduismus und Buddhismus: Interpretation und Kritik,* edited by Wolfgang Schluchter (forthcoming).

what makes caste in Weber's view a uniquely Indian or Hindu phenomenon is not hierarchy underwritten by the sanction of pollution, but its tie-in with the brahmanic karma doctrine of retribution, the most consistent theodicy ever produced, as he puts it.[7]

## 2

Analyses of the caste system, however much they may differ from each other, agree in at least one point. They all stress its immutability and total command over society. So also Weber's analysis. One may enter caste society as a group—by way of *Vergesellschaftung*—or one may leave it as an individual by renouncing the world, but the system remains unchangeable. Its grid can be endlessly refined, but it cannot be breached or transformed. In fact, Weber steps up and finalizes this line of thinking by bringing in the karma theodicy. In his view, this doctrine is the coping stone of the caste system, for it entails strict adherence to one's caste duties and rewards such adherence with the prospect of ever-improving rebirths, which will eventually lead to the ultimate goal of salvation. In this connection, Weber even comes to qualify the junction of caste and karma as a *Kastensoteriologie*.[8] And although he is perfectly aware that his intellectual doctrine cannot have been comprehended by all and sundry, Weber does argue that the promise of a progression to higher and better rebirths held out to the lower castes in a significant degree contributes to the latter's often observed conservatism.[9]

This linkage of caste and karma, Weber insists, is a pure product of rational ethical thought.[10] The caste order is in the last resort explained as the junction of two tendencies whose opposition is fundamental in Weber's thought. On the one hand, he analyzes caste society in magico-religious terms and qualifies it as thoroughly traditionalist and antirational.[11] On the other hand, it is inextricably linked with the ethical rationalism of the brahmanic karma theodicy. The remarkable point is that it is exactly this otherwise volatile mixture that is made responsible for the caste system's exceptional coherence and stability. If there is a paradox here, Weber does not seem to have been aware of it.

This does not mean, of course, that Weber was wrong in juxtaposing the two opposite principles of magico-ritualism and ethical rationalism. He shows himself, moreover, most sensitive to the tensions resulting from their competition and interpenetration.[12] However, in his view, this tension is blunted by an attitude of relative indifference or passivity toward the mundane order.[13] Deprived of its absolutist claim to transform the world, ethical rationalism gives way to the relativistic accommodation of an "organicist" social ethic.[14] In the Indian case, however, Weber argues that the perfect fit, the *sehr besondersartige Verknüpfung*,[15] of caste and karma did not produce just another accommodation but an absolute and unassailable social order. Far from prising it open, the ethical rationalism of the karma theodicy closed the mundane order of caste and sealed it with the prospect of ultimate salvation. The question is, Can we accept this monolithically coherent picture?

## 3

Now, Weber is certainly right in recognizing that in the Hindu view the mundane order is not as denuded of soteriological value as the prominence given to world renunciation may suggest. It is, however, more than doubtful whether this value can be located in the caste system. For one thing, the connection of caste with karma retribution is not as generally and unequivocally stated as the importance ascribed to it by Weber would require. We do find strong, authoritative statements to the effect that salvation is open, not only to the renouncer, but equally to the householder *(gṛhastha)*.[16] But it should be noted that it is the order of the gṛhastha—irrespective of caste—that is endowed with soteriological value, not caste as such. This may seem a quibble. The point, however, is that the nexus of caste and karma is far from unequivocal.

Let us look into it more closely. One should, of course, conform to the ways and habits of one's caste, for it is better to perform the duties of one's own caste, one's *svadharma,* indifferently than those of others with outstanding distinction. But what if these customs and duties, such as meat eating and impure occupations, are contrary to the precepts of dharma? For instance, to refuse to eat meat or, say, to participate in pig hunting if one happens to be a royal rājput would cause a scandal in one's community. Such refusal is therefore stated to be reprehensible. Conversely, one can not be blamed for following the code of conduct that is particular to one's community, even if it would constitute *adharma*.[17] In a similar vein, the authoritative *Mānava Dharmaśāstra* concludes its exposition of nonviolence *(ahiṃsā)* and the consequent prohibition of meat by saying that, after all, there is no sin in eating meat, this being simply the way of the world *(pravṛttir eṣā bhūtānām),* but that abstention *(nivṛtti)* is rich in religious reward.[18]

On the face of it, this statement may seem to be a rather lame attempt at harmonization. It does show, however, precisely where the problem lies. Ahiṃsā, abstention from destroying life, is an absolute, transcendent value, and for that reason, it is beyond the grasp of the world and totally at variance with normal practice, with *pravṛtti*. Pravṛtti, then, means going on with the business of life, following the practices of the community and thereby occasionally departing from the ultimate requirements of the dharma. As pointed out by Robert Lingat, there are no temporal sanctions against such ultimately adharmic behavior, nor can there be.[19] But one does not escape the religious or metaphysical sanction of one's karma. That is, as long as one follows the ways of the world, one is obliged to adhere to the customs of the community and so remains enclosed in it, for the inexorable karma accumulated by the faithful member of his caste will necessarily keep him in line with his community from rebirth to rebirth. And this situation will endure as long as the community—in contradistinction to the individual renouncer—does not conform its practices to the precepts of the dharma, a step that is nowadays known to sociologists by the confusing name "Sanskritization." However, such conformity can at best be only partial, for pravṛtti, going on with the business of life, as any community is bound to do, is incompatible with its opposite, nivṛtti, turning away from the ways of the world. On the other hand, the individual who would renounce his community's way of life would thereby break its rules and risk considerable scandal. Whichever way we look, the dilemma remains wide open.

Viewed in this light, the nexus of karma and caste does not look very promising as a way to ultimate salvation, and it is certainly wide off the mark to speak of a *Kastensoteriologie*. Incidentally, we can now well understand that insofar as the mundane sphere offers a way to salvation, it is not primarily attached to caste and hierarchy but, as we saw, to the dutiful performance of the householder's rites and duties enjoined by the Veda. This does not solve the essential problem either, but only moves it on to another field, namely, that of the relationship of the Veda to the mundane sphere.[20] This problem need not concern us here. At this point, it may be sufficient to note that insofar as a nexus between caste and karma is acknowledged, it can hardly lead to salvation. When caste is brought into play, it is not so much the loyal adherence to one's caste duties but the renunciation of the "fruit" of one's dutiful activity that neutralizes the inexorable law of karma and holds out the promise of salvation—an innerworldly renunciation through totally disinterested action, which then threatens the world with complete meaninglessness and so again leads to an unsoluble dilemma.

## *4*

More important, however, is that, as we saw, the dharma shows itself to be not so much a closed and fixed order as a wide-open problem. Now one may try to circumvent the problem by reasoning that dharma is not a law that is imposed, but one that is proposed, as Robert Lingat aptly puts it.[21] Or as Louis Dumont, borrowing the well-known phrase about constitutional kingship, says, "Le dharma règne de haut sans avoir, ce qui lui serait fatal, à gouverner".[22] However, whether dharma is only proposed without being imposed, or reigns from on high without actually governing the world, it cannot resign its function of ordering the affairs of the world. Here, as before, we come up against the unforgiving rift between the mundane sphere and otherworldly renunciation, between pravṛtti and nivṛtti. The dharma is and must be transcendent and eternal, but by the same token, it is divorced from the world. Coming down to the mundane sphere to govern it is indeed fatal for the dharma. Yet it cannot avoid doing so on pain of losing its universal validity.

Allegedly there once was a golden age, the *kṛtayuga,* when the dharma not only reigned from on high but fully governed man's affairs on earth. But even in that golden age, the matter was not unambiguous, for how is it that in spite of the dharma's governance, the world could progressively fall away from it till it reached our own wretched age, the irredeemable *kali-yuga,* fourth and last of the world periods? The answer, as given in a passage from the *Mahābhārata,* is in the very perfection of the dharma's governance.[23] We are told that in those blessed times, people protected each other with the help of the dharma alone *(dharmenaiva)*—as, of course, they should. But it is precisely thereby that, as our text dryly explains, the people became overwhelmed and confusion entered the world. This, then, is meant to explain the necessity of kingship. Now the king is indeed the mediator between dharma and world. But this does not solve the problem, for kingship could do little if anything to stop the progressive weakening and eventual dissolution of dharma in the successive world ages. The institution of kingship could only offer a focus for the unresolved and essentially insoluble tension. Far from patching over the rift, mythic imagination shows it to have been there from the very beginning, waiting to be focused on the king. We can now see how fatal its descent into the world is for the dharma, for in order to be universal, it has to accommodate within itself its own opposite, the principle of confusion and disorder. That, after all, is what is meant when the texts emphasize the utter subtlety of the dharma. This is not the subtlety of literate doctrine but the tension that only the sage can handle, even though he cannot resolve it.

## 5

When the dharma shows an essential "fault line," we should expect the caste order to be similarly broken. In fact, this has already become apparent from our discussion of the conjunction of caste and karma. Far from forming a coherent whole, caste and karma are at opposite ends and mutually disruptive. The point is that karma refers to the individual's fate; caste and its svadharma, however, refer to the collectivity. As we saw, it is the caste-bound collectivity that determines the individual's karma and thereby prevents him from working out his own salvation. Only when man realizes his individuality to the full extent and steps out of collectivistic society, will he be able to stop the inexorable karma mechanism. This, rather than an organistic theodicy, is the actual message of the karma doctrine. It breaks away from the collectivistic world toward individual salvation. Here the organicist restraints of caste are in conflict with the rationalistic karma doctrine. The juxtaposition of caste and karma, then, is indeed a volatile mixture. For the consequence of the karma doctrine is no less than a call to deconstruct the world. It is not fortuitous that its first formulation in the Upanishads takes the form of a secret doctrine not to be publicly divulged but to be discussed in private, outside the assembly.[24] Its ultimate consequence, world renunciation, threatens to break up society. Understandably, renunciation has always encountered muted but obstinate hostility.[25]

The conflict arose from the infusion of the renouncer's individualistic thought and rationalistic values into the otherwise devalued magico-religious world of caste. This created an irreparable rift, not only between the renouncer's otherworldly sphere and the mundane order of caste, but also within the caste world itself. Although usually supposed to be completely closed and internally coherent, caste does indeed show a rift. This is not just a matter of actual practices where the rift is obvious but all too easily dismissed as another instance of India's proverbial diversity. It is equally and clearly expressed in theoretical statements in the dharma texts. There we find at least two terms, *varṇa* and *jāti,* where we make do with only one, caste, suggesting an unbroken unity. Admittedly, varṇa and jāti are often used interchangeably, but the question is how the set of four varṇas are related to the practically innumerable jātis. One might, of course, take the jātis simply as subdivisions of the four canonical varṇas. The explanation of the dharma texts is, however, subtly different. The jātis, we learn, arose from marriages—that is, mixed marriages—between members of the "original" four varṇas.[26] This explanation has, of course, much to recommend itself. But the point is that here the preordained and immutable caste order breaks open. With a clarity that leaves nothing to be desired, we are told that the caste order with its innumerable jātis arose from the evil of *varṇasaṃkara,* the mixing of the varṇas. The caste order, then, is undermined from the beginning, built as it is on the "fault line" of varṇasaṃkara.

### *6*

Now it can be shown, as G. J. Held did almost half a century ago, that originally the varṇa concept, instead of prescribing strict separation, implied a system of connubial and other exchanges.[27] The decisive turning point was the rejection of such inter-varṇa exchanges and their replacement by the opposite rule, which set the varṇas rigorously apart from each other. It will not be possible to date this turning point in absolute chronological terms. It can, however, be related to the rationalized Vedic ritual outlined in the brāhmaṇa texts. Here, as also in the rise of Buddhism and Jainism, we find the reflection of India's version of the "Axial Age," or in Weber's terms, the onset of "disenchantment" and transcendentalism that split the world between two principles.[28] The unified world of sacrifice, held together by agonistic, potlatch exchanges is irreparably broken.[29] The new rationally systematized ritual excludes the community, and the mythical presence of the gods evaporates. Alone the sacrificer stands on his place of sacrifice. There, through the artifice of the ritual, he creates his own rigorously ordered universe separate from and transcending the mundane world.

The motive behind this radical change was the rejection of the ultimately self-defeating conflict and violence that were the essence of the original sacrificial exchanges. To eliminate conflict and violence, the community had to be broken up and the parties separated. This, not ethnic "apartheid," is the reason why the *ārya* and *śūdra* varṇas had to be separated from each other. Originally both had taken part in the agonistic sacrificial festival as opposite parties—a situation preserved in an innocuous form in the Vedic *mahāvrata* ritual, where the two parties are still described as contending with each other for the "goods of life."[30] In contrast, the rationalized Vedic ritual excludes the opposite party and sets the sacrificer apart in a transcendent world of his own. The end result is the individual sacrificer performing unaided and unopposed the sacrificial ritual in himself and by himself; in short, he is the ideal brahmin, in this respect, no different from the renouncer.

In the same way as the Vedic ritual, the varṇa theory breaks up society. It does not stop at dividing society into four strictly separate blocks but goes a long way in breaking down the internal cohesion of each varṇa too. This becomes clear when we look at the rules pertaining to marriage. One should, of course, marry within one's varṇa, but the rules about forbidden degrees of relationship (*sapiṇḍa* relatives) are such that they exclude the otherwise normal—even normative—practice of marrying within the circle of known relatives (such as one's mother's brother's daughter). If strictly adhered to—as, of course, it hardly ever is or can be—the prohibition would prevent the formation and maintenance over the generations of a web of marriage exchanges. The exclusion of the sapiṇḍa relatives would cause the affinal network to crumble with each new generation, leaving the single patriline isolated. The intention clearly is to atomize society.

## 7

Of course, no society can rest on the single principle of separation alone. And so varṇa, like dharma, has to encompass its own opposite, namely, varṇasaṃkara, the confusion of the varṇas, resulting in the proliferation of the innumerable jātis. The seemingly monolithic caste order, then, is torn apart by two diametrically opposed principles, strict separation as required by the varṇa theory and conflictual interlinking in the actual jāti order. To handle this unresolved tension is the function of the king. As upholder and mediator of the dharma, the king is called upon to set the world of jāti right when confusion and conflict are rife. However, belonging himself to the jāti world, he lacks the authority to do so. Such authority has to be derived from the otherworldly sphere and can only be imparted by the brahmin (or the renouncer).[31] For the brahmin is ideally above and beyond the jāti order. He is complete in himself and independent from the world. Only the brahmin can qualify for all six dharma activities—performing the ritual for himself as well as for others, learning and teaching, giving as well as receiving gifts. The two other "twice-born" varṇas, the kṣatriya and the vaiśya, are qualified for only one of each pair: sacrificing, learning, and giving, while the śūdra is only allowed to serve. That is, they are all dependent on others. Only the brahmin combines in himself both ends of each of the three pairs of activity and so he is, ideally, fully independent from others, transcending thereby the mundane order of conflict and interdependence. By the same token, however, he is—like the renouncer—cut off from the king's world. Indeed, if he is to preserve his transcendent authority, the brahmin must shun the king and all his works, even his gifts and benefices.[32] Yet he cannot live on his purity and transcendence. For his sustenance he is obviously, though contradictorily, dependent on the king whom he should avoid. So king and brahmin need but cannot reach each other, because the brahmin must opt out of the necessary compact.

So the unresolved tension within the worldly order of caste bears down in full force on the dual agency of king and brahmin. On the one hand, we find the collectivistic world of the jātis tenuously held together, or rather constantly rearranged, by the king; on the other hand, there is the brahmin whose individualistic varṇa concept is aimed at decomposing this world. In the open space circumscribed by these two opposite and incompatible principles, the arrangements for handling their tension have to be worked out time and again. The tension is insoluble and the arrangements for handling it therefore remain open to recall and replacement. In other words, the very insolubility of the tension provides a dynamic that opens up the world, invites new ways of handling it, and favors pluralism.

## *8*

One question remains. How is it that Weber, who otherwise was so sensitive to the tensions created by transcendental thought and world rejection and who shows the way to analyze such tensions, has failed to recognize and exploit them in his analysis of Hindu society? The answer, at least in part, is simply in the sources he had to use, notably, the Indian census publications and studies deriving from these materials. He had to base his theory on the view of Indian society, and in particular of caste, produced by the modern state for its own purposes. Now the modern state—in contradistinction to the ancien régime—is hived off from society and pretends to govern it by remote control as it were. To that end, it first of all needs an all-inclusive and immutable grid of rigidly bounded and inflexible categories. The grid can be refined, but it cannot be shifted or altered, on pain of losing its universal character and usefulness. This need for an immutable grid of categories was filled with deplorable obviousness by caste, seemingly custom-made for the purpose, especially in its brahmanic form of varṇa separation. Conversely, the modern state and its census grid of caste could not but project the image of an unchangeably fixed order of society. One may wonder whether and how far the notion of a never-changing, utterly tradition-bound, and stagnating India has been formed by the modern state's view of society. But this is another matter. For our present purpose, it may perhaps be relevant that the census definition of caste reached its height of authoritative elaboration with the censuses of 1901 and 1911, that is, at the time of Weber's study of Hinduism.[33]

Given this material and its background, we can hardly expect Weber to have set himself against the current of authoritative opinion in an area where he was a stranger. What he did achieve, though, was a highly original attempt at a consistent explanation of caste as it was presented to him, fitting it into his overall scheme of thought.

Incidentally, it may be that Weber's thoroughgoing "rationalization" of the still fairly chaotic and uneven information on caste may have contributed to his failure or, at least, to his ambivalence in recognizing the full impact on Hinduism of the "Zerspaltung der Welt in zwei Prinzipien" and the quality of the resultant tensions. He speaks of an ontological dualism of worldly transience and unmutable eternal order, but repeatedly refers to the transcendental sphere as a *Hinterwelt,* thereby suggesting the unbroken monism of the magico-religious world view.[34]

Returning to our query, the census view of caste created by the modern state will only provide part of the explanation for Weber's monolithic view of caste and karma—and the easy part at that. Perhaps, at a deeper level, Weber emotionally felt the need for the wholeness of a perfectly ordered world under the authority of a rational social ethic, while at the same time fearing its constricting consequences. Hinduism, then, may have been for him the screen on which to project this double and contradictory image. He seems to refer to this when, at the end of his chapter on caste, he points out that the very consistence, as he saw it, of caste and karma is a fearful perspective for the individual who asks for the meaning of life caught in the inexorable mechanism of repeated death.[35] Here Weber touches upon the inner rift of the caste order, for the tension created by the perspective of meaninglessness not only sets the mundane order apart from the renunciatory sphere, but breaks open the caste order.

# Abbreviations

| | |
|---|---|
| *AB* | *Aitareya Brāhmaṇa* |
| *ĀpDhS* | *Āpastamba Dharmasūtra* |
| *ĀpGS* | *Āpastamba Gṛhyasūtra* |
| *ĀpŚS* | *Āpastamba Śrautasūtra* |
| *AV* | *Atharvaveda Saṃhitā* |
| *AŚ* | *Arthaśāstra,* |
| *BĀU* | *Bṛhad-Āraṇyaka-Upaniṣad* |
| *BaudhGS* | *Baudhāyana Gṛhyasūtra* |
| *BaudhDhS* | *Baudhāyana Dharmasūtra* |
| *BaudhŚS* | *Baudhāyana Śrautasūtra* |
| *BhG* | *Bhagavad Gītā* |
| *JB* | *Jaiminīya Brāhmaṇa* |
| *JUB* | *Jaiminīya-Upāniṣad-Brāhmaṇa* |
| *KātyŚS* | *Kātyāyana Śrautasūtra* |
| *KB* | *Kauṣītaki Brāhmaṇa* |
| *KS* | *Kāṭhaka Saṃhitā* |
| *MānŚS* | *Mānava Śrautasūtra* |
| *Manu* | *Manusmṛti,* or *Mānava Dharmaśāstra* |
| *Mbh* | *Mahābhārata,* Ed. S. N. Joshi and R. C. Kinjvadekar. Poona, 1929–1933. |
| *MS* | *Maitrāyaṇī Saṃhitā* |
| *PB* | *Pañcaviṃśa Brāhmaṇa* |
| *Rām* | *Rāmāyaṇa,* Ed. W. L. Panśīkar. Bombay, 1930. |
| *RV* | *Ṛgveda Saṃhitā* |
| *ŚānkhGS* | *Śānkhāyana Gṛhyasūtra* |
| *ŚānkhŚS* | *Śānkhayana Śrautasūtra* |
| *ŚB* | *Śatapatha Brāhmaṇa* |
| *SvB* | *Ṣaḍviṃśa Brāhmaṇa* |
| *TĀ* | *Taittirīya Āraṇyaka* |
| *TB* | *Taittirīya Brāhmaṇa* |
| *TS* | *Taittirīya Saṃhitā* |
| *Vās* | *Vāsiṣṭha Dharmaśāstra* |
| *VS* | *Vājasaneyi Saṃhitā* |

# Notes

### *Introduction*

1. On the adaptiveness of tradition and the unsatisfactory tradition-modernity dichotomy, see L. I. Rudolph and S. H. Rudolph, Introduction to *The Modernity of Tradition: Political Development in India* (Chicago, 1967).

2. See Robert Lingat, "Time and the Dharma," *Contributions to Indian Sociology* 6 (1962): 7–16, esp. 14.

3. *ĀpDhS* 1. 7. 20. 6.

4. *Vās* 1. 6–7.

5. See chapter 1.

6. See especially chapters 2–7.

7. This would seem to be what is intended by J. F. Staal, "The Meaninglessness of Ritual," *Numen* 26 (1979): 2–22. Vedic ritual, on which Staal builds his case, consciously maximizes the potential of ritual for structure. It has structure instead of meaning. This, however, need not be the case everywhere for all ritual. I have expanded this theme in "The Ritualist's Problem," an article that will appear in a forthcoming volume edited by S. D. Joshi in honor of R. N. Dandekar.

8. See chapter 3.

9. See chapter 4.

10. See chapter 5.

11. Cf. chapter 2, section 6.

12. See chapter 6.

13. See chapter 7.

14. Cf. chapter 7, section 6, and Heesterman, "The Ritualist's Problem."

15. See chapters 8–10.

16. See chapter 8, especially section 7–11.

17. See chapter 9.

18. See chapter 10.

19. See chapter 11.

20. "Inclusivism" has been coined as a concept by P. Hacker. See his lecture in *Inclusivismus: Eine indische Denkform,* ed. Gerhard Oberhammer (Vienna, 1983), 11–28; also Oberhammer's "Nachwort," in ibid., 93–113. The phenomenon has more often been commented upon. See, e.g., Louis Dumont, "For a Sociology of India," *Contributions to Indian Sociology* 1 (1957): 7–22, esp. 21: "Hinduism has repelled the onslaught of christianity by integrating those christian values which were not dangerous to it."

21. See chapter 12.
22. See chapter 13.

## Chapter One

1. For the classical threat of scarcity and starvation, see E. Rau, *Staat und Gesellschaft im alten Indien* (Wiesbaden, 1957), 31.

2. One may compare the verbal contest, discussed in chapter 5, where the contestants strive to make their personal "subjective truth" prevail.

3. W. C. Neale, "Reciprocity and Redistribution," in *Trade and Market in Early Empires,* ed. K. Polanyi, C. M. Arensberg, and H. W. Pearson (Glencoe, Ill., 1957), 218–36; see also Neale's article in *Land Control and Social Structure in Indian History,* ed. R. E. Frykenberg (Madison, 1969), 5. On the complications of rights in the soil, see also chapter 12.

4. See O. Brunner, "Vom Gottesgenadentum zum monarchischen Prinzip," in *Das Königtum,* ed. Th. Mayer (Darmstadt, 1969), 289, on "der urtümliche Glauben dass die Enscheidung der Waffen 'Gott und das Recht' offenbare." In the same way, we can understand the feudal obligation of consilium binding both the lord and his men.

5. Louis Dumont, *Homo Hierarchicus* (Paris, 1967), 107.

6. Richard Lingat, *Les Sources du droit dans le système traditionel de l'Inde,* (Paris, 1967), 29–32.

7. Robert Lingat, "Time and the Dharma," *Contributions to Indian Sociology* 6 (1962): 13.

8. Dumont, *Homo Hierarchicus*. The point where I differ from Dumont primarily concerns the brahmin. Dumont views the brahmin as the priestly exponent of purity in the mundane order of society and therefore associates him with the king in an overall scheme of hierarchy. Against this view, I emphasize the scriptural statements that warn the brahmin against association with the king and stress his (ideal) independence (see below, chap. 10).

9. A. C. Mayer, *Caste and Kinship in Central India* (Berkeley, 1960), 33–47; also Mayer, "The Dominant Caste in a Region of Central India," *South Western Journal of Anthropology* 14 (1958): 407–27. Mayer's findings are also discussed by Dumont, *Homo Hierarchicus,* para. 36.

10. Brenda F. Beck, "The Right-Left Division of South Indian Society," *Journal of Asian Studies* 29, no. 4 (August 1970): 779–98.

11. Miss Beck's use of the latter term seems to echo Mayer's concept of "allied castes."

12. See Miss Beck's graph, where we find right-hand castes neatly ranked in an almost vertical row, while the left-hand castes are typically scattered and their rankings consequently vague. Thus, for instance, the left-hand merchant (no. 7) is, as may be expected, slightly higher than the artisan from the same division (no. 9). Yet the latter scores higher as regards brahminical conformity.

13. Mayer, *Caste and Kinship,* 37.

14. For a detailed discussion of this theme, see chapter 2.

15. See chapter 10.

16. *Manu* 9. 111.

17. The earliest manifestation of brahminical individualism is the insistence on the single sacrificer, who has the ritual performed for his own benefit, and the prohibition of collective sacrifices as a social event. *Sacra publica* are conspicuous by their absence, and even the royal consecration is represented as a single-sacrificer affair. But from the texts, it is clear that this one-sided stress on individualism rep-

resented a daring innovation on the part of the systematizers of the ritual. However, the innovation most probably was never fully put into practice, for next to it the nonsystematized ritual continued in full force.

18. M. N. Srinivas, *Caste in Modern India and Other Essays* (Bombay, 1962), chaps. 1 and 2; on the modernity of brahminical law, see L. I. Rudolph and S. H. Rudolph, *The Modernity of Tradition* (Chicago, 1967), 269–79.

19. It would, of course, be equally possible to study change by focusing on the cultural sphere. The pivotal point would then have to be the concept of "Hinduism" and its content, which, coming up in the thirties of the last century in English literature on India and expressing nothing more than an ill-assorted complex of social and religious customs, rites, and beliefs, both popular and scriptural, develops into a world religion, expressing the awareness of a new universalistic identity on the part of educated Indians.

20. On the Mughal Empire see chapter 11, sections 2–6. See also A. Wink, "Land and Sovereignty in eighteenth-century India" (Doctoral thesis, Leiden, 1984). In an analysis of the underlying ideas of the empire based on contemporary data, Wink emphasizes the element of conflict.

21. R. G. Fox, *Kin, Clan, Raja, and Rule* (Berkeley, 1971). Fox discerns five stages of a development cycle, moving from a segmentary lineage system through stratification to the breakthrough of ruling elements that "rip through the genealogical cover which had tied their political activities to the expansive familism of the group" (p. 159). Finally the system reverts again to the first stage. Though the analysis refers to the kinship-based rajput polity, the two main points of the cycle, dispersion and concentration of power, are generally relevant. We may also turn to Leach's analysis of the transition between the Kachin and Shan types of polity in *Political Systems of Highland Burma* (Boston, 1965).

22. Fox, *Kin, Clan, Raja,* 170.

23. See chapter 9.

24 . See D. H. A. Kolff, "An Armed Peasantry and Its Allies: Rajput Tradition and State Formation in North India, 1450–1900" (Doctoral thesis, Leiden, 1983).

25. See J. C. Heesterman, "Vrātya and Sacrifice," *Indo-Iranian Journal* 6 (1962): 1–37.

26. Beck, "The Right-Left Division", 780.

27. B. Stein, "Integration of the Agrarian System of South India," in Frykenberg, *Land Control,* 188ff.

28. W. Schlesinger, "Das Heerkönigtum," in Mayer, *Das Königtum,* 105–43.

29. S. N. Gordon, "Scarf and Sword," *Indian Economic and Social History Review* 6 (1969): 403–29; see also D. H. A. Kolff, "Sannyasi-Trader-Soldiers," and Gordon's comment, ibid. 8 (1971): 213–220.

30. Another way of describing this bifurcation would be in terms of the divorce of power and authority, the latter being beyond reach in the transcendent extrasocial sphere. See J. C. Heesterman, "Power and Authority in Indian Tradition," in *Tradition and Politics in South Asia,* ed. R. J. Moore (New Delhi, 1979), 60–85, and chapter 10 below.

31. It is perhaps not just accidental that the Prophet left no instructions as to the community's form of government.

32. *A'S* 7. 5. 49.

33. T. R. Metcalf, "From Raja to Landlord" and "British Land Policy," in Frykenberg, *Land Control,* 123–41, 143–62; P. D. Reeves, "Landlords and Party Politics," in *Soundings in Modern South Asian History,* ed. D. A. Low (Berkeley, 1968), 261–82.

34. For a case in point, see R. E. Frykenberg's study of local influence and central authority, *Guntur District, 1788–1848* (Oxford, 1965).

35. With regard to India's economic history in the nineteenth century, the seminal suggestions of M. D. Morris are particularly interesting. See M. D. Morris, ed., *Indian Economy in the Nineteenth Century: A Symposium* (Delhi, 1969).

36. R. Kumar, "The Political Process in India," *South Asia* 1 (August 1971): 97.

37. Ibid., 101.

38. Gandhi's role in the reorganization of the Congress comes out clearly in D. Rothermund, "Constitutional Reform versus National Agitation," *Journal of Asian Studies* 21 (August 1962): 505–21. See also chapter 11, section 8.

### Chapter Two

1. See Louis Dumont and David Pocock, *Contributions to Indian Sociology* 2 (1958): 58; also Dumont, "Caste, Racism, and Stratification," ibid. 5 (1961): 34–35.

2. See J. C. Heesterman, "Tradition in Modern India," *Bijdragen tot de Taal-, Land-, en Volkenkunde* 119 (1963): 149f. On "Sanskritization," cf. J. F. Staal, "Sanskrit and Sanskritization," *Journal of Asian Studies* 22 (1963): 261ff.; also Dumont and Pocock, "On the Different Aspects or Levels in Hinduism," *Contributions to Indian Sociology* 3 (1959): 40–45.

3. On brahminical rejection of priesthood, see also chapter 10.

4. For the following discussion of the Vedic ritual, I draw in part on a previous paper, "Vrātya and Sacrifice," *Indo-Iranian Journal* 6 (1962): 1–37, especially sections 4 and 6–9, where more detailed references may be found.

5. The exception is the *sattra,* or ritual session, in which a group of brahmins are at the same time patron and officiant, see below, section 9.

6. "The evil *(pāpman)* of the dīkṣita is divided in three ways. he who eats his food (takes) a third part; he who mentions his evil *(aślīla)* a third part; he who mentions his name a third part" (*KS* 23. 6). We are reminded here of the inauspicious "voice" *(aślīlā vāc)* that pursues Indra after his killing of Viśvarūpa. Indra—with whom the sacrificer is often identified—also disposes of his guilt, the impurity of death, in three ways (*TS* 2. 5. 1. 2–5). Eating the food of the dīkṣita is also forbidden by Manu, who brackets the dīkṣita with different kinds of impure people (*Manu* 4. 210).

7. *KS* 34. 7, 11; *TS* 7. 2. 10. 3.

8. *KS* 34. 8, 11; *TS* 7. 2. 10. 2; cf. also *ĀpŚS* 13. 6. 4–6.

9. For instance, if the cow whose milk is destined for the agnihotra offering sits down at the time of milking, this means that she has become aware of the yajamāna's evil. Therefore he should give this cow to a brahmin whose food he will not eat afterward. In this way, he fastens the evil onto the brahmin(*TB* 1. 4. 3. 2). The heinous sin of killing a brahmin is transferred to him who eats the food of a brahmin-killer (*ĀpDhS* 1. 19. 16). For the giving of cows to free oneself from evil, cf. also *Mbh* 13. 71. 50–51, 53. In general, liberality is considered a means of freeing oneself from evil, cf. *Manu* 4. 228; 2. 228; also *Mbh* 13. 93. 12c: *dānaṃ dadat pavitrī syāt*.

10. See also *Mbh* 13. 35. 23, where it is said that the acceptance of gifts extinguishes the brahmin's luster *(tejas)* (cf. Manu 4. 186) and where at the same time Bhīṣma warns against the brahmin who refuses to accept them.

11. *AB* 5. 24. 3; *KB* 6. 11.

12. For the patron's birth as a brahmin, "out of the sacrifice," "out of the *bráhman,*" cf. *ŚB* 3. 2. 1. 40; 13. 4. 1. 3; *AB* 7. 22. 4.

13. See *JB* 2. 369–70. Prajāpati is enveloped in pāpman at birth. Brahman delivers him from this evil in three moves (see the tripartite pāpman of the dīkṣita, n. 6); the pāpman then becomes Prajāpati's śrī.

14. See *ĀpŚS* 22. 1. 11–16, which deals with the twelve-day ritual, celebrated either as an ahīna or as a sattra. Though the ahīna, according to classical theory, is performed by one yajamāna assisted by sixteen officiants, it is striking that the *Āpastamba Dharmasūtra* and *Kāṭhaka Saṃhitā* consider the execution by a group of dīkṣitas assisted by non-dīkṣita officiants as the proper characteristic of the ahīna (cf. also *MānŚS* 7. 2. 1. 3). For the invited brahmin's question whether or not it is an ahīna, see *ĀpŚS* 10. 1. 3 with Caland's note and W. Caland and V. Henry, *L'Agniṣṭoma* (Paris, 1906–7), 4. See also Heesterman, "Vrātya and Sacrifice", 31–34.

15. See F. B. J. Kuiper, "The Ancient Indian Verbal Contest," *Indo-Iranian Journal* 4 (1960): 217–81.

16. It may not be a fortuitous invention that the *Mahābhārata* gives an elaborate identification of battle and sacrifice (*Mbh* 12. 98). Cf. Marcel Mauss's observation: "Le *Mahābhārata* est l'histoire d'un gigantesque potlatch" ("Essai sur le don," *Sociologie et Anthropologie* (Paris 1950), 243). Mauss's study is the starting point of G. J. Held, *The Mahābhārata: An ethnological study* (Leiden, 1936).

17. A. Hillebrandt, *Vedische Mythologie,* 2d ed. (Breslau, 1927–29), 260.

18. Cf. *ĀpŚS* 14. 19, 20.

19. *KS* 31. 15. *Samṛtayajñó vā́ eṣá yád darśapūrṇamāsaú, kásya yakṣyámānasya vā́ha devátā yajñám āgácchanti kásya vā ná* (*MS* 1. 4. 5; *TS* 1. 6. 7. 1). The point at issue is to whose sacrifice the gods will come (as guests).

20. For the gods and asuras competing in the ritual, see, e.g., *KS* 23. 7. See for the food exchanges, *JB* 1. 223 (Auswahl no. 83): "The asuras had swallowed poison from the gods; they had swallowed it unknowingly thinking it to be food." After what we have seen of the ideas underlying the gift, we can readily understand their feeling poisoned (cf. also *PB* 19. 4. 2). For the reversed relationship, see *JB* 3. 118: "In the beginning these worlds were in the possession of the asuras; the devas, intent on śraddhā and tapas, were dependent on them for their livelihood." Here we may compare *RV* 10. 151. 3, according to which the gods obtained śraddhā with the asuras. The reversible relationship between devas and asuras seems still to survive to some extent when it is related that the asuras had originally won command over the universe from the gods, that the gods overcame the asuras, but that later on, the asuras will again conquer the gods. Similarly, when Indra has won Śrī from Bali, Bali says that at a future occasion there will again be a *devāsuraṃ yuddham,* in which he will win (*Mbh* 12. 225. 31).

21. *KS* 25. 7; *MS* 3. 8. 6.

22. *ĀpŚS* 22. 3. 13f.

23. *BaudhŚS* 18. 20.

24. *JB* 3. 18 (Auswahl no. 136).

25. It is noteworthy that in the Āditya-Angiras story the parties exchange competing invitations and participate together in the ceremony. In the case of Keśin and Khaṇḍika, each performs his own separate ceremony, only announcing it to the opponent. These ceremonies are supposed to bring about their result automatically, by means of the classical arsenal of normalized liturgical operations in which there is no place for a real contest.

26. J. C. Heesterman, *The Ancient Indian Royal Consecration* (The Hague, 1957), 141f., 150f. *ŚānkhŚS* 16. 18. 1–7 fittingly assigns the brahmin's role in this verbal exchange to the sole brahman officiant.

27. *ŚāṅnkhŚS* 16. 8. 8.

28. This idea also survives in the classical Soma ritual in the restricted and mitigated form of a begging tour *(saniyācana),* see below, chapter 6, section 7.

29. *ŚB* 11. 6. 2. 10.

30. Brahmins acting as kṣatriyas are mentioned, e.g., *Mbh* 12. 22. 6. It is said of Indra that he is a son of Brahman but has become a kṣatriya through his works *(karmaṇā)* (*Mbh* 12. 22. 11). For Indra as a brahmin, cf. also the subrahmaṇyā recitation, where Indra is addressed, among other epithets, as *kauśika brāhmaṇa* (see *SvB* 1. 1. 21; and Caland and Henry, *L'Agniṣṭoma,* no. 49). See also H. P. Schmidt, *Bṛhaspati und Indra* (Wiesbaden, 1958), 237–39.

31. *Mbh* 3. 117. 12; 12. 49. 64. Cf. *AB* 8. 21. 8, where it is a mythical king, Viśvakarman Bhauvana, who having conquered the earth offers her to Kaśyapa at the occasion of a horse sacrifice at which Kaśyapa is the chief officiant. See also *ŚB* 13. 7. 1. 15.

32. Heesterman, *Consecration,* 203ff. Cf. also E. W. Hopkins, "The Position of the Ruling Caste," *Journal of the American Oriental Society* 13 (1889): 99ff. In connection with the king's court, Hopkins notes that the brahmins "seem a gradual intrusion on the knightly assembly."

33. Of course there will have been some priestly specialists, who seem to have been amalgamated in the group of sixteen or seventeen officiants assisting the yajamāna in the classical ritual. But it would seem to me that specialized priesthood was not necessarily characteristic of the bearers of the brahman.

34. "Das vedische Opfer ist durch alle wesentlichen Einzelheiten seiner Form und seines Verlaufs definiert als ein stilisiertes Gastmahl" (P. Thieme, "Vorzarathustriches bei den Zarathustriern," *Zeitschrift der Deutschen Morgenlämdischen Geschicte* 107 (1957): 90. This refers to a banquet offered to the gods, but it is also offered to the brahmins, who are the "human gods." Elsewhere, Thieme suggests that the dakṣiṇā is a "Gastgeschenk" *(Der Fremdling im Rigveda* [Leipzig, 1938], 27; previously, *Indo-Iranian Journal* 3 (1959): 255, n. 36). I have doubted this interpretation, but I now recognize that the rendering "Gastgeschenk" seems to touch the essence of the matter.

35. *PB* 19. 4. 2, cf. also above n. 20.

36. *Mbh* 12. 8. 34ff.

37. Mauss, "Essai sur le don," 149–53.

38. See *JB* 2. 183 (Auswahl no. 144) for the meaning of *jana,* "other people." Cf. also *ṢvB* 1. 7. 3: "Food leaves him, who though fit to eat food yet does not eat food . . . . Especially by the food of the other people *(janyam annam)* he becomes a food-eater." Caland renders *jana* "die Ferne" or "die Fremde." It would seem that what was originally meant was the opposite party in the ritual. In the *Jaiminīya Brāhmaṇa* passage quoted above, *jana* is explained as vaiśya or bhrātṛvya. *AB* 8. 26. 3 calls the rivals *janyāni (sapatnā vai dviṣanto bhrātṛvyā janyāni).* Interesting also is the *janya,* or *janyo mitram,* who participates in the unction ceremony (Heesterman, *Consecration,* 114). In the *Ṛgveda Saṃhitā, jánya* and *jáne mitrá* occur in the sense of matchmaker (cf. L. Renou, *Études sur le vocabulaire du Ṛveda* [Pondichéry, 1958], 35) and thus possibly denote affinal relationship. Such a relationship may well be in keeping with the ambivalence of the rivalry and cooperation between the parties.

39. "He who sees diversity here, in this world, moves from death to death" (*BĀU* 4. 4. 19). The words suggest that it is still the relations with the others that implies recurrent death.

40. *JB* 2. 69–70 (Auswahl no. 128). In *JUB* 2. 10. 1 it is made clear that the Prajāpati-Mṛtyu contest continues the older idea of the contest between devas and asuras.

41. *PB* 16. 7.

42. This means also that the agonistic rites have in fact no place in the classical ritual. Thus, for instance, the chariot race is relegated to the outskirts of the ritual. *JB* 2. 193, dealing with the vājapeya, even discusses the question whether one should perform it, because "those who go outside the vedi stray from the sacrifice." It is also typical that in this connection the chariot race is equated with a liturgical element, the *rathantara* melody, whose name recalls the chariot, *ratha*. In the case of the vājapeya, the chariot race is preserved. The *Jaiminīya Brāhmaṇa* in this instance recommends that it be observed in both ways: the liturgical "race" of the gods (the rathantara) and the real race of man. But elsewhere the substitution has been completed, as in the case of the sādyaskras, mentioned above, to which the viśvajicchilpa also belongs. In this ceremony, the chariots are replaced by simple liturgical "wheels" (*PB* 16. 15. 3–4).

43. Cf. *ŚB* 10. 5. 2. 23; 10. 6. 5. 8; *BĀU* 1. 2. 5.

44. Cf. W. Caland, *Altindische Zauberei* (Amsterdam, 1908), no. 117; *MS* 2. 2. 6.

45. Instances of this kind can easily be multiplied. In the first instance, we may think here of the *sava* ceremonies involving an unction, such as the rājasūya, where we see the rival actively participating in the unction ritual. The vrātyastomas may also be quoted. It is also interesting that the *tānūnaptra* rite in the normal Soma sacrifice (Caland and Henry, *L'Agniṣṭoma,* no. 45) is mythologically explained in the same way as the saṃjñāneṣṭi (cf. the *Maitrāyaṇi Saṃhitā* passage quoted above with MS. 3. 7. 10).

46. cr. also *'SB* 11. 1. 8. 6.

47. *BĀU* 3. 2. 13; 4. 4. 5.

48. On the individual, inalienable quality of karma, cf. also *Mbh* 12. 321. 47, 58: *Na tatra saṃviyujyate svakarmabhiḥ parasparam,* "One is not separated from one's works" or "One does nos exchange one's work with another."

49. Cf. also *ŚB* 12. 8. 1. 17, "Where the trunk is pure, the limbs are pure," said of yajamāna and officiants. The development of ritual thinking naturally left its imprint on the ritualists' view of the dakṣiṇā. *ĀpŚS* 21. 1. 5–7 gives two diametrically opposed views. "One should not officiate (for a yajamāna) at the twelve-day sacrifice, so as to avoid evil" (because through accepting the dakṣiṇās one would "eat what falls off from the head" of the yajamāna [*TS* 7. 2. 10. 4]). In this statement, the preclassical idea is reflected. The adaptation to the classical line of thinking is given in the next statement: "Prospers who gives (at a twelve-day sacrifice); prospers who accepts" (*KS* 34. 9, cf. *JB* 3. 4). *AB* 4. 25. 2 also expresses this latter opinion, but it is interesting that this is mythologically explained by the exchange between Prajāpati and the months, mentioned above, section 4. Reinterpretation is all but palpable here. Through their exchanges, Prajāpati and the months "become firmly established in each other." This leads straight up to the classical doctrine: Prajāpati and the months are no longer different from each other. Prajāpati is the whole, the year, of which the months and the seasons are the integral parts.

50. According to *BaudhŚS* 18. 25, the saṃjñāneṣṭi was part of the vrātya alliance ritual.

51. Cf. *ŚB* 14. 1. 1. 32.

52. The loss in meaning that the sacrificer-officiant bond underwent in the classical doctrine seems to be underlined by the ritual dissolution of the bond at the end of the Soma sacrifice (Caland and Henry, *L'Agniṣṭoma,* no. 251), corresponding to the tānūnaptra rite at the beginning. It is perhaps significant that Caland notes (*ĀpŚS* 13. 18. 2) that there is no older authority for this rite of dissolution. In the classical

doctrine, the sacrifice is a closed circuit and stands outside the religious life of the community as a whole. Theoretically there is a possibility here for a viable relationship between patron and officiant. The patron is transformed into a brahmin for the duration of the sacrifice through the dīkṣā (in the classical doctrine it is the dīkṣā, not the sacrifice, that purifies the patron and transforms him into a brahmin). At the end of the ceremony, he returns to his previous status and the bond with the officiants is dissolved. But viewed in this way, the patron-officiant relationship is merely theoretical. The only practical point is that the dakṣiṇās stay with the officiant. The officiant might, in his turn, act as a patron, but this would imply a relapse into the dualist system of exchanges. The classical system, when fully developed, had sealed its own end.

53. Mauss, ''Essai sur le don,'' 243, n. 3.

54. *AśvGS* 4. 7. 3; *Manu* 3. 177.

55. *Manu* 3. 148.

56. *Manu* 3. 125–26.

57. *Manu* 3. 138ff.; *Mbh* 13. 90. 41ff.

58. *ĀpDhS* 2. 17. 8–9; *Manu* 3. 141; *Mbh* 13. 90. 46.

59. This would seem to be reason why the *Mimāmsā,* after discussing the point, decides that the dakṣiṇā is not a gift but a salary for services rendered (see Charles Malamoud, ''Terminer le sacrifice,'' in *Le Sacrifice dans l'Inde ancienne,* ed. Madeline Biardeau and Charles Malamoud [Paris, 1976], 155–204, esp. 179–82). This view, which makes the service and its payment an incidental transaction, ''desacralizes'' the dakṣiṇā and thereby neutralizes the danger the gift holds for the brahmin's purity and independence.

60. *Vyāvṛtya* (*TB* 2. 2. 5. 1).

61. Mauss, ''Essai sur le don,'' 248f.

62. *ŚB* 13. 4. 3. 14.

63. *JB* 3. 94–95 (Auswahl no. 180); *PB* 13. 3. 12.

64. *Manu* 4. 218; *Mbh* 13. 35. 23.

65. *Manu* 3. 64, 153; 4. 85f.

66. E.g., *Mbh* 13. 93. 130; 94. 33.

67. *Mbh* 12. 767.

68. The commentary of Nandanācārya reads *dānayuddhapradhānāśca,* ''very liberal men and those delighting in strife.'' One is tempted to render it as: ''those engaging in gift-giving contests,'' because nothing could be wrong with liberality, unless it were in an agonistic context.

69. *Manu* 4. 205.

70. *Manu* 3. 130, 132.

71. *AŚ* 3. 10. 44. Cf. S. C. Dube, *The Indian Village* (London 1955), 116. Hereditary ritual office is sometimes held by caste fellows, as for instance the dasayas of the vokkaliga caste. See also T. S. Epstein, *Economic Development and Social Change* (Manchester, 1962), 136.

72. By interiorization I do not mean to suggest a dichotomy between ''external'' and ''internal'' sacrifice or the replacement of the former by the latter. The ritual act is both, as is shown, e. g., by *ŚB* 10. 4. 3. 9, where the agnicayana ritual is both ''internal'' knowledge *(vidyā)* and ''external'' act. The differentiation arose as a result of the ritual's interiorization and could be valid only from the point of view of the individualized sacrifice (cf. J. F. Staal, *Advaita and Neoplatonism* [Madras 1961], 71f.)

73. See Louis Dumont, ''World Renunciation in Indian Religions,'' *Contributions to Indian Sociology* 4 (1960): 33–62. Dumont endeavors to build up a unified

picture of Hinduism by viewing it as "the dialogue between the renouncer and the man-in-the-world."

74. Cf. *BĀU* 4. 5. 15.

75. *BhG* 6. 29.For this expression and for related ones referring to the vision of the self (seeing the self in the self, through the self), cf. P. Hacker, *Saeculum* 12 (1961): 371ff.

76. *Manu* 6. 25,38.

77. *BaudhDhS* 2. 18. 8–9. The ātmayajña is closely connected, if not identical, with the so-called *prāṇāgnihotra,* the offering of food in the (fires) of the breaths *(prāṇa),* i.e., a ritualized form of taking food. For the internal or mental sacrifice, see J. Varenne, *La Mahā-Nārāyaṇa-Upaniṣad,* (Paris, 1960), 2: 53. For the prāṇāgnihotra see the texts collected by Varenne, ibid., 69ff., and H. W. Bodewitz, *Jaiminīya Brāhmaṇa 1. 1–65, with a Study of Agnihotra and Prāṇāgnihotra* (Leiden, 1973). Though the ātmayajña in Baudhāyana's dharma-sūtra is explicitly meant for the renouncer, Bodewitz points out that the prāṇāgnihotra is equally available to the brahmin householder and that consequently there need not be a specific, close connection with renunciation (ibid., 323). For our purpose, however, the essential point is the inner logic of the development that led from "external" to "internal" sacrifice. The latter promises independence from the outside world. Because of his extrasocial outerworldly stance, this is of no less importance for the brahmin householder than it is for the renouncer (see also chapter 6, section 8).

78. M. Winternitz ("Zur Lehre von den Āśramas," *Festschrift für Hermann Jacobi* [Bonn 1926]) and F. Weinrich ("Entwicklung und Theorie der Āśrama Lehre," *Archir für Religionswissenschaft* 27 [1929]) emphasize the opposition between brahmin orthodoxy and renunciation. Cf. also the guarded pronouncements of Renou and Filliozat, *L'Inde Classique,* nos. 768, 1236.

79. On brahmacārin and vrātya, cf. M. Bloomfield, *The Atharvaveda and the Gopatha Brahmana* (Strassburg, 1909), 94. J. W. Hauer rejects this connection on the ground that the vrātya book, *AV* 15, does not mention brahmacarya (*Der Vrātya* [Stuttgart, 1927], 16.f.). Hauer further considers the vrātya as an exponent of nonbrahminical religion and therefore has to separate him rigidly from the brahmacārin. In my opinion, both vrātya and brahmacārin belong to the preclassical stage of development, where the meaning of brahmacārin was certainly not yet limited to that of a young man learning the Vedas. On the vrātya as predecessor of the classical dīkṣita, see my "Vrātya and Sacrifice," 11ff.

80. *JB* 2. 183. Cf. *ĀpŚS* 17. 26. 14ff.

81. On *jana,* see above, note 38.

82. On the exiled king, see W. Rau, *Staat und Gesellschaft im alten Indien* (Wiesbaden, 1957), 129.

83. *Mbh* 12. 10. 17.

84. *ŚānkhŚS* 16. 15. 20f. Cf. *ĀpŚS* 20. 24. 16; *ŚB* 13. 6. 2. 20 (where the rule obtains for the puruṣamedha).

85. *Maitrī Upaniṣad* 1. 1; 6. 26.

86. *Manu* 6. 83 prescribes the recitation of texts bearing on (a) ritual equivalences *(adhiyajñaṃ brahma),* (b) macrocosmic equivalences *(ādhidaivikam),* (c) the equivalences referring to the self *(ādhyātmikam),* and (d) vedānta *(vedāntābhihitaṃ ca yat).* A hierarchical gradation seems to be intended, building up to the meditation on the (interiorized) ritual.

87. Chapters 12 and 25, quoted by L. Alsdorf, *Beiträge zur Geschichte von Vegetarismus und Rinderverehrung* (Wiesbaden, 1962), 47f. It is interesting to note that the Jaina monk appears on the place of sacrifice to ask for a share of the sacri-

ficial meal. His upbraiding of the sacrificing brahmins strangely recalls the figure of the "reviler" in the mahāvrata (*PB* 5. 5. 13, see also below, chap. 5, sect. 5). It is tempting to see in the monk's appearance on the place of sacrifice a distant echo of the preclassical pattern of ritual.

88. There can be difference of opinion on doctrines and practices, and these differences have often taken the form of remarkably acrimonious disputes and rivalries. But these conflicts differ from "worldly" conflicts. They turn ostensibly on doctrine. Conflict in society concerns one's place, rights, and duties in the community, but it presupposes one's belonging to it. Doctrinal conflict, on the other hand, makes one's belonging dependent on allegiance to the right doctrine. It brings the individual and his choice into sharp focus. Thus the sharply profiled contrast or conflict between the householder-sacrificer and the renouncer is not identical with the divide between the social world and world renunciation. Even if the householder-sacrificer can be made out to stand for society, his opposition to the renouncer proper is primarily one of doctrine. Both partake of the individualized sphere characterized by renunciatory values. Their conflict is fought on the other, nonworldly side of the barrier.

89. Of the vānaprastha it is said that he should always give but not receive *(dātā nityam anādātā),* (*Manu* 6. 8). The sannyāsin, on the other hand, receives gifts but does not give (*Kaṭhaśruti Upaniṣad* 3). The pivotal point seems to be that relations of reciprocity involving gift exchanges are barred. *Manu* 1. 88 (cf. 10. 75) describes the activities of the (ideal) brahmin as teaching and learning, sacrificing and officiating, giving and receiving. At first sight, this would seem to go straight against the renunciatory ideology. In the first place, if this statement refers to reciprocal relations (which seems doubtful), it is clear that such relations would only be possible for the brahmin within the brahmin community. However, from the following verses dealing with the activities of kṣatriyas and vaiśyas another interpretation seems to emerge. Out of the six activities allowed to the brahmin only three are allowed to the kṣatriya and vaiśya: learning, sacrificing, and giving. That is, only the brahmin is complete and independent in that he alone encompasses both sides of the relationships involved.

90. *Mbh* 3. 206. 33ff.

91. *Mbh* 12. 261. 19ff.

92. *Manu* 12. 125; cf. 12. 91, 118.

93. *BhG* 6. 29.

94. *Mbh* 12. 237. 11.

95. *Mbh* 13. 90. 43; *Manu* 3. 138.

96. *Mbh* 13. 90. 38.

97. *Manu* 3. 135.

98. *BĀU* 4. 4. 23.

99. *TB* 2. 3. 2. 1.

100. This does not mean, of course, that the actual brahmin is necessarily a renouncer; usually he is not. But it is the ideal image of the brahmin that is the mainspring of brahminical prestige. Brahminization (I prefer this term to Sanskritization) is therefore not simply the imitation of the local brahmin; it refers to the ideal brahmin. The non-brahmin is thus enabled to "out-brahmin" the brahmin. To a great extent, this may be the ideological background of "anti-brahminical" movements, past as well as present.

### *Chapter Three*

1. Cf. H. Oldenberg, *Die Weltanschauung der Brāhmaṇa-Texte* (Göttingen, 1919), 150; S. Lévi, *La Doctrine du sacrifice* (Paris, 1909), 9. Also, above, chapter 2, section 6.

2. E.g., at the agnyādheya, *ĀpŚS* 5. 10. 4; at the sādyaskra, ibid. 22. 3. 13–14. See chapter 2, section 3.

3. *ŚB* 3. 8. 3. 11, 28–29; cf. *TS* 6. 3. 7. 4; *MS* 3. 10. 3. See also K. Rönnow, "Zur Erklärung des Pravargya, des Agnicayana und der Sautrāmaṇī," *Monde Oriental* 25 (1930): 137.

4. E.g., *ŚB* 1. 2. 1. 2; *TB* 3. 2. 8. 3.

5. E.g., *ŚB* 1. 3. 3. 12.

6. E.g., *ŚB* 1. 4. 5. 5; 3. 7. 4. 7.

7. E.g., *KS* 24. 8; *ŚB* 3. 2. 3. 20.

8. E.g., *KS* 25. 8, 9, 10; 26. 1; *ŚB* 3. 5. 3. 2.

9. E.g., *TS* 6. 5. 1. 1–2; *KS* 27. 10.

10. E.g., *TS* 6. 4. 9. 1; *KS* 27. 4.

11. E.g., *KS* 29. 4.

12. E.g., *TS* 2. 1. 7. 1; *KS* 13. 8.

13. E.g., *ŚB* 14. 1. 1. 10; *KB* 8. 3.

14. J. C. Heesterman, *The Ancient Indian Royal Consecration* (The Hague, 1957), 222ff.

15. See chapter 2, section 6. The actual killing of the victim is performed outside the place of sacrifice, the technical terms is, euphemistally, *saṃjñapayati,* "to cause to consent," while for sacrificing an animal the term *ālabhate,* "to take hold of," is used.

16. A. Bergaigne, *La Religion Védique,* reprinted. (Paris, 1963), 2: 80–83.

17. Only Namuci is characterized as a demon throughout. Dadhyañc puts his head at the disposal of the devas to conquer the asuras. Makha is identified with Viṣṇu, who also is an intermediary, for instance, in his role at the churning of the ocean. Viśvarūpa, "sister's son of the asuras," officiates for the devas while secretly promising a share to the asuras.

18. On these myths, see Rönnow, "Zur Erklärung." On Dadhyañc, cf. also F. D. K. Bosch, "De god met de paardekop," *Tijdschrift Bataviaas Genootschap* 67 (1927): 124–53.

19. His name connects him with the curdled milk, cf. F. B. J. Kuiper, "The Three Sanskrit roots *añc-* /*añj-*" *Vāk* 2 (1952): 63 ("showing the curdled milk")

20. In *RV* 10. 8. 9, Indra not only cuts off Viśvarūpa's three heads but also drives away his cattle. Wealth in cattle being the substance of sacrifice, this feature of Indra's heroic act aptly illustrates the actual treasure associated with the "head of the sacrifice." On Viśvarupa, see A. Hillebrandt, *Vedische Mythologie* (Breslau, 1929), 2: 206, 384–86.

21. On Makha, see the materials in J. Gonda, *Aspects of Early Viṣṇuism* (Utrecht, 1954), 167f. Though the etymology remains unclear (cf. M. Mayrhofer, *Kurzgef. Etym. Wb. des Altindischen,* s.v.), Grassmann's rendering "Kämpfer" is still interesting. According to Renou, *makhá* is a "simple variante phonique du mot maghá," "wealth, gift" (*Et. Véd. et Pan.* 4: 62; 8: 69). If these notions of festival, contest, and wealth or gift are combined, Makha turns out to be a complete personification of the potlatch-like festival.

22. Cf. *ŚB* 14. 1. 1. 18, where it is said that Dadhyañc knew "this essence *(etaṃ śukram),* this sacrifice, how the head of the sacrifice is restored, how this sacrifice becomes complete."

23. Cf. *TS* 6. 4. 9. 1; *MS* 4. 6. 2; *KS* 27. 4.

24. The Aśvins are especially fond of the madhu beverage, *madhupātama* (*RV* 8. 22. 17).

25. The notion of a contest for the secret also seems present in the version given in *ŚB* 14. 1. 1. 18–24. Indra forbade Dadhyañc to teach the secret on pain of having his head cut off. The Aśvins cheat Indra by giving Dadhyañc a horse's

head. Indra cuts off the horse's head, and the Aśvins restore Dadhyañc's own head.

26. P. Thieme, "Vorzarathustrisches bei den Zarathustriern," *Zeitschrift der Deutschen Morgenlämdische Geschicte* 107 (1957): 90. See also above, chapter 2, section 4, note 34.

27. And, one might add, in actual reality. One may compare contemporary "village festivals" involving or resulting in intervillage fighting. Intervillage fighting seems to be too much of a stereotype to be simply a question of a festival accidentally degenerating into a riot. The fighting seems to belong to the festival. See, e.g., A. R. Beals, "Conflict and Interlocal Festivals in a Southern Indian Region," *Journal of Asian Studies, Supplement* 23 (June 1964): 99–113.

28. A. Hillebrandt, *Ritualliteratur* (Strassburg, 1897), 80; See also my brief remarks in a review of L. Alsdorf, "Vegetarismus and Rinderverehrung," *Indo-Iranian Journal* 9 (1966): 148.

29. For the identification sacrificer-victim, see, e.g., *TB* 2. 1. 5. 2.

30. *TS* 2. 5. 1–2; *KS* 12. 10; *MS* 2. 4. 1; *ŚB* 5. 6. 3. 1ff. See also above, note 20.

31. W. Caland, "Eine Vierte Mitteilung über das Vādhūlasūtra," *Acta Orientalia* 6 (1927): fragm. 108.

32. It would seem to me that in this third intermediary element resides the brahman. Its mythical representatives are characterized as brahmins; their slaying is a brahmahatyā.

33. In my opinion, this is implied when it is stated that at the end of the ceremony the sacrifice leaves the sacrificer, i.e., the host, and goes to the nonsacrificer, i.e., the guest (*TS* 6. 6. 7. 3; *MS* 4. 8. 6; *KS* 29. 4). *KS* 25. 10 calls the nonsacrificer *bhrātṛvya,* "rival."

34. Thus also the sacrificer's consecration *(dīkṣā)* can only express the aspect of rebirth; its concomitant, death, is explicitly mentioned only in *JUB* 3. 9. 4, but it cannot be made tangible.

35. For a summary of this ritual, see Hillebrandt, *Ritualliteratur,* 161–65.

36. The relevant passages are *ŚB* 6. 2. 1. 1–2. 15 and *KātyŚS* 16. 1. 1–43.

37. *KātyŚS* 16. 1. 18. Cf. J. Schwab, *Das altindische Thieropfer* (Erlangen, 1886), 111ff.

38. *KātyŚS* 16. 1. 33; *ŚB* 6. 2. 1. 37–39. *BaudhŚS* 22. 2: 119. 9 also mentions golden or clay heads. *Vādhūla* keeps the human head (obtained outside the ritual) but substitutes for the other victims animals made from flour *(piṣṭapaśu)* (Caland, *Acta Orientalia* 4 [1926]: 165).

39. It is perhaps not without interest that his name occurs elsewhere in agonistic contexts (see A. H. Macdonnel and A. B. Keith, *Vedic Index* [London, 1912] s.v.) as does his ancestor's Sāyaka (cf. *JB* 1. 337).

40. For the relevant passages, see *TS* 5. 1. 8 and 5. 5. 1. 1–4; *MS* 3. 1. 10 and 3. 2. 7; *KS* 19. 8 and 20. 8; *ĀpŚS* 16. 6. 2–8. 10; *BaudhŚS* 10. 9; 22. 2; 25. 29; *Vādhūla* (Caland's extracts 59 and 108–10, *Acta Orientalia* 4: 168f. and 6: 229–33); *MānŚS* 6. 1. 2. 23; 3. 1–17.

41. Cf. *Vādhūla,* extract 110: "Previously they used to immolate a man for Prajāpati." When the gods retired from the sacrifice, the human victim was replaced by a he-goat. Apparently there was a basic rule of five "animals" interpreted in different ways by the two branches of the Yajurveda. The Black Yajurveda fills out the number five by replacing the human victim with the Prajpāti he-goat. The more systematic White Yajurveda opts for the abstract solution and systematizes the five-animal sacrifice as it stands, taking over the substitute Prajāpati he-goat as an alter-

native to the complete five-animal sacrifice. The complete sacrifice apparently originated with the Black Yajurveda since it is ascribed, by *ŚB* 6. 2. 2. 1, to the Carakas. The Vāyu he-goat may have been an original alternative.

42. The following considerations, though not strictly necessary for the argument, should illustrate the full extent of the aporia created by the classical system of ritual.

Completing the sacrifice with all five victims obviously leaves open the problem of the heads. The problem is stated in these terms: on one hand, completing the sacrifice with all five victims would "exhaust" the heads; on the other hand, taking them out of the sacrifice would disrupt the ritual. The solution preferred by the Black Yajurveda is to have it both ways: start with all five, take four of them out after consecration, and complete the ritual only with the Prajāpati he-goat. Since the goat replaces the human victim, whose head is obtained in a nonsacrificial way, the sacrifice itself does not involve decapitation (*TS* 5. 1. 8. 3; *MS* 3. 1. 10; *KS* 19. 8). This comes as near as possible to squaring the vicious circle, except for the fact that taking out consecrated victims goes against the grain of the system's closed circuit. It implies the recognition that besides the closed universe of sacrifice something else, outside it, is needed to make it fulfill its purpose (as is also clear from the fact that the human head has to come from elsewhere).

The White Yajurveda knows a similar start-with-five, end-with-one rule, but it cannot serve the same purpose as in the Black Yajurveda. The White Yajurveda has opted for the complete system and nothing but the system. The head cannot be taken outside the sacrifice; nor is there any sense in substituting an animal for the human victim, since one would still have to obtain the human head from outside. The solution attempted is to sever and keep the five heads within the sacrifice but to throw four of the bodies into the water from which the clay for the construction of the altar is to be taken. In itself, this practice may be old; moreover, it neatly expresses the idea of cyclical disintegration and reintegration: disintegrated bodies are reconstructed in the form of the altar and joined again with the heads. In terms of the system, however, the rule seems to have a somewhat different meaning. As the *Śatapatha Brāhmaṇa* puts it, by completing the sacrifice with all five victims, one "would reach the end of the fire altar," but one would not be able to collect the clay for building it (*ŚB* 6. 2. 1. 7, 13). That is, the sacrifice would be final and complete in itself (as it should be), but one would not be able to build the altar. Or, in other words, the sphere outsude the sacrifice cannot be ignored. Whereas the Black Yajurveda acknowledges this fact by giving the outside sphere its due, the White Yajurveda has to integrate it. Throwing the bodies into the water, from where the clay is later taken, it extends the sacrificial sphere so as to include the outside world.

43. *BaudhŚS* 10. 9: 8. 8: *Dīvyanta, ṛṣabhaṃ pacante vṛṣṇiṃ ca bastaṃ ca.*

44. The moment is exactly indicated (*BaudhŚS* 10. 9: 8. 19), namely, after the acts described by Schwab, *Das altindische Thieropher,* no. 26; cf. *BaudhŚS* 4. 3: 112. 9.

45. See J. C. Heestermann, "Vrātya and Sacrifice," *Indo-Iranian Journal* 6 (1962): 1–37.

46. *BaudhŚS* 18. 24: 372. 4: *Te yam ajaṃ pramāthaṃ pacante, sa eṣāṃ paśuḥ.*

47. *ĀpŚS* 16. 6. 2; *MānŚS* 6. 1. 2. 23.

48. *BaudhŚS* 10. 9: 8. 7: *Saṃgrāme hatayor aśvasya ca vaiśyasya ca.*

49. *ŚB* 6. 3. 3. 8; 4. 15.

50. *KS* 22. 10 *Prajāpatir vā ukhyam agnim abibhas, tasya śiraḥ prāvartata, tena devā aśrāmyaṃs, tasyaitacchiraḥ pratyādadhur yad ukhā.*

51. *ĀpŚS* 16. 27. 7.

52. *TS* 5. 1. 2–5; *MS* 3. 1. 3–6; *KS* 19. 2–5; *ŚB* 6. 3. 1. 22–4. 4. 22; *ĀpŚS* 16. 1–3; *BaudhŚS* 10. 1–4; *MānŚS* 6. 1. 1; *KātyŚS* 16. 2. 1–3. 13.

53. *MS* 3. 1. 3: *Áśvena vaí devā́ ágre víjitiṃ vyàjayanta, yád áśvena yánty, víjityai.*

54. *TB* 2. 4. 2. 9.

55. *MS* 3. 1. 4; *ĀpŚS* 16. 2. 6.

56. *MS* 3. 1. 3: *Vājam evá téna tásmād vr̥ṅkte*. Cf. *KS* 19. 2; *TS* 5. 1. 2. 5. Vādhūla, *Acta Orientalia* 4 (1925): 163, even adds the words *Vājam te vr̥ñje,* "I wrest the force from you," to the mantra.

57. *TS* 4. 1. 2h, k.

58. In the White Yajurveda, the place of the enemy is taken by an *anaddhāpuruṣa* (Eggeling: "shamman") to whom the mantra is addressed and who accompanies the procession (*ŚB* 6. 3. 3. 4; 4. 4. 14). He is said to be the substitute the gods saw for the human victim, and the meaning of the word is somebody "who pleases neither gods, nor the fathers, nor men" (*ŚB* 6. 3. 1. 24). I am inclined to view this in the light of *MS* 4. 8. 6 (cf. *KS* 29. 4): *Vídevo vā́ ījānáh, sádevó 'nījānaḥ,* "The gods are absent from one who has offered sacrifice, they are with him who has not offered sacrifice." In my opinion, the anaddhāpuruṣa represents the "host party" that has delivered "the head." (On this word, cf. also D. S. Ruegg, "Védique *addhā́,*" *Journal Asiatique,* 1955, 167.

59. *MānŚS* 7. 1. 2. 36; *VārāhaŚS* 3. 1. 2. 3.

60. See also Heesterman, *Consecration,* 20, 167, 170.

61. *KS* 20. 8; *TS* 5. 1. 8. 1; *ĀpŚS* 16. 6. 3; *BaudhŚS* 10. 10: 9. 13. This, in my opinion, explains why the anthill is not used in the making of the ukhā, as is done in the case of the pravargya pot; the anthill is to be used in the ritual pertaining to the human head.

62. *BaudhŚS* (dvaidhasūtra) 22. 1: 117. 8.

63. See J. Gonda, *The Savayajñas* (Amsterdam, 1965), 224f., and the literature mentioned there.

64. Cf., e.g., *SB* 1. 2. 5. 17; 6. 3. 1. 38; 8. 5. 1. 25. Gonda notes the connection purīṣa-cattle.

65. *PB* 13. 4. 13.

66. *ĀpŚS* 2. 3. 5.

67. In this connection, it may be interesting that the words Baudhāyana uses for describing the posting of the vaiśya *(tāṃ dakṣiṇato gopāyann āste)* could be interpreted as "he keeps himself south of it (the anthill), acting as a cowherd." The anthill and the loam pit thus seem to be simple emblems of what the systematized rite actually stands for, conquest of head and cattle (see also above, n. 20).

68. *MS* 4. 3. 5; *KS* 27. 10.

69. Heesterman, *Consecration,* 129.

70. Thus when *ŚB* 3. 8. 3. 28–29 characterizes offerings from the head as asuric and therefore prohibits them, this seems to indicate a rejection not of "asuric" religion, but of the dualistic pattern in which devas and asuras contend. The rival, the asura, is then excluded.

71. Cf., e.g., Louis Dumont, *Une sous caste de l'Inde du Sud* (The Hague, 1957), 378: "L'animal est décapité d'un coup d'aRuval. La dépouille, *le plus souvent la tête,* part du prêtre, reçoit une pūjā."

## *Chapter Four*

1. See M. Winternitz, "Die Flutsagen des Altertums und der Naturvölker," *Mittheilungen der Anthropologie Geschicte in Wien* 31 (1901): 305–33. Winternitz

observes: "In zahlreichen Sagen wird gar keine Ursache angegeben, sondern einfach constatiert, dass eine Überschwemmung hereinbrach" (315). Man's sinfulness seems to be a prominent motif in a minority of seventy-three flood stories listed by Winternitz.

2. *ŚB* 1. 8. 1. 1–11. See A. Weber *Indische Studien* 1 (1850): 161ff. H. Usener, *Die Sintflutsagen* (Bonn 1899), 25–28; A. Hohenberger, *Die Indische Flutsage und das Matsyapurāṇa* (Leipzig, 1930), 4–6; S. Lévi, *La Doctrine du sacrifice dans les brāhmaṇas,* reprinted. (Paris, 1966), 115–17.

3. Cf. Winternitz, *Die Flutsagen,* 327. For Manu's being instructed to take seeds on board his ark see *Mbh* 3. 187. 32; *Matsyapurāṇa* 2. 11; *Agnipurāṇa* 2. 12; *Bhāgavatapurāṇa* 8. 24. 34; *Daśāvatāracarita* 1.32.

4. As Eggeling observes *iḍayā carati* has the double meaning of proceeding with the Iḍā ceremony and of living with Iḍā *SB* 1.8 1. 11).

5. *KS* 11. 2: 146. 6–8; see W. Caland, *Altindische Zauberei: Darstellung der altindischen Wunschopfer* (Amsterdan, 1908), 117 (no. 170), for the sacrifice for which the story should account.

6. See, e.g., *RV* 4. 42. 4; 7. 86. 1; cf. also *RV* 1. 103. 2; 2. 11. 7; 2. 15. 2. *RV* 10. 31. 6 ("This benefactor's favor having spread out with [to the extent of], the earth became the primordial cow") may contain a hidden reference to Iḍā or, as suggested by Geldner, the *dakṣiṇā* cow (the two are intimately connected). Such conflation of different themes is proper to the rhetoric of the *Ṛgveda* but in order to be rhetorically effective the themes have to be different. For the cosmogonic scenario involving the *instabilis terra,* its riveting and spreading, see F. B. J. Kuiper, "Cosmogony and Conception: A Query," *History of Religions* 10 (1970): 91–138, esp. 107–10.

7. *KS* 29. 3: 171. 14.

8. See A. Hillebrandt, *Vedische Mythologie* (Breslau, 1927), 2: 145–53, on Agni's flight and hiding place in the waters.

9. W. Caland, "Vierte Mitteilung über das Vādhūlasūtra," *Acta Orientalia* 6 (1927): 110–20. The ritual context is the offering cake for Agni, made of rice or barley.

10. For a similar succession of immolations of the *medha,* see ŚB 1. 2. 3. 5–7.

11. Caland, *Altindische Zauberei,* 119.

12. See M. Defourny, "Note sur le symbolisme de la corne dans le Mahābhārata et la mythologie brahmanique classique," *Indo-Iranian Journal* 18 (1976): 17–23. Insofar as the fishes in both cases can be put on a par, Vādhūla seems to lend credibility to Defourny's suggestions, but the possible associations of the horm seem too diverse to allow a confident identification. If Defourny is right, it would make Manu the victim attached to the *yūpa*. This is in itself not impossible, the sacrificer (represented by the sacrificial victim) being, ideologically, himself the victim. But the *Śatapatha's* telling of the flood story in no way supports this consequence. At any rate, the fish in the flood story does indeed seem to represent, if not sacrifice itself, at least the life-creating force that is inherent in sacrifice.

13. See W. Caland and V. Henry, *L'Agniṣṭoma* (Paris, 1906), 397 (no. 254d).

14. Ibid., 406–9.

15. Cf. *ŚB* 1. 1. 1. 12; 3. 1. 4. 15; *TB* 3. 2. 4. 1; *MS* 4. 1. 4: 6. 1; *AB* 2. 20. 11; *KB* 12. 1.

16. For the invocation *(iḍopahvāna),* see *ŚānkhŚS* 1. 11–12. For the complex of rites involved in the Iḍā ceremony, see A. Hillebrandt, *Das altindische Neu- und Vollmondsopfer* (Jena, 1880), 122–130; *ĀpŚS* 3. 1. 6–3. 1.

17. See J. C. Heesterman, "Reflections on the Significance of the *dakṣiṇā,*" *Indo-Iranian Journal* 3 (1959): 241–58.

18. *TS* 2. 6. 7. 1. The verb *karoti* in this passage is rendered by Keith as "to produce," by Caland (*ĀpŚS* 3. 1. 7) as *verwenden,* "to utilize." The expression is rather cryptic and possibly goes back to a sacrificial riddle. In this connection, it may be mentioned that *karoti* can, in the context of the ritual, occur in the sense of "to kill." In that case, the passage may originally have referred to the miraculous capacities of the cow as a sacrificial victim. As will be argued, this may be relevant for the goddess Iḍā.

19. Cf. *MS* 4. 2. 13: 36. 3–7, where Mitra and Varuna fashion the (Iḍā) cow out of an *indigesta moles* produced by the gods (see below).

20. Cf. *RV* 1. 128. 1; 2. 10. 1; 3. 23. 4; 3. 29. 4; 6. 1. 2; 10. 1. 6; 10. 70. 1; 10. 191. 1; *TS* 3. 5. 11. 1(d). For the ghee-footed goddess Iḍā, see *RV* 10. 70. 3. For "the head of the earth," on which the ghee libation is made, as the archetypal place of sacrifice, see *TS* 6. 1. 8. 2.

21. Cf. *RV* 3. 29. 3 and 6. 52. 16. Also A. Bergaigne, *La Religion Védique,* reprinted. (Paris, 1963), 2: 11.

22. See W. Caland and V. Henry, *L'Agniṣṭoma,* 37–40 (no. 31).

23. Cf. *ŚB* 3. 3. 1. 12.

24. See *Indo-Iranian Journal* 3 (1959): 254.

25. *MS* 4. 2. 1: 21. 11–12.

26. *MS* 4. 2. 13.

27. See Caland and Henry, *L'Agniṣṭoma,* 36f. (no. 30). For the mantras see *TS* 1. 2. 4f–o.

28. Cf. Lévi *Doctrine du sacrifice,* 118–20. In most versions, the wife is let off, but according to *ŚB* 1. 1. 4. 14–17, she is immolated without scruple.

29. *ŚB* 11. 4. 3. 1–2.

30. Cf. *ĀpŚS* 8. 11. 12. This sacrifice is part of the autumnal *sākamedha.*

31. Cf. *ĀpŚS* 5. 19. 4. For many cows being slaughtered, see *BaudhŚS* 2. 15: 57. 12–15. Significantly, the cow staked in the gambling may be replaced by a (vegetal) rice mess *(odana).*

32. *TS* 1. 2. 5d–e.

33. *MS* 4. 2. 3: 24. 16–25. 5.

34. For the rivalry of gods and asuras for the Iḍā (and cattle), see *TS* 1. 7. 1. 3. In connection with violent conflict, one might also adduce Rudra's shooting at and fatally wounding Prajāpati to punish him for his incestuous behavior toward his daughter. This theme is associated with the "foreportion" *(prāśitra)* of the sacrificial cake given to the brahman priest. Though relevant to our argument, it is mythologically kept apart from the Iḍā theme and dealt with separately in the ritual.

35. See *TS* 1. 7. 1. 4; 2. 6. 8. 2; *ŚB* 1. 7. 4. 19.

36. *TS* 1. 7. 1. 1.

### Chapter Five

1. On the vāda expositions and their development into treatises on logic, see Gerhard Oberhammer, "Ein Beitrag zu den Vāda-Traditionen Indiens," *Weiner Zeitschrift für die Kunde Süd - und Ost asiens* 7 (1963): 63ff.

2. On this meaning of the contest, see F. B. J. Kuiper, "The Ancient Aryan Verbal Contest," *Indo-Iranian Journal* 4 (1960): 218ff.

3. L. Renou, "La Notion de *bráhman,*" *Journal Asiatique* 237 (1949): 7ff.; also, "Le Passage des Brāhmaṇa aux Upaniṣad," *Journal of the American Oriental Society* 73 (1953): 138ff. Cf. P. Thieme, "Bráhman," *Zeitschrift der Duetschen Morgenlämdischen Gcschicte* 102 (1952): 91–129. Thieme argues that Renou's "riddle formulation" is at best an intensified or special meaning of the general "formulation." (p. 102).

4. For instance, the Kurus remain silent on a question put to them by the Pañcālas and are therefore defeated. The solution is not stated but give outisde the dialogue by the narrotor (*JB* 1. 262); cf. also *ŚB* 1. 5. 4. 6, where the asuras remain silent in the fifth round, thus yielding victory to the devas.

5. As does, e.g., Janaka in the first round of the debate cycle with Yāhñavalkya (*ŚB* 11. 6. 2. 4); this is possibly also the case with Uddālaka when he refuses to answer, giving his answers only afterward to his pupils (*JB* 1. 296). This withdrawal still seems to be reflected in Caraka's vāda rules, where the winning party is said to sit down leaving the decision to the assembly *(pariṣad)*—of course after having made certain that the assembly will hand him the palm (*Caraka Saṃhitá* 3. 8. 25)

6. *Ví yás tastámbha ṣáḷ imā́ rájāṃsy ajásya rūpé.*

7. *Tisró mātṝ́s trī́n pitṝ́n bíbhrad éka ūrdhvás tasthau ném áva glāpayanti.*

8. Verse 34: *Pṛchā́mi tvā páram ántaṃ pṛthivyā́ḥ, pṛchā́mi yátra bhúvanasya nā́bhiḥ, pṛchā́mi tvā vṛ́ṣṇo áśvasya rétaḥ, pṛchā́mi vācáḥ paramáṃ vyòma.*

9. Verse 35: *Iyám védiḥ páro ántaḥ pṛthivyā́, ayám yajñó bhúvanasya nā́bhiḥ, ayáṃ sómo vṛ́ṣṇo áśvasya réto brahmā́yám vācáḥ paramáṃ vyòma.*

10. It is no mere coincidence that these two verses, *RV* 1. 164, 34–35, form the conclusion of the well-known brahmodya after the immolation of the sacrificial horse (cf. *ŚB* 13. 5. 2. 21; *VS* 23. 61–62). For this brahmodya, cf. also Renou, "La Notion de *brāhman,*" 32.

11. This mystery is also expressed in the ritual copulation of the queen with the dead horse (a contradiction) and in the exchange of obscene verses at this scene.

12. According to the Black Yajurveda, this verse is indeed spoken by the brahman officiant, who thereby triumphantly concludes the brahmodya of the horse sacrifice (cf. *ĀpŚS* 20. 19. 8). Enunciating the final *bráhman,* he shows himself a true *brahmán.*

13. At this point, I should warn that though I am indebted to Renou's study, the above exposé is not covered by the authority of the great savant. The main difference is the emphasis I place on antithetical formulation, as against mere identification. Silence is the outcome of the verbal contest, not merely a stage on the way to the final formulation. Renou seems to suggest a similar line when he tentatively suggests that the classical brahmodya is 'peut-être dégradé" with regard to "l'énigme essentielle du védisme ancien," but he does not follow this up. This does not preclude the possibility of riddles with explicit solutions at particular occasions. However, the oldest texts seem exclusively to give enigmatic formulations without explicit answers, as Renou also observes ("La Notion de *bráhman,*" 41).

14. This self-assertion in lieu of solution recurs also in other places of the aśvamedha brahmodya. The officiants take turns questioning each other. Thus, at the question of the brahman officiant concerning the three places *(padá),* the udgātṛ answers, "I am in those three places" (*VS* 23. 50); next the two partners change roles, and the udgātṛ questions the brahman, who ends his answer with "you are not superior to me in *māyā*" (*VS* 52); this seems to be final, as now two other debaters take over. Next again brahman-udgātṛ and vice versa; when it is the brahman's turn to answer, he simply states, "I know the navel of the world," without any further explanation (*VS* 60). Finally, in a last round, the sacrificer challenges the brahman ("I ask you . . . "), who then concludes, as we saw, with the triumphant answer ("I am the highest extension of speech . . . ").

15. *ŚB* 11. 6. 3. 11. Cf. the following brahmodya passages:

10. 3. 3. 5: Dhīra goes up to Jābāla, who challenges him with questions, but Dhīra is equal to the occasion. Jābāla gets dọwn from his seat and becomes Dhīra's pupil.

10. 3. 4. 2: (Uddālaka Āruṇi) questions Vaiśvārasavya, whom his son had retained

as a hotṛ officiant. Not knowing the answers to the second set of questions, Vaiśvārasavya becomes Uddālaka's pupil.

11. 4. 1. 9: Uddālaka Āruṇi, though recognized as "a brahman and son of a brahman who will cause his challenger's head to fly off," is nonetheless silenced by Svaïdāyana and, with the characteristic act of bringing firewood, becomes the latter's pupil.

11. 5. 3. 13: Śauceya, outwitted by Uddālaka, whom he has challenged, surrenders, firewood in hand, and becomes Uddālaka's pupil.

11. 6. 2. 1; 4. 10: Janaka challenges three brahmins; among them is Yājñavalkya. The latter proves himself the most knowledgeable and is given a thousand cows by Janaka, who then goes off leaving Yājñavalkya with a last unanswered question. Yājñavalkya goes after Janaka to challenge him but in fact becomes his pupil. Having received Janaka's teaching, Yājñavalkya grants Janaka at his request the right to question him in his turn; thereby Janaka, though a kṣatriya, becomes a brahman.

The last episode clearly shows the pattern of challenge and reversal: First Janaka asks the questions, then it is Yājñavalkya's turn, and finally Janaka again challenges Yājñavalkya with questions. In a similar way, we see Uddālaka first as challenger and then being challenged himself by Svaidāyana and becoming his pupil. The contestants in the brahmodya of the horse sacrifice also take turns. The contest, then, goes on indefinitely, cyclically alternating the roles.

16. See, e.g., *ŚB* 11. 6. 2. 4.

17. See chapter 2, especially sections 5 and 6.

18. L. Renou, "Le Passage des Brāhmaṇa aux Upaniṣad," *Journal American Oriental Society* 73 (1953): 138–44.

19. For these formulas, cf. *TĀ* 3. 1. 1 (daśahotṛ); 3. 2. 1 (caturhotṛ); 3. 3. 1 (pañcahotṛ); 3. 5. 1 (saptahotṛ); 3. 6. 1 (saḍḍhotṛ).

20. *TB* 2. 2. 1. 4: *etád vaí devā́nāṃ paramám gúhyaṃ bráhma, yáccáturhotāraḥ*.

21. *PB* 4. 9. 12; *AB* 5. 25. 22; *KB* 25. 4; *TB* 2. 3. 5. 1. Cf. *ĀpŚS* 21. 11. 12ff.

22. It is interesting that something of the original openness of the contest is still discernible in the description of this brahmodya: "Some say, 'Agni is the gṛhapati,' . . . some say, 'Vāyu is the gṛhapati,'. . . some say, 'The one that burns yonder (the sun) is the gṛhapati' " (*AB* 5. 25. 22).

23. In this connection, it may be noted that according to *TB* 2. 3. 5. 5, the knowledge that the caturhotṛ formulas are the whole cosmos gives victory in debate.

24. *PB* 5. 5. 13; cf. *KS* 34. 5. According to the *Taittirīyaka*s and the *Jaiminīya Brāhmaṇa,* the praising and reviling are done by the two champions who fight for the hide (cf. *TS* 7. 5. 9. 2; *TB* 1. 2. 6. 7; *JB* 2. 405). The abhigara and the apagara are further mentioned in the list of officiating participants at the serpent sattra (*PB* 25. 15. 3). That these two particular officiants are not just an incidental feature is suggested by the fact that at least one of them, the abhigara, has found a place in Baudhāyana's list of officiants in the standard Soma sacrifice, though no specific function is assigned to him. He occurs there together with the *dhruvagopa* (the guardian of the Soma beverage, not mentioned otherwise) and the *saṃśrāva* as an acolyte of the equally elusive *sadasya* (apparently the representative of the guests) (*BaudhŚS* 2. 3.: 37. 1). Obviously, a praising and reviling contest cannot be part of the explicitly nonagonistic classical ritual, and it is hardly surprising that the abhigara's counterpart, the "reviler," has been suppressed. It is to be noted that his fellow acolyte, the *dhruvagopa,* who guards the permanent Soma draught—against whom?—and who is a *rājapūtra,* also seems to be a contestant (on the side of the host and sacrificer). This suggests that the contest between "praiser" and "reviler"

originally was an important feature of the ritual in general, not just of the mahāvrata in its classical form. This conclusion is further strengthened by the fact that in the pañca- and ṣaḍḍhotṛs we find an abhigara. Indeed, in the latter we even find two *yajnasya abhigarau,* which probably means both abhigara and apagara (*TĀ* 3. 6. 1; 5. 1).

25. *TB* 1. 2. 6. 7: "These (sacrificers) cause upheaval *(udvāsikāriṇaḥ),* these have caused misfortune *(durbhūta).*"

26. Insofar as sacrifice still involved the death of the victim, the actual killing was removed from the place of sacrifice, the victims being immolated in a separate shed outside the ritual enclosure. Even so, from the point of view of the classical ritual, it could only be viewed as an embarrassing breach, that is, an "error." Hence the connections between violent death in sacrifice and the concept of the ritual error (see my article "Vrātya and Sacrifice," *Indo-Iranian Journal* 6 (1962): 22–24).

27. *ŚB* 11. 4. 2. 17–20.

28. Cf. *PB* 15. 6. 5; *ĀpŚS* 21. 9. 7–9, with Caland's notes. This tenth day seems to have been a problem for the classical ritualists. It is called *avivākya,* "on which no declaration of errors should be made." However, only *AB* 5. 22. 5 gives this rule simply. The other texts discuss at length whether "declaration" is or is not to be made, the conclusion being that it is to be made. The central problem, however, seems to be another one, By whom is it to be made? The term *avivākya* implies that a declaration is to be made, but by somebody else. Thus *AB* 3. 35. 4 says that no "declaration" of possible errors in the recitation of the āgnimāruta śastra (in the normal Soma sacrifice) is to be made and that (therefore) one should provide for a separate "declarer" *(tasmād āgnimārute na vyucyam, eṣṭavyo vivaktā),* whom "one thus makes into a bridge for passing," meaning that the "declarer" takes the onus of the error or, originally, the onus of death. (One may also interpret the passage as an unresolved mīmāṃsā, simply stating the two theses). It would seem that the problem arose with the elimination of the contest, verbal or otherwise, from the classical ritual.

29. Cf. *PB* 4. 9. 14; *ĀpŚS* 21. 11. 13ff. *KātyŚS* 12. 4. 19–20 makes the reviling of Prajāpati the substance of the brahmodya and calls it *aguṇākhyāna,* tale of the negative qualities. *AB* 5. 25 and *KB* 27. 5 give, instead of blame, the enumeration of Prajāpati's "bodies" ("eater of food and mistress of food," "the fair and the beautiful," etc.), thus eliminating the controversial nature.

30. As such it occurs in the brahmodya hymn *RV* 1. 164. 33.

31. Cf. *PB* 17. 5. 1; *TS* 2. 5. 1. 2; *KS* 12. 10.

32. *AB* 7. 27–28.

33. *AB* 7. 27. 1 *(pāpasya . . . karmaṇah kartāraḥ, apūtāyai vāco vaditāraḥ)*

34. The word *itthaṃvid* recalls the well-known phrase (found especially in the *Śatapatha Brāhmaṇa*) *ya evaṃ veda,* "who knows thus," namely, the connections or identifications of the cosmic with the ritual elements. In our passage, the knowledge does not seem to refer to identifications so much as to antithetical relations, essential to the verbal contest.

35. The story is used to legitimate the separation of the varṇas, who should not eat each other's food, that is, should not maintain commensality. But it fails to explain why the kṣatriya is excluded from the Soma drink, whereas Indra, as Rāma Mārgaveya explains, later won back the Soma drink at Tvaṣṭṛ's sacrifice. The difficulty seems to be that Indra regained the Soma drink in a contest, which is out of the question in the classical ritual. Moreover, the doctrine of the sacrificial drink proper to each of the varṇas seems to have originally referred to each of the four classificatory groups having charge of a particular kind of food, which is exchanged

with the others. At least this is implied in Rāma's statements that partaking of the food from another varṇa brings about a change of varṇa among the partaker's progeny in the second or third generation. It might be interesting to compare on this point Held's theory on the origin of the classical varṇa from tribal clan organization (G. J. Held, *The Mahābhārata: An Ethnological Study* [Leiden, 1936], chap. 1).

36. The fact that the dispute develops into a treatise on food does not mean a later accretion but is quite consistent with the central concern of this contest (the goods of life). It may be noted that the mahāvrata is also consistently considered as (Prajāpati's) "food."

37. Indra, as Bergaigne already noted, is about the only god in the *Ṛgveda* whose existence seems to be doubted. See *La Religion Védique,* (Paris, 1963) reprinted. 2: 166.

38. *Yáṃ smā pṛchánti kúha séti ghorám, utém āhur naíṣó astíty enamsó aryáḥ puṣṭīr víja ivā́ mināti, śrád asmai dhatta, sá janāsa índraḥ.*

39. Oldenberg in his *Rigveda-Noten* admits to some doubt, but he does not go into the matter.

40. Cf. *RV* 8. 100. 3; 5. 30. 1; 6. 18. 3; 6. 27. 3; 8. 64. 7; 10. 22. 1.

41. Cf. H. P. Schmidt, *Bṛhaspati and Indra* (Wiesbaden, 1968), 237f. Schmidt specifically refers to Indra's priestly characteristics, also indicated by epithets sometimes given to Indra, for example, *ṛṣi, kavi, vipra*. What is of interest to us here is Indra's apparently shifting nature. Schmidt wants to harmonize these shifting traits into a single consistent image of a king-priest. My approach is different in that it emphasizes as essential Indra's ambiguity and alternation between the two roles, corresponding to the alternation and exchange between sacrificial patron and brahman.

42. *RV* 5. 30. 2: *Ávācacakṣaṃ padám asya sasvár.*

43. *RV* 5. 30. 3: *Védad ávidvāñ chṛṇávac ca vidvā́n váhate 'yám maghávā sárvasenaḥ.*

44. *RV* 6. 18. 3: *Ásti svin nú vīryàṃ tát ta indra, ná svid asti, tád ṛtuthā́ ví vocaḥ.*

45. Cf. also the questions "Where is the bull?" "To whose Soma drink will he come?" and "Who is nearest to you at the time of recitation?" (*RV* 8. 64. 7–9). Similarly, *RV* 10. 22. 1–2, where the question "Where is Indra's fame heard, among which people is he heard of as an ally" is followed by the triumphant answer "Here Indra's fame is heard."

46. Cf., e.g., *RV* 4. 24. 3; *PB* 9. 2. 22.

47. *TB* 1. 4. 6. 1: *Ékaiko vaí janátāyām índrah. ékaṃ vā etáv índram abhí sáṃ sunutaḥ, yaú dvaú saṃ sunutáḥ. prajā́patir vā́ eṣá vítāyate, yád yajñáḥ. tásya grā́vāṇo dántāḥ, anyatarám vā́ eté samsunvatór nírbapsati*. Cf. in this connection the formula, recorded in the *Sāmavidhana Bráhmaṇa,* for success in a verbal contest in the gathering (pariṣad): *Rājanvān aham, arājaskas tvam,* "I have the king (on my side), you have no king" (2. 7. 13).

48. From this point of view, a separate investigation—which cannot be undertaken here—of terms like *mṛdhravāc, avāc, vivāc* might be worthwhile. See Kuiper, "The Ancient Verbal Contest," 273. On *saṃsava,* see chapter 2, section 3.

49. *RV* 8. 100. *Prá sú stómaṃ bharata vājayánta, índrāya satyáṃ yádi satyám ásti, néndro astī́ti néma u tva āha, ká īṃ dadarśa, kám abhí ṣṭavāma;* Verse 4: *Ayám asmi jaritaḥ pásya mehá.*

50. *Yám krándasī saṃyatī́ vihváyete páré 'vara ubháyā amítrāḥ, samānáṃ cid ráthan ātasthivā́ṃsā nā́nā havete, sá janāsa índraḥ*. The image of the two on the same chariot seems to be an expression for the two partners bound together in the common endeavor of the cosmic fight for the goods of life. The sacrifice is equally

a battle, albeit that in the classical conception there is no opposite party. It is interesting, though, that the vedi in the classical animal sacrifice should have the measurements of a chariot (*ĀpŚS* 7. 3. 7).

51. Cf. *JB* 2. 1: *Yām imāṃ (vācam) śreṣṭhinas tūṣṇīm āsinasyaiva jijñāsante*. On the *śreṣṭhin,* see W. Rau, *Staat und Gesellschaft im alten Indien,* (Wiesbaden, 1957), 74.

52. See chapter 2, section 3; Heesterman, "Vrātya and Sacrifice," 27ff.

53. On the connection of the sacrificer's ritual birth and his dakṣiṇā distribution, see J. C. Heesterman, "Reflections on the Significance of the *dákṣiṇā,*" *Indo-Iranian Journal* 4 (1959): 241ff.

54. See J. C. Heesterman, *The Ancient Indian Royal Consecration* (The Hague, 1957), 141; also below, chapter 10, section 6.

55. See above, section 4.

56. The king, though, is beaten, according to the White Yajurveda (See Heesterman *Consecration,* 141.

57. Ibid., 103ff.

58. On this point, cf. Oberhammer, "*Beitrag zu den Vāda-Traditionen,*" 72.

***Chapter Six***

1. On the relationship of the dharma with the Veda, see J. C. Heesterman, "Die Autorität des Veda," in Gerhard Oberhammer *Offenbarung: Geistige Realität des Menschen,* ed. (Vienna, 1974), 29–40.

2. Madeline Biardeau and Charles Malamoud, *Le Sacrifice dans l'Inde ancienne* (Paris, 1976).

3. I refer to the agnicayana performance recorded by J. F. Staal and R. Gardner. For a full description, see J. F. Staal, ed., *Agni* 2 vols., (Berkeley, 1983).

4. A. Hillebrandt, *Ritualliteratur* (Strassburg, 1897), 75.

5. On the prāṇāgnihotra see below, section 7.

6. Robert Lingat, *Les Sources du droit dans le système traditionel de l'Inde* (Paris, 1967), 239.

7. Birardeau and Malamoud, *Le Sacrifice,* 153.

8. The question is also posed by Professor Biardeau: "Le problème soulevé maintenant est donc de savoir si le sacrifice n'est plus effectivement qu'une affaire de langage" (ibid., 81). She concludes, however, that even the confrontation with world renunciation could not dislodge sacrifice from its central position. See my review of her study, *Indo-Iranian Journal* 21 (1979): 47–49.

9. The expression is L. Renou's. See "Le Destin du Veda," *Études védiques et paṇinéennes* 6 (1980): 2.

10. On the problem of ahiṃsā, cf. L. Alsdorf, *Beiträge zur Geschichte von Vegetarismus und Rinderverehrung in Indien* (Wiesbaden, 1962); H.-P. Schmidt, "The Origin of *ahiṃsa,*" in *Mélanges d'Indianisme à la mémoire de Louis Renou* (Paris, 1968), 625–55; also my review of Alsdorf, in *Indo-Iranian Journal* 9 (1960): 147–49. For the classical Mīmāṃsā view denying ahiṃsā ultimate authority, which it reserves for the Vedic injunction of animal sacrifice, see W. Halbfass, *Śankara und Kumārila, Studien zur Indologie und Iranistik* 9 (Reinbek, 1983), 2–9. For our purpose, the main point is the unresolved and indeed insoluble conflict between Vedic sacrifice and ahiṃsā.

11. For a critique of current explanations of sacrifice, see J. van Baal, "Offering, Sacrifice, and Gift," *Numen* 23 (1976): 161–78. Van Baal stresses the communicative function of sacrifice.

12. Marcel Mauss, "Essai sur le don," *Année Sociologique*, n.s. 1 (1924): 30–186; reprinted in Mauss, *Sociologie et Anthropologie* (Paris, 1950).

13. *RV* 10. 90. 16 ( = 1. 164. 50): *Tā́ni dhā́rmāni prathamā́ni āsan.*

14. *ŚB* 3. 6. 3. 1: *Yajnáṃ hyèvédáṃ sárvam ánu.* H. Oldenberg, *Die Religion des Veda,* (Stuttgart and Berlin, 1923), 321; Oldenbergg, *Die Weltanschauung der Brāhmaṇa-Texte* (Göttingen, 1919), 150; S. Lévi, *La Doctrine du sacrifice,* reprint ed. (Paris, 1966), 9. It is perhaps significant that this idea finds it most systematic expression in the speculations on the agnihotra sacrifice, which will be discussed below, sections 6–8.

15. E.g., *ŚB* 12. 2. 3. 12. See J. C. Heesterman, "Opferwildnis und Ritualordnung," in *Epiphanie des Heils,* ed. Gerhard Oberhammer (Vienna, 1982), 13–25.

16. The legend is found in *AB* 7. 13–18 and *ŚānkhŚS* 15. 17–19 (cf. F. Weller, *Die Legende von Śunaḥśepa* [Berlin, 1956]). The sons who rebel against the adoption are expelled by their father with the words: "Your progeny will have the end (or the ends, *antam, antān)* as its share." This refers to the far out areas at the end of the world, where, as the text says, they will become the peripheral tribes of Andhras, Puṇḍras, Śabaras, Pulindas, and Mūtibus (or Mūcipas). But the word *anta-* seems to refer to death and impurity as well. The expelled sons are burdened with the evil of death, as is in keeping with their impurity as tribals on the fringes of brahminic civilization. The commentator Sāyaṇa speaks here of "caṇḍālas and the like."

17. *JB* 2. 297–99 (Auswahl, no. 156).

18. According to *JUB* 4. 26. 12, the center of the earth is only one span to the north of this spot.

19. The idea of the fallen warrior's ascent to heaven is found in India in various forms, especially as salvation in later times. Thus, for instance, the demon who attains salvation when slain by the goddess or Śiśupāla's fiery essence being united with the divine Kṛṣṇa after the latter has decapitated him with his discus weapon (*Mbh* 2. 45. 25–29; Viṣṇu-Purāṇa 4. 15. 12–15; in the second passage, the salvation motif is stressed). See, in general, J. Filliozat, 'L'Abandon de la vie par le sage et les suicides du criminel et du héros dans la tradition indienne," *Arts Asiatiques* 15 (1967): 65–88. In this connection, it is interesting that the victim of violent death and the deceased ascetic are put on a par as beneficiaries of the Nārāyaṇabali sacrifice (H. Krick, "Nārāyaṇabali und Opfertod," *Wiener Zeitschrift für die Kunde Süd und Ostasiens* 21 (1977): 71–141.

20. *JB* 2. 297 (Cf. n. 17).

21. *JB* 1. 337.

22. E.g., *Mbh* 2. 22. 17; 5. 141. 29ff; 12. 98. 12ff. It is not fortuitous that Śiśupāla's decapitation by Kṛṣṇa (see above, n. 19) takes place in the context of the rājasūya sacrifice.

23. *Mbh* 1. 2. 12; cf. 7. 11. 43: *yugasyeva paryāsaḥ*. For the interpretation of the *Mahābhārata* war as a sacrifice, see H. Gehrts, *Mahābhārata* (Bonn, 1975), 162ff., 234ff. Also above, chapter 2, section 3 and note 16.

24. *Mbh* 2. 12. 29–30, 46. 7–17.

25. On the kalivarjyas, see P. V. Kane, *History of Dharmaśāstra,* 2d ed., (Poona, 1973), 3: 926f.

26. *Manu* 1. 86. See also Robert Lingat, "Time and the Dharma," *Contributions to Indian Sociology* 6 (1962): 7–16.

27. See above, chapter 3. For the popular buffalo sacrifices (where the victim is immolated by decapitation), see Biardeau and Malamoud, *Le Sacrifice,* 144–53.

28. E.G., *ŚB* 11. 6. 2. 6–10. Though the idea of cosmic circulation is clearest in the Upaniṣads (Cf. E. Frauwallner, *Geschichte der Indischen Philosophie* (Salzburg, 1953), 49f; U. Schneider, Die altindische Lehre vom Kreislauf des Wassers, *Saeculum* 12 [1961]: 1–11), it is no less important in ritualistic thinking. For an early instance, see *RV* 1. 164. 51.

29. See above, chapter 5, section 5, and especially note 26.

30. For the noncommunal, strictly individual nature of Vedic ritual, see chapter 2, especially sections 6 and 7. Cf. also *Manu* 3. 151, 164; 4. 205; 11. 198.

31. For a detailed description according to the śrautasūtras see P. E. Dumont, *L'Agnihotra* (Baltimore, 1939). The explanations in the brāhmaṇa texts have been gathered, translated, and annotated by H. W. Bodewitz, *The Daily Evening and Morning Offering according to the Brāhamaṇas* (Leiden, 1976).

32. Oldenberg, *Weltanschauung;* P. E. Dumont, L'Agnihotra, vii–ix; Bodewitz, *Evening and Morning Offering*, 2–5.

33. *ŚB* 2. 3. 1. 11–12.

34. *TB* 2. 1. 5. 3.

35. *ŚB* 1. 2. 1. 20; 2. 2. 2. 1; 3. 9. 4. 2; 4. 3. 4. 1; 11. 1. 2. 1.

36. *Manu* 3. 68.

37. *ŚB* 11. 6. 1; *JB* 1. 42–43. Cf. H. W. Bodewitz, *Jaiminīya Brāhmaṇa 1.1–65*, translation and commentary (Leiden, 1973), 99ff. See also Schmidt, "Origin of *ahiṃsā*," 644f.

38. For the need of expiation, see *TB* 2. 1. 5. 3; for food as the remainder of the agnihotra, see *ŚB* 2. 3. 1. 11f.

39. See the passages translated by Bodewitz, *Evening and Morning Offering*, 155–7. Though these passages do not directly refer to expiation but the subduing of death—equated with the fire—by the food offering, the link with the expiation of the sin of "killing" the food can hardly be overlooked. These passages keep strictly within the compass of the ritual and its cosmic mechanism without dealing with the worldy matter of food and its provenance.

40. *TB* 2. 1. 5. 11.

41. *MS* 1. 8. 9: 130. 9; *TB* 1. 4. 4. 10; *ŚB* 12. 4. 1. 2; *JB* 1. 51; *AB* 7. 12. 3; *ĀpŚS* 9. 10. 15–17 (cf. also 9. 6. 11 and 14. 31. 2).

42.*ĀpŚS* 9. 11. 1–4. This recalls the misfortune of Sthūra and similar cases of slain sacrificers, discussed above, section 3.

43. *JB* 2. 69–70. See chapter 2, section 6.

44. *ĀpŚS* 6. 15. 10; *MS* 1. 8. 7: 126. 17. See further, P. E. Dumont, *L'Agnihotra*, 37f., 87f., 136; Bodewitz, *Evening and Morning Offering*, 116f.

45. The sacrifice, of course, involves a sacrificial meal. Hence its character of a "stilisiertes Gastmahl" (P. Thieme, "Vorzarathustrisches bei den Zarathustriern," *Zeitschrift der Deutsche Morgenlämdische Geschicte* 107 [1957]: 90). The sacrificial meal as a communal feast was, however, broken up and eliminated from the śrauta ritual. See J. C. Heesterman, "Veda and Society," *Studia Orientalia* 50 (1981): 50–64.

46. For the dīkṣita's setting out on a chariot, see *ĀpŚS* 10. 19. 6ff.; for his alms begging tour *(saniyācana)*, ibid. 10. 18. 4ff. Though the two activities are treated by the śrauta rules as two separate episodes, they are clearly connected. Moreover, it would otherwise be inexplicable why the dīkṣita should travel at all. The combination of chariot and "begging" brings us back to the original raiding habits that belong to the ancient sacrificial scenario. Here we see how the ritualists "defused" the warrior aspect of the dīkṣā, namely by disjoining and isolating its elements. In a

similar way, the battle for "the head of the sacrifice" was defused and its separate elements made innocuous, albeit at the price of each becoming in itself inexplicable (see chapter 3).

47. For the impurity of the dīkṣitā, see J. C. Heesterman "Vrātya and Sacrifice," *Indo-Iranian Journal* 6 (1962): 11–15.

48. See J. C. Heesterman "Householder and Wanderer," in *Way of Life: Essays in Honour of Louis Dumont,* ed. T. N. Madan (New Delhi, 1982), 251–71, esp. 255.

49. *BaudhDhS* 2. 12. 1–15 and 2. 18. 8–9. See also chapter 2, note 78 and the literature cited there. For the prāṇāgnihotra as "a ceremony for dining," see Bodewitz, *Jaiminīya Brāhmaṇa,* 256, 310.

50. *MS* 3. 6. 6: 67. 6; 3. 6. 10: 74. 7; *KS* 23. 7: 82, 21; *ŚB* 12. 3. 5. 3; *JB* 2. 38 (Auswahl no. 120); *KB* 7. 3; *ĀpŚS* 10. 14. 4–7; 16. 11; 17. 8.

51. In this respect, it may be significant that among the Nambudiris in Central Kerala, whose remarkable devotion to Vedic śrauta ritual has kept its practice alive till the present day (see above, n. 3), the great landed families do not appear, as a rule, to perform these sacrifices. A traditional explanation has it that such families have performed them in the past up to ninety-nine times; one more time would make them equal to Indra, which would be too dangerous an ambition. One might also say that they have to the extent of the humanly possible left sacrifice behind them. But they help and encourage their lesser brethren to perform śrauta sacrifices among themselves.

### *Chapter Seven*

1. The relationship between the Upaniṣads and early Buddhism is a much debated but still unresolved question. The conclusion so far is that they represent two parallel but separate developments that do not show unequivocal evidence of mutual contact or influence (see P. Horsch, "Buddhismus und Upaniṣaden," in *Pratidānam: Studies Presented to F. B. J. Kuiper* [The Hague, 1968], 462–77). They seem to have their homelands in different though adjoining areas. Buddhism arose in the periphery of the brahmanized regions of present-day Bihar, while the Upaniṣads have their home in the ancient "Middle Country" to the west. Even though the eastern homeland of Buddhism was already "profondément brahmanisé," its brahmanism "n'est pas le Brahmanisme des Brāhmaṇas et des Upanishads" (L. de la Vallée Poussin, *Indo-européens et Indo-iraniens,* revised ed., [Paris 1936], 312). The same author's wise but inconclusive summary still holds: "á l'époque des Unpanishads et du Bouddhisme, comme plus tard, les écoles exploitaient, chacune á leur manière, un certain fond commun, très riche, et que nous ne connaissons pas parfaitement" (ibid., 314).

Caution is equally needed with regard to the view that assigns the exploitation and "recycling" of the common body of ideas to kṣatriya circles, which then come to be seen as the first "carriers" of the new doctrinal systems—whether Upaniṣadic or "heterodox"—as against the obtusely ritualistic brahmins. Much will eventually depend on the view of Vedic ritualism and of what it may tell us about the development of the varṇa concept and the emergence of the brahmin.

2. See H. Bechert, "Einige Fragen der Religionssoziologie und Struktur des südasiatischen Buddhismus,"*Internationales Jahrbuch für Religionssoziolgie* 4 (1968): 251–95, esp. 260f. The starting point of formal relations between the temporal power and the sangha was the momentous purge of the internally divided sangha by the Maurya king Aśoka (see H. Bechert, "Aśoka's Schismenedikt und

der Begriff *sanghabheda,*" *Weiner Zeitschrift für die Kunde Süd - und Ostasians* 5 [1961]: 18–52.

3. See J. C. Heesterman, *The Ancient Indian Royal Consecration* (The Hague, 1957), 226.

4. L. Renou, "Le Destin du Veda dans l'Inde," *Études védiques et paninéennes* 6 (1960): 2.

5. See J. C. Heesterman, "Veda and Dharma," in *The Concept of Duty in South Asia,* ed. W. D. O'Flaherty and J. D. M. Derrett (New Delhi and London, 1978), 80–95; also above, chapter 6, section 2.

6. On the terms *śruti* and *smṛti,* see A. Ludwig, *Der Rigveda* (Prag, 1878), 3: 21–24.

7. *ĀpŚS* 24. 1. 31.

8. K. Jaspers, *Vom Ursprung und Ziel der Geschichte* (Zürich, 1949), 24.

9. H. Oldenberg, *Die Weltanschauung der Brāhmaṇa-Texte* (Göttingen, 1919), 1. Cf. also S. Lévi, *La Doctrine du sacrifice dans les Brāhmaṇas,* 2d ed., (Paris, 1966), 3f., where the systematic, "scientific" nature of the texts is given equal attention.

10. Thus Max Weber stresses priestly magic as "das absolut beherrschende Element" *(Gesamonelte Aufsätze zur Religionssoziologie* [Tübingen, 1920], 2: 136).

11. *RV* 1. 164. 50 ab; 10. 90. 16 ab.

12. Thus, for instance, the interesting attempt to study "le tronc commun de l'hindouisme . . . antour de la notion de sacrifice" (Madeline Biardeau and Charles Malamoud, *Le Sacrifice dans l'Inde ancienne,* [Paris, 1976], 13). See above, chapter 6, section 2.

13. *ĀpŚS* 24. 1. 33; cf. S. N. Dasgupta, *A History of Indian Philosophy,* reprint ed. (Cambridge, 1969), 1: 405.

14. Cf. *AB* 6. 34. 4.

15. Cf. *AB* 7. 27.

16. *Mbh* 12. 8. 34–37.

17. *ŚB* 6. 8. 1. 1. See J. C. Heesterman, "Opferwildnis und Ritualordnung," in *Epiphanie des Heils,* ed. Gerhard Oberhammer (Vienna, 1978), 13–25, esp. 14f.

18. *JB* 2. 299 (Auswahl no. 156); see above, chapter 6, section 3.

19. Hesiod, *Works and Days,* 161–65; see P. Walcot, "Cattle Raiding, Heroic Tradition, and Ritual," *History of Religions* 18 (1979): 326–51, esp. 327.

20. *JB* 2. 68–69 (Auswahl no. 128); see above, chapter 2, section 6.

21. See L. Renou and L. Silburn, "Sur la notion de *bráhman,*" *Journal Asiatique,* 1949, 7–46 (reprinted in Renou, *L'Inde fondamentale: Études d'indianisme réunies et présentées par Charle Malamoud* [Paris, 1978], 83—116).

22. See above, chapter 6, sections 3 and 4.

23. Renou, "La Notion de *bráhman.*"

24. See J. C. Heesterman, "Vrātya and Sacrifice," *Indo-Iranian Journal* 6 (1962): 1–37, esp. 23f. Also above, chapter 6, sections 7–8.

25. In a performance of the *agnicayana* ritual by Nambudiri brahmins of Kerala in 1975 (recorded on film and tape by J. F. Staal and R. Gardner), the whole of the ritual emplacement was even burned. The spectacle distinctly brought to mind the *pralaya* conflagration at the end of a world period.

26. See Weber, *Religionsozialogie,* 1: 465; Wolfgang Schluchter, *Rationalismus der Weltbeherrschung* (Frankfort/Main, 1980), 16.

27. *Mbh* 12. 225. 30–36.

28. See Max Weber, *Wirtschaft und Gesellschaft* (Studienausgabe hrsg. von J. Winckelmann) (Cologne and Berlin, 1964), 396.

29. *ŚB* 2. 3. 1. 5.

30. Interestingly where *tyāga* occurs in the *Ṛgveda,* it is the giving up of his life by the warrior in (sacrificial) battle (4. 24. 3).

31. On the chief meritorious act of each of the four *yugas,* see *Manu* 1. 85–86; also Robert Lingat, "Time and the Dharma," *Contributions to Indian Sociology* 6 (1962): 7–16.

32. *Manu* 3. 64, 153; 4. 84–85, 218. See above, chapter 2, section 9.

33. See above, chapter 6, section 8.

34. *ŚB* 6. 8. 1. 4.

35. Jaspers, *Vom Ursprungund Zeil,* 33.

36. *ŚB* 1. 4. 1. 10–17.

37. *TB* 1. 8. 4. 1–2; *ŚB* 5. 5. 2. 5. See W. Rau, *Staat und Gesellschaft im alten Indien* (Wiesbaden, 1957), 15. On the *vrātya* expeditions of the "sons of the Kuru-brahmans," *Staat und Gesellschaft,* see also *BaudhŚS* 18. 26: 374. 8.

38. Rau, *Staat und Gesellschaft,* 51–54.

39. On *yoga* (yoking) and *kṣemya,* see H. Oertel, *The Syntax of Cases* (heidelberg, 1926), 223–27 (Excursus on . . . *yogakṣema*); also J. C. Heesterman, "Householder and Wanderer," in *Way of Life; Essays in Honour of Louis Dumont,* ed. T. N. Madan (New Delhi, 1982), 251–71.

40. *AB* 2. 37. 1; *KB* 7. 7.

41. On the geographical and historical context of Zarathustra and on his reform of sacrifice, see K. Rudolph, "Zarathustra: Prieter und Prophet," *Numen* 8 (1961): 81–116 (reprinted in *Zarathustra,* ed. B. Schlerath [Darmstadt, 1970], 270–313).

42. Jaspers, *Vom Ursprung und Zeil,* 43.

### Chapter Eight

1. The material on the ancient Indian oligarchies has been conveniently assembled by J. P. Sharma, *Republics in Ancient India,* (Leiden, 1968). The title implies an emphasis on the difference between "republics" and "monarchies," in my opinion, an overemphasis. See also chapter 10, section 4.

2. For instance, A. S. Altekar, *State and Government in Ancient India,* (Benares, 1949); U. N. Ghoshal, *A History of Indian Political Ideas* (Bombay, 1959). It should be recognized that scholarly works of this type had an obvious place and function in the wider context of modern national thinking, which necessitated a rethinking of the received texts. In this respect, these works are akin to much of nineteenth-century European historiography. It may also be a sign of the changing times that Indian historians are at present directing their attention to social and economic history rather than to ancient political institutions.

3. Cf., e.g., *Nārada Smṛti* 18. 20; *Mbh* 3. 185. 26.

4. *Mbh* 1. 42. 27–31.

5. *Nar̃ada* 18. 21.

6. *Mbh* 12. 63. 25.

7. *Mbh* 1. 41. 27; 105. 44; 5. 39. 78; 12. 67. 4; *Rām* 2. 67. 9ff.

8. See W. Rau, *Staat und Gesellschaft im alten Indien* (Wiesbaden, 1957), 34, 59ff., 104.

9. *Manu* 4. 85–86; cf. *Mbh* 13. 126. 9. Since the *Manu* passage is preceded by a reference to the non-kṣatriya king, it might be thought that the following condemnation of the king equally refers to the non-kṣatriya king. Thus, for instance, Robert Lingat, *Les Sources du droit traditionel de l'Inde,* (Paris, 1967), 234. However, in other passages, it is the king in general who is condemned. Moreover, his

being a kṣatriya would not make things any better, for the kṣatriya is reputed to perpetrate all sorts of impure and sinful acts, so that the brahmin is forbidden to officiate for him at the daily agnihotra. See chapter 6, section 7.

10. *Mbh* 12. 228. 78; *AŚ* 1. 15. 3. Cf. J. J. Meyer, *Trilogie altindischer Mächte der Vegetation* (Zürich, 1937), 2: 129f.

11. *Viṣṇu Purāṇa* 1. 13. 16–18. See also below, note 22.

12. *RV* 10. 93. 14. Cf. also *AV* 4. 1. 1, where Vena is said to have disclosed the *bráhman*.

13. *Manu* 7. 9.

14. See J. Gonda, "Ancient Indian Kingship from the Religious Point of View," *Numen* 3 (1956): 56.

15. *AV* 11. 5. 17.

16. E.g., *Manu* 7. 4–7 (Indra, Vāyu, Yama, Āditya, Agni, Varuna, Soma, and Kubera); *Rām* 3. 40. 12 (Agni, Indra, Soma, Yana, and Varuna); *Mbh* 12. 68. 41ff. (Agni, Āditya, Mṛtyu, Vaiśravaṇa, and Yama); *Nārada* 18. 26 (Agni, Indra, Soma, Yama, and Kubera).

17. *Manu* 7. 8.

18. *Mbh* 12. 59. 131.

19. *RV* 10. 164. 50.

20. E. g., *Manu* 5. 93; 8. 311; *Vās* 18. 48; 19. 2; *AŚ* 1. 19. 33. For the purānic royal rituals and conception of kingship, see R. Inden, "Ritual, Authority, and Cyclic Time," in *Kingship and Authority in South Asia*, ed. J. F. Richards (Madison, Wisc., 1978), 28–73.

21. Lingat, *Les Sources du droit*, 260–62.

22. According to *Harivaṃśa* 5, Vena indeed proclaims himself to be the only recipient and celebrant as well as the sacrifice itself: *aham ijyaśca yaṣṭā ca yajñaśca*. On the sacrality of kingship, see also below chapter 10, section 6.

23. See J. C. Heesterman, "Priesthood and the Brahmin", *Contributions to Indian Sociology*, n.s. 5 (1971): 43–47; also above, chapter 2, section 9.

24. See *Manu* 7. 2, which reserves kingship for the kṣatriya, who has duly received the *brāhma-saṃskāra-*. Most commentators do not take this *saṃskāra* to be the rājasūya or another abhiṣeka but the *upanayana*, which any member of the "twice-born" varṇas must undergo (Lingat, *Les Sources du droit*, 234, n. 1).

25. See J. C. Heesterman, "Opferwildnis und Ritual Ordnung," in *Epiphanie des Heils*, ed. Gerhard Oberhammer (Vienna, 1982), 13–25; also above, chapter 6, section 7.

26. See J. C. Heesterman, *The Ancient Indian Royal Consecration* (The Hague, 1957), 75–78.

27. See E. Benveniste, *Le Vocabulaire des institutions indo-européennes* (Paris, 1969), 2: 7–15.

28. Rau, *Staat und Gesellschaft*, 68–70.

29. Lingat, *Les Sources du droit*, 235.

30. Herein, it would seem, lies the essential difference with Machiavelli, who decisively breaks away from the concept of politics as part and parcel of the scholastic *philosophia ethica* (or *moralis*). Kauṭilya's sobriquet "Indian Machiavelli" is all too glib.

31. Cf., e.g., *ŚB* 4. 1. 4. 3, 6.

32. See also below, chapter 10, section 9. I am indebted for this view to the works of Louis Dumont (see in particular "World Renunciation in Indian Religions," *Contributions to Indian Sociology* 4 [1964]: 33–62). I differ, however, with

respect to the brahmin, whom Dumont views as the opposite of the renouncer, while my reading of the texts puts him on a par with the renouncer (cf. above, chapter 1, esp. n. 8, and "Priesthood and the Brahmin.")

33. *Mbh* 12. 69. 79ff.; 70. 6–25; 92. 6; 139. 10; *Manu* 9. 301f.

34. See Hesterman, *Consecration,* 143–46, 151–56.

35. Ibid., 156.

36. See, e.g., the passages quoted by Rau, *Staat und Gesellschaft,* 59–61.

37. *ÁS* 6. 2. 22–28; *Manu* 7. 155–58; also Harmut Scharfe, *Die Staatsrechtslehre des Kauṭalya* (Wiesbaden, 1968), 120–27. See also below, chapter 10, section 5.

38. *ÁS* 6. 2. 39.

39. Scharfe, *Die Staatsrechtslehre,* 125f,

40. *Viṣṇu Smṛti* 3. 28, 48; *Yājñavalkya* 1. 335–37.

41. Lingat, *Les Sources du droit,* 256.

42. *Manu* 7. 54ff; *Mbh* 12. 87. 7ff.

43. *Mbh* 5. 34. 38.

44. *AB* 8. 17. 5.

45. E.g., *Mbh* 13. 85. 35; *Sukranīti* 2. 274. cf. also *Jātakas,* nos. 73, 432. The problem may be compared to that of kingship-by-the-grace-of-God and the right of resistance (see O. Brunner, "Vom Gottesgnadentum zum monarchischen Prinzip," in *Die Entstehung des modernen Souveränen Staates,* ed. H. H. Hoffman [Cologne and Berlin, 1967], 115–136).

46. On the much debated question of the king's "legislative" authority, see Lingat, *Les Sources du droit,* 251ff.

47. *Manu* 7. 203; *Yājñavalkya* 1. 342.

48. *Manu* 8. 41; *Yājñavalkya* 2. 192; *Nārada* 13. 2; *Bṛhaspati* 2. 28.

49. *Manu* 8. 46.

50. *ĀpDhS* 1. 7. 20. 6.

51. *ĀpDhS* 1. 7. 20. 7.

52. On the so-called Tegernseer Ludus or Ludus de Antichristo, see K. Langosch, *Lateinische Dramen des Mittelalters* (Darmstadt, 1961), 216: *Deponam vetera, nova iura dictabo.*

53. *Manu* 7. 13; 9. 275; *Yājñavalkya* 2. 186. The commentators are generally at pains to restrict this to occasional orders regarding, for example, the organization of festivals; one may also think of what we call administrative law. But the point to bear in mind is that the texts do not make such distinctions; dharma has to comprehend all or nothing. Moreover, elsewhere the king is instructed to prohibit those customs that are contrary to his wishes or interests (*Nārada* 10. 4).

54. *AŚ* 3. 1. 39. Further on, however, the same text does not mention rājaśāsana as a source of law (3. 1. 43).

55. *Mbh* 12. 59. 87ff.

56. Probably the next cycle of seven kings (or eight, if Visnu, the divine founder, is counted as the first, as the text does) should start with equally dismal risks and failures. The number seven recalls the seven kings of Rome.

57. *Mbh* 12. 67. Cf. also the Buddhist notion of the king as the *mahāsaṃmata* (see Ghoshal, *Political Ideas,* 258–60, and the interesting observations of Louis Dumont, "The Conception of Kingship in Ancient India," *Contributions to Indian Sociology* 6 (1962): 61–64, contrasting the Buddhist and the brahmanic view).

58. *AB* 8. 5. 1. Cf. also *Visṇu Dharmottara Purāṇa* 1. 162, which prescribes the yearly repetition of the abhiṣeka.

59. See, e.g., B. Stein, "Integration of the Agrarian System of South India," in *Land Control and Social Structure in Indian History,* ed. R. E. Frykenberg (Madison, 1969), 175–216, which clearly bears out the importance of the opposition.

60. *Mbh* 3. 314.

61. See N. Falk, "Wilderness and Kingship in Ancient South Asia," *History of Religions* 13 (1973): 1–15, which deals mostly with Buddhist materials. We may also think of the wilderness as the "conquest of kings" *(TB* 1. 7. 3. 8: *rā́jnām áraṇyam abhíjitam),* which can help us understand why one should ask the king for a place of sacrifice although it is situated outside the grāma, in the wilds (cf. W. Caland and V. Henry, *L'Agniṣṭoma* [Paris, 1906], 6). The soma plant, which in the context of the ritual is referred to as "the king," very clearly belongs to the jungle.

62. *Grāme dīkṣate, araṇye yajate* (quoted by Caland and Henry, ibid., 26). The texts give detailed instructions for the march toward the place of sacrifice.

63. See Heesterman, *Consecration,* 71, 95, 116.

64. Ibid., 147. I have suggested that the unction in the rājasūya originally took place while the king was seated on the throne. Such unctions on the throne do indeed occur in similar rituals, but in the rājasūya, as the texts describe it, unction and enthronization are separated by a significant intervening rite. I shall try to show that this is not accidental.

65. For instance, Rau, *Staat und Gesellschraft,* 89f.

66. See Heesterman, *Consecration,* chap. 16.

67. Ibid., 91, 98, 226. Originally the ritual will have been a public, cyclically repeated regeneration festival. In the textual form we know, however, the public is excluded, sacrifice having become a purely private affair. Against this background, we can understand why, as already noted, the king *qua talis* has no place in the ritual except as a sacrificer like any other. In this way, we may also understand why the rājasūya, or even the single abhiṣeka, is not considered by the majority of commentators on *Manu* 7.2 to be the decisive royal "sacrament" (cf. note 24 above). In fact, though there are many rites that might be used (generically known as *Sava*), there is none that is specifically prescribed for the purpose.

68. *Manu* 11. 11–15.

69. See Heesterman, *Consecration,* 191.

70. *TB* 1. 8. 4. In fact, there may even be two cycles: one formed by unction, samṣrps, and daśapeya, the other, greater one by unction-daśapeya (these two being formally connected by the use of the same lot of soma stalks acquired at the outset of the unction festival), prayujāṃ havīṃsi, and the haircutting solemnity.

71. *ĀpŚS* 22. 28. 2–10.

72. *BaudhŚS* 11. 7; 74. 10, 75. 8; 11. 12; 81. 2.

73. *ĀpŚS* 18. 4. 12–6. 6.

74. *ĀpŚS* 18. 7. 17.

75. *ŚB* 5. 2. 1. 19.

76. *Vaikhānasa Srautasūtra* 17. 18; 248. 2: *kṣatravṛttiṃ nivartuyet.*

77. *Lāṭyāyana Srautasūtra* 18. 7. 10; 18. 12. 1.

78. *Vādhūlasūtra,* in W. Caland, *Acta Orientalia* 4 (1926): 168f.

79. Ibid., 169.

80. *AB* 8. 10–11.

81. *AB* 8. 21.

82. See Caland and Henry, *L'Agniṣṭoma,* 19.

83. *TS* 6. 1. 4. 1; *MS* 3. 6. 8: 70. 16; *KS* 23. 4: 79. 11.

84. For the scepter, see Benveniste, *Vocabulaire,* 2: 29–32. In this way, we can

perhaps also understand the carrying of the daṇḍa at the division of the inheritance, because division of inheritance implies departure and settling elsewhere (*Kauśikasūtra* 23. 9–11).

85. See Heesterman, "Vrātya and Sacrifice," *Indo-Iranian Journal* 6 (1962): 1–37.

86. There are different possible moments for handing over the daṇḍa to the maitrāvarūna: see *ĀpŚS* 10. 27. 2 (after the buying of the soma; ibid. 11. 18. 6 (at the end of the "intermediate dīkṣa"); *MānŚS* 2. 2. 5. 7 (after the pravara of the *agniṣomīya* animal sacrifice).

87. Heesterman, *Consecration,* 202.

88. Cf. *ŚB* 5. 3. 4. 12; 5. 4. 3. 2, 21; *TS* 5. 6. 2. 1; *TB* 2. 7. 6. 1; *ŚankhŚS* 15. 13. 4.

89. Cf. *ŚB* 5. 4. 3. 2; 5. 4. 5. 1; *TB* 1. 8. 1. 1; 1. 8. 5. 1; *MS* 4. 3. 9: 49. 4; *PB* 18. 9. 1; *JB* 2. 202. See also, Heesterman, *Consecration,* 177. This is not the place to go into the matter, but it may be observed in passing that there seems to be an interesting alternation between Varuṇa and Indra. The strength that Varuṇa loses is his *indriya-vīrya-,* his Indra-power. It is Indra who then consistently takes over, or is born out of the sacrifice, and starts out on the warrior phase. In this connection, it is interesting that the rājasūya's unction festival is especially dedicated to Varuṇa, "for it is Varuṇa whom they consecrate" (*ŚānkhŚS* 15. 13. 4). But the cow sacrifice, which comes after the unction festival and precedes the samsṛp offerings and which in the Soma ritual is normally performed for Mitra and Varuṇa, is here dedicated to Indra, who is said to be born out of it (Heesterman, *Consecration,* 170). That is, Indra is born after the disintegration of Varuṇa, at the start of the warrior phase. Moreover, the cow sacrifice seems to have been one of the possible "boxes" of the abhiṣeka, as indeed it seems to be in the punarabhiṣeka of the *Aitareya Brāhmaṇa* (8. 5. 1–2). On the return Varuṇa takes over again, as seems to be borne out by another ritual, namely the *Varuṇa-praghāsa,* which apparently referred originally to the return of a war band at the end of the hot season (see below chap. 9). The handing over of the daṇḍa to the maitrāvaruṇa officiant seems to point in the same direction. Varuṇa, then, seems to be connected with the enthronement, which may explain the vacillation in the rājasūya as to whether the unction should be performed on the throne. According to *JB* 3. 152, Varuṇa, wishing to become king, goes out to be taught by Prajāpati—in other words, to obtain authority—and on his return is honored by the gods, who place him on the throne and then give the abhiṣeka. Moreover, when the king has sat down on the throne, he is equated to Varuṇa (*TS* 1. 8. 16f.).

90. *Mbh* 2. 12; 1. 46; 9. 49; 9. 50; *Rām* 7. 83. See also H. Gehrts, *Mahābharata: Das Geschehen und seine Bedeutung* (Bonn, 1975), 166.

91. *Mbh* 14. 3. For the aśvamedha as a penance for slaying a brahmin, cf. *Manu* 11. 75, 83.

92. Elsewhere I have called the cyclical pattern of ritual "preclassical" (see above, chap. 2).

93. See below, chapter 10, section 7.

94. *Mbh* 12. 99. 12.

95. *Mbh* 12. 103. 16–22.

96. See above, chapter 2, section 3.

97. See *ĀpŚS* 20. 2. 12f.

98. Cf. *Bṛhaspati* 1. 23. 17–19; *KātyŚS* 801.

99. See S. N. Biswas, "Über das Vrātya Problem in der Vedischen Ritualliteratur," *Zeitschrrift der Deutschen Morgenlämdische Gesellschaft* 105 (1955): 53f.;

also Heesterman, "Vrātya and Sacrifice," *Indo-Iranian Journal* 6 (1962): 27–29.

100. On the concept of *brahman,* cf. L. Renou, "La Notion de *brahman,*" *Journal Asiatique,* 1949, 7ff.; P. Thieme, "Brahman," *Zeitschrift der Deutschen Morgenlämdishe Gesellschraft* 102 (1952): 91ff. Also see above, chapter 5.

101. *JB* 2. 55–56, (Auswahl no. 125). For Hṛtsvāśaya Āllakeya as a king of the Mahāvṛsas, see *JB* 1. 234 (Auswahl no. 87).

102. Cf. *JB* 1. 341, where the text's lectio facilior *śārdūlājinam* should be amended to *śāmūlājinam.*

### *Chapter Nine*

1. I refer in particular to R. P. Kangle's edition and translation (Bombay, 1960–1963); F. Wilhelm, *Politische Polemiken im Staatslehrbuch des Kauṭalya* (Wiesbaden, 1960); D. Schlingloff, "Arthaśāstia Studien," *Wiener Zeitschrift für die Kunde Süd- und Ostasiens* 9 (1966): 1ff. H. Scharfe, *Untersuchungen zur Staatsrechtlehre des Kauṭalya* (Wiesbaden, 1968); and T. R. Trautmann *Kauṭilya and the Arthaśāstra,* (Leiden, 1971).

2. See Scharfe, *Untersuchungen,* 177–190. Scharfe in my opinion conclusively argues that the *samāhartṛ* is a provincial administrator.

3. *Daśakumāracarita* 8.

4. *AŚ* 2. 9. 34.

5. *AŚ* 2. 7. 41.

6. *AŚ* 1. 1. 1: *pṛthivyā lābhe pālane ca.*

7. *AŚ* 1. 2. 11. On the term *ānvīkṣikī* meaning "Untersuchung mit Gründen," see P. Hacker, "Ānvīkṣikī," *Wiener Zeitschrift für die Kunde Süd- und Ostasiens* 2 (1958): 54–83.

8. In this connection, it seems interesting that, as Wilhelm has shown, the wording of the quotations of opponents' views stems from Kauṭilya himself (*Politische Polemiken,* 140). Even though, as Wilhelm concedes, these quotations might represent real school views, they would seem to serve primarily as models for the articulation of debate.

9. See Kangle, *Arthaśāstia,* 3: 116.

10. *AŚ* 1. 13. 5–14.

11. J. Gonda, "Ancient Indian Kingship from the Religious Point of View," *Numen* 3 (1956): 36.

12. *PB* 2. 7. 5.

13. For a fuller exposition of this point, see J. C. Heesterman, "Power and Authority in Indian Tradition," in *Tradition and Politics in South Asia,* ed. R. J. Moore (New Delhi, 1979), 60–85, and below, chapter 10.

14. *AŚ* 1. 6. 1. See below, chapter 10, section 9.

15. B. Breloer, *Kauṭilya Studien* (Leipzig, 1934), 3: 248.

16. *AŚ* 2. 7. 16–25.

17. *Aś* 2. 7. 24–25. *Pracārasamaṃ mahāmātrāḥ samagrāḥ śrāvayeyur aviṣamamantrāḥ, pṛthagbhūto mithyāvādī caiṣām uttamaṃ daṇḍaṃ dadyāt.* Scharfe translates: "den, der verfahrensgerecht war, sollen die sämtlichen mahāmātra einstimmig verkünden; wer von ihnen zich ausschliesst oder unwahr redet, soll die höchste Strafe geben."

18. Scharfe, *Untersuchungen,* 229.

19. See Ch. Johnson, *Dialogus de Scaccario* (London, 1950), xxxv.

20. Unless we follow Kangle's translation, which renders the crucial phrase *samagrāḥ śrāvayeyuḥ* with "they should render accounts in full," taking *samagrāḥ* in

the improbable sense of "full (accounts)" as the object of the verb *śrāvayeyuḥ*. In that case, we are left in the dark as to the identity of the auditing authority. Since they would then have to "proclaim" *(śrāvayeyuḥ)*—not just "render"—their accounts, Kangle's translation leads to the conclusion that the assembled mahāmātras sit in judgment on each other's accounts. Such a procedure obviously would be undesirable, if not down right impossible, from the point of view of proper auditing.

21. Scharfe, *Untersuchungen,* 231. For the varuṇapraghāsa sacrifice, cf. A. Hillebrandt, *Ritualliteratur* (Strassburg, 1897), 116f.; *ĀpŚS* 8. 5. 1.

22. See above, chapter 2.

23. This does not mean, of course, that the varuṇapraghāsa is exactly identical with the festival that Kauṭilya had in mind. Rather it appears that this sacrifice in its systematized classical form derives from a similar festival on the full-moon day in Āṣāḍha. Thus its rites and the speculations connected with it can lead us to the meaning of the original festival. For the rest, one might also think of a sacrifice like the sautrāmaṇi—another sacrifice of reparation and atonement—which according to *Baudhāyana Śrautasūtia* also falls on the full-moon day of Āṣāḍha or Śrāvaṇa in the rājasūya cycle. The agnicayana—Prajāpati's reintegration—is, according to some authorities, also to be started in Āṣāḍha (*ĀpŚS* 16. 1. 2).

24. Thus *TB* 1. 6. 4. 1; cf. also *ŚB* 5. 2. 4. 1f.

25. *MS* 1. 10. 10; *KS* 36. 5.

26. *ĀpŚS* 8. 6. 20.

27. See, e.g., *AB* 7. 13.

28. *ĀpŚS* 8. 6. 22; *TB* 1. 6. 5. 2: *Priyám jñātíṃ rundhyāt,* "She would lose a dear (or close) relative."

29. *TB* 3. 8. 4. 1. The two affines should lead the dog that is bathed with the horse and then killed as a scapegoat (*ĀpŚS* 20. 3. 6). It is perhaps not surprising that *BaudhŚS* 26. 10 replaces the two relatives with slaves.

30. *TB* 1. 4. 6. 12. Cf. W. Caland, *Altindsche Zauberei* (Amsterdam, 1908), no. 184.

31. A similar arrangement is to be found in the sautrāmaṇi sacrifice.

32. *TB* 1. 6. 5. 4.

33. *MS* 1. 10. 12; *KS* 36. 7.

34. *ŚB* 2. 5. 2. 6; cf. also *MS* 1. 10. 10 and *KS* 36. 5.

35. *TB* 1. 6. 5. 1, 4.

36. *ĀpŚS* 8. 6. 19; *TB* 1. 6. 5. 2–3.

37. *TS* 1. 8. 3d.

38. Perhaps the same idea can be discerned in *AB* 3. 22. 7, where the gods obtain a share in Indra's booty through his wife, Prāsahā, who is at the same time his "weapon" *(senā)*. The gods put her to shame by saying to her, "Ka ("who," or Prajāpati, her father-in-law) sees you." Thus cowering Indra's *senā,* they manage to obtain a share. In the above case of the karambha offering on the southern fire, at which Indra and the Maruts are invoked, the Maruts, or the viś, in the same way are not only bound but also obtain their share.

39. *ŚB* 2. 5. 2. 23. This idea is also expressed in another way. The adhvaryu makes an image of a ram from barley groats, the pratiprasthātṛ, an image of a ewe. After being baked in the fire, the ewe is placed in the Varuṇa milk dish on the northern vedi, the ram in the Marut milk dish on the southern vedi. Then the positions are reversed, the ewe being placed in the Marut dish, the ram in the Varuṇa dish. Here again the explanation given refers to marital union through which the creatures are released from Varuṇa's bonds (*ŚB* 2. 5. 2. 17, 36). It is to be noted that these are not real animals; they are, as *MS* 1. 10. 12 and *KS* 36. 6 say, *anṛta-*

*paśu,* "false animals," and thereby the creatures are freed from anṛta and from Varuṇa's noose.

40. *TB* 1. 6. 4. 1; cf. *MS* 1. 10. 10; *KS* 36. 5.

41. *TB* 1. 6. 2. 2; cf. *MS* 1. 10. 6, 10; *KS* 36. 5.

42. Perhpas we should go even further: the original opposition seems to be between Varuṇa (or, in the decisive phase of the ritual, Indra) and the Maruts. This opposition was then partially replaced with the one between Prajāpati, the epitome of the classical theory of sacrifice, and his prajāḥ.

43. *ŚB* 2. 5. 2. 1, 16. Cf. *KS* 36. 5: *jagdhād vai Varuṇo gṛhṇāti.* On the evil or sin involved in appropriating food, see above, chapter 6, section 5.

44. *KS* 36. 6.

45. For this passage, see J. C. Heesterman, *The Ancient Indian Royal Consecration* (The Hague, 1957), 209–11; W. Rau, *Staat und Gesellschaft im alten Indien* (Wiesbaden, 1957), 15. A remote echo of this cycle can still be heard in *ĀpGS* 22. 12ff. Immediately after the rules for the aṣṭakā rites in the cold season, a mantra is prescribed for going out to beg; the text then goes on to explain the rules for mounting a chariot, which should face east.

46. See J. C. Heesterman, "Vrātya and Sacrifice," *Indo-Iranian Journal* 6 (1962): 15–18. Also above, chapter 8 sections 7–9. For the ambivalence of the Maruts, see A. Bergaigne, *Mythologie Védique* (Paris, 1963), 2: 401; 3: 38. The Maruts are known to have fallen out with Indra. The word praghāsa refers to the (sinful) eating of Varuṇa's barley (*ŚB* 2. 5. 2. 1).

47. In the *Dialogus de Scaccario,* this is indeed made explicit in the obvious comparison with chess-play: "Sicut in lusili pugna committitur inter reges, sic in hoc inter duos principaliter conflictus est et pugna committitur, thesaurarium scilicet et vicecomitem qui assidet ad compotum" (Johnson's edition, 7). At the board the officers of the king's household, like Kauṭilya's mahāmātras, also sit as witnesses and judges. The difference is, of course, that the English king's household officers are not the same as the vicecomites, while with Kauṭilya it is exactly these persons that are included among the mahāmātras.

48. *AŚ* 2. 4. 10.

49. *ĀpDhS* 2.25.

50. See H. Losch, *Rājadharma* (Bonn, 1959), 51, 313.

51. It is therefore easy to understand why some texts read *deśarakṣitṛ,* although, as Losch makes clear, *akṣarakṣitṛ* is the right reading.

52. See Heesterman, *Consecration,* chap. 17.

53. Ibid., 153f.

54. On this point, see Heesterman, "Power and Authority in Indian Tradition," and chapter 10. It is to be noted that the king is also considered the husband of the viś.

55. *AŚ* 5. 6. 34: *Ayaṃ vo nikṣepaḥ, pitaram asyāvekṣadhvaṃ sattvābhijanam ātmanaśca, dhvajamātro 'yam, bhavanta eva svāminaḥ, kathaṃ vā kriyatām iti.* Scharfe takes *ātmanaḥ* as referring to the pretendent (*Untersuchungen,* 219); it would, however, seem that an appeal to the mahāmātras' own quality and honor as masters of the realm is perfectly in keeping with the context.

56. *TB* 1. 7. 3. 1.

57. See W. C. Neale, "Reciprocity and Redistribution," in *Trade and Markets in Early Empires,* ed. K. Polanyi et al. (Glencoe, 1957).

58. *AŚ* 2. 10. 31. One is tempted to compare this with Elphinstone's "the Ceded Districts plan of having a Double Dufter," that is, the appointment of two *dafterdars,* record keepers, of equal rank as the chief Indian officials in the district, so that they could be used as a check upon each other. See K. A. Ballhatchet, *Social*

*Policy and Social Change in Western India, 1817–1830* (London, 1957), 92; also E. Frykenberg, *Guntur District, 1788–1848* (Oxford, 1965), 127.

59. *AŚ* 2. 4. 29–30.

**Chapter Ten**

1. Louis Dumont, "Kingship in Ancient India," *Contributions to Indian Sociology* 6 (1962): 48–77, esp. 52 and 54.

2. See chapter 2, section 12, and J. C. Heesterman, "Priesthood and the Brahmin," *Contributions to Indian Sociology,* n.s. 5 (1976): 46–49.

3. See Harmut Scharfe, *Die Staatsrechtslehre des Kauṭalya* (Wiesbaden, 1968), 138ff. Scharfe illustrates both meanings, land as well as people, separately. For the undifferentiated unity of land and people, cf. O. Brunner, *Land und Herrschaft* (Darmstadt, 1970), 234f. The undifferentiated people-cum-territory is discussed by Louis Dumont, "Nationalism and Communalism," *Contributions to Indian Sociology* 7 (1964): 30–70, esp. 60ff. For the rise of the clearly defined and compact territory as the basis of national unity, see J. R. Talmon, *The Origins of Totalitarian Democracy,* reprint ed. (London, 1906), 109f.; and J. C. Heesterman, "Two Types of Boundaries," *Felicitation Volume for S. N. Eisenstadt,* ed. E. Cohen (forthcoming).

4. One may compare E. R. Leach's observation on the use of the jural idom of local group endogamy for legitimizing membership: "Anyone who was acceptable as a Pul Eliya landowner and was also acceptable in the capacity of brother-in-law to an existent Pul Eliya landowner would, in practice, be treated as of our *variga*" (*Pul Eliya,* [Cambridge, 1961], 303). Compare also the *mutha,* or "clan" territory, as described by F. G. Bailey, actually a group of lineages living in the same territory and expressing this fact as conventional agnation (*Tribe, Caste, and Nation* [Manchester, 1960], 47ff.). See Dumont's remarks in *Contributions to Indian Sociology* 7 (1964): 72.

5. See, for instance, the remonstrances against the rulers (apparently strengthened by their alliance with the British) by the clan-brethren, to whom the ruler is only a primus inter pares, in J. Todd, *Annals and Antiquities of Rājhasthan,* pop. ed. (London, 1914), 159ff. (app. to book 2).

6. J. C. Heesterman, *The Ancient Indian Royal Consecration* (The Hague, 1957), chap. 6.

7. See R. S. Sharma, *Aspects of Political Ideas and Institutions* (Delhi, 1968), 145.

8. The procedure may be compared with the yearly ceremonies described by A. Béteille (*History of Religions* 5 [1965]: 85), where the central temple is visited by parties carrying the *mūrti,* the image, of the deity of the outlying temples. Next the central mūrti goes on a circuit visiting the associated outlying temples.

9. See W. Rau, *Staat und Gesellschaft im alten Indien* (Wiesbaden, 1957), 107; also Scharfe, *Die Staatsrechtsleure,* 158f.

10. Or he is the king himself. This, at least, is the opinion of the *Śatapatha Brāhmaṇa,* which has the sacrificer himself in the place of the rājanya or rājan. *MS* 4. 3. 8, on the other hand, distinguishes the rājan from the sacrificer.

11. This group recalls the first four of the eight so-called *vīras,* or "heroes," who sustain kingship (*PB* 19. 1. 4). This group comprises the king's brother, the king's son, the purohita, and the first consort, followed by *sūta, grāmaṇī, kṣattṛ,* and *saṃgrahītṛ.*

12. I refrain from translating these terms since this would only give them a de-

ceptive air of precision, without clarifying the context. So much is clear, however, they do not indicate specific administrative charges, but rather functions in agonistic potlatch festivals. Thus *sūta, grāmaṇī, saṃgrahītṛ,* and *rathakāra* are connected with chariot racing and chariot fighting. One commentary consideres the *kṣattṛ* to be a charioteer, although he seems to be connected instead, together with the *govikarta,* with the slaughter and cooking of the cow that is staked in the royal game of dice. The *akṣavāpa* clearly serves the king in the dicing match, while the *takṣan* is described elsewhere as cutting off and receiving the head of the sacrificial victim (*MS* 2. 4. 1)—a custom eliminated in the normalized śrauta ritual. The point to be retained is that all these personages are assocaited with contests (chariot racing, dicing) and their prizes (the cow in the game of dice).

13. *ŚB* 13. 4. 1.

14. *ĀpŚS* 20. 5. 9.

15. *ŚB* 13. 5. 2.

16. See Heesterman, *Consecration,* chap. 14. The four-five schema seems to be fairly current in India as a numerical formula of sociopolitical organization. The epic relates that Yuddhiṣthira, the leader of the five Pāṇḍava brothers, asked, by way of compromise, for a kingdom of only five villages, one for each of his four brothers and one, presumably the central one, for himself (see Heesterman, "Two Types of Boundaries"). Another example is offered by S. Sinha's study of the principality Barabhum, which consisted of a central tract, or *taraf,* and four outlying *tarafs*. The four-five schema forms a striking parallel with the Javanese *mantjapat*. On the two-three and four-five schemas and on their conjunction, see P. E. de Josselin de Jong, *Minangkabau and Negri Sembilan* (Leiden, 1951), 106.

17. See Heesterman, *Consecration,* 143–45.

18. See G. J. Held, *The Mahābhārata: An Ethnological Study* (Leiden, 1936), 89–97. Held derives the varṇa system from a clan system, or more precisely, from "a circulative marriage system with a four-clan arrangement (ibid., 95).

19. See *ĀpŚS* 18. 19. 7f.

20. Claude Lévi-Strauss, *Les Structures élémentaires de la parenté,* 2d ed. (Paris, 1967), 306.

21. E. R. Leach, *Political Systems of Highland Burma,* reprint ed. (London, 1964), chap. 6.

22. Josselin de Jong, *Minangkabau,* 71ff.

23. Ibid., 105.

24. There is, in my opinion, no need for a historical reconstruction of the different phases through which the republic developed out of elected kingship, finally ending in a monarchical system, as proposed by J. P. Sharma, *Republics in Ancient India* (Leiden, 1968), 17f. As Sharma makes clear, the monarchical order existed all the time, side by side with the "republican" one.

25. Louis Dumont, *Une sous-caste de l'Inde du süd* (Paris, 1957), 143f.

26. *TS* 2. 6. 2. 1.

27. *ŚB* 1. 6. 3. 18–22.

28. *ŚB* 1. 6. 3. 23.

29. *AŚ* 1. 15. 34–40.

30. See above, chapter 6, especially section 3.

31. *AŚ* 6. 2. 13–28; cf. Scharfe, *Die Staatsrechtslehre* 122–27. See also above, chapter 8, section 5.

32. *AŚ* 6. 1. 13–15. The state is said to consist of eight elements; however they are unspecified (*Mbh* 15. 5. 8; 12. 122. 8).

33. *AŚ* 6. 2. 25.

34. See Scharfe, *Die Staatsrechtslehre,* 123–26, where the two schemes have been lucidly disentangled.

35. L. Renou, "La Notion de *bráhman,*" *Journal Asiatique,* 1949.

36. J. C. Heesterman, *Consecration,* 141, 150; also above, chapter 5, section 8.

37. *Manu* 5. 96; 7. 4; 7. 7; 9. 303–11. In connection with the paired ratnins discussed above, it is interesting that in *Manu* 7. 7 the eight gods seem to form four pairs: Agni and Vāyu (Fire and Wind), Sūrya and Soma (Sun and Moon), Yama and Kubera, Varuṇa and Indra. For eight gods representing kingship, cf. also *BĀU* 1. 4. 11. In other texts the number is five (*Nārada Smṛti* 18. 26; *Rām* 3. 40. 12; *Mbh* 12. 68. 41ff.).

38. *JB* 3. 94 (Auswahl no. 180); cf. *PB* 13. 3. 12.

39. See above, section 1.

40. See chapter 7.

41. See chapter 2, section 6.

42. *ŚB* 1. 1. 1. 6; 1. 9. 3. 23.

43. Robert Lingat, *Les Sources du droit dans le système traditionel de l'Inde,* (Paris, 1967), 234, n. 1.

44. *ĀpŚS* 18. 8. 1.

45. See chapter 2, section 9, note 59.

46. See above, note 2.

47. *AŚ* 1. 6. 1; 1. 7. 1. See above, chapter 9, section 3.

48. *AŚ* 1. 9. 11.

49. *AŚ* 1. 7. 9.

50. See H. Bechert, "Einige Fragen der Religionssoziologie und Struktur des Südasiatischen Buddhismus," *International Jahrbuch für Religionssoziologie* 4 (1968): 251–95, esp. 200f.; also Bechert, "Aśokas Schismenedikt und der Begriff *sanghabheda,*" *Wiener Zeitschrift für die Kunde Süd - und Ostasians* 5 (1961): 18–52.

51. *Mbh* 12. 59. 14–15.

### *Chapter Eleven*

1. Anil Seal, *The Emergence of Indian Nationalism* (Cambridge, 1968), 351.

2. Interestingly, the organizaiton of the British Indian administration seems to have been very well geared to accommodate dissension through its "dual alignment" of authorities at each rung of the hierarchy. See R. E. Frykenberg, *Guntur District* (Oxford, 1965), 237f.

3. See J. C. Heesterman, "Political Modernization in India," in *Traditional Attitudes and Modern Styles in Political Leadership* ed. J. E. Legge (Sidney, 1973), 29–56, esp. 48.

4. On this problem, see chapter 8, section 4, and chapter 10, sections 1, 7, and 8.

5. See G. M. Carstairs, *The Twice-Born* (London, 1957), 143.

6. See Irfan Habib, *The Agrarian System of Mughal India* (Aligarh, 1963); J. F. Richards, *Mughal Administration in Golconda* (Oxford, 1975).

7. W. Foster, ed., *The English Factories in India* (Oxford, 1906–27), 5: 204.

8. "Ample evidence from the archival remains demonstrates that the organization of the empire was both impressive and effective. The total impression conveyed by these documentary sources is that of a great machine, built and organized for continuous expansion and gradually intensifying control from the centre." (Richards, *Mughal Administration,* 311).

9. J. N. Sarkar, *History of Aurangzib* (Calcutta, 1912–30), 3: 283–364.

10. Satish Chandra, *Parties and Politics at the Mughal Court, 1707–1740* (Aligarh, 1959), xliii–xlvii.

11. Habib, *Agrarian System* 317–51.

12. Richards, *Mughal Administration,* 306–10.

13. M. Athar Ali, "The Passing of Empire: The Mughal Case," *Moderan Asian Studies* 9 (1975): 385–96.

14. See also articles from the Symposion on the Decline of the Mughal Empire by M. N. Pearson, J. F. Richards, and P. Hardy in *Journal of Asian Studies,* 35 (February 1976): 221–63.

15. H. Dunlop, ed., *Bronnen tot de geschiedenis der Oostindische Compagnie in Perzië* (The Hague, 1930), 204. This opinion was not particularly original. For contemporary Turkish opinions to the same effect, see Bernard Lewis, "Some Reflections on the Decline of the Ottoman Empire," in *The Economic Decline of Empires,* ed. C. M. Cipolla (London, 1970), 215–34. See also Fernand Braudel, *La Méditerranée et le monde méditerranéen à l'époque de Philippe 2* 2d ed. (Paris, 1966), 2: 47.

16. Richards, *Mughal Administration,* 316. In this respect the evidence given by Richards for the remarkable recovery of the two main centers of Golconda under a forceful governor in the 1720s after a period of confusion and decay seems indicative of the system's resilience (ibid., 304ff.).

17. M. Athar Ali, *The Mughal Nobility under Aurangzeb* (London, 1966), 92–94, 173; Habib, *Agrarian System,* 269–73.

18. See Richards, *Mughal Administration,* 157–62.

19. See Habib, *Agrarian System,* 230.

20. Ibid., 242; See also W. H. Moreland, *The Agrarian Systems of Moslem India* (Cambridge, 1929), 107, 133ff.

21. Moreland, *Agrarian Systems of Moslem India,* 204; Habib, *Agrarian System,* 236ff., 249.

22. See W. H. Moreland, *India at the Death of Akbar* reprint ed. (Delhi, 1962), 126–29; 248–53; Moreland, *From Akbar to Aurangzeb* (London, 1923), 202f., quoting Bernier's letter to Colbert.

23. W. H. Moreland, *Relations of Golconda* (The Hakluyt Society, 1930), 77. Though the reference is to Golconda, there is no reason to assume that the picture of the countryside in the Mughal area was essentially different.

24. Moreland, *India at the Death of Akbar,* 104; also Habib, *Agrarian System,* 78.

25. *AŚ* 4. 1. 65. Perhaps a not unsimilar outlook, stressing the warrior-administrator's point of view while disregarding commerce, can also be found with the British-Indian administration. For instance, it is remarkable that while Governor-General Wellesley, like a true "warrior-administrator," discussed the annexations of 1801 exclusively in terms of their strategic importance and their revenue resources, his brother Henry was particularly enthusiastic about their commercial potentialities (see P. J. Marhsall, "Economic and Political Expansion: The Case of Oudh," *Modern Asian Studies* 9 [1975]: 465–82, esp. 481; cf. also E. Stokes, "Agrarian Society and the Pax Brittania," ibid., 505–28, esp. 507). Even though "there is no evidence that commercial considerations played a part in his brother's (the governor-general's) decision to take teritory," the two sets of considerations were, of course, to a great extent interdependent. The governor-general's exclusive emphasis on strategic and land revenue arguments may have been determined by the boundaries of the warrior-administrator's legitimizing idiom, which precludes the commercial argument's

expression. Generally speaking, the British-Indian administration's marked preferences for peasants and landlords and its disregard or contempt for urban traders and financiers seems to have this background.

26. For a good example, see, for instance, one Koldinder Ranga Razu, mentioned by Richards (*Mughal Administration,* 270), an important landholder and *deshmukh* of Eluru, who owned ships and carried on coastal trade as well. In fact this is not very surprising, except when we think, as we are prone to do, in terms of the neat Census of India categories.

27. Irfan Habib, "Aspects of Agrarian Relations and Economy in a Region of Uttar Pradesh during the Sixteenth Century," *Indian Economic and Social History Review* 4 (1967): 205–32, esp. 216.

28. See J. P. Musgrave,"Landlords and Lords of the Land: Estate Management and Social Control in Uttar Pradesh, 1860–1920," *Modern Asian Studies* 6 (1972): 257–75, esp. 268ff.

29. M. N. Pearson, "Political Participation in Mughal India," *Indian Economic and Social History Review* 9 (1972): 113–31, esp. 129.

30. A well-known example is the career of Mir Jumla, who started out as a self-made merchant, became a powerful minister of Golconda, and went over to the Mughal side as a high-ranking mansabdār (Manucci, *Storia do Mogor,* trans. W. Irvine [London, 1907–8], 1: 231). His official position seems to have been closely tied in with his extensive commercial operations.

31. See, for instance, the case of Chinana Chetti, younger brother and successor of the east coast commercial magnate Malaya, who appears to have held various public offices and on occasion to have commanded troops in the field (Moreland, *From Akbar to Aurangzeb,* 156). For a late example of the tie-in of finance, commerce, and military affairs, see K. Leonard, "Banking Firms in Nineteenth-Century Hyderabad," *Modern Asian Studies* 15 (1984): 177–201.

32. B. S. Cohn, "Political Systems in Eighteenth-Century India: The Benares Region," *Journal of the American Oriental Society* 62 (1962): 312–20, esp. 313. Though Cohn refers to the eighteenth century, the system of relative weakness and management by conflict is equally relevant for the sixteenth and seventeenth centuries—as it is for traditional empires in general. See also A. Wink, "Land and Sovereignty under the eighteenty-century Marāṭha Svarājya" (Doctoral thesis Leiden, 1984), chap. 1.

33. William Hawkins, *The Hawkins Voyages,* ed. C. R. Markham, Hakluyt Society, vol. 57 (1878), 433. For this well-known stereotype, cf. also Bernier's classical statement in his letter to Colbert (A. Constable's edition, revised by V. A. Smith, of *Bernier's Travels in the Mogul Empire* [Oxford, 1914], 202f.).

34. See Habib, *Agrarian System,* 68f.; Richards, *Mughal Administration,* 190.

35. See J. C. Heesterman, "Littoral et intérieur de L'Inde," in *History and Underdevelopment,* ed. L. Blussé, H. L. Wesseling, and G. D. Winicus, (Leiden, 1980), 87–92.

36. W. H. Moreland, *Jahangir's India: The Remonstrantie of Francisco Pelsaert* (Cambridge, 1925), 58f.; see also D. H. A. Kolff and H. W. Van Santen, *De Geschriften van Francisco Pelsaert over Mughal India, 1627* (The Hague, 1979), 307.

37. For the easy transition from robbery to blackmail and transit dues, see Moreland, *From Akbar to Aurangzeb,* 289.

38. Ibid., 288.

39. Moreland, *Jahangir's India,* 59; Kolff and Van Santen, *Geschriften van Franciso Pelsaert,* 308. See also Habib, *Agrarian System,* 69, n. 42, for references

to the activities of Meos and Jats between Agra and Delhi, the Rajputs of Baghelkhand, and the Kolis in Gujarat.

40. For these terms, see Habib, *Agrarian System,* 331, n. 5. According to Habib, the term *mawās* is not found in the dictionaries. It is, however, given in J. Platts's *Dictonary of Urdū, classical Hindī, and English* in the sense of "protection, refuge, asylum, shady grove or wood," which from the "rebel's" point of view, makes perfect sense. Cf. also H. H. Wilson, *A Glossary of Judicial and Revenue Terms* (London, 1855), s.v. *mawāshī* ("cattle"), and J. T. Molesworīh, *Marāṭhi-English Dictionary,* 2d rev. ed. (Bombay, 1957), s.v. *mavāsī* ("life and practices of a *mavās* or leader of a horde of banditti"). The combination of cattle keeping and transhumance with "rebelliousness" and warrior bands in the interstitial areas is easily explicable (see below and n. 41).

41. Richards suggests that Aurangzeb might have paused in 1687 to negotiate some form of tributary relationship with the Maratha king (*Mughal Administration,* 310). This would have enabled the emperor to organize the newly conquered Deccan kingdoms of Bijapur and Golconda. Such a course of action might have alleviated, at least temporarily, the pressure, but it would not have changed the structural problem, since it is not clear what would have kept the Marathas from building up strength and renewing their inroads.

42. For the opposition between "nuclear areas" of settled agriculture and the wastes with their warriors, see B. Stein, "Agrarian Integration in South India," in *Land Control and Social Structure in Indian History,* ed. R. E. Frykenberg (Madison, 1969), 175–216, esp. 188, 192, 206. Stein concentrates on the "nuclear areas" and their institutions, but their relationship with the "tribal" areas is also made clear. Though he deals with South India, there is no reason to assume that the opposition was limited to the South. In fact, it is not limited to India either, see, for instance, *Land* as against *wald* (in O. Brunner, *Land und Herrschaft,* 6th ed. (Darmstadt, 1970), 185ff.; also W. Berges, "Land und Unland in der Mittelalterlichen Welt," *Festschrift Hermann Heimpel* (Göttingen, 1972), 399–439. The opposition recalls the ancient one of *grāma* and *araṇya,* see chapter 8, section 7.

43. L. P. Tessitori, "Bardic and Historical Survey of Rajputana: A Progress Report," *Journal of the Asiatic Society of Bengal,* n.s. 15 (1919): 33f., 39f.

44. Rather than the well-known Turner thesis of the American frontier, I am indebted to P. Witteks view of the frontier marches and their warriors (*The Rise of the Ottoman Empire* [London, 1938], 16–32). Wittek sees the origins of the Ottoman Empire in the warrior bands of *ghāzīs,* ("warriors of the faith") with their distinctive culture and institutions, operating in the marches—shared by them with the Byzantine *akritai*—between the Islamic and Byzantine worlds. In many ways the Mughal Empire seems reminiscent of this situation. One might even say that the Mughals never quite overcame their frontier situation. They remained based in it in a way that the Ottoman Empire did not. See also O. Lattimore, "The Frontier in History" *Relazioni: X Congresso Internazionale di Scienze Storiche,* 1 (1955): 103–38.

45. On the institution of *bhūmiyāwat,* see W. H. Sleeman's *Rambles and Recollections,* revised and annotated by V. A. Smith (Karachi, 1973), 245–52.

46. Perhaps the Mughal bureaucracy's dual alignment of military and financial offices, putting at least two officers in charge of each post, can be viewed more as an adaption to the fractional structure, than a purely rational division of tasks. Thus a provincial revenue officer could equally well intervene militarily, especially in the reserved crown domains. (For a not dissimilar alignment in the British Indian administration, see above, n. 2). The formation of semiindependent regional principalities,

as in the case of Bengal or Hyderabad, started with a pulling together of both functions by the "protodynast" (see P. B. Calkins, "The Formation of a Regionally Oriented Ruling Group in Bengal, 1700–1740," *Journal of Asian Studies* 29 [1969–70]: 799–806, esp. 802, on Murshid Quli Khan; see also Richards, *Mughal Administration,* 277, on Mubariz Khan in Hyderabad).

47. See Marshall, "Economic and Political Expansion." Characteristically, British commercial interests in the area strongly opposed the annexations of 1801.

48. See T. R. Metcalf, "From Raja to Landlord," and "Social Effects of British Land Policy in Oudh," in Frykenberg, *Land Control,* 123–62.

49. See B. S. Cohn, "Structural Change in Rural Society, 1596–1885," in Frykenberg, *Land Control,* 53–121, esp. 113.

50. A case in point is the one analyzed by Frykenberg *(Guntur District),* of a district chief clerk, who, combining various interests, managed to build up a tightly controlled network. In other words, he had used the bureaucratic facilities to build his own "dependency" in much the classical way. Interestingly, the conspiracy was broken by the efficient cooperation of an English administrator and his Indian chief clerk, the latter belonging to the same background and community as the guilty head of the district bureaucracy. Probably it was his particular knowledge and understanding of the utterly tangled and particularistic situation that made the inquiry a resounding success. It almost looks as if the English had to use—albeit unknowingly—the potentialities of intracommunal factionalism in order to break the conspiracy, that is, they acted in the "traditional" way.

51. On the increase of resources, see M. D. Morris, "Towards a Reinterpretation of Nineteenth-Century Indian Economic History, *Journal of Economic History,* 33, no. 4 (1963), reprinted with critical comments in *Indian Economic and Social History Review* 5 (1968): 1–100. See also Morris's rejoinder, ibid., 319–88. On the development of local positions of strength and their supralocal connections, see, e.g., D. Washbrook, "Country Politics: Madras, 1880–1930," in *Locality, Province, and Nation,* ed. J. Gallagher, G. Johnson, and A. Seal, (Cambridge, 1973), 155–211; and C. A. Bayly, "Patrons and Politics in Northern India," ibid., 29–68.

52. An illustration is provided by the unrest in the Punjab canal colonies, where wealthy peasants had built up their strength and, using their rural-urban networks, undermined bureaucratic rule. See N. G. Barrier, "The Punjab Disturbances of 1907," *Modern Asian Studies* 1 (1967): 353–83.

53. On the institution of world renunciation, see Louis Dumont, "World Renunciation in Indian Religions," *Contributions to Indian Sociology* 4 (1960): 33–62; for a different view, cf. chapter 1.

54. Notwithstanding Gandhi's professed disregard for constitutional niceties, the Congress constitutions of the interbellum period clearly bear the inprint of his considerable organizational talent and ideas. See D. Rothermund, "Constitutional Reform versus National Agitation," *Journal of Asian Studies* 21 (1962): 505–22.

55. On the friction over the relationship between the governmental apex and the congressional center, see S. Kochanek, "The Indian National Congress: The Distribution of Power between Party and Government," *Journal of Asian Studies* 29 (1965–66): 681–97.

56. It is, of course, too early to view recent developments in their proper perspective. However, it may well be that in the end it is not so much the state that will have eliminated society's encroachment on its grounds, but, on the contrary, particularistic society and its turgid procedures that will take over the seat of government.

57. See F. Robinson, *Separation among Indian Muslims: The Politics of the United Provinces, 1860–1923* (Cambridge, 1974).

***Chapter Twelve***

1. See, for instance, H. Yule and A. C. Burnell, *Hobson Jobson: A Glossary of Anglo-Indian Colloquial Words and Phrases,* 2d ed. (London 1903), s.v. "caste."

2. Ibid. But note the early orientalist H. T. Colebrooke's casual idea of caste: "In practice, little attention is paid to the limitations to which we have alluded" (*Remarks on the Husbandry and Internal Commerce of Bengal,* [London, 1806]), 31.

3. See A. C. Mayer, *Caste and Kinship in Central India* (Berkeley 1960), 30–47; also chapter 1, section 2.

4. Best known is Charles Metcalf's minute in *Report from the Select Committee in the House of Commons* 3 (1830), appendix 84. Cf. Louis Dumont, "The 'Village Community' from Munro to Maine," *Contributions to Indian Sociology* 9 (1966): 67–89.

5. See chapter 11, section 7; also J. C. Heesterman, "Political Modernization in India," in *Traditional Attitudes and Modern Styles in Political Leadership,* ed. J. D. Legge (Sidney, 1973), 29–56, esp. 35–37, 46–48.

6. For this section I am greatly indebted to discussions with Frank Perlin and to his work on and expert knowledge of the rich Marāṭhi material on seventeenth- and eighteenth-century Western India. This does not necessarily mean that he concurs with my views. Cf. his "Of White Whale and Countrymen in the eighteenth-century Maratha Deccan," *Journal of Peasant Studies* 5, no. 2 (1978): 172–237; and "To Identify Change in an Old Regime Polity," in *Asie du Sud: Traditions et Changements,* ed. M. Gaborieau and A. Thorner (Sixth European Conference on Modern South Asian Studies, Paris, July 1978).

7. H. D. Robertson, in *Selections of Papers from the Records of the East India House* (London 1826), 6: 416, quoted in V. T. Gune, *The Judicial System of the Marathas* (Poona 1953), 4.

8. Conquest does not normally change the existing order of rights and holdings. Against this background M. Athar Ali's statement that "Aurangzeb's annexations in the Deccan were not the work of a military steam-roller, but of a slow and cumbrous machine, which sought energy and strength by recruiting deserters bribed to come over from the enemy" gains in depth (*The Mughal Nobility under Aurangzeb* [London, 1966], 173). The "deserters" were clearly important figures in the intricate web of rights and holdings, in which the conquering power had to gain a foothold.

9. Perlin, "Of White Whale," 177.

10. Ibid., 183.

11. A particularly illustrative specimen is contained in W. H. Sykes, "Land Tenures of the Deccan," in *Parliamentary Papers* (London, 1866), vol. 3, no. 22b, 17–32. The document quoted by Sykes gives a detailed account of a long, drawn-out conflict over a village headmandship.

12. Perlin, "To identify Change," 8, 12.

13. Ibid., 7ff.

14. See W. Rau, *Staat und Gesellschaft im alten Indien* (Wiesbaden 1957), 34f.

15. Perlin, "To identify Change," 10. Perhaps the "eating" metaphor has an added dimension, namely, that the "food" miraculously does not diminish when wisely "eaten," even when the eating has continued for generations.

16. See G. R. B. Inden and R. W. Nicholas, *Kinship in Bengali Culture* (Chicago, 1977), 17–19, 29–31, 80–81.

17. It may be noted that here the criterion for status is not "purity" (as in Dumont's treatment of caste), but "honor."

18. Sykes, "Land Tenures," 30.

19. Perlin, "To Identify Change," 7.

20. Incidentally, this also means that caste is not naturally bound up with peasant life. We therefore need not be surprised to find it again in modern city life in new and possibly even sharper forms in some respects.

21. Louis Dumont, *Homo Hierarchicus,* trans. M. Sainsbury (London, 1972).

22. See ibid., 93ff. (para. 32), for Dumont's view of the way the theoretical scheme of the four varṇas accounts for power and allows the hierarchy of purity, headed by the brahmins, to be conjugated with power represented by the second, kṣatriya, varṇa. Dumont recognizes that the varṇa scheme is not based on purity. But, although it gives a place to the kṣatriya, it cannot establish a valid relationship between the kṣatriya and the brahmin. The principle of the varṇa scheme is strict separation. On the problematic relationship, or rather the chasm, between king and brahmin, see chapter 10, esp. sections 1, 7–10.

23. Dumont, *Homo Hierarchicus,* 107 (para. 24).

24. Ibid., 268 (para. 106).

25. Ibid., 107 (para. 24).

26. R. B. Inden, *Marriage and Rank in Bengali Culture* (Berkeley, 1976); Veena Das, *Structure and Cognition: Aspects of Hindu Caste and Ritual* (Delhi, 1977).

27. Inden, *Marriage and Rank,* 102.

28. Ibid., 47, 106.

29. This is argued by Madeline Biardeau and Charles Malamoud, *Le Sacrifice dans l'Inde ancienne* (Paris, 1976), esp. 13, 153, 197. But cf. chapter 6.

30. Inden, *Marriage and Rank,* 91.

31. See J. C. Heesterman, "Veda and Dharma," in *The Concept of Duty in South Asia,* ed. W. D. O'Flaherty and J. D. Derrett (Delhi and London, 1978), 80–95; also above, chapter 6.

32. Das, *Structure and Cognition,* 22–26. It is interesting that later on the Caturvedis lose their status and resort to a śūdra life, apparently through lack of faith in their divine calling, when their relationship with a heterodox king forces them to an ordeal (ibid., 26–31). The Trivedi brahmins—that is, those who are less perfectly in possession of the Vedas, having only three out of the total four—go through with the ordeal and win. Though the text does not connect the two episodes, the lesson seems to be that this world does not tolerate perfection. The less perfect Trivedis, closing their eyes to the incompatibility of power and purity, accept King Rāma's largesse and manage to come through, while the perfect Caturvedis try the humanly impossible and fail.

33. See above chapter 10, section 8.

34. Marcel Mauss, "Essai sur le don," in *Sociologie et Anthropologie* (Paris, 1950), 243, no. 3. See above, chapter 2, section 9.

35. On the division of the "grain heap," see W. C. Neale, "Reciprocity and Redistribution," in *Trade and Markets in Early Empires,* ed. K. Polanyi et al. (Glencoe, 1957), and Louis Dumont, *La Civilisation indienne et nous* (Paris, 1964), 19. For a contemporaneous description of the procedure, see M.-L. Reiniche, "La Notion de Jajmāni," *Puruṣārtha* 3 (1977): 71–107.

36. In her analysis of the division procedure, Miss Reiniche wants to stress the symbolical aspects of the distribution as a sacrificial act tying the participants to-

gether in hierarchical exchange and interdependence ("l'ensemble sacrifice-sacrifiant-spécialistes" forming "un modèle pour l'activité de la société et sa reproduction"). Her analysis, which also brings in the ritual gift *(dakṣiṇā)* is certainly interesting. It is also interesting that she has recourse to the idiom of differential or shared rights—as apparently do her informants, who seem less interested in the sacrificial model but prefer to explain the procedures in terms of *kāṇiyāṭci,* holding of a right or share (ibid., 73 and passim).

37. This may explain the otherwise strange fact that although the texts seem to suggest that the king's part of the harvest is related to his protection of the people, his right to part of the produce is not dependent on the performance of this duty (see Robert Lingat, *Les Sources du droit traditionel de l'Inde* [Paris, 1967], 237; U. N. Ghoshal, *A History of Indian Political Ideas* [Oxford, 1966], 536f).

38. At first sight, this would seem to come down to the integral unity of the village. However, the important feature is the dispersion and interspersion of rights, irrespective of boundaries, bringing about a complex integration. The counterpart of this integration—bringing together many varied, often rivalling, holders of rights in the same good—is conflict, which all the time threatens the comprehensive order of rights.

39. This concept of property was introduced through Cornwallis's Permanent Settlement (1795). Whether the owner was to be the *zamīndār* ("landholder"), the *ryot* ("peasant"), or even the village community made corporate is, of course, a pragmatical question.

### *Chapter Thirteen*

1. Max Weber, *Wirtschaft und Gesellschaft,* Studienausgabe hrsg. von Joh. Winckelmann (Cologne and Berline, 1964), 684.

2. Louis Dumont, "Caste, Racism, and Stratification," *Contributions to Indian Sociology* 5 (1961): 23f.

3. *Wirtschaft und Gesellschaft,* 685.

4. Ibid., 29–31; see also Reinhard Bendix, *Max Weber: An Intellectural Portrait,* (Garden City, N.Y., 1962), 476.

5. For example, by Dumont, see above, note 2.

6. This may be helpful in dealing with the occurrence of Hindu and Muslim castes. When too narrowly defined as a specific Hindu phenomenon, the otherwise obvious and justified use of the term "caste" becomes unnecessarily problematic (see Louis Dumont, *Homo Hierarchicus* [Paris, 1966], 255–263, paras. 102, 103.

7. Max Weber, *Gesammelte Aufsätze zur Religionssoziologie* (Tübingen, 1920), 2: 118, 122, 131.

8. Ibid., 367.

9. Ibid., 120, 122; *Wirtschaft und Gessellschaft,* 344.

10. *Religionssoziologie,* 2: 131.

11. Ibid., 109.

12. See, for instance, ibid., 1: 540–42.

13. *Wirtschaft und Gesellschaft,* 462.

14. *Religionssoziologie,* 1: 551f.; cf. Wolfgang Schluchter, *Rationalismus der Weltbeherrschung,* (Frankfortam/Main, 1980), 16.

15. *Religionssoziologie,* 1: 552.

16. P. V. Kane, *History of Dharmaśāstra* (Poona, 1930–62), 2: 424. On the *gṛhastha* as an example of "innerweltliche Askese," see A. Wezler, *Die wahren "Speiseresteesser,"* (Mainz, 1978), 118. Weber deals briefly with the notion of

disinterested, and therefore karma-free, action as a this-worldly way to salvation in *Religionssoziologie,* 2: 195.

17. For the avoidance of acts that, though dharmic, cause scandal *(lokavikruṣṭa),* see *Manu* 4. 176; see also Robert Lingat, *Les Sources du droit dans le système traditionel de l'Inde* (Paris, 1967), 214. On the blameless practice of local custom even if contrary to the dharma, see Kane, *History,* 3: 861, and Lingat, *Les Sources du droit,* 220f.

18. *Manu* 5. 56; Cf. L. Alsdorf, *Beiträge zur Geschichte von Vegetarismus und Rinderverehrung in Indien* (Mainz, 1961), 17–21.

19. Richard Lingat, "Time and the Dharma," *Contributions to Indian Sociology* 6 (1962): 13f.

20. See J. C. Heesterman, "Householder and Wandered," in *Way of Life: Essays in Honour of Louis Dumont,* ed. T. N. Madan (New Delhi, 1982), 251–71.

21. Lingat, "Time and Dharma," 12.

22. Dumont, *Homo Hierarchicus,* 107.

23. *Mbh* 12. 59. 14–15; see also chapter 10, section 10.

24. *BĀU* 3. 2. 12.; see also chapter 2, section 7.

25. See Kane, *History,* 2: 424.

26. *Manu* 10. 5–56; see also chapter 12, section 4.

27. G. J. Held, *The Mahābhārata: An Ethnological Study,* Leiden, 1936), 89–97.

28. *Wirtschaft und Gessellschaft,* 409f.; *Religionssoziologie,* 1: 541. Cf. Schluchter, *Rationalismus,* 15ff.

29. See chapter 7.

30. See A. Hillebrandt, *Ritualliteratur* (Strassburg, 1897), 58. Weber mentions this ritual in *Religionssoziologie,* 2: 58. On the mahāvrata see also chapter 2, section 6. It is in the context of the mahāvrata that the texts place the mythical fight between Prajāpati and Death, which ended with Prajapati's definitive victory and the elimination of sacrificial battle.

31. On the problematic relationship of king and brahmin, see chapter 10, sections 7–10.

32. See J. C. Heesterman, "Priesthood and the Brahmin," *Contributions to Indian Sociology,* n.s. 5 (1971): 43–47; also above, chapter 2, section 12.

33. The foremost authority at the time was Sir Herbert Risly (see *Religionssoziologie* 1: 1, n. 1) who served as census commissioner for the 1901 decennial census of India. His code of regulations formed the basis on which the census of 1901 and of 1911 were conducted. It is not without interest that his *The People of India* (1908) was felt at the time to overstress in the matter of caste "its modern, rigid form" (second, posthumous, edition, edited by W. Crooke, [Calcutta, Simla, London], 1915, xvii). On one hand, early on, British officials evinced "a tendency to emphasize the caste category at the expense of all others," thereby making caste more comprehensive and rigid than warranted (see C. A. Bayly, "Indian Merchants in a 'Traditional Setting,' " in *The Imperial Impact,* ed. C. Dewey and A. C. Hopkins, [London, 1978], 180, n. 54). On the other hand, F. Buchanan, in the beginning of the last century, still spoke of the warlike Sakarwars of the Benares, Shahabad, and Bihar districts adopting "the doctrine of caste and rules of *modern* purity" (see D. H. A. Kolff, "An Armed Peasantry and Its Allies," [Doctoral thesis, Leiden, 1983], 139, 149).

34. Wirtschaft und Gesellschaft, 410, *Religionssoziologie,* 1: 366; 2: 122, 374, 377.

35. Ibid., 1: 132f.

# Index


*Abhigara*. *See* Praiser
*Abhiṣeka*. *See* Unction
Act of truth, 135
Adharma. *See* Dharma
*Adhvaryu* officiant, 125
Aditi, 67
Ādityas, 29, 209n. 25
*Adṛṣṭa*, 101
Agni, 62, 65, 86
*Agnicayana*. *See* Fire altar
*Agnihotra*, 89, 93, 102, 226n.14, 227n.38
Agriculture, 62, 106
*Āhavanīya*, 40
*Ahiṃsā* 82, 96, 98, 196, 225n.10
*Ahīna*, 209n.14
*Akṣapaṭala*, 132, 137
*Akaṣarakṣitṛ*, 137
*Akṣavāpa*, 137, 239n.12
"Alighting," 120
*Aṃhas*, 105, 134
*'Āmil*, 165
*Anaddhāpuruṣa*, 218n.58
*Anāśyānna*, 37
Angirases, 29, 54, 209n.20
*Anṛta*. See Untruth
*Anṛtadūta*, 79
Anthill, 54, 55, 218n.61
*Ānvīkṣikī*, 130, 131, 235n.7
*Apagara*. *See* Reviler
*Apratigṛhya*, 37
*Āpta*, 115
Apūrva, 101, 125
*Araṇya*. *See* Wilderness
*Arghya*, 48
Arthaśāstra: on brahmin, 21; and dharma, 111; on financial audit, 6, 132f.; on merchant, 165; and nationalism, 128; purpose of, 130; on renunciatory virtue, 156; on territory, 143. *See also* "Circle of Kings"; Conqueror; Kauṭilya
*Arthavāda*, 99, 104
Ascent to heaven, 120
Aśoka, 20, 228n.2
*Āśrama*, 40
Asuras. *See* Devas
*Aśvamedha*. *See* Horse sacrifice
Aśvins, 47f., 215nn.24, 25
Athar Ali, M., 161, 245n.8
*Ātman*, 39
Aurangzeb, 20, 161, 243n.41
Authority: of brahmin, 111, 141, 155, 201; dispersed, 147, 148, 150; and king(ship), 6, 24, 117; separated from power, 157, 187; transcendent, 125, 127; universalistic, 177, 179
*Avabhṛtha*. *See* Final bath
*Avivākya*, 223n.28
Axial Age, 95, 96, 106, 107, 200
Axial breakthrough, 4f., 157
Ayasthūṇa, 75

Baal, J. van, 225n.11
Bali, 101
*Bandhu*, 71, 80
Baudhāyana, 52, 53, 55
Beck, B. F., 13, 206n.12
Bhīsma, 116, 125
*Bhrātṛvya*. *See* Rival

Bhr̥gu, 90
*Bhūmiyāwat,* 243n.45
Biardeau, M., 81, 82, 246n.29
Bodewitz, H. W., 213n.77
"Boxing device" of ritual, 118
*Brahmacārin,* 40, 73, 126, 213n.79
*Brahmahatyā,* 76
*Bráhman:* birth from 208n.12; as enigmatic formulation, 4, 71; as intermediary element, 216n.32; and *kṣatra,* 112, 141f.; and wilderness, 126. *See also* Brahmán; *Brahmodya*
*Brahmán:* at *brahmodya,* 72, 221n.12; as healer of sacrifice, 27; Indra qualified as, 77, 210n.30, 224n.41; and king, 79, 151, 154; and sacrificer, 6, 28; as sacrificial officiant, 30, 71, 79, 220n.34. *See also* Brahmin
*Brāhmaṇa* (text), 97
*Brahmavādin,* 73
Brahmin: desacralized, 155; duties of, 214n.89; as guest, 30; holds authority, 111, 141, 155, 201; not a priest, 150; proclaimed, 154, 208n.12; as renouncer, 4, 43f., 145, 155, 160, 200, 232n.32; sits below king, 142; stands apart, 38, 103, 201, 246n.22; takes over death, 31, 37; as warrior, 3, 106, 126, 210n.30. *See also* King.
Brahminization, 12. *See also* Sanskritization
*Brahmodya,* 71–74, 76, 100, 126, 150, 221nn.13, 15
Breloer, B., 132
*Br̥haspatisava,* 120
Brotherhood, 185–87, 189
Buddhism, 95f., 228n.1

Calkins, P. B., 244n.46
Cash nexus, 164, 166–68
Caste: alien term, 180; "allied," 12f.; and census, 8, 202, 248n.33; and karma, 195, 197; and modern state, 192; and peasant society, 180, 246n.20; and *Stand,* 194; right-left division of, 13. See also *Varṇa; Jāti*
Cattle corral, 56
*Cātvāla,* 56
Census, 175, 182, 202, 248n.33
Chariot: alighting from, 121; driving on, 99, 119, 125; mounting on, 237n.45; oblation on, 145; and ritual, 28, 92, 106, 224n.50; 227n.46; war and racing, 29, 120, 148, 211n.42
"Circle of Kings," 6, 18, 21, 103, 149f.
Civil disobedience, 177
Cohn, B.S., 176, 242n.32
Commensality, 223n.35
Community, settled, 6, 118f., 243n.42
Conflict, 148, 167, 171, 177f., 185, 214n.88 *See also* Devas
Congress. *See* Indian National Congress
Connubium, 135, 138, 145
Conqueror, 103, 149
Conquest of the senses, 131f., 156
Consensus, 178
Consilium, 130
Contest: and sacrifice, 28f., 32–34, 92, 152f.; for secret, 215n.25; verbal, 75, 80, 223n.28. See also *Brahmodya;* Reviler
Cosharers, 18, 133, 139, 156, 184
Cosmic circulation, 88, 227n.28
Cosmic man, 46, 84
Cow, 65, 67, 220n.31. See also *Dakṣinā; Iḍā*
Custom, 11, 196f., 248n.17
Customary law, 10

Dadhyañc, 47, 215n.17
*Dakṣiṇā,* 27f, 30f., 46, 64f., 79, 211nn.49, 52, 225n.53
*Daṇḍa,* 122, 234n.84
Das, Veena, 246nn.26, 32
*Daśapeya,* 30, 120
Death, 33, 153
Deccan, 161, 163
Defourny, M., 219n.12
Devas: and conflict with the asuras, 47, 49, 57, 79, 90, 209n.20, 210n.40, 215n.17; driving of, 99, 107; non transcendence of, 88, 155
Dharma: and adharma, 2, 111, 196; based on *śruti,* 11, 81, 82f., 96, 156; dilemma of, 11; and king, 108, 115, 232n.53; rule of, 156f., 198; and wilderness, 118
Dhīra, 221n.15
*Dhruvagopa,* 85, 222n.24
*Dīkṣā,* 27, 92, 119, 216n.34
*Dīkṣita:* and *daṇḍa,* 122; as impure, 27, 92, 208nn.6, 9, 228n.47; proclaimed a brahmin, 154; in search of knowledge, 126; as warrior, 40, 86, 92, 227n.46
Disenchantment, 101, 200

Division of harvest, 139, 191
Dumont, L.: on brahmin, 206n.8, 231n.32; on caste and hierarchy, 12f.; on dharma, 197; on encompassment, 187f.; on Hinduism, 212n.73; on Kallar chieftainship, 147; on kingship, 141, 152; on power and purity, 246n.22
*Dvādaśāha* 27, 209n.14
*Dviṣat*. *See* Rival

"Eater": of the people, 109; of rights, 185, 186
Empire, traditional: of Mauryas, 20, 96; of Mughals, 16–20, 160–73, 243n.44
Encompassment, 104, 187f
Enigmatic formulation, 71–73, 79. See also *Brāhman*
Enthronization, 119
Epics, pattern of, 41, 87, 123, 148
Equivalence. *See* Identification
Error in ritual, 75, 88, 90, 223nn.26, 28
Evil: of death, 85; passed on, 32, 135; of sacrificer, 79, 208nn.6, 9; turned into opposite, 27f., 219n.13. *See also* Brahmin
Exchange: connubial, 199; of food, 209n.20; hierarchical, 191; in sacrifice, 30, 50, 72, 79, 200; and sharing, 185
Exchequer, 133

Factionalism, 140, 148
Final bath, 61, 63, 120
Financial audit, 132
Fire altar, 46, 50, 57, 103, 225n.3, 236n.23
Fish, 59f., 62f
Flood story, 59f
Four-five scheme, 145, 239n.16
Four-Hotṛ formulas, 74
Frykenberg, R. E., 244n.50

Gambling, 67, 112f., 137f., 220n.31
Gandhi, M. K., 23f., 177, 179, 244n.54
Gift, 31, 36f., 83, 102, 188, 189
Gods. *See* Devas.
Gonda, J., 131
*Goṣṭha*. *See* cattle corral
*Govikarta,* 239n.12
*Grāma*. *See* Community, settled
Great Rebellion (1857), 175
*Gṛhastha*. *See* Householder
Guest, 30, 48, 144, 210n.34, 216n.33

Hacker, P., 205n.20
Hariścandra, 84
Hauer, J. W., 213n.79
Head: of Aditi, 67; contest for, 47, 49, 57; of enemy, 53; knowledge of, 49; problem of, in building of fire altar, 50–52, 217n.42; of victim, 4, 218n.71, 239n.12; victim's, not be be severed, 46, 50
"Head of the sacrifice," 4, 46, 48, 53, 57 *See also* Dadhyañc; Makha; Namuci; Viśvarūpa
Headmanship, 184
Held, G. J., 199, 209n.16, 224n.35, 239n.18
Hesiod, 99
Hierarchy, 12–14, 35, 146, 188, 247n.36
Hinduism, 81, 207n.19, 212n.73
Honor, 191, 246n.17
Hopkins, E. W., 210n.32
Horse sacrifice, 57, 72, 122, 124, 125, 221n.10, 234n.91
Host, 30f., 216n.33, 218n.58. *See also* Guest
Householder, 40, 196, 247n.16
Hṛtsvāśaya Āllakeya, 126, 235n.101

Iḍā, 60, 64–67
Identification, 33, 73, 80, 94
Immobilism, 182
Immolation, 51, 87, 98, 215n.15, 221n.10, 223n.26, 226n.27 *See also* Head
Incest motif, 60, 76
Inclusivism, 7, 205n.20
Inden, R. B., 246n.26
Indian National Congress, 23, 177
Individualization, 34, 41, 154, 206n.17
Indra: contest of with Bali, 101; cuts off heads of Namuci and Viśvarūpa, 47, 215n.20; plunders Maruts, 86; presence of denied, 77f.; qualified as *brahmán,* 77, 210n.30, 224n.41; reviled, 76, 208n.6; and Varuna, 234n.89, 237n.42; and his wife, 236n.38
Inner frontier, 7, 170–73, 175
Interiorization, 41, 212n.72
Interstitial areas, 169, 170
Irfan Habib, 161
Islam, 160, 179
*Itthaṃvid,* 223n.34

Jābāla, 221n.15
*Jāgīr,* 20, 162, 165, 172

*Jāgīrdār,* 166
*Jajmān,* 88, 188
*Jana,* 210n.38
Janaka of Videha, 30, 221n.5, 222n.15
*Janapada,* 141
Jaspers, K., 95, 105, 107
*Jāti,* 8, 103, 190, 199. See also *varṇa*
Jester, 155
Joint family, 15
Josselin de Jong, P. E. de, 146, 239n.16

Kachin, 146
*Kalivarjya,* 87
Karma, *karman:* individualized, 30, 198, 211n.48; ritual work, 34, 80; and theodicy, 195
*Kastensoteriology,* 195, 197
Kauṭilya, 6, 108, 111, 128, 130, 132, 140, 148f., 156, 231n.30. *See also* Arthaśāstra
Keśin Dārbhya, 29, 209n.20
King: and brahmin, 7, 15, 112, 114, 131, 142, 154f., 189; and dharma, 108, 115, 154, 198; exiled, 41, 149; "maker of the age," 112; number of mythic, 232n.56; primus inter pares, 131, 146; proclaimed *brahmán,* 79, 96; and *ratnins,* 143–46; relationship of with people, 109, 131, 138, 144; ritual beating of, 232n.56; and self-discipline, 131f.; share of; 139, 247n.37; shunned by brahmin, 103, 246n.32; transfer of function of during horse sacrifice, 125; *See also* Kingship
Kinglessness, 116
Kingmakers, 114, 138f
Kingship: connective, 6, 151; dispersed, 147, 148, 151; multiple, 147, 148, 151; mythic origin of, 115f., 142; problematic character of, 5, 108, 118; sacral, 110f., 131, 151
Kinship, 144, 210n.38
Knowledge, 44, 48, 49, 94
Kolff, D. H. A., 207n.24
Kṛṣṇa, 226nn.19, 22
*Kṣatra,* 112, 141f.
*Kṣatriya:* and brahmin, 246n.22; duties of, 214n.89; exclusion of from sacrifice, 77, 91; impurity of, 92; transformation of into brahmin, 29f.
*Ksattṛ,* 239n.12
*Kṣemya,* 106

Kuiper, F. B. J., 209n.15, 219n.6
Kurukṣetra, 48, 98
Kurus, Kuru-Pañcālas, 49, 120, 149, 221n.4, 230n.37

Land, private ownership of, 174, 175, 182, 192
Landholder, 165
Land revenue, 139, 163, 164, 168, 192
Leach, E. R., 146, 238n.4
Lévi-Strauss, C, 146
Lingat, R., 110, 196, 197, 230n.9
"Little kingdom," 17, 18, 22, 25

Macchiavelli, 231n.30
*Madhu,* 47, 48, 215n.21
*Mahāmātra,* 132, 138, 237n.47
*Mahāsaṃmata,* 232n.57
*Mahāvrata,* 32, 75f., 200, 224n.36
*Maitrāvaruṇa* officiant, 122
Makha, 47, 215nn.17, 21
Malamoud, Ch., 212n.59
*Maṇḍalayoni. See* "Circle of Kings"
*Mansabdār,* 162, 166
*Mantjapat,* 239n.16
*Mantra,* 97. *See also* Consilium
Manu, 59f., 116
Market towns, 167, 169
Maruts, 86, 135, 137, 237nn.42, 46
Mauryas. *See* Empire
Mauss, M., 31, 36, 83, 148
Mayer, A. C., 12f
*Mawās,* 170, 171, 243n.40
Merchant, 165f
Middle of the world, 85, 226n.18
*Mīmāṃsā,* 73, 125, 225n.10
Minangkabau, 146, 147
*Mithuna. See* Pair, Pairing
Mitra and Varuṇa, 61, 65f.
*Mitravindeṣṭi,* 66
"Mixed" marriages, 146
Modernity, 9, 15, 23, 25
Moiety, 145
Monarchy, 108, 132, 146, 239n.24. *See also* King; Kingship
*Mṛtyu. See* Death
Mughals. *See* Empire
Mughal-Rajput alliance, 171f.
*Mulkgīrī,* 7
Multiple kingship, 147, 148

Nambudiri, 228n.51, 229n.25
Numuci, 47, 215n.17
*Nāstika,* 70, 75, 80
National unity, 24, 178
Nation state, 21, 157
*Nivṛtti,* 196, 198
Noncooperation, 177
Nyāya, 71

Oberhammer, G., 220n.1
*Odana,* 138, 220n.31
Officiant, sacrificial, 38, 100, 155, 211nn.49, 52
Oldenberg, H., 98
"Opting out," 12

Pair, Pairing, 136, 145, 240n.37
*Pākayajña,* 68
Pālāgala, 79
*Pancāyat,* 134
Pañcāyatī rāj, 181
Pāṇḍavas, 149
*Pāpman. See* Evil
Paraśurāma, 30, 142, 152
*Pargana,* 167
*Parivrājaka,* 42
Peasant, 164
Pelsaert, 168f.
People, 113. *See also* King
Perlin, F., 245n.6
Permanent Settlement, 21, 174, 247n.39
*Piṣṭapaśu,* 216n.38; 236n.39
Plakṣa Prāsravana, 85
Power: and authority, 141, 157, 187; dispersed, 114, 147, 148, 150, 167
Praiser, 75f., 80, 222n.24
Prajāpati: and contest with Death, 33, 94, 153, 210n.40; as creator, 134, 136; head of, 53; incest of, 61; as personification of systematized ritual, 50; reviled, 76; and sacrificer, 27
*Prakṛti* 113, 149
*Pralaya,* 229n.25
*Prāṇāgnihotra,* 4, 42, 93, 103, 213n.77
Prāsahā, 236n.38
*Prāśitra,* 220n.34
*Pratirājan,* 30, 79, 123
*Pratyavarohaṇīya. See* "Alighting"
*Pravṛtti,* 196, 198
*Pravrājaka,* 40
*Prayujāṃ havīṃṣi,* 120
Priesthood, 141, 151–53, 157
Pṛthu, 116
*Punarabhiṣeka,* 117, 234n.89. *See also* Unction
*Punarmṛtyu. See* Re-death
*Purīṣa,* 55f.
*Purohita,* 37f., 42, 144, 151, 155
*Puruṣa. See* Cosmic man

Raiding. *See* Transhumance
*Ra'īyatī,* 169
*Rājābhiṣeka,* 120. *See also* Unction
*Rājadharma,* 109
*Rājan,* 111, 144, 146. *See also* King
*Rājaśāsana,* 115, 232n.54
*Rājasūya,* 5f., 111, 117, 118–24, 133, 137, 143; does not create king, 154
*Rājaputra,* 222n.24
Rājputs, 12, 17, 171f.
Rāma, 123, 189, 246n.32
Rāma Mārgaveya, 76
*Rāṣṭra,* 141
*Rāṣṭrabhṛt,* 145
Rathor, 171
Rational order, 102
Rationalism, ethical, 195
*Ratnin,* 137f., 143–46, 148
Rebirth, 195, 197
Reciprocity, 31, 36, 83, 190, 214n.89
Re-death, 32, 34, 202
Regeneration of cosmos, 26
Regionalism, 177
Reiniche, M.-L., 246nn.35, 36
Renou, L., 71, 73, 96, 221n.13
Renouncer, 23, 41, 43f., 177, 193, 197
Renunciation, 41f., 192, 197, 199
Republic. *See* Monarchy
Revelation, 97
Reviler, 75f., 80, 214n.87, 222n.24
*Rex,* 111
Richards, J. F., 161, 162, 243n.41
Rights, landed: fractionized, 184, 186; inalienable, 191; of the king, 139; and personal relationships, 14, 143, 182; saleable, 165, 175; shared, 247n.36
Risley, Sir Herbert, 248n.33
Ritual, Vedic: *adṛṣṭārtha* as, 3; breaks agonistic pattern, 6, 33, 57, 87, 107;

controversial, 96; individualized, 34, 88, 206n.17; interiorization of, 39, 41f.; rationalized, 45; and sacrificial meal, 48, 89; stands apart from society, 125. *See also* Sacrifice
Ritual enclosure, 90
Ritualism, 41, 91. 93, 98, 100, 103; certainty of, 91, 93, 98, 100; outlaws conflict, 103
Rival: exclusion of, 153; relation to own party, 56, 144; in ritual, 29, 45; vaiśya as, 40, 54f. *See also* Sacrifice
Rönnow, K., 50, 56
*ṛṣi*, 97
*ṛta*, 134
*ṛtvij*. *See* Officiant
Rudra, 220n.34
Ryot, 164

*Sabhā*, 137
Sacrality: devalorized, 6, 155, 157; of king, 110, 131, 151, 155; as opposite of transcendence, 157; and violent death, 3
*Sacra publica*, absence of, 3, 88, 206n.17
Sacrifice: as absolute order, 84, 88f., 156; agonistic, 28f., 81; and battle, 3, 99, 125, 148, 209n.16; catastrophic, 86; cyclical, 92; without dakṣiṇā best, 38; human, 50, 56, 216n.41; internal, 39, 42, 213n.77; and meal, 64, 89, 93; as model of society, 82, 188; reformed, 5, 50, 87, 91, 106; replaced by ritualism, 100. *See also* Ritual; Ritualism
Sacrificer: as host, 36f.; identifical with Prajāpati, 27, 34; and officiants, 36, 211nn.49, 52; set apart, 103; single individual as, 27, 88; and victim, 216n.29
*Sadasya*, 222n.24
*Sādhu*, 115
*Sādyaskra*, 29, 211n.42
Śākalya, 73
Salary of priest, 155
*Samāhartṛ*, 129
*Saṃjñaneṣṭi*, 34, 211nn.45, 50
*Saṃjñapana*. *See* Immolation
*Saṃkhyāna*, 33
*Saṃnyāsin*, 40, 214n.89. *See also* Renouncer
*Saṃpad*, 33
*Samṛtayajña*, 29
*Saṃsāra*, 88
*Saṃsava*, 29, 33, 78
*Saṃskāra* of king, 111, 154, 231n.24
*Saṃśrāva*, 222n.24
*Saṃsṛp* offerings, 120
*Śāmūlājina*, 126
*Sangha*, 96, 157, 228n.2
*Saniyācana*, 92, 119, 227n.46
Sanskritization, 9, 16, 26, 197, 214n.100
*Sapatna*. *See* Rival
*Sapiṇḍa* relatives, 200
Sarkar, Sir Jadunath, 161
*Sarvamedha*, 41
Satish Chandra, 161
*Sattra*, 38, 74, 85, 105, 151, 209n.14
*Satya*, 134
*Satyadūta*, 79
*Sātyadūtahavīṃṣi*, 30
Śauceya, 222n.15
Śaulvāyana, 75
*Sautrāmaṇi*, 117, 236nn.23, 31
Scepter, 122, 233n.84
Scharfe, H., 113, 133, 235n.2, 249n.34
Schluchter, W., 248n.14
Schmidt, H.-P., 224n.41
Seniority, 186
Seventh step, 65, 67
Sharing, 185. *See also* Cosharer
Sharma, J. P., 239n.24
Silence, 71, 72, 73, 78
*Śiṣṭa*, 115
Śiśupāla, 226nn.19, 22
Social ethic, 195
Soma, 76f., 87, 92
*Śraddhā*, 79
*Śrāddha*, 37, 209n.20
*Śrauta* ritual. *See* Ritual, Vedic
*Śreṣthin*, 78
*Śrī*, 28, 40, 47, 66, 209nn.13, 20
*Śrotriya*, 37, 38
*Śruti:* dharma based on, 11, 156; revelation, 97; set apart, 87; threat of, to dissolve relationships, 103
Staal, J. F., 205, 212n.72
State: formation of, 18; and interstate relations, 113; and kinship, 144; modern, 21, 157, 174, 182, 192, 202; problem of, 5, 132, 140. *See also* King; Kingship
Stein, B., 243n.42
Sthūra, 85f.
*Streitwagenvölker*, 106
Śunaḥśepa, 84f.

*Sūrā* beverage, 47
*Sūta,* 151
*Svadharma,* 196, 198
Svaidāyana, 222n.15
Śyāparṇas, 76

*Tantrayukti,* 130
*Tānūnaptra,* 36, 211nn.45, 52
Territorial units, 175, 182
Theodicy, 195
Thieme, P., 48, 210n.34, 220n.3
Trade, role of, 164
Trade routes, 167f
Tradition, 2, 9, 10f., 12–16, 120, 183
Transcendence: and brahmin, 201; and mundane reality, 5, 101, 201; as opposite of sacrality, 156; and ritual, 97, 101, 103; and sacrifice, 81f., 94; and tradition, 11. *See also* Renouncer; Renunciation.
Transhumance, 19, 105
Tryaruna, 37
Two-three scheme, 145, 147, 239n.16
*Tyāga,* 102, 230n.30

Uddālaka (Āruṇi), 221nn.5, 15
*Ukhā,* 53
*'Umma,* 20
Unanimity, 133
Unction, 117–19, 145, 153, 231n.24, 232n.58, 233nn.64, 67, 234n.89
*Universitas christiana,* 20
Untruth, 134, 236n.39. See also *anṛtadūta*
*Upanayana,* 154, 231n.24
*Upaniṣad,* 34, 74, 95, 228n.1

*Vāda,* 70, 80, 81, 221n.5
*Vaiśvadeva,* 134
Vaiśvārasavya, 221n.15
*Vaiśya,* 2, 40, 55, 214n.89
*Vājapeya,* 120
*Vajra,* 90, 122
*Vānaprastha,* 40, 214n.89
*Varṇa:* contrast of with *jāti,* 8, 103, 145, 199; and separation, 200, 202, 214n.89, 223n.35. *See also* Caste; *Jāti*
*Varṇasaṃkara,* 190, 199, 200
Varuṇa: bonds of, 134–36; and Indra, 234n.89, 237n.42; and Maruts, 137; and Mitra, 61, 65f.
*Varuṇapraghāsa,* 133, 134–37, 234n.89, 236n.23
*Varuṇasava,* 123
Veda. *See* Ritual, Vedic
Vedānta, 74
*Vedi* 56, 135, 226n.50
Vena, 109, 231nn.12, 22
*Vihava,* 78
*Vijigīṣu. See* Conqueror
Village, 8, 181, 183f.
Village festivals, 216n.27
*Viś,* 135. *See also* People
Vision, 97
Viśvāmitra, 85
Viśvantara Sauṣadmana, 76
Viśvarūpa, 47, 49, 215nn.17, 20
*Vivaktṛ,* 76, 223n.28
*Vrata* milk, 93
*Vrātya,* 19, 52, 122, 126, 211nn.45, 50, 213n.79, 230n.37
Vṛśa Jāna, 37
Vṛtra, 49, 87

Warrior-administrator, 163, 165, 167, 241n.25
Weber, A., 106
Weber, M., 5, 101f., 194, 201f., 229n.10
Wezler, A., 247n.16
Wife of sacrificer, 134–36
Wilderness, 6, 84, 118, 126, 233n.61, 243n.42
Wilhelm, F., 235n.8
Wink, A., 207n.20, 242n.32
Wittek, P., 243n.44
Womb: of kingship, 135, 142, 144; of sacrifice, 61, 66
World eras, 87, 99, 112, 157, 198

*Yajamāna. See* Sacrificer
*Yajña. See* Sacrifice
Yājnavalkya, 35, 221n.5, 222nn.15
Yajurveda, 28, 51f., 57, 216n.41, 217n.42
*Yātsattra,* 105
*Yoni. See* Womb
Yuddhiṣthira, 99, 110, 115, 118, 123, 149, 239n.16

*Zamīndār. See* Landholder
Zarathsutrian reform, 107